WHO'S IN CONTROL?

*Polar Politics
and the
Sensible Center*

Richard Darman

SIMON & SCHUSTER

SIMON & SCHUSTER
Rockefeller Center
1230 Avenue of the Americas
New York, NY 10020

10   9   8   7   6   5   4   3   2   1

Library of Congress Cataloging-in-Publication Data

Darman, Richard Gordon, date.
   Who's in control? : polar politics and the sensible center /
Richard Darman.
      p.   cm.
   Includes bibliographical references and index.
   1. United States—Politics and government—1981–1989.
2. United States—Politics and government—1989–1993.
3. United States—Politics and government—1993–.
4. Right and left (Political science).
I. Title.
E876.D36   1996
320.973—dc20   96-24939   CIP
ISBN 0-684-81123-5

For:
Kathleen Emmet Darman
William Temple Emmet Darman
Jonathan Warren Emmet Darman
Christopher Temple Emmet Darman

CONTENTS

Prologue: Missing in Action   9

PART ONE: GOING FOR THE BOLD—
            And the Power of the Mainstream

1 The Buckaroo Stops Here: 27
   The Reagan Revolution Comes to Town

2 "P Hit/Fighting":   47
   Who's in Control?

3 Victory in the Fog: 63
   The Ranch in the Sky

4 Voodoo Politics: 72
   A Faustian Bargain

5 The Fall Offensive: 93
   The Kingdom for a Mouse

6 Symbols and Substance: 120
   "You Ain't Seen Nothin' Yet"

7 The Levelers' Mandate: 145
   Tax Reform—Dead or Alive

8 Buckner's Bobble—   164
   And the Cowboys' Farewell

9 The Reagan Restoration: 175
   Who's in Control? (Revisited)

PART TWO: RESTORING THE BALANCE—
Of Prudence and the Future

10 Read My Lips: 187
    Back to the Future

11 An Awkward Two-Step: 198
    From Now-Now to New Balance

12 Ted Williams and BUBBA: 230
    "Read My Lips Is History"

PART THREE: THE VISION THING—
Struggling to Be Reborn

13 Neo-Media-Pop-ism: 269
    Trashing the 1990 Budget Deal

14 The Clinton-Gingrich Co-Presidency: 299
    A Field of Stones

15 Reviving the Sensible Center: 321
    Beyond the Politics of Polarization

Epilogue: Looking for Heroes   345

Bibliographic Note   351
Acknowledgments   365
Index   369

Prologue:
Missing in Action

AMONG POLITICAL OBSERVERS and sports fans—that is, among most Americans—there is a tendency to observe cycles. Cycles, of course, vary in importance and significance. Some may be profound; others trivial. And somewhere in between are countless observations like this one: Every four years, in the fall, attention to elections surpasses baseball as America's pastime. That observation might well be dismissed as uninteresting if it were not for a related curiosity. In 1996, it seemed that things might be different.

As the last presidential election before the turn of the century approached, the presidential contest promised to command less interest than baseball's pennant races. It was not that baseball was so exciting. Indeed, many found it boring. It was that enthusiasm for presidential politics seemed remarkably low.

It had become customary for about half of America's eligible voters not to go to the polls. But even among those who did intend to vote, large numbes were disenchanted. There was a widespread feeling that the political process was letting the public down.

The country was strong in many fundamental respects. Still, it had real problems, for which politicians offered few credible solutions. As usual, their rhetorical posturing combined promise and partisanship. But political language had lost much of its meaning. It was notoriously unreliable as a guide to post-election performance. Worse still, in 1996, the choice between the major parties' presidential candidates left much of the public highly uncertain about what might actually follow in the way of governance.

Indeed, governance itself had been in abeyance since 1994, the midterm election year. Who or what was in control—if anyone—had become unclear. America's politics had become polarized.

For most of the post-World War II era, it had been otherwise. The rhetorical positions of the two major parties had differed, of course, as had their policy leanings. But, in practice, the parties had shared a large amount of common ground in the broad middle between ideological extremes. And they had routinely come together in order to govern.

In recent years, however, they had been pulled apart—like continents shifting toward the poles. One party was led by a President who was prone to drift away from the center when elections were behind him. The other was moved by a Speaker of the House who consciously fostered a clear divide—not just in rhetoric and ostensible ideology, but in political practice. As he did so, as the practical divide was widened, inhabitants of the more temperate zones of policy and politics were left on increasingly tenuous ground. It was in these zones that the processes of constructive compromise had ordinarily been managed. But in the world of polar politics, compromise was denigrated as unprincipled behavior. And without compromise, the American system did not function. The result was not the triumph of one extreme at the expense of another. It was simply an unbridged gap, an unproductive stalemate.

Arguably, the increased ideological separation had begun in 1980 with the election of President Ronald Reagan. But in practice, the "Reagan Revolution" had been more a matter of rhetoric than reality. Though ideologically committed, President Reagan had understood well that pragmatic compromise was necessary in order to govern. It was the rise of the less compromising Newt Gingrich to the speakership of the House that moved the ideological divide beyond rhetoric into practice, producing the frozen stalemate of polar politics.

Yet, though Gingrich's rise crystallized differences between Democrats and Republicans, the extent to which these differences were mirrored by the parties' presidential candidates in 1996 was blurred. Both candidates were naturally inclined toward compromise. And both knew that they had to appeal to the center in order to win. So, from time to time, as the election approached, it appeared that the ground in the center was being reclaimed. But the public was understandably skeptical.

The issue of interest was how each candidate would govern, not how he might campaign. And for many, that issue was hard to assess. Would a reelected President Clinton become the New Democrat he had claimed to be in seeking election in 1992? Or would he, the former McGovernite, take another sharp turn to the left, as he had done in 1993 after winning the presidency? Would a newly elected President Dole define what he thought was best for the country, separate himself from righter-than-right factions, build the coalition necessary to govern, while drawing on the strengths of character that had guided most of his life? Or would he yield to congressional leadership by a reenergized Speaker Gingrich, as he had done in 1995? It was amazing, in a way, that with such well-known candidates, the answers to these rather basic questions could seem so uncertain. But they did.

And there was this further complication: It was not entirely clear what was really at stake. Was there a serious threat that American government might turn toward one extreme or another? Was the future of "big government" fundamentally at issue? Many people acted as if answers to such basic questions were obvious; but at least as many others were far from sure.

To me, one point did seem clear. To begin to answer such questions sensibly, one had to step back from the candidates, the rhetoric, and the partisan posturing. One needed a broader perspective with which to frame the issues that the country was facing. Not knowing the future, I tried to look at the recent past. My hope was that a bit of history might yield a more meaningful sense of where the American political system was headed—and what that might mean for people's choices as they thought about exercising a right that was once widely treated as precious.

Part of the process of gaining perspective required a look at the candidates' performance in 1996. But it soon became obvious that looking at 1996 alone was not likely to provide much help. That should have been expected, perhaps, because election years are typically strange and often misleading. Yet the start of 1996 seemed unusually bizarre to me. Distorted images floated over and through each other across the screen. It was surreal.

Four things, in particular, were striking. First, there was the change in Bill Clinton. He had always had a remarkable capacity to adapt to his audience and to transform himself to gain political appeal. But as he took center stage for the semiofficial start of his reelection campaign, on January 23, he reached a new level. For one compelling hour, as he delivered his State of the Union address, he seemed oddly like a cross between a President and a Mighty Morphin Power Ranger—a Mighty Morphin President.

Like most Americans, I watched from afar via television. In prior administrations I had had a front-row seat, and had come to appreciate the show. It had degenerated into a sporting event that some thought a bit grotesque. But it was still an important annual rite of renewal. It commenced with the President's triumphal entry as a conquering hero through a cheering crowd: the proverbial man in the arena. There was little danger, however, other than the risk of boredom. The only bull that entered the ring showed up as lines moving across a TelePrompTer. The scene was, in fact, more like raucous theater than any athletic challenge. Yet, as a sometime aficionado of this peculiar art form, I had to admit: President Clinton put on a first-class performance.

He had not always looked or performed so well. But he and his handlers had managed a fantastic transformation. About a year before, his advisers had persuaded him to stop being seen in public doing the Clinton shuffle. Until they did so, he had jogged almost daily before attendant TV cameras. His style was not that of a classic runner. And his rest stops at McDonald's did not accentuate his athletic prowess. But that was not the problem. His advisers felt there was something more basic that was wrong with the image he was communicating. That image was somehow internally conflicted. In doing his special shuffle, the President wore a baseball cap with one or another middle-American advertisement on the visor. He also wore a distinctively short pair of short-shorts, which commentators tended to mock. In its way, this combination was fitting. It was consistent with the new breed of yuppie populism that the Oxford-and-Yale Arkansan had cultivated. But Americans seemed to want a bit more dignity in a President of the United States.

So, after the crushing congressional electoral shift of 1994, President Clinton was persuaded that he had to seem more like a strong American leader. At a minimum, he had to look more like a composed and conventional adult. The short-shorts suddenly went the way of his late-night saxophone. They disappeared. And the President who, for his first two years, had appeared routinely in casual attire underwent a sartorial metamorphosis. In public, he was seen almost exclusively in buttoned suits, dressed like a bona fide grown-up.

I had had a year to adjust to this newfound presidential appearance. So, seeing the President look dignified as he delivered his address was not what seemed surreal. What seemed odd was more fundamental. What caused the clash of images was the character the President had chosen to adopt for this occasion. Along with most other Americans, I had seen him advertise his youthful connection with President John F. Kennedy, and then consciously mimic JFK's distinctive hand gestures and cadences. But superimposed upon the Kennedy image was something new. On national television, in prime time, with a straight face, President Clinton did a full-fledged imitation of none other than the President whose policies he had long ridiculed, Ronald Reagan.

It wasn't merely that he adopted such Reagan techniques as saluting heroes carefully placed in the House balcony. It was the substance of what he had to say. This alleged role model for the profligate star of the best-selling political novel *Primary Colors* presented himself as a stern protector of traditional values. And this recent advocate of one of the most interventionist policy proposals in American history, the Clinton-Magaziner health plan, elicited applause from both Republicans and Democrats with a line that was as disingenuous as it was popular. It became the headline for the speech: THE ERA OF BIG GOVERNMENT IS OVER.

The line played like a declaration of victory in a long and difficult war. It was blazoned across newspapers throughout the land. And amazingly, it was taken seriously. Even the leading conservative journal of opinion, *The Weekly Standard*, featured the line on its cover. "The Era of Big Government Is Over," it repeated, along with this attribution: "Bill Clinton, announcing the surrender of modern liberalism." This was the subtitle to the *Standard*'s even bolder declaration: "WE WIN."

For me, this was the second major oddity of 1996. I liked and respected the *Standard*'s editor and publisher, Bill Kristol, a smart and sophisticated analyst of the American political scene. Yet I wondered what on earth he may have had in mind in declaring, "We win." Who was the "we"? Conservatives were not exactly one big happy family. And what was the "win"? The federal government's share of gross domestic product (GDP) was almost identical to what it had been when Ronald Reagan took office, promising to reduce it radically.

The accompanying *Standard* editorial noted that the Clinton "concession" was "rhetorical and insincere." "But," it went on, "rhetoric matters." This was a respected tenet among merchants of language. And I happened to agree with it. Still, I thought, reality matters as well!

To me, the reality did not seem to be one that conservatives should have been celebrating. Bill Clinton was in the process of rehabilitating himself yet again. Often criticized for shuffling back and forth on matters of policy, he was now seen as staking out a firm claim to the broad middle of the American political spectrum. Indeed, with his Reaganesque act, he had just successfully stolen a march to the center, where American presidential elections are won or lost.

And while President Clinton was reclaiming the center, the Republican party seemed to be tearing itself apart, with internecine warfare over who and what were righter than right. Respected moderates shied away from the fray. Jim Baker, Dick Cheney, and Colin Powell—leaders in the dramatic Gulf War victory—had decided to forgo a primary contest for the Republican nomination. So had Jack Kemp, a confessed "bleeding heart conservative." He had found himself at odds with the House Republicans' one-dimensional focus on cutting government spending. But the remaining field of would-be presidential contenders was hardly shy about cutting itself to pieces. Ronald Reagan's eleventh commandment—speak no ill of fellow Republicans—was but a nostalgic memory, if that.

Malcolm S. (Steve) Forbes, Jr., started the bloodletting in

New Hampshire and Iowa with a barrage of negative advertisements. Its size and concentration were unprecedented for these
states. Forbes, like Ross Perot before him, was a multi-hundred-
million-dollar populist, who could finance his own campaign.
His ads attacked the respected Republican Senate Majority
Leader, Bob Dole, conservative Texas senator Phil Gramm, and
former Tennessee governor Lamar Alexander. Their offense,
according to Forbes, was that they had all participated in raising
taxes.

Forbes proposed to scrap the current tax system and substitute a 17 percent flat tax on earned income. His proposal
seemed simple. And its in-your-face, anti-government boldness
attracted a popular following. But whatever popularity the flat
tax might have had was soon limited by counterattacks from almost all visible Republicans—ranging from Alexander, who
criticized it as "nutty"; to Dole, who expressed concern about its
effect on the deficit; to Speaker of the House Newt Gingrich,
who dismissed parts of the Forbes plan as "nonsense."

As if this were not enough, Pat Buchanan advanced his
own, very different, brand of populism—nativist, protectionist,
and isolationist. He was consciously running against much of
what mainstream Republicans stood for. As was increasingly
common, he claimed to be adamantly against government—except that he saw the need for government to thwart immigration, stop imports, and impose his own set of values. He was, in
fact, against Washington government more for its being out of
touch with the concerns of ordinary Americans than with its
"bigness." His message appealed to many working Americans,
who were sick of political hypocrisy, alienated by modern liberalism, and fearful of the forces of change. That was no small
number of Americans. But for every American Buchanan attracted, he scared many more.

He and Forbes were very different in their policy orientation, with Forbes being much more market-oriented and tolerant. Together, however, they made a powerful assault on the
conventional Republican establishment. For some time, that establishment had failed to communicate that it really understood the economic worries of the middle class and the fears
associated with the breakdown of traditional values. It did not
seem adequately to care. Nor did it seem energized for a serious

fight to restore the American Dream. Clearly, these were fatal flaws for a group that meant to govern. The establishment did, indeed, need a wake-up call.

But the Buchanan-Forbes wake-up call amounted to more than just a telephone ring or the hum of a clock radio. Theirs was a full-blast air-raid warning. Indeed, they meant to do more than just warn; they meant to complete a disabling attack.

Their first target was the natural Republican front-runner, the distinguished and dedicated Senate Leader, Bob Dole. Buchanan showed surprising strength by winning the New Hampshire primary. Conventional wisdom correctly said that neither he nor Forbes could be the ultimate Republican nominee. Still, they had significant effects.

Bob Dole and Lamar Alexander were then the leading Republican candidates who defined themselves as alternatives to the "extreme." But while separating themselves from the polarizers, they were also tilting further to the right. Both Dole and Alexander were, in fact, moderate personalities with centrist balance. Yet the primary process made caricatures of their better selves. Dole, whose character and leadership abilities were proven strengths, was made to play defense on others' turf. And Alexander, who was capable of thoughtful advocacy, felt obliged to pose as a plaid-shirted populist. Buchanan and Forbes dismissed both derisively. If, as some claimed, the purpose of this conflict was to elevate discussion of policy ideas, such elevation was not the dominant impression. Alexander, who was normally temperate, was reported to have likened Buchanan to the discredited Senator Joe McCarthy. Buchanan then termed Alexander's newly acquired campaign chairman, the conservative Bill Bennett, a "Beltway blowhard." The quality of debate did not seem to be helping advance anyone or anything.

By forcing the Republican party to the immoderate right, the polarizers allowed candidate Clinton to occupy the abandoned middle ground without much contest. And by framing a stark, sometimes scary, contrast, they were making it easy for the newly presidential Clinton to appear as a moderate and reassuring presence. They were making his reelection campaign so much easier that *Wall Street Week*'s iconoclastic TV host, Louis Rukeyser, suggested that Bill Clinton himself must have been behind all this.

Respected conservative columnist Charles Krauthammer lamented what he described as the "calamitous political immaturity of contemporary conservatism," noting, "Republicans seem unable to realize that they are no longer the party of protest but the party of governance."

Even the conservative editors of the *Wall Street Journal* were alarmed. In an editorial entitled "McGovern Republicans," they criticized Republican party activists and professionals for "Borking" each other:

> Put simply, Republicans are on the verge of transforming their party into the mirror image of the loser Democrats: A party in which the only people who can win can't be nominated, and a party in which the only people who can be nominated are people who can't win. . . . Republicans in general and the religious right in particular are behaving like McGovern Democrats. That is, like losers.

As images from Iowa and New Hampshire were televised across the land, the political dynamics seemed like theater of the absurd. And yet this was all unquestionably real.

There was a third oddity that struck me in this surreal mix. Though others acted as if they knew, I couldn't quite figure out what was really meant by the assertion "The era of big government is over." At one level, of course, the meaning was obvious. In switching from mimicking JFK to mimicking Ronald Reagan, President Clinton meant to signal that he understood what poll after poll made clear: In the period since the Kennedy assassination, the public had steadily lost confidence in government.

The confidence of the Kennedy era had been high. It was naively optimistic, perhaps; but well within the tradition of the American Romance. In his famous inaugural address, President Kennedy had offered a "revolution of hope." He knew and communicated that America was meant to be special—special in its place, special in its mission, special in its promise. The idea of America was meant to be liberating. The spirit of hope was meant to soar, to mount up with wings as eagles. Having written of America as *A Nation of Immigrants*, Kennedy understood the boldness of spirit that gave life to each new wave and each new generation. With confidence in what government and Americans together could do, he linked past, present, and future to the American Revolutionary spirit:

> We dare not forget today that we are the heirs of that first revolution. Let the word go forth from this time and place, to friend and foe alike, that the torch has been passed to a new generation of Americans. . . . Since this country was founded, each new generation of Americans has been summoned. . . .
>
> Now the trumpet summons us again—not as a call to bear arms . . . but a call to bear the burden of a long twilight struggle . . . against the common enemies of man: tyranny, poverty, disease, and war itself. . . . And so, my fellow Americans: Ask not what your country can do for you—ask what you can do for your country.

Yes, this had a fair degree of adolescent romanticism to it. But as one of the adolescents who had been inspired by the Kennedy promise, I could attest to the force of its appeal. Back in those days of Camelot, a whole new generation was inspired by hope and a confident sense of the possible. Government was not the enemy. Public service was a noble calling.

But a generation later, when President Clinton declared the era of big government over, the mood had certainly changed. It had become politically fashionable to treat government as the enemy. And there was not much evidence of a soaring sense of promise.

Given America's remarkable achievement, there should have been some confidence in her political system's capacity to deliver. In two short centuries, America had risen from colonial upstart to leader of the world. She had attracted more of the world's immigrants, assimilated more races, given opportunity to more of the earth's diverse ethnic groups than any society in history. There was obvious reason to marvel at the American political system's endless renewal. It had inspired the whole world's move toward freedom and market-oriented pluralism. America had become the sole politicoeconomic superpower. To many, she seemed to be fulfilling the mission that had guided her founders' hopes: becoming the proverbial "city upon a hill."

Abundant natural resources, a market economy, and a strong work ethic undoubtedly had much to do with the success story. But America's government had played a major role throughout—from developing the railroads and opening the West to educating the public, pioneering new technologies, winning two world wars, assuring the collapse of imperial communism, landing on the moon, and beginning to explore the reaches of space. Yet, all of this was somehow irrelevant to the mood of diminished confidence.

Notwithstanding the record of success, the change in national mood was clear. And it had an understandable basis in reality. America had suffered from a host of traumatic shocks in the post-Kennedy period. Not only had the President and his brother been assassinated; so, too, had Martin Luther King and Malcolm X. The "best and the brightest" had failed to deliver either their intended Great Society or victory in Vietnam. Watergate had broken a basic bond of trust. The Arab oil embargo had called attention to America's interdependence in a changing global economy. The Iranian hostage taking had made an American President seem impotent. And even after the Reagan restoration of hope, there was a sense of disappointment.

The trillion-and-a-half-dollar federal budget, and the mounting public debt, seemed to produce little in the way of public satisfaction. The economy continued to grow. But inner cities were decomposing. Children were seen to be at risk of abuse in homes, schools, streets, and the emerging electronic media. Middle-aged workers feared restructuring. Older Americans were often ignored, isolated, and underused. Civility seemed to decline, and violence to increase. The media had become more adversarial. Television's emphasis on entertainment had given greater visibility to the extremes, increasing the power of political polarizers. The system seemed, too often, to find itself in unproductive stalemate. Fulfillment of the American Dream was thought to be in jeopardy.

But still, I found myself asking, did those who proclaimed the end of an era mean to suggest that all these problems were the result of government that had grown too big? It didn't quite add up. The connections between many of the perceived problems and "big government" were, at best, unclear. And more simply, it was unclear whether "big government" had really grown so big.

It depended how one measured. Government's share of the economy was actually much smaller than in most other developed countries. And in relation to the U.S. economy, the federal government had been relatively stable for two decades. Even in relation to the Kennedy era, it was only modestly larger (4 percent of GDP) than it had been. And that increase was accounted for almost entirely by transfer payments—the growth of social insurance, which went primarily to the middle class, and which the middle class showed no eagerness to give up.

Further, it seemed clear that, though many Americans were disappointed, few were volunteering to give up on America's pursuit of the Dream. Ironically, their disappointment was a testament to the Dream's continuing power. It was the standard against which the system was being measured. Indeed, the struggle over tax and spending policy in the latter part of the twentieth century was not merely about the size of government. It was, more important, a struggle about whether and how the federal government should best assure that the American Dream might be fulfilled. Whatever may have been meant by the facile assertion that "the era of big government is over," one thing it certainly did not mean was that the struggle about how to achieve the Dream had reached its end.

Far from it. That struggle promised to be one important focus of the presidential election—which brings me to the final thing that struck me as odd about the start of 1996: Republican leaders of what Colin Powell had termed the "sensible center" seemed to be missing in action.

The center had played a crucial role in the domestic policy struggles of the past quarter century. But since the midterm election of 1994, the center had not been part of an effective governing coalition. There was no such governing coalition. To many, it seemed as if no one was in control. And at the start of 1996, in the face of what promised to be a historic national referendum, the Republican center was keeping its collective head down, as if in hiding. No Republican leader had yet felt comfortable defining a centrist vision, or even just an effective case for a centrist.

Of course, even as Buchanan and Forbes enjoyed their temporary highs, I knew that a degree of centrism was likely to return as the general election approached. And on March 5, Junior Tuesday, the possibility of a centrist revival suddenly began to suggest itself. Bob Dole won eight out of eight primaries.

His moderate competitors dropped out of the race, leaving him as the sole representative of moderation. Appropriately, Dole declared himself to be like the Energizer bunny, who beats his drum and keeps going, and going, and going.

His immediate problem, however, was that his polarizing critics were refusing to accept the reality or legitimacy of his likely convention victory. They seemed characteristically uncompromising in the pursuit of their objectives, determined to keep shooting holes in the Energizer's drum. Buchanan, in particular, continued to denigrate Dole. And he promised his followers that he would fight to assure that the Republican platform reflected his views, and that Colin Powell would be denied the vice presidential nomination.

In time, of course, the Forbesians and Buchananites would yield to reality. But their extended opposition was symptomatic of a longer-term problem that showed no signs of passing. In the Republican party of the mid-1990s, there were powerful factions that considered moderation a vice. They made it difficult for centrists to lift their heads aboveground without fear of "friendly fire."

Dole himself was not one to be intimidated. He was a battle-tested soldier—"tested, and tested, and tested," as he justifiably emphasized. But still, his practical problem remained: He might have to spend so much attention protecting his right flank, or mollifying its intemperate leaders, that he would be denied the opportunity to use his unquestioned skills as a centrist leader. Looking too much to the right could hurt doubly. For a conservatively oriented centrist who was interested in governing, the dilemma was first this: Accommodating the polarizers in the campaign could cost the election. But then, second, if the election were nonetheless won, accommodating excessive demands from the hard-right Gingrichians in Congress could mean a failed presidency. To be elected and then effective, Dole had to strengthen his base in the middle. And yet that is exactly what the polarizers on the right meant to prevent.

As a creature of the center, I found its predicament disconcerting. And as a citizen, I found it disturbing. This was not merely a partisan matter. Clearly, Republicans who practiced the politics of polarization—not just Forbes and Buchanan, but the Gingrichians as well—had made it easy for Bill Clinton to steal his election-year march to the middle. Yet to me, the issue seemed larger.

The American political system was meant to be governed at the center. Pat Buchanan did not believe that; nor did the hard-right Gingrichian faction in the House of Representatives. But they were wrong. And a majority of Americans understood that they were wrong. That was part of the reason presidential elections ended up being a contest for the American middle. The 1996 election would be no exception. Yet even as a degree of centrism reappeared in the general election, as was to have been expected, that was not enough. The country needed a full-time governing centrism, not just periodic posturing for the middle.

The system was not intended either to jump to extremes or to polarize itself in unproductive stalemate. To move forward in its historic quest, the American system required not only bold vision and consistent conviction; it also required creative mediation and constructive compromise. That was what a vital center was supposed to provide. Yet, in recent years, it had not been able to do so. The polarizers' perceived power, and their evident contempt for mediating forces, were keeping the system from its normal tendency toward constructive compromise and forward movement. That was not healthy.

Having participated directly in many of the heated policy battles of the 1980s and early 1990s, I was inclined to wonder what accounted for the center's predicament. How had the system—and the public debate—come to this curious pass? Would the rise of the politics of polarization permanently weaken the forces of constructive moderation? How and when might a creative center be seriously revitalized—not just for campaigning, but for governing? Who or what was to assume effective control?

I didn't have entirely satisfactory answers. It was obvious that one would have to look back at more than just the election year to begin to understand what really might be meant by this odd swirl of forces: the evident populist frustration; the rise of the polarizers; the weakness at the Republican center; and the remarkable Clinton declaration, "The era of big government is over." I reflected on my experience in several Republican administrations. It alone could not produce the missing answers.

But the experience seemed to me to provide a perspective that might help.

That perspective has led me to think that, in addition to important issues of ideology, Americans must consider a related choice. It is a choice among governing styles: whether, on the one hand, to tolerate a continuation of polarized politics; or, on the other, to return a degree of power and legitimacy to the sensible center.

In the past, our political system has been threatened by the prospect or pleadings of one extreme or another. And it has consistently demonstrated both its stability and its capacity for self-correction. So it is not the risk of the "extremes" that concerns me. There is more than enough counterbalance to keep that risk low. What should be of special concern now, I think, is the risk of continued stalemate. It is not only unproductive. It is also corrosive of the confidence on which our system depends for its energy, creativity, and ultimate sustainability.

In its remarkable history of progress, America has moved through cycles of romantic hope and disappointment, of establishmentarian complacency and populist correction. Indeed, the past two decades might be viewed as an extended wave of populist correction. In many respects, that correction has been valuable. But from my perspective, the correction that is called for in looking toward the next presidential term is this: The politics of posturing and excessive polarization should be put behind us. It is time, once again, for governing—bearing in mind that, in the American system, that requires an effective political center.

An elaboration of what has led me to this perspective follows. It grows out of a story that starts where much of the recent struggle over "big government" and "the Dream" started: with the Reagan Revolution. The story tries to show what has really come of the "revolution"—and how the system and its elected leaders have steered us to where we are today. Then it uses this perspective to frame a look toward the future. It does so in the hope that, with this bit of history in view, one might better assess the continuing arguments over the future of "big government," the American Dream, and the role of the center. In the process, it may imply an answer to the related issue that elections periodically settle: What kinds of characters should the people put "in control"?

PART ONE

GOING FOR
THE BOLD—

And the Power
of the Mainstream

1

The Buckaroo Stops Here:

The Reagan Revolution
Comes to Town

PRESIDENTS ARE OFTEN thought to be powerful. At the President's desk the proverbial buck is said to stop. But, of course, we're all taught that power is intentionally divided and shared in the American system. Power often seems like mercury. One may think it fixed in a neat silver ball, only to find it break into little pieces, and slip in all directions.

Presidents, especially, know the frustration. President Harry Truman offered a somewhat sarcastic lament for his successor, General Dwight Eisenhower, the heroic leader of World War II. "Poor Ike," he suggested, would find the presidency very different from the military. A President might say, "Do this, do that," and find that nothing happened. Two of Ike's successors, Presidents Lyndon Johnson and Richard Nixon, must have felt that frustration in the extreme. Each won a large electoral victory, and then was forced to relinquish power ahead of his intended time. President Johnson had to withdraw from his reelection campaign in the face of insurgent "flower children." He had failed to gain sufficient support for either the war in Vietnam or a full-scale war on poverty at home. And President Nixon was forced to resign in the face of threatened impeachment. His final tearful press conference, before backing away with a last double-armed salute, remains a telling reminder of how ephemeral the illusion of power can be.

Yet, though power skitters about, the ball of mercury does seem to land in the hands of the people from time to time—at least during elections. The process may seem surreal. Choices may be disappointing. Yet when the people vote, they do make one point clear: The buck may stop at the President's desk; but the people decide who sits behind that desk—with what support, for how long. And when the public becomes disturbed, its will can strike with a suddenness that rivals that of the executioner. It is almost cruel to watch. Indeed, eyes turn quickly to the new holder of the big silver ball, who is suddenly invested with euphoric hopes and a new mandate to use his "power" and lead.

So it was in 1980, when Americans decided that they were fed up with governmental ineffectiveness and the floundering of the 1970s. Abruptly, unequivocally, they brought on a new act. They sought relief in the American Romance, the mythic imagery of America's limitless potential and special mission. They summoned a cowboy hero out of the West, a nostalgic flashback out of the heart of America.

Though he had risen to national prominence, Ronald Reagan remained the quintessential hometown boy, a friendly reminder of America's simpler past. He was the embodiment of traditional Americana, from *Boy Meets Girl* to *Hellcats of the Navy*. He personified heroic folklore from Knute Rockne and the Gipper to General Electric and the cowboy tales of *Death Valley Days*. And on November 4, 1980, this friendly cowboy was suddenly the President-elect of the United States.

On that election night, the suspense ended early. Among Washington's Georgetown dinner party set, many lamented that President Carter's concession came before cocktail ice had even begun to melt. This was as troublesome in the East as disenfranchisement was to the late-voting electorate in the West. There, people were informed of the election result before they got a chance to vote.

The press, in their characteristic way, immediately forgot their too-close-to-call reporting. They hailed the dawn of a "new era." The page one headline of the *Washington Post* captured the new wisdom of the herd, "A Sharp Right Turn: Republicans and Democrats Alike See New Era."

What exactly would define the new era remained to be determined. The principal contenders were diverse: a revivalist conservatism, a cowboy nostalgia, a market-oriented modernism, a nascent neoliberalism, or a higher synthesis still struggling to be born.

But uncertainty about the ultimate outcome did not tone down either the established national newsmagazines or their hitherto obscure conservative counterparts. Together, they proclaimed a "Reagan Revolution."

In voting for Ronald Reagan, the electorate had not actually affirmed any particular "Reagan Revolution." At the time of his election, the terms of the "revolution" had not yet been specified in any detail. The notion of a Reagan Revolution had meaning for a small group of hard-core conservatives and long-time Reagan activists, known as "Reaganauts." But for much of the majority who voted for Ronald Reagan, the use of the phrase "Reagan Revolution" was taken to be largely sloganeering or media hype. They had voted for a change of direction, but not really a hard-right revolution.

Candidate Reagan had, in fact, campaigned on popular general themes that were hardly revolutionary: restoring American strength; ending "the failed policies of the past" and the liberal excesses of "tax-and-spend." He had flirted with a fundamental shift of power to the states; but, as a practical matter, had abandoned any radical proposal before the general election. The same was true of his inclination to privatize Social Security. He did say he would cut personal income tax rates across the board by 30 percent. And he promised to cut federal spending down to 19 percent of GDP. But he didn't say exactly how.

More than an affirmation of a specific program, the vote for Ronald Reagan was a vote for a nostalgic hero and a rejection of the frustrations of the years before. It was a vote against the disappointment that had started in the aftermath of the Kennedy assassination, deepened with the failures of Vietnam, and expanded steadily with the seemingly endless crises of the 1970s.

Of course the prior decade and a half had not been entirely without its moments of confidence. In one triumphant display, fulfilling the Kennedy commitment, Americans had actually reached the moon. That was a heroic and inspiring achievement, seemingly impossible before it was done. The first human to set foot on the moon, Neil Armstrong, captured the spirit of the moment in a single, powerful sentence: "That's one small step for man, one giant leap for mankind." But clearly, this was far from the norm.

In some adolescent quarters, there had been hopeful talk of "the dawning of the Age of Aquarius . . . when peace will guide the planets, and love will steer the stars." So, at least, went the dawning of *Hair, the American Tribal Love-Rock Musical.* The Age of Aquarius promised to be an age of liberation—not only from earthly bonds, but from virtually everything. At *Hair*'s dawning, the liberation was mainly symbolic: from codes of dress. Youthful Americans, who found it only partly satisfying to mock Victorian standards by adopting Edwardian attire, took this form of protest to the next natural level. Where humankind, in its thousands of years since the fall, had clung to a curious insistence on clothing, young Americans appeared without any attire at all. The concept of liberation extended beyond such superficia, however. It extended to "the system" itself. Many adolescents approached the bicentennial celebration of the American political system in the spirit of *Hair:* looking confidently forward, in naked innocence, with "revolution" on their minds. For more traditional Americans, this was not an entirely comfortable prospect.

In reality, America in the 1970s was more bogged down by its sense of crisis than uplifted by any revolutionary spirit. Washington disturbed itself constantly with images of challenge that threatened risks of disaster. The classic Kennedy crisis, the Cuban missile crisis, had had a heroic quality and a somewhat satisfactory ending. The crises of the 1970s, however, didn't quite measure up. They just proliferated. In foreign affairs, some tended to be exaggerated, like President Ford's *Mayaguez* crisis. Others were mismanaged, like Vietnam generally, or President Jimmy Carter's treatment of the Near-Eastern "arc of crisis." And in domestic affairs, the crises seemed to make up in number what they lacked in quality.

The following is a selection of 1970s "crises" that were identified by the national news media. They are listed in alphabetical order, for most proved to be recurrent: crises of the budget, capitalism, child care, cities, competitiveness, conscience, credit, crime, the dollar, drugs, energy, environment, ethnic pride, fiscal responsibility, health, high blood pressure, higher education, housing, hunger, illegal aliens, inflation, intergenerational relations, leadership, manpower, medical malpractice, modernity, municipal finance, political participation, race relations, rural poverty, school finance, Social Security, social services, tax fairness, teenage alcoholism, transportation, un-fulfilled expectations, welfare, and White House management.

In part because these were not handled satisfactorily, there were also "the crisis of confidence," "the economic crisis," "the crisis of Western democracy," "the crisis of spirit," and "the cri-sis of competence" (not to mention the likes of "the lingering crisis," "the hidden crisis," and "the coming crisis"). To this al-ready excessive list developed by the media, academics added still more: "the intellectual crisis," "the crisis of understanding," "the crisis of uncertainty," and so on. (In academese these might be termed a set of meta-crises.) It was crisis identifica-tion, more than the human spirit, that seemed to know no earthly bounds.

In 1979, frustrated by the energy crisis and other woes, President Carter retreated to Camp David, the local Catoctin mountaintop, to reflect upon what had been wrought. There-upon he pronounced a more basic domestic malaise: "a crisis of confidence," "a crisis that strikes at the very heart, soul, and spirit of our national will . . . threatening to destroy the social and the political fabric of America." His Democratic challenger, Senator Ted Kennedy, accused him of "lurching from crisis to crisis" in foreign affairs. This was not without reason: Eritrea, Nicaragua, Iran, Yemen, Cuba, Afghanistan. The President him-self termed the Afghan crisis "the most serious threat to world peace since the Second World War." Then, turning inward again, he suddenly ordered a crash revision of his weeks-old budget, declaring a national economic crisis. A sense of pro-portion seemed lost. The Carter White House's chief of staff, Hamilton Jordan, captured the spirit of the times by titling his memoirs with this one word: *Crisis.*

At the time, I said that America was exhibiting the symp-toms of a "crises crisis." The phrase was half-facetious. But clearly something was wrong—whether the underlying reality, or its characterization, or both. America was describing herself in a schizophrenic way: a society uniquely capable of problem solving; a society continually plagued by intractable national crises. And both parts of the schizophrenic character were based in an odd reality. America was uniquely capable. But in the post-Kennedy period, America had been peculiarly clumsy.

By the end of the 1970s, the American standard of living was in decline. The global poor continued to mount. Africa had been liberated from colonialism, but enslaved by domestic poverty and authoritarianism. War-torn Southeast Asia was destroying what remained of itself. Latin America was in latent turmoil, but largely ignored. The global balance seemed unstable. America's ability to project military power was in doubt. An Iranian cleric held Americans hostage. And an American President seemed almost impotent.

The capacity to destroy had at many turns outpaced the capacity to create. Disquieting strains of change were more deeply marked than ephemeral streaks of hope. The vision of youthful promise seemed a distant hope for those who still dared dream. Clearly, the Age of Aquarius and other fantasies of an adolescent America had not yet fulfilled the promise of their dawning.

For much of the nation, the characteristically confident American spirit had flagged. That, I thought, was a serious problem. Since John Winthrop had first sermonized about colonial America as "a city upon a hill," in 1630, America had consistently defined herself as an inspirational force. So, as the 1970s malaise deepened, I imagined profoundly troublesome consequences if America were to lose her special sense of mission.

Yet before these troubles could materialize, a process of self-correction triggered itself into action. The American Romantic spirit, I discovered, could not long remain subdued. The rhythm of reality shifted. Through a clear populist reaction, America summoned a primal image of herself.

On the cover of *Time*, the hero brought forth out of the West smiled at the nation. He was an American icon, Ronald Reagan, captured perfectly by a Michael Evans photo. From under the cocked brim of his cowboy hat, the new President smiled his confident smile as if to say that all would soon be as thoroughly hopeful as, in America, it was meant to be.

The broad crowd of populists who had become upset with government's failures were suddenly given a renewed basis for hope. I myself looked forward to several things I thought a Reagan presidency could reasonably be expected to produce: a healthier and more market-oriented economy, a stronger America in a still-dangerous world, and a renewed sense of national confidence. But, like a majority of other Americans who had voted for Ronald Reagan, I did not actually expect a hard-right revolution. I didn't take the talk of a conservative revolution much more seriously at the start of the 1980s than I had taken the talk of a liberal revolution at the dawning of the Age of Aquarius. The use of the word "revolution" seemed way overblown.

Further, I had some doubts whether the incoming Reaganauts would even be able to get effective hold of government. They did not control the Congress. And it was unclear to me whether they had a working understanding of the governing culture for which their rhetoric had shown contempt. I suspected they did not. But I also suspected that the rest of us probably did not understand how the governing culture would handle the populist infusion.

So it was with considerable curiosity that I watched when high noon approached on Tuesday, January 20, 1981, as Ronald Reagan prepared to take a few last steps as a private citizen. His gait had a little hitch in it, like that of a seasoned bronc-buster. He sometimes explained that an old injury had left one leg slightly shorter than the other. Commonly pictured in Western clothes and a cowboy hat, he was viewed as too much of a gun-slinger by what was left of the old establishment. But he was somberly dressed for this occasion. His sure right hand was ready. He lifted it to the hip that had often been seen with six-gun and holster. Then he moved it on up to the traditional position from which to take the oath. Within seconds, he was sworn in as President of the United States.

President Carter looked on—defeated, but apparently serene. President Reagan observed:

> The orderly transfer of authority as called for in the Constitution routinely takes place, as it has for almost two centuries. And few of us stop to think how unique we really are. In the eyes of many in the world, this every-four-year ceremony we accept as normal is nothing less than a miracle.

There was a little hyperbole in this observation. It linked politics and metaphysics. But it accurately communicated a sense of wonder. President Reagan suggested that America's traditional pride was about to be renewed. A natural American exceptionalist, he clearly appreciated the specialness of the American system.

Official accounts noted that President Reagan had become the fortieth U.S. President. This went unrebutted, except by the President himself. From time to time, he took friendly pleasure in pointing out the error. By his reckoning, the Reagan presidency could be termed the fortieth presidency. Yet he, Ronald Reagan, was only the thirty-ninth individual to become President. Statisticians mistakenly counted Grover Cleveland twice. Cleveland was responsible for two presidencies (separated by the Benjamin Harrison presidency). But he was really only one President. On this, as on many other issues, President Reagan preferred his own math. And in this case, he was right. But right though he was, and thirty-ninth President though he may have been, he was nonetheless consistently referred to as the fortieth President of the United States.

Even a favorite presidential gift got it wrong. It was a Western-style belt buckle. The buckle is still worn proudly by several grateful recipients. On each buckle is a classic image of Reagan-style power. It is a cowboy on a bucking bronco in front of the White House. It bears this bold imprint: "The Buckaroo Stops Here." Yet on the flip side of every one of these buckles is an inscribed message, "With best wishes, Ronald Reagan, 40th President of the United States." This unyielding little inscription is a hidden reminder of the limits of presidential power. As Presidents come to know better than most, once even rather small things get established, it typically takes more than presidential words to change them.

The Reagan presidency, of course, came to demonstrate this point dramatically with regard to larger matters of accountancy. In his inaugural address, the new President lamented debt and promised "to get government back within its means." But in his first year, President Reagan signed a bill that "temporarily" allowed the federal debt to exceed $1 trillion. The President also promised to balance the budget and begin retiring the debt by 1983 (soon revised to 1984). Yet by 1984, it was to become clear that he would have to raise the debt ceiling to more than $2 trillion; and it would keep rising with $200 billion deficits as far as the eye could see.

The governmental bronco was to show that it had a strong head of its own. Yet on inauguration day, that evident truth in no way humbled the new buckaroos. They were ready to mount, and to turn into bronc-busters.

As it happened, I ended up joining these new buckaroos. I served in the Reagan White House, with pride, as assistant to the President and deputy to the chief of staff.

One might well wonder, as I sometimes did, what I was doing among the would-be bronc-busters. How did a member of the Kennedy-inspired generation of youth get associated with the Reagan Revolution? Was this just an unusual case of wandering, or had the country moved so far to the right that this was to have been expected?

Answers differed for different people. The generation that had gone adrift in the late 1960s and early 1970s had begun to regain its bearings. By the late 1970s, even famous radical activists had moved back into "the system." Tom Hayden became an elected assemblyman and California state senator. His former wife, Jane Fonda, the heroine of the anti–Vietnam War culture, was marketing exercise videos to what had become the "me generation." Eldridge Cleaver ran for the U.S. Senate from California—as a Republican! The once-notorious Chicago Eight were beginning to look like establishmentarians. Jerry Rubin was a successful businessman, and Rennie Davis was preaching risk-aversion as an insurance salesman.

In my own case, I had never drifted far from center. Yet, like the scientist who is still part child, I was still part adolescent in my attraction to idealistic hopes. I had not lost the youthful dream that somehow we might "explore the stars, conquer the deserts, eradicate disease." In this sense, I was still very much imbued with the spirit of the Kennedy era. That spirit had been lost in the aftermath of the assassination and the unsuccessful Johnson presidency. And though I had served in the subsequent Nixon and Ford administrations, I had to acknowledge that they, too, had failed to renew the sense of the American Romance. Under President Carter, the once-powerful sense of romance had been reduced to a pervasive malaise. Yet, in contrast, it seemed that Ronald Reagan, in his own distinctive way, had some of the same confident, romantic spirit that had once inspired America. Along with millions of other Americans, I found that spirit attractive.

Even so, for many people like me, a journey from the mainstream toward the right bank did seem an odd crossing. Among those close to me, it seemed especially odd to my wife, Kathleen Emmet. She and I had been classmates at Harvard College. She had gone on to get her Ph.D. in English literature, and had become a writer. She had her own perspective on government, and was not a natural enthusiast for my association with the politics of a White House. She was certainly not inspired by the prospect of a trip to the right. Indeed, she would have preferred a tilt to the left. But odd as it may have seemed to Kath, to others, and even to me, the journey that some of us took seemed even odder to those standing solidly on the right bank.

My service in prior Republican administrations had earned me the epithet "Washington insider." As such, I was understood to be of some possible use to the new administration. But to the newly empowered Reaganauts and movement conservatives, "Washington insider" was not a flattering concept. To them, I was clearly a cultural and ideological outsider.

One of my early mentors had been Elliot Richardson, with whom I first served when he was secretary of Health, Education, and Welfare (HEW) in the first Nixon term. HEW was then the biggest government department, with a budget larger than all other federal departments combined. (It was later split into smaller pieces.) Richardson was serious, highly intelligent, and as consistently decent a person as I have ever met. He was also a sometime adversary of the then-governor of California, Ronald Reagan.

Featured as "Super-Secretary" in the national press, Richardson set an American record, becoming a cabinet officer in four departments. As he moved, I was fortunate to be able to move with him. I went to the Pentagon as special assistant to the Secretary of Defense, then on to Justice from which Richardson (and I) later resigned on the occasion of the Saturday Night Massacre, and on to Commerce in the Ford administration, where I served as assistant secretary for policy. Clearly, my rapid rise in the Washington system was inextricably associated with Richardson's. For me he became not only an admired mentor, but also a close and continuing friend. He was a quintessential "moderate."

I was somewhat more conservative than Richardson, but

did not define myself as ideological. I was highly committed to the virtues of markets and pluralism, and strongly opposed to statism and totalitarianism. Yet I had never found it particularly useful to divide Americans according to ideological categories. Rarely had I encountered serious and sustained ideological conflict within the United States, except in academic courses and intellectual debates. In the world of practical America, there were competing labels and slogans; but ideology tended to be blurred, confused, often hypocritical, and routinely put aside. The gap between left and right was much narrower in America than in most societies. And most Americans were prepared to be flexibly pragmatic within America's traditional democratic bounds.

So it was new to me to find ideology to be the driving force for many of the Reaganauts. They used it as a litmus test by which to separate the black hats from the white hats. And their version of the purity test was one I could not pass. Indeed, in their minds I was disqualified for having been so clearly associated with moderates. "Moderate" was a term I had been taught to think of as a virtue. With experience, I had come to believe it clearly was a virtue. But hard-right conservatives were trained to treat it as a vice.

In joining the Reagan White House, I had been exempted from the litmus test. I came straight from a position on the post-election transition team, which I owed to Jim Baker, the newly designated White House chief of staff. Being hooked on public policy making, and genuinely disturbed by America's having lost her way under President Carter, I had approached Baker the moment his appointment was announced. He promptly named me executive director of the White House transition, from which I moved to the White House as his deputy.

Baker and I had served together at Commerce, where he was undersecretary when I was assistant secretary. We had worked together closely and well. He had a natural gift for governing responsibly. An unusual combination of Princetonian and Texan, he was both smooth and tough, moderate and conservative, broad-gauged and focused. He had a remarkable ability to earn people's confidence and respect almost immediately. And he used this, with skill and grace, to help people put away their lesser interests and find their way to constructive agreement. In this, he was ideally suited for coalition building—as he was later to show not only in managing divided government at home, but in building creative alliances abroad.

Baker had left Commerce to lead the 1976 Ford campaign to its convention victory over candidate Ronald Reagan. Tried-and-true Reaganauts, some of whom had been with Ronald Reagan since the wilderness days of 1964, were upset by the new President's choice of Baker as White House chief of staff. But I viewed the announcement of Baker's appointment as a highly encouraging initial step. Among other reasons, it seemed to confirm what I had guessed: that President Reagan would govern with a degree of pragmatic balance.

That was exactly the attitude that earned me the kind of skepticism that greeted Baker. I was actually greeted by somewhat greater skepticism from the right than had greeted Baker—and understandably so. I had not worked in the Reagan campaign, or any other campaign for that matter. I was not part of the organized conservative movement or any other organized movement. Movement activism (right, left, or center) was foreign to me.

Further, I was from New England. The new governing culture was much more Californian and Western. Unlike many of the new buckaroos, I didn't wear Western cowboy boots. I tended to wear beat-up Bass Weejuns. They were part of my former school uniform—an Ivy League uniform, of all things. My version of that uniform lacked any style, even Eastern style. I remember Nancy Reagan's look of shock when I first visited President Reagan in his study. Her eyes fixed on something that I had not noticed until I caught her stare. She was looking at my shoes, not my eyes. I had dressed early, in the dark. My shoes were utterly plain. But one turned out to be black and the other brown. It was obvious that I had not set foot—either foot—on Beverly Hills's posh Rodeo Drive.

The only substantial contact I'd had with California was as a teenager. And that was highly indirect. My father had me go "west" to South Barre, an old mill town, out toward the western part of Massachusetts. There I worked two shifts a day in a mill that processed raw wool. On one shift, I cut open fleeces from all over the world. On another, I had to spread them around in a dark, putrid, two-story interior silo. All the fleeces were filthy. But it was easy to recognize those from California. They were dryer than the others. When hit by the knife that cut them open, or when dropped from above in the silo, they produced distinctive clouds of California dust. The clouds were like smoke signals from the dry California ranges. But I could not decipher their meaning.

Clearly, I was not a natural for the Reagan White House. Still, I felt strongly that America needed to refind her historic place. In pursuit of this, I saw the Reagan phenomenon as a potentially useful corrective. America also needed a successful presidency. And for that, I was arrogant enough (many would say more than arrogant enough) to believe that I could make a useful contribution. I didn't take the ideological differences to be as significant as some did. On the basis of Ronald Reagan's record as a labor negotiator and governor, it seemed to me that, though he might talk like an ideologue, he might govern with a reasonable degree of moderation. In any case, I tended to give considerable weight to the inertial tendencies of the American political system.

As it turned out, I spent the entire four years of the first Reagan term in the White House, and several hours of every day with the President. I came to respect him personally and professionally to a far greater extent than most of my moderate and liberal friends would have thought likely.

Initially, I was given responsibility for coordinating all staff work intended for the President or issued on his behalf. I was known as the "last stop" for all paperwork on its way to the President's desk. My out-box was the President's in-box, and vice versa. Steadily, additional responsibilities were given to me. I coordinated the work of the Legislative Strategy Group and the President's Budget Review Board; became a routine member of the President's traveling core group; oversaw presidential speechwriting; and attended most meetings of the cabinet and National Security Council. I also became a consistent participant in most of the smaller groups where the management of the presidency was really conducted.

In his personal qualities, President Reagan was as good as he seemed: decent, principled, patriotic, concerned, likeable, and gracious. He was also better than he seemed. Far more than we condescending Easterners had assumed, or than he let the general public know, he was intelligent, disciplined, and hardworking. Admittedly, he was a biased empiricist, tending to remember only the evidence that reinforced his ideological predilections. And he was often oddly passive. But in the period when I worked with him, long before his Alzheimer's disease took its tragic hold, he still had a near-photographic memory. He had a clearheaded capacity for writing and editing, a compulsive insistence upon completing whatever work was given him—and, when he applied himself, a natural analytic facility. (This last had been underused because his charm, good looks, and memory served to get him a long way without additional effort.)

Beyond these personal qualities, I came to respect President Reagan's profoundly important historical contribution to the restoration of the American spirit. Still, I never really became a Reagan revolutionary in the indiscriminately anti-government sense of those who used the phrase. And though it took me a while to accept, at no point was my presence accepted by the hard right. My moderateness (compounded, no doubt, by my arrogance) permanently disqualified me.

When I had become established in the Reagan White House, I assumed there might be some grudging conservative accommodation to the reality of my position. But I couldn't have been more wrong on that point. The editor of *Conservative Digest* reminded me of the counterreality with this lively handwritten note:

Dear Richard:
    You slay me! What a wry sense of humor! You're "frankly somewhat disappointed" to read in my column that I think your appointment was a "mistake"? Wow. . . .
    "Somewhat disappointed" indeed. Think how we feel, Friend, think how we feel!

Best regards,
John [*Lofton*]

When President Reagan was sworn in, I didn't really have an informed sense of the serious ideological conflict that was ahead. At most, I had incomplete inklings.

Immediately after his inaugural address, the new President performed his first official act. At 1:00 P.M., in the President's Room of the Capitol, he signed a Federal Employee Hiring Freeze. He ordered "a strict freeze on the hiring of federal civilian employees to be applied across the board." He did so after removing a little note I had attached. It was the first of what would be thousands of such notes I addressed to the President, indicating what each associated memorandum was about and what action was recommended. This initial action was largely symbolic. But symbolism was an important part of the three-month action plan that had been developed to create a sense of motion and change. And symbolic action was to become an important part of the Reagan presidency.

As his second official act, done within minutes of the first, the President began to hire some new civilian employees. He nominated his cabinet. Having just signed a hiring freeze, some might have said there was a little irony in this. But it went unnoticed.

At 9:25 the next morning, right after breakfast, the President went downstairs to the East Room of the White House. There, he participated in the swearing-in of the first new hired hands: the senior White House staff. I stood among the Californians, Jim Baker, and many others in this band of new hires as we were all sworn in together.

The ceremony was impersonal. It was not exactly in the American individualist tradition. In retrospect, I came to think we were arranged like the staff of some European manor. But the brief show was reasonably dignified. The Marine band played. Chief Justice Warren Burger led the recitation of the oath of office. The President said we were a team. (I presumed he would be correct; but "team" turned out to be more aspiration than description.) He rightly said that "our loyalty must be only to the nation and to the people that we represent."

As I looked at the classical lines of the East Room, and the panels depicting Aesop's fables above, I didn't think of cowboys or much else. I suppose I might have thought of the famous stories of President John Adams's family hanging laundry in the East Room; or of Union troops occupying the room in the Civil War; or of Amy Carter roller skating on the polished parquet floor; or of President Kennedy lying in state there. But the truth is this wasn't the kind of ceremony I had much interest in. I was thinking mainly that there was important work to be done.

Our little ceremony ended, and several of us went off to a cabinet meeting for the official start of what was supposed to be cabinet government. In general, cabinet meetings did not turn out to qualify as the kind of important work I had in mind. The

President himself later joked that the plaque on his cabinet room chair should read, "Ronald Reagan slept here." But cabinet meetings required attendance.

At 10:15, the President entered the cabinet room through the door that connects it with the Oval Office's outer office. A large portrait of Calvin Coolidge was by that door. At the direction of John Rogers, the paintings had been changed immediately upon the change of presidency. Rogers, who was the new head of White House administration, had a keen eye for aesthetics. But the Coolidge portrait had not been selected for its artistic quality. President Reagan had selected it for another reason, the irony of which was not yet to be appreciated. He had chosen Coolidge out of respect for his budget balancing.

We all stood up, and the President said, "Don't get up." He did so in a characteristic way that communicated two important messages at once. With his bearing he said, yes, treat the presidency with special respect. With his eyes and expression, he said, no, don't think I'm anything other than a regular American guy.

Throughout his presidency, we always disobeyed and stood up. And throughout, he managed to maintain just the right corrective balance between the casualness of the Carter era and the imperiousness of Nixon's. (In symbolic terms, his style was just about halfway between a Carter cardigan and the braided epaulets once contemplated by the Nixonians.)

To relieve tension—whether a group's or his own—the President was a chronic joke-teller. He led off with a joke for newcomers. It was about confused Army recruits trying to learn how to salute. They tried one way, then another, then another, until one of them took command and said, "Wait, wait. Just do it like they do it in the Army!" Although not exactly hilarious, the joke got a nervous, supportive laugh.

At 10:20, the press were ushered in for an opportunity to photograph the proceedings. At 10:22, the President made a few remarks for their benefit, and they were ushered out. This, plus the opportunity to witness our swearing in, provided the only direct exposure to the President that the press would have as they developed their authoritative accounts of the first day's White House news.

With the press removed, the substantive business began. But it wasn't clear that the press was missing much. There was little that seemed revolutionary. And if anyone was inspired to build a city on a hill, it was not immediately apparent.

Eight of the ten agenda items involved the budget. They began with a review of the freeze and ended with a discussion of spending controls. David Stockman, the brilliant young budget director, provided most of the content. He had been a revolutionary of the left in his student activist days in the 1960s, but was accepted in early 1981 as a full-fledged Reagan revolutionary. This curious incongruity was treated as no more peculiar than the fact that the new Secretary of Energy had been trained as a dentist. And with the fervor of the converted, Stockman dominated.

He had not participated in the development of the abstract economic plan that candidate Reagan had run on. Yet he was unquestionably a strong advocate of spending reform. And after the election, under the watchful eye of proven Reaganauts, Stockman led a crash effort to give the plan concrete meaning—and to make it workable. That was a large challenge, which Stockman rose to as well as anyone could possibly have done.

In the cabinet meeting, the President himself showed a keen interest in spending control. But he was especially focused on what seemed surprisingly minor matters. He did not offer any grand vision of program elimination, or restructuring, or privatization, or devolution of responsibility to the states. He did recommend a report on the efficient operation of a motor pool.

This turned out to be a common characteristic of the Californian Reaganauts. Led by presidential counselor Ed Meese they tended to think the enormous federal budget could be dramatically reduced by cutting administrative overhead to increase efficiency. This was also the conventional businessman's point of view. Though seemingly commonsensical, and clearly appropriate in some contexts, it was a deficient notion when applied to the federal government. Overhead reduction, though desirable, could not be a panacea. It could not be a significant cure for the problems of "big"ness that were widely seen as offensive.

Many people had a picture of federal inefficiency and bureaucratic foolishness that was born of their experience with federal regulation. To them, it was obvious that the federal government promulgated much incomprehensible regulatory gobbledygook. In important ways, this regulation affected states, localities, and the private sector. In the process, it almost always increased their overhead. In many cases, the regulations were justifiably viewed as ridiculous. That led naturally and understandably to an image of the federal government as inefficient at best, a horde of bureaucrats tripping over each other to do things that were somewhere between useless and absurd.

In reality, however, the problem with the federal government was far more basic than "overhead." The problem was much more the substance of offensive regulations than the administrative inefficiency of those who produced them. And when it came to addressing the federal budget, the image of excessive overhead and administrative incompetence—however well earned—was actually an unhelpful distraction. Stockman knew that well.

The federal government was largely a dispenser of money to entities other than the federal bureaucracy. The amount it transferred to individuals, states, localities, and private entities was close to one hundred times larger than the administrative cost of running the federal government. The federal government was actually relatively efficient as a check-writing transfer agent. What was typically inefficient or ineffective was the use of federally transferred funds by others, who were forced to operate within convoluted program structures and extensive federal constraints.

There was money to be saved from reducing program overlap, making greater use of vouchers and market incentives, and transferring more flexible authority to states and the private sector. Such reforms were well known among federal policy anaysts. (These were reforms that I myself had worked on at Harvard in the late 1960s. And at HEW, in the early 1970s, Elliot Richardson had integrated a set of related proposals in a single comprehensive reform. Its title, the "Mega" proposal, revealed both the scope of its authors' ambition and our lack of schooling in populist communication.) But such basic structural reforms went far beyond overhead. For exactly that reason, they amounted to a far more significant political undertaking than improving administrative efficiency.

Thinking primarily in terms of overhead could not generate the political strategy necessary for the more basic reforms.

Indeed, no such broad strategy was seriously advanced until the Gingrichian revolution of 1995. And the difficulty that strategy encountered only underlined how large an undertaking serious structural reform really was.

Be that as it may, back in 1981, overhead is not where the proverbial Willy Sutton would have looked for savings in the federal budget. Apart from fundamental structural reform, the big money was in defense and "entitlements," a euphemism for mandatory income transfer programs and health insurance payments. (Interest on the federal debt later became a third major component of federal spending. But it was not so significant until the big run-up in federal debt.) Because the Reaganauts wanted a strong increase in defense spending, a serious reform of entitlements was necessary if significant overall budgetary savings were to be achieved.

This was an inescapably important point. But it constituted a fundamentally troublesome dilemma. A serious reform of entitlements would have had to go beyond restraint on programs for the poor because most of the entitlement programs and dollars went to the middle class. Yet political support from the middle class was essential for the rest of the Reagan agenda. The dilemma was straightforward. There was no way the cut-taxes-increase-defense-balance-the-budget math could work without an attack on middle-class entitlements. But there was no way the politics could work with one.

The initial discussion of the budget saw no dilemmas, however. The implied premise was that, with a sharp eye on things like wasteful motor pools, all would be well. That, of course, was to prove absurd.

After the lesson on motor pool management had been recommended by the President, the Secretary-designate of Labor offered an idea of his own. He suggested it would be good if the government could organize all our nation's youth to work and save as a way of paying off the national debt. It was curious that this supposed conservative was volunteering a suggestion that was half-socialistic.

While some eyes glazed over, a few others opened with wonder. Seeming to sense he did not yet have full command, this new bronc-buster beat a quick retreat. He said he recognized that his idea was "perhaps too idealistic." And, as it was to turn out, debt reduction was not to be the way by which the Reagan presidency would define itself for history.

Clearly, buckaroos had stopped at the White House. Out of the West, the Reagan Revolution had come to town. The new cowboys were ready to take what they thought were the reins of power. But it wasn't yet clear just where they'd end up—or how long they would ride.

2

"P Hit/Fighting":

Who's in Control?

THE NEW BRONC-BUSTERS had hardly taken hold of the reins when an ugly shot of reality hit. The illusion of a pleasant ride along happy trails went poof. In a way that few old-time scriptwriters would have allowed, the cowboy in the white hat was suddenly blown out of the saddle.

For all the promise of a "new beginning," the Reagan Revolution was almost over before it began. And the system was put to an interesting test. Who would assume control? And what would be the fate of the Reagan Revolution?

At 2:28 P.M., on March 30, 1981, shots were fired at the President. That much was immediately clear. But all other early reports were confused.

Some suggested that one more presidency—this one less than three months old—was suddenly to fall, the victim of yet another assassin's bullet. Everyone had seen replays of the Kennedy assassination video, with the youthful President's head blown forward and back; and his wife climbing out the back of the open limo in her bloodstained pink suit. But at the first news of a shooting involving President Reagan, all was still too uncertain for such dire images. It was not even clear that the President had been shot.

Several of us on the White House staff gathered immediately in the large corner office of the chief of staff, Jim Baker.

Blocks away, Jerry Parr, the President's lead Secret Service agent, had thrown the President to the floor of the presidential

47

limousine. The President himself did not think he had been shot. Parr's shove was a standard precautionary measure.

At 2:30, when Parr saw the President coughing bright red blood, he ordered the limo to George Washington University Hospital. He and the President thought that Parr's protective shove must have broken one of the President's ribs and punctured a lung. That was the President's self-diagnosis as he started to walk into the hospital. Then his knees buckled as he gasped for air.

A nurse, a paramedic, and two Secret Service agents helped carry the President to a trauma bay. One nurse started tearing off his clothes. "I knew I wouldn't wear that suit again," the President later remarked. But as the suit was actually being cut away, the President was in no position to joke. Another nurse was taking his blood pressure. Above the noise of the crowded emergency room, she shouted, "I can't get a systolic pressure."

Technically, the Secret Service worked for the Secretary of the Treasury, Don Regan. He, too, had rushed to Baker's office in the West Wing of the White House. The office had an understated spartan style that suggested discreet order. (It would later become Regan's office, and assume a corporate plushness. But it was still four years before the Baker-Regan job switch.)

The Treasury Secretary had his own full-time Secret Service detail. This was an excessive perquisite of power. It had been added by one of Regan's self-aggrandizing predecessors. But it was one more mark of Regan's classic American climb. That climb had taken him from the poorer side of the tracks in Cambridge, Massachusetts, to Harvard, then to the Marines and some of the toughest battles of World War II, on to the top of the Wall Street pyramid, and then on toward the top of the Washington power culture. His progress was like that of the Merrill Lynch bull he had helped make famous.

Through his agents he was able to communicate directly with the President's. At 2:40, the Secret Service reported to Regan, and he reported to us: The President was not hit.

At the same moment, I looked over Jim Baker's shoulder. He was on the phone with Mike Deaver. Among members of the White House staff, Deaver had the closest personal relationship with the First Family. He had been in their service for most of his adult life. He himself had just narrowly missed a bullet, and was at the hospital with the President.

Baker was taking notes. I watched as his black felt tip pen scrawled: "P hit/fighting."

I then thought of the Kennedy assassination and all the associated images. So did Deaver. But his Kennedy flashback was more focused. He recalled the Parkland Hospital in Dallas, from which President Kennedy emerged as a corpse.

Deaver put Dave Fischer, the President's personal aide, on the phone. I picked up a second receiver. Fischer was like a loyal son to the President, and was on the verge of breaking up. He said the problem was with the President's chest, and he wondered aloud whether it might be a coronary. The President was having trouble breathing.

At 3:00, the Secret Service confirmed Deaver's report. The President had been hit. His condition was serious, but stable.

Within a short time, things began to sort themselves out. A command center was established at the hospital, with Baker in charge. Cabinet officers and White House staff gathered around the heavy wooden conference table in the White House situation room. It was just down the hall from my office, and much less impressive than outsiders might have imagined: small and windowless, but secure.

The President's National Security Adviser, Dick Allen, calmly coordinated. It was not always easy.

At 4:09, Secretary of State Alexander Haig twisted to look up at the television set. He was seated next to me at one corner of the table. The TV set was behind and above us on the wall. Haig was staring intently.

Larry Speakes, the deputy press secretary, was on the screen. A few minutes before, Haig had proclaimed, "The helm is right here in this chair" (meaning his own). Since it was the chair right next to mine, I suppose I might have felt some sense of respect. But no one seemed to pay much serious attention. Mentally, I dismissed Haig's statement as utterly absurd.

At 4:10, a press questioner asked Speakes whether the Vice President would assume "emergency powers." "Would there be a division of labor of any kind?" Speakes responded innocently enough, "Not that I'm aware of. We just haven't crossed those bridges yet."

Within the hour, the situation room group would make a false start across "those bridges"—the bridges of succession to the presidency. But no one knew that at the moment.

"Who's running the government right now?" another questioner asked. "Would Vice President Bush become Acting President?" The issue wouldn't go away.

"I cannot answer that question at this time," Speakes said.

"Larry, who'll be determining the status of the President and whether the Vice President should, in fact, become the Acting President?" asked another reporter. "Pardon?" said Speakes. "Who will be determining the status of the President?" the questioner repeated.

"I don't know the details on that," Speakes replied honestly. But he communicated a degree of unsureness that some found a bit unsettling. Many people were looking for whatever reassurance certainty might bring.

Annoyed at the slowness with which Speakes was providing details, CBS's persistent Lesley Stahl asked, "Why the time lag?" Speakes's response showed both the need for prudence and the inherent difficulty that faced us all. "Lesley, I would assure you there is no reason except we want to be completely sure of our facts."

As Speakes tried to handle these questions, I could see the emotion rising in Haig's eyes.

From the moment he had arrived at the White House an hour and a quarter before, it was evident that he wanted to take charge. Wearing a trench coat with shoulder pads and epaulets, he had marched into Baker's office like a modern-day soldier-bureaucrat's version of Patton or MacArthur. The office had once been his. The big, wood-paneled wall desk was right where it was when he had taken it from Bob Haldeman eight years before. He seemed intent upon repossessing it.

But by the time he reached his old office, people were scattering to the hospital and the situation room. There was, in reality, little for him to command. Authority for most key functions rested with others.

Haig, the former four-star general and former Nixon chief of staff, was not in control. He moved to the situation room where, like the rest of us, he sat around the table seeking and reviewing information—with relatively little that could be done. His one assignment came from Baker. It hardly seemed worthy of his past. He was to ensure that any White House public statements were coordinated with the command group at the hospital.

Speakes had been at the hospital. Baker had sent him back to the White House with instructions on what to say. Having his instructions, Speakes had gone straight to the press room. He had not stopped in the situation room or checked with Haig.

Initially, Haig didn't sense that Speakes had entered his domain. Then he noticed the familiar blue White House press room backdrop behind Speakes on television. His jaw tensed as he realized that the one thing he was assigned to control was operating completely independently of his command. "He's right upstairs here!" he said of Speakes in near disbelief. He glared at the screen with an intensity that made his eyes seem like two remote control laser beams trying to shut Speakes off. But Speakes kept talking.

Haig erupted. He jumped up to leave the room. With four bullish strides he reached the door, charging forward. I could tell he intended to go to the press room and thought of lassoing him to hold him back. But I had neither the authority nor a lasso.

Haig said he was going to "repair" what Speakes had done. That turned out to have been a poor choice of words.

Dick Allen seemed to try to restrain him by tugging at his elbow. But off Haig went, with Allen hanging on.

Haig charged up the stairs. Several of us followed. And at 4:14, Haig began what were to become his most famous public remarks.

"I just wanted to touch upon a few matters associated with today's *tragedy*," he said. No one had yet officially used such a strong word.

"The *Crisis Management* is in effect. . . ." Most of the public had no idea what that was. But it sounded ominous.

"Constitutionally, gentlemen," he said to the women and men of the press as if he were addressing a group of junior, male military officers, "you have the President, the Vice President, and the *Secretary of State* in that order." That, of course, was not correct. It was a hint that Haig was on the edge of experiencing a heightened delusion of his own grandeur.

"As of now," he went on—perspiring, tense, seeming almost to tremble—*I am in control* [sic] here, in the White House. . . ." That line became the most memorable of his entire career. His delusion of grandeur seemed beyond the ordinary.

It was reminiscent of Dr. Strangelove. Haig intended to calm the nation. He unnerved the world.

George Will later offered television commentary on the scene. He noted that Haig's performance was either politically insensitive or Constitutionally illiterate. It was both.

When we got back to the situation room, the chain of command issue got hotter. The Secretary of Defense, Cap Weinberger, calmly intoned that the alert status of the bombers had been raised slightly. This was directly at odds with what Haig had just told the press and the world. Haig blew up.

Weinberger was receiving and reviewing military situation reports every few minutes. He explained the change in alert status as essentially a matter of prudence in light of minor shifts in Soviet forces. I suggested that if there was to be any public comment on the change, it ought to emphasize that this was strictly a standard precautionary measure. I was anxious to avoid excessive reactions, both internally and externally.

But Haig was anxious about something else: authority. He challenged Weinberger, a distinguished graduate of Harvard Law School, saying Weinberger didn't know his Constitutional law. Haig's argument was wrong and somewhat off point. Weinberger was acting in accord with the National Command Authority, the law and regulations governing the chain of military command from the President on down. He knew what authority he had. And he knew that neither the Constitution nor any law placed Haig immediately after the Vice President in the line of succession. Nor did they place the Secretary of State in the military chain at all.

In his calm way, Weinberger exhibited a quiet contempt for Haig's claim of authority. As Haig continued his blustering, Weinberger made him look the more absurd with incisive remarks that were barely audible, but clearly cutting. Allen supported Weinberger on the issue of authority. They were among the few who seemed to understand the matter correctly.

The President's counsel, Fred Fielding, and I quietly took Weinberger aside as he answered a call in the larger monitoring room that enveloped the small conference room. We told him we, too, knew he was right. We all wanted things to cool down at the moment. But if the authority issue were to be seriously contested, we said we would produce the relevant documents.

It was a bit odd. Here, in the inner sanctum of the national security system, were most of the highest officials of the executive branch. Some had enjoyed the trappings of power in previous administrations. Although occasionally they displayed the frenetic enthusiasm of kids playing capture the flag, in general they took to the closed world of national security with high self-seriousness. But a high school civics class knew almost as much about the Constitution as this distinguished crew.

So Fielding and I prepared to conduct a little adult education course if we had to. We each sought relevant papers from our offices. I was gone for only a few minutes. When I returned, Fielding was with Haig and the Vice President's chief of staff, Dan Murphy, at one end of the sit room table. They were looking over documents.

But the documents weren't the Constitution or the relevant law and regulations. They were actual succession documents, letters drawn up in accordance with the Twenty-fifth Amendment to the Constitution. They were addressed to Strom Thurmond, President pro tempore of the Senate, and Thomas P. O'Neill, Jr., Speaker of the House. And they were available for possible execution by the assembled members of the cabinet—with places for signature neatly arrayed in two columns, beginning with the Vice President and ending with the Secretary of Education. There had never before been a transfer of power under the Twenty-fifth Amendment. But one quick pass around the room, and the group might have begun the effective removal of the President of the United States.

I had worked briefly with both Haig and Murphy when they wore their military uniforms. (Like Haig, Murphy was also a retired four-star—in his case, from the Navy.) Our careers had all overlapped at the Pentagon. When I was a young assistant to the Secretary of Defense, Murphy was his principal military assistant, and Haig was vice-chief of the Army. That was in 1973, before I moved with Richardson to Justice, where I had my first dramatic encounter with Haig's approach to command. Among other excesses of clumsy authoritarianism, Haig helped engineer the firing of Watergate special prosecutor Archibald Cox. He thus forced Richardson's resignation in the Saturday Night Massacre and crystallized the public perception of President Nixon's guilt. In the process, Haig had the FBI seize and seal our offices at Justice. Though overdrawn, I could never forget my Saturday Night Massacre image of him as commissar of a police state.

We got along superficially in the Reagan administration; but Haig and I remained suspicious of each other. He was thoroughly engaging at times; and treated me like an old Army buddy, slapping me on the back and calling me "tiger." But he was rightly skeptical of my willingness to follow orders in the style of the military. And I was highly skeptical of his tendencies under stress.

About Murphy, I had no such reservations. He had been a model of prudent balance when I knew him at Defense. Even so, I didn't like the image that ran through my head as I looked toward the end of the sit room table. Although they were both wearing well-tailored civilian suits, I couldn't help seeing Haig and Murphy as if they were still in military dress: two four-stars arranging the succession to the presidency of the United States. It didn't seem quite democratic.

Images aside, it seemed unnecessarily risky to deal with signable succession documents in that context. No doubt those involved thought it only prudent. But all things considered, it seemed to me unwise. The group in the situation room had shown itself capable of chaotic, emotional, half-informed discussion. We did not need a general outbreak of that. There was a strong possibility of misleading leaks (as when press secretary Jim Brady was mistakenly declared dead). And there was little to be gained from a discussion of presidential succession just then—later perhaps, but not then.

The Vice President was in an airplane. The plane was hardly an ideal command center. It did not even have a capacity for secure voice communications (an oversight that was subsequently corrected). What capacity for voice communication it did have was subject to frequent breakup. That failing was immediately evident. When Haig first called the plane to tell the Vice President of the situation, he had to repeat his name three different times, finally bellowing it, in order to be understood. This weakness in the communication system presented practical difficulties that argued against moving formal authority to the plane.

There was also a narrower administrative problem. For the Vice President to become Acting President, the Twenty-fifth Amendment required transmittal to the congressional leadership of a "written declaration." But since the Vice President was in the air, he would be unable to deliver any succession documents bearing his personal signature until his return. His return had been accelerated, but was not expected until about 6:30. It didn't seem reasonable that the written declaration should be delivered unsigned. And though it was possible to execute a signature on the Vice President's behalf, I didn't think it desirable for him to take over the presidency on the strength of an automatic signature pen. The Justice Department was inclined to argue that the documents simply had to be "transmitted," not actually delivered or received. With this interpretation, the Vice President could sign his declaration on the plane, and then deem himself to be transmitting it. But this seemed to me to be a legalistic argument that was better not joined unless it had to be. So I concluded that, as a practical matter, there was no fully credible way to transmit succession documents for at least two hours. And in two hours, we might know a lot more.

In the interim, the national command authority existed to assure timely military decision making through authorized channels. It was designed to serve even if the President or the Vice President were unable to communicate. It had weaknesses, both technological and political. But it could handle this situation as well as it could handle most other contingencies—whether a military "black bag" (bearing codes for the management of nuclear war) falling off a horse on a mountain ridge, or the temporary sedation of a President for a medical procedure.

The fact was, however, that there was no evidence to suggest that there was any military dimension to the shooting. The Attorney General, William French Smith, was a longtime Reagan loyalist. The director of Central Intelligence, Bill Casey, was hardly a naïf. Both reported that there was no sign of conspiracy or organized foreign threat. Indeed, Smith said that investigators had already found the name of the would-be assassin's psychiatrist, and that all available information suggested a lone actor. Smith and Casey remained firm even when pressed by a suspicious Haig, who took pains to remind us of foreign connections in the Kennedy assassination.

Apart from military contingencies, there were no presidential actions required in the next few hours. And of some relevance, surely—or so it seemed to me—there had not yet been a clear determination as to the President's medical condition and prospects. Further, there was something unseemly about a rush to succession. For a moment, I had something like that half-sick feeling that Hamlet expressed when his uncle so quickly assumed the throne upon the death of his father: "O God! a beast that wants discourse of reason / would have mourned longer."

Quietly, I made several of these points (excluding the Hamlet reference) to the little Fielding four-star group. I suggested that I should take the succession documents for safe-keeping until their use was deemed appropriate. And I removed the documents from the table.

Then I got Baker on the open line that connected us with the hospital. I told him what I had done. I suggested that there should be no action on our end until there was a formal medical determination on his end, and asked him for his backing if I needed it. He readily agreed. Indeed, he said that at the hospital, huddled in a half-closed space for privacy, they had considered having the President execute a temporary transfer of power. They had rejected the idea.

So, I took the first succession documents in America's history to be readied for execution under the Twenty-fifth Amendment. I put them in my personal office safe, unexecuted.

When I went back to the sit room, at 4:43, the group was watching a videotape replay of the Haigian melodrama. Several people laughed, including Haig. It was another reminder of the wonders of television as an entertainment medium. Then, at 4:44, Haig got on the phone with President Nixon. Images from the past, from Kennedy's assassination to Watergate, were overlaid on the present. Like fast-forward and reverse on the videotape machine, time seemed to be jumping around.

At 4:48, Regan half-jokingly told Marty Anderson, the President's rather libertarian policy adviser, "Better get started on our policy on handgun control." Then Regan was given a note from his Secret Service link saying the President would be out of surgery in ten minutes.

Haig said to prepare a public statement on this, "an international hand-holder." Remarkably, he saw himself as the voice of reassuring calm.

At 6:15, Jim Baker returned to the sit room and took over effective control of the group. A close personal friend of the

Vice President's, Baker was one of the few whose power could be expected to increase, not decrease, if there were a Bush presidency. The power-sensitive sit room group showed a little extra gravitational pull in his direction.

Allen was going over the next day's schedule. Baker said, "Don't get involved in questions of succession. By tomorrow, the President will be able to make a decision." Allen then noted that a bill had to be signed. "It'll be a historic signature. They'll want to know how his hand moved."

At 6:30, the Vice President's plane landed at Andrews Air Force Base. In the sit room, we were tuning in the early feed of the CBS news, getting it from Baltimore half an hour before its Washington airtime. Upon seeing the news, Haig said we had to get a press plan. This was ironic. His "I am in control" show was one of the most glaring press problems. He later attributed this to "the way in which the tape was edited, especially by CBS." He termed this "the most effective bit of technical artistry to appear on television since that unfriendly makeup man touched up Richard Nixon's five o'clock shadow before his first debate with John F. Kennedy." Unfortunately for Haig, no one else—except perhaps President Nixon—interpreted his problem as sabotage by television. Television had simply brought into every home, live and in color, a telling glimpse of this particular character under stress.

Regan correctly added that we needed public statements prepared before the financial markets opened. Baker noted, "We've got to get the doctor's prognosis first." Somehow people seemed to keep overlooking this. Caught up in the heady atmosphere of crisis, some tended to interpret events so as to keep the crisis alive.

Vice President Bush joined us in the situation room at 6:59. His manner was at once dignified and matter-of-fact. He had helicoptered from Andrews to the Vice President's residence, and had come by motorcade from there. Helicopter landings on the White House lawn were ordinarily reserved for the President. The Vice President had discreetly chosen not to assume that privilege. He received reports from several of those assembled. Then he said that he wanted to postpone any discussion or paperwork concerning a possible transfer of power—that a transfer of power would be a bad signal.

At 7:30, Dr. Dennis O'Leary briefed the nation on the President's condition. (Brady was still in surgery.) He said that the President was "clear of head" and that the prognosis for recovery was "excellent." Like the rest of the nation, we who were watching on the sit room screen breathed a collective sigh of relief.

When the doctor got through answering the press, Lyn Nofziger took the remaining questions. He had been President Reagan's press secretary in the California days and had joined the White House as assistant for political affairs. With his distinctively disheveled look (and Mickey Mouse tie loosened at the neck), he was, in his own way, a reassuring Reaganite symbol of continuity.

"Have you considered invoking the Twenty-fifth Amendment?" Nofziger was asked. "No," he said, "we have not considered it. We have not considered invoking it. No." As far as Nofziger and most other people knew, that was correct. Shortly thereafter, the sit room group disbanded.

By 8:50, the President was joking in the recovery room. With tubes in his mouth, he wrote an old W.C. Fields line, "All in all, I'd rather be in Philadelphia." The White House press office released the quip. The President's humor deepened the national sigh of relief. It was exactly the right touch. No amount of press planning could have done better.

At 11:00 P.M., I prepared to go home. I had one last task. I got S-509, a milk price support bill, ready for the President's consideration and signature. It was the kind of entitlement a Reagan revolutionary should have wished to veto. But for political reasons, the President's advisers—including all the Reaganauts—unanimously recommended that he sign it. Although it was obviously not the story of the moment, that little fact was an important harbinger of things to come.

In his hospital bed, at 7:00 the next morning, the President borrowed Baker's cheap plastic felt tip pen. It was the same pen that only sixteen hours and twenty minutes before had scratched out "P hit/fighting." With a noticeable downward wobble on the Ronald, the President signed the bill.

Without any change in the formal authority structure—without any need for change—the business of American government went on. The system managed to preserve its equilibrium. The sense of crisis passed. A calmer reality returned. And the

Reagan Revolution, which less than a day before looked as if it might suddenly be over, was left to follow what course it would. What that course would be, in the aftermath of the attempt on the President's life, and what the system would do with the Reagan Revolution was much less clear to me.

It is a testament to the power of the televised image that people remember Haig's "I am in control" as clearly as the attempt on President Reagan's life. The Haigian moment suggested that not just some crazed assassin, but perhaps the system itself had gone awry. It quickly became evident, of course, that the Constitutional system remained intact. (And it was soon to become clear that the system would remove from power a character whose delusions of grandeur seemed likely to become dangerous if left unchecked.) But what interested me, especially, was the question introduced by Haig's memorable assertion: Who really was in control?

The assassination attempt led me to wonder, once again, about the relative "control" a President really had within the system. My wonderings were a bit more particular than the questions raised in civics: What would have happened if President Reagan had been unable to resume the duties of his office, and power had been shuffled at the top? Would that have made a fundamental difference in the ultimate fate of the Reagan Revolution?

At the time of the shooting, I thought surely it would. Initially, looking around the situation room while the President was in surgery, I couldn't help thinking that many of the faces would change if Vice President Bush were to take over. The influence of several of President Reagan's old cronies would certainly be reduced. I thought power would be taken away from several people who seemed to have less competence than a President could or should attract. As a general matter, I thought that displacement of America's most ideological President would be bound to mean that the administration would move toward the political center.

Even as the President came home from the hospital, I thought his fate—and, therefore, the fate of the Reagan Revolution—was still very much in doubt. With ruddy cheeks, a bright red sweater, and an even brighter smile, the President looked as chipper as could be. A delighted crowd applauded his arrival. He acknowledged the crowd with a characteristic wave as he walked into the south entrance of the White House. He seemed like a championship golfer strolling toward the eighteenth green. But in reality, he had risen to the occasion with a bit of an act.

Just how much of an act I learned the next morning. At 10:00 I got into the President's private elevator on the ground floor of the White House, and went up to the President's living quarters, known as "the residence." An usher showed me into a sitting room. I was joined by Mike Deaver and Helene von Damm. (She had long been the President's devoted personal secretary, later became ambassador to her native Austria, and wrote a book on the fairy-tale quality of her life.) Deaver and von Damm had been extraordinarily helpful in integrating me into the President's immediate office, which they ran. That morning, we were in the residence to discuss the President's work routine for the period of his recuperation.

When the President came in, I was shocked by his appearance. He was obviously uncomfortable walking. In the bright morning sunlight, his face looked deathly pale. His skin had a pallid, see-through quality. His distinctive smooth voice—the voice that had soothed listening audiences since his early days in radio—was lost. In its place was a low, raspy substitute. He had to strain visibly to ease himself into a deep sofa.

The First Lady entered. The President's ordeal had been especially difficult for her, and she was understandably protective of him. She was not hospitable. There was a special coldness in her treatment of von Damm. Nancy Reagan's wide eyes, frozen open, could stare adoringly at her Ronnie. But von Damm could make the President's eyes return the sparkle of her own. The two women seemed to have neither a sparkle nor a stare for each other. Without any small talk, the First Lady said she was going to be consulting about new draperies and wall covering in the area where we were sitting. She asked us to move.

The President was a bit reluctant. But straining again, he winced as he pulled himself up dutifully, and we moved to another area. "I've never understood why she cares so much about those things," he said quietly, as a courtesy to us.

The stiffness of his walk made clear that he had mustered a good show for the crowd the day before. But the most surprising thing to see was something that the First Lady ordered an usher to place on the table beside the President: a large, portable, hand-squeezed respirator. The inescapable impression was that the President was a great deal weaker than the public and most of the White House staff then knew.

We did our business rather quickly. It was clear the President was tired and not yet comfortable with extended periods of concentration.

To lighten his load, we agreed to such things as auto-penning certain classes of documents that I had previously been giving the President for his personal signature. I was among the few with authority to direct the use of the automatic signature pen. It was an excellent forger, with the capacity to execute "Ron" and "Dutch" as well as the more formal Ronald Reagan. Such pens are commonly used in large bureaucracies and most congressional offices. They are often necessary, given the large volume of paper requiring signature. But equally necessary is a system for assuring that their use is strictly controlled. For the period of the President's recuperation, my discretionary authority had to be expanded considerably.

As I left the residence that morning, I was much more worried about the President's health than I had expected to be. Thoughts of a prolonged recuperation, such as Eisenhower's, ran through my head. Even worse, I imagined the possibility of a Woodrow Wilson–type disability, with various people acting on the President's behalf. But I didn't share the wanderings of my imagination with anyone.

It turned out to have been just as well. Within a few weeks, the President seemed to have been miraculously transformed. His color was back, along with the bounce of his step. One day when I went up to the residence, I found him dressed in a T-shirt, sweatpants, and running shoes. He'd become an enthusiast for his exercise program. Not long before, I had worried about a Wilson parallel. Now it suddenly seemed more reasonable to imagine a parallel with Charles Atlas, "Rambo" Stallone, or Arnold Schwarzenegger.

The President's physical strength recovered remarkably. Indeed, his regimen made him stronger after the shooting than before. And as his physical strength grew, so, too, did the perception of the President as a strong leader.

As time passed, however, I was to notice a more and more curious development. Although Vice President Bush did not in any respect take over, the things that I had first imagined would come with such a transition nonetheless took place. President Reagan was unquestionably President. But, after a brief flurry of initial "supply-side" boldness, his administration was steadily to move toward the middle.

The purist Reagan revolutionaries lamented this. They alleged that those of us who were called "the pragmatists" were the cause. But though we were partly responsible, the allegation gave us credit for far more power than we had. I wondered more and more: Who or what really was in control?

It seemed a rather basic question for anyone who might invest hope in one vision or another. Increasingly I came to the view that, although Presidents were thought to be very powerful, their degree of control was even more limited than civics books taught. Gradually I was led to this conclusion: President Reagan undoubtedly had effects of historic proportions in slowing the growth of interventionist government and accelerating the decline of the Soviet empire. Yet these achievements were largely consistent with the objectives of the American mainstream. As for the full Reagan Revolution sought by hard-right conservatives, in most programmatic respects it was left undone.

Many assumed the contrary. They treated the Reagan Revolution as if it actually came to full fruition under the strong leadership of a bold and uncompromising President. Since my point of view is rather different, I will try to explain it.

3

Victory in the Fog:
The Ranch in the Sky

MY SUGGESTION about the limited power of Presidents—and the limited effect of Reagan revolutionaries—might be misunderstood if the argument were carried too far. I do not mean that individuals cannot make a difference. Nor would I suggest that real-world change is always within boring and predictable bounds. Clearly, some individuals seem to make a significant difference. And change can be quite surprising.

This much is true: America is naturally progressive. And though uniquely tolerant of diversity, the American system has traditionally resisted the extremes of left and right. Those with delusions of grandeur have generally been checked in their quest for power. And most American change has proceeded incrementally along a broad middle path. That does sound rather boring and predictable—stable and progressive, perhaps, yet still boring and predictable.

But there have been exceptions to the general pattern of middling incrementalism. In science and technology there have been bold leaps forward. Even in the remarkably stable American political system, there have been important cases where individuals have gone against conventional wisdom—have gone for the bold—and have successfully forced dramatic change upon the system.

The more compelling examples, which stand out in American history, are well known: President Abraham Lincoln decided to end slavery and endure the trauma of civil war, thereby expanding civil rights and strengthening the American union. Presidents Wilson and Franklin Roosevelt decided to leave America's insular past and join world wars, expanding America's global reach as a protector of freedom. President Kennedy decided to ignore the views of his science advisers and commit America to go to the moon, expanding both the frontier of human exploration and mankind's sense of the possible. These were acts of genuine historical importance, by individuals who countered the inertia of the status quo.

Reagan revolutionaries have tended to argue that a similar place in history should be claimed for President Reagan's effort to reduce radically the burden of taxation and government. That claim is excessive. President Reagan never even proposed a detailed budget that could bring spending down to the level he had promised in the 1980 campaign. And even that level was not exactly radical; as a share of the economy, it would have been about the same as in the Kennedy era.

It is reasonable to suggest, however, that President Reagan helped prevent America's slide toward a statist, European-style, mixed economy. He did. And there can be little doubt that he put conventional wisdom aside, went for the bold, and in one respect got it. Though in the course of the two Reagan terms much of the Reagan revolutionary program was rejected, its centerpiece was enacted: major tax rate reduction across the board, along with increased incentives for business investment. As enacted, the Reagan tax cut was the largest in American history. That was neither boring nor widely predicted. By American standards, it went far beyond the ordinary pattern of change. It was unquestionably bold.

And, as has since been widely observed and debated, the tax cut alone was ultimately to have major consequences for the American economy. What those effects were is arguable—and still argued to this day. Liberals have blamed it for helping the wealthy, hurting the middle class, and constricting creative policy initiative. Supply-siders have praised it for stimulating the longest period of economic growth in peacetime. One of its progenitors, David Stockman, was rather less enthusiastic in hindsight. In a rare public interview years after leaving office, Stockman said, somewhat repentantly, "No one imagined how bad the outcome would be. It was really an unnecessary chapter. It got away from us. It would have been far better had it not happened." And, troubled by the fiscal policy dilemma that persisted into the 1990s, President Reagan's former chairman of the Council of Economic Advisers, Murray Weidenbaum, of-fered this somewhat ambiguous lament: "Stockman's plan is still working. It's very hard to explain. The farther away in time one gets, the harder it is to explain. Something from 1981 is de-termining the present."

Whatever one's point of view on the economic effects of the Reagan tax cut, there can be little disagreement on this point: Directly and indirectly, it was to have a powerful effect on American politics and the shape of public argument for years and years to come.

And whatever else may be said of it, there can be little ques-tion about this related point: The bold Reagan tax cut ran counter to the prevailing conventional wisdom. It is true that there was legitimate justification for tax rate reduction. Marginal tax rates were so high that they discouraged work, increased the use of tax avoidance schemes, and increased ani-mosity toward government. There was also good reason to crit-icize Keynesianism and the Phillips curve (the staples of the liberal economics establishment). And, within reasonable bounds, it was clear that debt, investment, and some forms of tax reduction could pay for themselves. But the Reagan tax cut's supply-side enthusiasts took these defensible positions be-yond their natural bounds. They transformed them into an ex-treme form of free lunch theory.

Their argument was that the economic growth stimulated by deep tax cuts would increase revenues more than enough to offset the revenue lost by reducing tax rates. Fittingly, the free lunch theory, and the Laffer curve that described it, had been most memorably recorded on the back of a napkin. And while few doubted that tax cuts could be stimulative, the analysis sup-porting the free lunch theory was seen as amateurish at best within the economics establishment.

Of course, the opposition of the economics establishment wasn't necessarily a compelling argument against supply-side wisdom. But the political establishment wasn't much more fa-vorably disposed than the professional economists.

Traditional liberal Democrats were naturally opposed. They preferred higher marginal tax rates and bigger govern-ment. They also led the House of Representatives. The rising generation of new, young Democrats was ambivalent. In the words of one, then a thirty-four-year-old Arkansan named Bill Clinton, "Reagan's budget mathematics don't work." But these Democrats were less relevant than others in 1981. It was conservatively oriented Democrats who held the votes that were ultimately key to the Reagan tax cut's passage. And they were highly skeptical. They feared the consequences of its effect on the federal deficit.

Even within the President's own party there were major doubts and doubters. The Senate Majority Leader, Howard Baker, publicly called the Reagan tax plan a "riverboat gamble." The Republican chairman of the Senate Budget Committee, Pete Domenici, expressed strong reservations in private. So, too, did several senior members of the President's White House staff. And the sitting Vice President of the United States, George Bush, had once campaigned against it, dismissing it as "voodoo economics."

Yet, remarkably, it happened. The riverboat gambler won his bet. Improbably, he beat the House. On August 14, 1981, the Reagan tax cut became the law of the land, the Economic Recovery Tax Act.

Though it was not revolutionary, the bold 1981 tax cut was clearly outside the bounds of conventional incrementalism. And though I myself helped make it happen—I believed that some tax rate reduction was clearly desirable—I didn't really expect that a tax cut of that magnitude would actually be enacted. Like many other people, I had assumed that countervailing pressures would produce a more moderate result. But they didn't.

So it is interesting to consider: How did the boldness of 1981 overcome the system's forces of moderation? And how was the system eventually to recover its habitual balance?

On the day of the tax cut's signing, however, I wasn't caught up with these questions. That was to come in the months and years that followed—when the deficit problem burgeoned, and I found myself continually struggling with further adjustments to the 1981 act.

In those years that followed, I was ultimately to feel like a Br'er Rabbit victim, punching at the deficit tar baby while getting more and more stuck to it. (I viewed my plight more melodramatically in the successor Bush administration. I imagined myself as a modernized whaling captain pursuing the public policy equivalent of an elusive great white whale.) But at the bill-signing ceremony, I found myself merely noting a curious clash of lesser symbols.

President Reagan chose to sign the centerpiece of his economic program in a place that was very special to him. It was an earthly dream world. Not quite a city on a hill, it was a rolling hilltop ranch set in the ridges of the Santa Ynez Mountains, 2,250 feet above the Pacific Ocean, that much closer to heaven. The rugged terrain, still largely virginal, was little different from when first traversed by pioneers of the West. The name of the ranch seemed to come from a Hollywood script. But it was appropriate: Rancho del Cielo, ranch in the sky. There, the President looked forward to linking his view of paradise with his Program for America's Economic Renewal. He wanted to do so before the press and cameras, in the open air, where one could breathe free, up close to the wide Western sky.

The imagery was powerful.

The ranch evoked both the frontier settler and the Western cowboy. With Barney Barnett, his former driver and fellow ranch-hand, Ronald Reagan had cleared the brush, built the fences, and rebuilt the old adobe ranch house. With evident pride, he would tell visitors how he and Barney, by themselves, had moved and laid the very stones the visitors were then standing upon.

Yet, though unquestionably rustic, the ranch had some Hollywood qualities. Central casting seemed to have sent a city-lover to play the cowboy's wife. She obviously had no taste for the hot sun, dusty trails, rattlesnakes, swarms of gnats, and cold nights. There was a canoe by the artificially aerated pond. It was there more for the picture than for any canoe trip. The whole pond was only a few canoe-lengths long. An outhouse stood within sight of the porch. Inside, the President had hand-printed an ode to the old two-holer titled "Lest We Forget." It concluded with the line, "No 'powder room' can ever take its place." But apparently something else could; for this was a non-functioning replica.

Even the tack room had a Hollywood touch. It provided a uniquely American variation of oil portraits in a European castle: well-framed movie posters of Ronald Reagan and Nancy Davis stared down on the bridles and saddles.

There was a touch of irony as well. This Western mountain ranch, with its precious sense of natural freedom, was a refuge for one who campaigned against the evils of government. Yet the preservation of its beauty was due, in large part, to governmental tax incentives and direct governmental measures to protect the environment. On the day of the big bill signing, however, one couldn't see much of government.

The press were herded up to the ranch in the sky via the winding mountain road. When they made it to the top, they were corralled in a rope-bound pen in front of the ranch house. Horses meandered nearby in corrals of their own. The rest of us, along with the First Lady, were carefully placed outside of camera angle. The wooden outdoor luncheon table was moved from near the triangular calling iron, under the porch roof, to where the light was better. On this sturdy table sat the giant tax bill and its companion spending bill.

The small Spanish-style ranch house was the intended backdrop. One wasn't able to see much else.

It was summer recess, and none of the legislative authors or cabinet officers was invited to the photo opportunity. As special mementos for them (and for ourselves), we decided to have the President use an extraordinary number of signature pens. Unlike many standard ceremonial pens distributed after bill-signings, these were actually to be used in the signing. So there on the table—right in the middle of the photo, like tiny stand-ins for the normal crowd of VIPs—were two dozen signature pens.

With the stage thus set, at 10:30 in the morning, the President strolled out of the ranch house on cue. Wearing faded blue denims and cowboy boots, he looked as if he was stepping out of one of his own cowboy movies. Cameras snapped and whirred. The cowboy-President sat down at the table. The wind blew at his hair and at the pages of the bills, adding a little motion for the still photos. Then, the President introduced the business at hand:

> These bills that I'm about to sign—not every page—represent a turnaround of almost a half a century of a course this country's been on, and mark an end to the excessive growth in government bureaucracy, government spending, government taxing.

This didn't turn out to be quite true. But to most Americans it sounded good. The President finished his brief remarks after noting, characteristically, "The real credit goes to the people of the United States, who finally made it plain that they wanted a change."

Then he picked up one of the pens. There were exactly twenty-four. This let him use one pen for each letter of the two "Ronald Reagan"s. Each of the twenty-four signature pens had already been assigned its ultimate destination.

At just this essential moment of the intended Reagan Revolution, the President got things off to a mathematically awkward start. He signed two letters with only one of the pens. That left twenty-three more pens, but only twenty-two more letters. "Oops," he said, "one letter too many. I'll have to catch up here someplace!"

To one inclined to look for symbolism, the "I'll have to catch up here someplace" moment seemed doubly significant.

But if one wanted to find awkward symbols, one hardly had to look so closely. There was something a great deal more obvious. For all the planning, for all the staging, for all the hopes of grand Western vistas, there was one element that conspicuously failed to follow the intended script.

Entering stage left, stage right, stage everywhere were puff after puff and gust after gust of thick white fog. It was relentless. The ranch in the sky had become a ranch in the clouds. One could see neither hills, nor valleys, nor even the backdrop. Indeed, the television cameras could not get a completely clear view of the President only yards away.

The inescapable fact of the matter was that the President of the United States was enacting his would-be revolutionary economic program in a cloud of fog.

The two bills he signed totaled over a thousand pages. The legislative language was often impenetrable. Neither bill had been read in detail by the senior White House staff or the President. In signing the bills, the President relied primarily on the analysis of the Office of Management and Budget (as had long been customary). But OMB itself had performed its detailed analysis only after the President had gone on television to argue for the bills' enactment, and after he had celebrated the victories of their congressional passage.

The dictates of political management in the television era had led the President to support the bills visibly and unequivocally before the final compromises were struck. In what was consciously advertised as a fundamental test of the Reagan presidency, there was little room or time for cautious qualification.

At the time of the crucial votes, few in the Congress could themselves have claimed honestly that they knew everything of importance in the bills they were voting on. Indeed, many were embarrassed when it emerged that the actual bills were so crudely slapped together they included cut-and-pasted pieces of Xerox paper taped to the conventional parchment. Among these was a reference to a previously obscure congressional staffer's name and telephone number. For any member who wanted more detail, her name and number were written into law. (Her name was Rita Seymour. Her telephone number, which I hope and presume was changed, was forever inscribed as 255-4844.)

When I received the cut-and-pasted bills at the White House, I thought some mistake had been made. But I was assured these were exactly what the Congress had passed and what were now being presented to the President for his signature.

As the President actually did provide his signature, I couldn't quite get the symbols out of my mind: telephone-for-details, signing-in-a-fog. But no one else seemed to make much of the symbolism.

That was understandable. The substance of the bills alone was sufficient to command one's full attention. Personal income tax rates were cut by almost 30 percent across the board, and indexed so they would not rise again with inflation. Tax incentives for business investment were substantially increased. Over a hundred individual domestic programs were cut or reoriented. Entitlements for the poor were restrained (although, more significantly, the larger entitlements that benefited the middle class were barely touched). With twenty-four little pen strokes, a major portion of the gross national product was shifted around. The two new laws were the largest single spending control bill and the largest single tax reduction bill in the history of the American republic.

A few months before, after recovering from being shot, the President had made a dramatic appearance before a joint session of Congress to appeal for this program. In his speech, he referred to the space shuttle, which had just been launched for the first time. He said, "It raised our expectations once more; started us dreaming again." He repeated the familiar Sandburg quote:

> *"The republic is a dream.*
> *Nothing happens unless first a dream."*

"That's what makes us Americans different," he said, celebrating again American exceptionalism. Then he went on with lines written largely in his own hand: "We've been courageous and determined, unafraid and bold. Who among us wants to be first to say we no longer have those qualities?"

The speechwriter's version of the closing was the conventional, "All we need to do is act." Recalling the Sandburg quote, the President added, "And that dream will come true."

With an eye on the dream, President Reagan had gone for the bold. And with the signing at the ranch in the sky, the frontier virtues of courage and determination were underlined.

As a matter of awkward reality, I had noted the Hollywood staging, the mathematical "oops!," and other such bits of possible symbolism. But as a matter of romance, the signing was seen as a heroic triumph. The American cowboy not only had gone for the bold; he was getting it. And he promised to make the American dream come true.

What was actually to come of that promise is a slightly more complicated story. But the 1981 tax bill was clearly of fundamental significance, and way out of the ordinary. It seems important, therefore, to understand just how this unusually bold change happened to become law—as one considers what it may have wrought.

4

Voodoo Politics:

A Faustian Bargain

IN SOME WAYS, the Dream did begin to come true. And it wasn't just on Wall Street, as many have said of the 1980s. Ultimately, however, a price was also paid—by the country and, as it happened, by several of us who were caught up in the shaping and reshaping of American economic policy.

The economic growth of the 1980s accounted for impressive job creation all across America—eighteen million net new jobs, and the highest labor force participation of the twentieth century. Abroad, America's increasing economic strength contributed fundamentally to American primacy. It accelerated both the decline of imperial communism and the remarkable expansion of market-oriented democracy. This was not the stuff of small dreams.

It is true that the out-of-balance economic program of 1981 scared financial markets with the prospect of what Stockman later termed "two hundred billion dollar deficits as far as the eye could see." But after an initial deepening of the recession, the economy turned around.

The 1981 tax rate cuts and investment incentives encouraged more work and innovation. Paul Volcker and the Federal Reserve brought inflation down. The Volcker Fed also provided necessary liquidity after its initial anti-inflationary shock treatment. And a degree of market confidence in the government's fiscal policy was restored with a series of corrective tax increases.

The biggest and most controversial of these was known as TEFRA. It was mainly a set of corporate reforms and "loophole" closers. Passed in the depth of the 1981–82 recession, this Reagan tax increase was, at the time, the largest single tax increase in history. It was far larger than the much-maligned 1990 act, and not challenged for primacy until the Clinton tax act of 1993. It did not undo the tax rate cuts. But because the very fact of a tax increase went against supply-side doctrine, it put some conservatives on the edge of apoplexy. It led them to demand Baker's and my resignation. (This was a phenomenon I was to become very familiar with, in time.)

Several lesser tax increases followed in 1982, 1983, 1984, 1986, and 1987. And the economy went forward to achieve the longest period of uninterrupted peacetime economic growth in American history.

But while the economic growth of the 1980s was much to be appreciated—and I am proud to have been associated with an administration that helped produce it—there is no escaping the fact that an unwelcome price was paid: the legacy of multi-trillion-dollar federal debt for the 1990s and beyond.

The promise of a balanced budget by 1983 or 1984 proved to be a chimera. Stockman's revised prediction of $200 billion deficits was ultimately fulfilled, and then some. In the Reagan years, more federal debt was added than in the entire prior history of the United States. Interest costs alone rose to hundreds of billions of dollars per year. For federal policy-makers, the large deficit became an obsession and an albatross.

Further, though the economy grew, prosperity remained elusive for millions of Americans. Urban civilization continued to decompose. For many in the middle class, the American dream seemed further away, not closer, at the decade's end. The 1981 economic program was viewed increasingly as a mixed blessing.

The Dream that was promised at the ranch in the sky remained a long way from fulfillment. Creative public policy was put on hold awaiting the resolution of the fiscal problem. Yet there was no easy or prompt resolution. The gap between promise and reality was to prove haunting for years to come. For many, the dream come true seemed more and more like debts come due.

One had to wonder. How did it come to pass that the good news of the 1980s was offset by such a large, inhibiting, unintended effect: the enormous increase in deficits and debt?

. . .

Of course, the promise inspired by euphoric hopes at the 1981 act's signing was hardly the first presidential promise to fall short. Nor was this the first bill enacted where the parties were shown to have had less than complete understanding of the consequences of their action.

In the presidency just before Ronald Reagan's, President Carter had promised a New Beginning and "fresh faith in the old dream." But his presidency had come to a disappointing end, mired in recession and crisis. Prior to that, President Nixon had promised a New American Revolution. It came to nothing. And just before that, President Johnson had promised a Great Society. It was enacted with much the same bustle and fanfare as accompanied the Reagan Revolution. Yet it became the classically cited example of promise that exceeded performance.

The centerpiece of the Great Society had been the Community Action Program. Former Professor Daniel Patrick Moynihan was among the core group of Johnson administration officials involved in its conception. (Back then, he was already well on his way to becoming an interesting and entertaining original.) Moynihan analyzed the origins of the Johnson program in a book published shortly after he joined the Nixon White House. It had a marvelous title for a tale that could have applied to a host of governmental initiatives, *Maximum Feasible Misunderstanding.*

In it, Moynihan frankly evaluated the Johnson effort of which he had been a part: "This is the essential fact: *The government did not know what it was doing.* It had a theory. Or rather, a set of theories. Nothing more. . . . A big bet was being made."

These were almost exactly the lines used later by many critics of the Reagan Revolution. But to the extent the Reagan Revolution was in fact a poorly understood gamble, it was not alone in this similarity to the Great Society. Much the same might have been said of Roosevelt's New Deal or of hundreds, perhaps thousands, of less grandiose initiatives.

What was extraordinary in the case of the dramatic Reagan tax cut was not the fact that it was a gamble. It was that the gambler won in the face of overwhelming odds against.

Enactment of the large 1981 tax cut violated the abstract

dictates of conventional wisdom and American incremental-ism. In doing so, it overcame such practical obstacles as the fol-lowing. It was explicitly opposed by the Congress's Democratic leaders, and initially resisted by the two leading tax legislators from the President's own party. In the Senate, Finance Com-mittee Chairman Bob Dole told the press that the tax bill would have to be significantly diluted, and would be. When Dole spoke, there was reason to listen. In the House, the respected ranking Ways and Means Committee member, Barber Conable, stated firmly and publicly that he opposed the across-the-board rate cut. He went further, saying: "I don't think for a minute that if the President proposes a flat-rate cut, Congress will agree."

Conable must have been surprised to find that exactly such a cut was passed by both houses of the Congress, with the sup-port of Senator Dole and other skeptics. In an especially ironic turn, the ultimate bill bore the name of one Barber Conable as its principal co-sponsor.

Conable and Dole weren't the only ones who were sur-prised. I myself was among the many who incorrectly predicted that the dramatic form of the tax cut would not survive.

On January 5, 1981, I wrote a memo to Jim Baker titled "Heresy: The Politics of the Economic Program." This was be-fore the Reagan inaugural. At that time, the general outline of the program was still being filled out. Specific details to give the outline meaning were being developed by a group under Stock-man's direction. His team was working in coordination with the supply-side Treasury and the more conventionally conservative Council of Economic Advisers, with policy oversight from two tried-and-true California Reaganauts, Ed Meese and Marty Anderson. There was close to zero centrist influence within this group.

In the memo I noted, "The $620 billion FY '81 spending target announced by RR on September 9 cannot be achieved. That is a simple practical fact." This observation turned out to be correct. Outlays for that year actually ended up at $678 billion, even after the highly touted Reagan "spending reduc-tions." I noted, also, "For those particularly interested in budget balancing [a group that included the new President], the easi-est way to balance the budget within the next few years is to fail to get a major tax cut. . . . I'm not recommending this. . . . I'm just offering this as a reminder for perspective." I observed, further: "This failure is likely to be achieved." That is where I was more than a little bit off.

The purpose of the memo was clear. It suggested that there was a need "to analyze the politics of compromise—in detail—even as the no-nonsense-no-time-for-temporizing talk is mouthed." It was my view that, given liberal Democratic control of the House and moderate control of the Senate, there was bound to be compromise. Further, internal inconsistencies in the program would have to be straightened out. I thought they should be, and could be, worked out sensibly in the process of compromise. What I was arguing was straightforward. The dynamics of compromise should be addressed in advance in order to maximize the chances of a responsible and satisfactory outcome.

The memo went on: "The political strategy for the budget [should be] worked out and approved before any Presidential rhetoric on the subject is approved." This was a point I would have to argue again eight years later, when candidate Bush was considering his famous pledge, "Read my lips: no new taxes." But of course I didn't imagine that then.

At the time, the fact that there was a need to plan for compromise didn't even appear to me to merit argument. It seemed obvious and commonsensical. I wondered that I even had to emphasize it. But in 1981, in spite of the liberal-to-moderate leadership of the Congress, planning for compromise was not viewed as politically correct by many of the Reaganauts. They were inclined to see any talk of compromise as beyond the self-defeating, bordering on the traitorous.

Not all of them felt that way, however. Among the program's designers, there were early worries that the numbers would not add up right. Squaring the circle required a wildly optimistic economic forecast, with very high real growth rates, low money supply growth, low inflation, and an implied velocity of money turnover that was implausible at best. The chairman of the Council of Economic Advisers, Murray Weidenbaum, would not accept the initial version. He insisted that the forecast be modified. It was brought into a range that was "rosy," but not wild.

The potential deficit problem remained. Dave Stockman and Marty Anderson became particularly concerned. They were conservative, intelligent, thoughtful, and serious about governing. In early February, with the prospect of Reagan-induced deficits looming larger and larger, Stockman and Anderson pressed for consideration of alleviating measures. They advanced four kinds of proposals: an attack on "tax expenditures," especially for the rich; a reduction in the proposed sweetening of business depreciation allowances; a reduction in the proposed rate of increase in defense expenditures; and a delay in the effective dates for personal income tax rate reductions.

Ed Meese and the President resisted. They still thought the deficit gap could be closed by reducing what was known as "f.w.a"—fraud, waste, and abuse. As of February 16, the internal estimate of required savings from f.w.a. stood at an impossibly high level. The year when the budget was supposedly going to balance had been slipped from 1983 to 1984. But even with this switch, additional f.w.a. savings of $50 billion per year were needed. That was a lot.

To achieve such savings would have required far more draconian measures than improving the efficiency of motor pools. It would have required highly unpopular cuts in middle-class entitlement programs—including Social Security, Medicare, student loans, farm price supports, veterans benefits, and so on. The substance of the cuts could be identified easily. But it was another thing to enact them politically.

This rather basic problem was treated as a nonproblem by the President and Meese. Conceiving government as largely "extravagance and waste," they seemed to think the additional cuts could in fact come from f.w.a., and would therefore be doable. So, the worries of Stockman, Anderson, and other insiders were put aside. The program was presented to Congress on February 18, with its large structural deficit built in.

This deficit was offset on paper by a single line in the budget. It highlighted the need for additional cuts to close the gap. It was not hidden, as some have assumed. It was printed in black and white and explicitly labeled: "savings to be identified later."

As the months went by, however, it became clear that the "savings to be identified later" would not materialize. The premise that tax cuts would be accompanied by commensurate spending reduction was evidently falling apart. The Reaganaut cabinet found less f.w.a. than had been imagined to exist. And political resistance to middle-class entitlement reform showed itself to be far more powerful than some had assumed.

The practical fact was that spending was not going to be restrained to anywhere near the extent that Reaganauts had supposed. That reality should have made the giant tax cut's chances even slimmer. But, in fact, the tax cut got bigger and bigger as it moved through the legislative process, toward the ranch in the sky.

At the hilltop bill signing, the President got more than he had asked for in tax reduction. But unfortunately, he got only about half his intended spending reduction. That disparity became one of the major causes of the fiscal deficits that followed. Ultimately, the revenues from the enacted program came in at 18.5 percent of GDP. That was one full percentage point below the level put forth in candidate Reagan's September 1980 plan. At the same time, spending stayed up in the 22 to 24 percent range.

The process of legislative compromise had not resolved internal inconsistencies in any coherent way. The dynamics of compromise had managed to widen, rather than narrow, the gap between spending and revenue.

At one level, that was all too easy to understand. Tax cuts are popular. Spending reduction, though popular in the abstract, tends to lose its popularity when it becomes particular. But if that were all there was to it, the government would long since have gone bankrupt.

At the start of the Reagan administration, it had not done so. In reality, the American government had managed to keep its debt within reasonable bounds. In 1981, gross federal debt equaled only one third of a year's gross domestic product. Debt held by the public equaled about one quarter of GDP. That was easily financed; and it left a healthy margin of safety for debt to expand in time of war or national emergency. After two hundred years, the national balance sheet had been left in pretty good shape.

Further, deficits themselves were consistently unpopular with the general public. Even when traded against tax cuts, deficits were viewed as undesirable. A CBS/ *New York Times* election day poll of the 1980 electorate found voters rejected the proposition that "cutting taxes is more important than balancing the federal budget." The rejection was by 53 to 30 percent.

Nonetheless, a program that was likely to cause a major increase in deficits got enacted. It was curious, to say the least.

If the American political system had acted the way it normally does, it would have lopped off the extremes, and forced compromise within moderate bounds. But in this case, even as it became absolutely clear that necessary spending control would not be achieved, the system allowed a way-out-of-the-ordinary-sized tax cut to become law. It didn't do what highly experienced legislators like Dole and Conable (and their Democratic counterparts, Russell Long and Dan Rostenkowski) had expected and predicted. It didn't pare the tax cut back. Instead, the system threw itself out of fiscal balance.

One did, indeed, have to wonder. What accounted for this deviation from the ordinary pattern?

I puzzled over that for a long time. Many others tried to explain the improbable occurrence. Again, Moynihan proved to be one of the more provocative explainers. He offered his perspective formally in 1987 at what seemed a carefully chosen moment: shortly after the stock market crash. Many were then pointing to the looming deficits as an important contributing factor. Curiously, Moynihan did not apply the theses he had used to explain the origin of the Great Society's Community Action Program. To some degree, those earlier theses could have applied again. But he abandoned both his innocent "big bet" thesis and his "government did not know what it was doing" thesis.

Moynihan jumped to the other extreme. Drawing on the perspective of Stockman and the supply-side publicist Jude Wanniski, he adopted (as Wanniski did) a somewhat Leninist view of history. He (and they) gave almost exclusive weight to the thoughts and actions of a small band of would-be revolutionary intellectuals. Moynihan concluded that the 1981 act was the product of a thoroughly conscious conspiracy. "Persons of deeply radical and disruptive purpose . . . set about creating a fiscal crisis which they hoped would produce a political transformation." He then tried to dismiss this as revolutionary game playing, which he termed an "infantile disorder" (quoting Lenin).

With reason, Moynihan asked to hear from the grown-ups. But his theory of the intentional creation of a fiscal crisis was

way overdrawn. It is true, of course, that following the enactment of the 1981 program, budget deficits increased. The
deficits in turn inhibited the creation of new runaway spending
programs. In an indirect way, they ultimately helped force the
spending reforms of 1990 and 1995. And along the way, they
had the effect that Moynihan assumed had been a matter of intent: To a degree, they restrained both expansive governmental
action and creative policy initiative. But the notion that this was
all a matter of conscious conspiratorial design, back in 1981,
gives too much credit (and blame) to the alleged conspirators.

To the extent that the conspiracy theory applied in 1981, it
applied only to a few. And to those few, it applied only in part.
President Reagan did justify the threat of a fiscal crisis as having
the virtues of a "children's allowance." But at the same time, he
believed the fiscal crisis could be avoided through the self-
financing magic of the Laffer curve. So, he was not exactly a
single-minded conspirator. Similarly, Stockman argued, "The
politicians, including the cabinet, would have to dismantle
bloated, wasteful, and unjust spending enterprises—or risk national ruin." He thought he had consciously "made fiscal necessity the mother of political invention." But, in his own way,
he was also ambivalent. He worked as hard as anyone to raise
taxes to close the deficit gap.

Even putting their ambivalence aside, the Reagan-Stock-
man attraction to the logic of a children's allowance was about
as far as the alleged conspiracy went. In reality, there were few
others in 1981 who knowingly participated in the presumed
conspiracy. Further, while a President and a budget director are
not insignificant, in our democracy large-scale change cannot
be achieved without the support of the political middle. There
must be overt complicity by those representing the broad-based
center. And that hardly qualifies as conspiracy.

Something more than a conspiracy theory is required to
account for the extraordinary 1981 act. I myself am still not satisfied with any single explanation. Indeed, I am sure there is no
single reason for the 1981 act. To my mind, there are at least
ten significant reasons. They are tedious to recite. But it takes
all ten to form an explanation.

The first reason is more negative than positive: The country had become profoundly dissatisfied with the status quo. The

Carter leadership did not inspire confidence. There was uncomfortable talk of America being in decline. And the "misery index" (inflation plus unemployment) was unusually high. So, the public was willing to take its chances with an out-of-the-ordinary bet.

A second reason reinforced the first: There was a new kind of populism abroad in the land. It was not angry at banks, the rich, or Wall Street in the way that American populism ordinarily had been. It was an anti-government, anti-tax populism. It had been rising since the late 1960s and early 1970s, when Alabama's George Wallace and California's Howard Jarvis had given this new wave of populism national life.

Ronald Reagan's intended economic cure was completely consistent with the populist mood. Inflation had driven middle Americans into higher and higher tax brackets. They were more than ready for across-the-board rate cuts, even if "the rich" would benefit—for the tax system was treating the middle as if it were "the rich." Government had demonstrated its wastefulness and ineffectiveness in a host of ways. So the public was also ready to accept excessive estimates of fraud, waste, and abuse. Thus, in the context of rising populist discontent, the Reagan program's populism (more than any supply-side theory) resonated. It resonated deeply.

A third reason made the new populism more broadly acceptable. Ronald Reagan was somehow reassuring. Although he was an ideologically based populist, he did not show the rigidity of an ideologue or the angry resentment of many populists. His manner was genial, kindly, confident, respectful of others. And although his program in some ways favored the rich, and he himself was moderately wealthy, he still seemed to be a man of the people. He had a natural blue-collar appeal. He had none of the upper-class mannerisms of the Northeastern elite. He remained the small-town lifeguard, the Midwestern sportscaster, and the American cowboy.

Further, his program even promised to attend to the weak and vulnerable, to protect the "truly needy," to preserve the "social safety net." And best of all, his program proposed to pay for itself—without any pain. It was to do this either with the increased revenues that the Laffer curve said would flow from lower tax rates, or with spending cuts in fraud, waste, and abuse that were widely presumed to be easy. In short, the Ronald Reagan version of his program did not seem as threatening as some might have expected.

A fourth reason related to political management. The Reagan team artfully used the concept of a "mandate," and supported it with a well-conceived legislative strategy and a disciplined approach to public relations. The team did this in spite of the fact that the actual mandate was highly abstract.

The 1980 Reagan election campaign had been light on programmatic detail, heavy on generality and anecdote. During the campaign, the "details" of the economic plan were not made public until September 9, 1980, at which point they were blessed by Alan Greenspan. (He was then a former Council of Economic Advisers chairman and a future Federal Reserve Board chairman.) Greenspan's blessing managed to compensate for the fact that, at the time, the details comprised less than one full page of numbers. (Few of the plan's actual details were developed until Stockman began to provide them in December, after the election.)

Most analysts correctly argued that the election was more a referendum on the failures of the Carter presidency than on the merits of particular Reagan proposals. Yet when the full Reagan plan was put forward in February and March of 1981, and in every subsequent discussion, the illusion was fostered that "this was exactly what the election was about." The President had a "mandate" from the people, and this was it. Further, the congressional votes were framed in relation to comprehensive packages allegedly embodying the mandate. This allowed all the complex issues to be reduced to a simple yes-no choice: Do you or don't you support the program the people sent President Reagan here to enact?

A fifth reason grew out of the first four. Democratic members of Congress recognized President Reagan's populist appeal among blue-collar and Southern Democrats, and feared his potential to force party realignment. As a result, many hesitated to put any distance between themselves and what President Reagan said the people wanted.

A sixth reason was the length of the Reagan honeymoon. The new President was given the customary benefit of the doubt in his initial honeymoon period. The quick and highly visible launch of his program was intended to take advantage of this before the expected erosion of public support. But shortly after the launch, President Reagan was shot. One might have thought this would slow momentum. Ultimately, it had the reverse effect. When the President recovered and went again before a joint session of Congress to plead for his program, he was everyone's returning hero. Just when the honeymoon might ordinarily have been expected to begin to fade, it was deepened and extended.

A seventh reason may seem academic, but it was of enormous practical consequence. It derived from this general rule of politics: A coalition can agree on a position even when the arguments of its supporters are inconsistent with each other. It was obvious that there were fundamental disagreements about the likely effects of the tax cut. Yet to the extent that the merits mattered, much of this disagreement nonetheless did not.

Two of the leading academic analysts of this bit of history, Joseph White and Aaron Wildavsky, neatly summarized the basic arguments that were used to support the view that the proposed tax cut would not cause a deficit problem: It was not really much of a tax cut. It was a dramatic change that would create enough economic growth to pay for itself. And it would create deficits, but deficits themselves would restrain spending and thus eventually eliminate deficits. These three arguments were logically opposed to each other. But they all supported the point that, one way or another, the deficit issue could be put aside.

An eighth reason was much more personal: David Stockman. He was correctly viewed as brilliant and intensely committed to his work. His command of both information and the budget process allowed him to have extraordinary influence. He had a chronic need for comprehensive solutions; the intellectual capacity to invent them; and, not least, the confidence to pursue them. Without his continuing to push, drive, organize, negotiate, trade—beyond the point where others would have given in—the full tax bill would undoubtedly have failed to get the necessary votes. A more conventional compromise would have been struck.

A ninth reason involved the group of us known as "the moderates" or "the pragmatists." (Both of these were terms of derision in the minds of purist conservatives.) Within the White House, our group included Jim Baker, Mike Deaver, Dave Gergen, Max Friedersdorf, Ken Duberstein, Craig Fuller, and me—along with Stockman, who was both ideological and pragmatic. We operated through a group called the Legislative Strategy Group (in which Ed Meese, Marty Anderson, and Treasury Secretary Don Regan were also active participants). I had recommended the creation of the group. Baker chaired it, and I coordinated its work. As a group, we were generally thought to have skills in the management of legislative strategy, public affairs, and policy development. Inevitably, we found ourselves managing the processes of compromise.

We were thus naturally at odds with the self-styled purists, who were fundamentally opposed to compromise. But in the case of the 1981 tax cut, we did something that was uncharacteristic. We forged a rare moderate-conservative alliance, and gave it practical effect. Rather than restrain the movement toward an unbalanced bill, we ended up using our skills to help achieve a result that was not moderate. We met daily in Baker's office to review strategy, plan tactics, and coordinate execution of anything and everything necessary to advance the President's legislative program. On hundreds, perhaps thousands, of issues we shaped the decisions and actions that allowed the giant tax bill to become enacted. If we had not done so—or if we had dragged our feet—I doubt that the full Reagan tax cut would have passed.

A tenth and final reason for the bill's enactment involved hubris. More particularly, it involved the curious interaction of Stockman's overconfidence with my own. He and I became good friends. We shared an excessive regard for our own and for each other's brainpower. In moving the President's legislative program forward, we coordinated with each other on what was almost a moment-to-moment basis. Our close operational coordination was an important key to the unusual moderate-conservative, pragmatist-ideologue alliance. We both knew the President's program was out of balance. But we both worked to advance it nonetheless. Each of us favored large portions of the spending and tax reduction program. Our problem was with the built-in imbalance between the two. Yet each of us was confident that, in one way or another, we could solve that problem.

In Stockman's case, he had excessive and misplaced confidence in his ability to use the imbalance to force additional spending reforms. I specifically thought he was wrong about that. But in my own case, I had excessive and misplaced confidence in our ability to arrange whatever corrective compromises might be necessary. I assumed we could do this, if not with our first legislative effort, then with a subsequent compromise later in the first Reagan year. Stockman, the sometime ideologue, was overly confident that the system would fully accommodate his ideological preference. I, the ofttimes moderate, was overly confident that the system would not do so—or that if it did, it would quickly bring itself back to balance. I failed to appreciate soon enough that the times were out of joint. We were dealing with voodoo politics.

Our assumptions about our ability to make the political system produce intellectually coherent policies were excessively hopeful. We were unable to make the political system produce either Stockman's intended coherence on the right, or my intended coherence in the middle. Together, in our differing ways, Stockman and I fooled ourselves.

Looking back now at all the reasons that the imbalanced 1981 program was passed, I am struck the more by how improbable the enactment of the full 1981 tax act really was. Of the ten basic reasons for its enactment, at least six were themselves highly unusual: a dominating anti-government populism; a majority party fear of realignment; Ronald Reagan; an extended honeymoon; David Stockman; and a pragmatist-ideologue alliance. Of these six unusual phenomena, probably at least five were required for enactment. The odds of those five coinciding could reasonably be assessed at something like one in a million.

Yet it happened.

In reflecting upon the causes, I myself have been inclined, like Moynihan, to give too much attention to a single explanation. Where Moynihan concentrated excessively on the ideological "conspirators," I've focused on those of us who were "the pragmatists." In a way, I wish I did not have to. And I recognize that doing so may be too self-centered. But I do think it unlikely that a small band of "revolutionaries" could have succeeded without at least two conditions having been met. The popular mood had to be on their side (which undermines the very concept of conspiracy). And the pragmatists had to help.

If I am right about this last requirement, the question naturally arises: Why did the pragmatists help? Why were the moderates immoderate?

The answers are several.

It was partly that we assumed that, one way or another, there would be a conventional compromise. Indeed, at one key point, House Ways and Means Chairman Dan Rostenkowski did offer the expected split-the-difference solution. He proposed to reduce the across-the-board rate cut from 30 to 20 percent, and to delay the points at which it was to be phased in. But in the curious context of the times, the middle ground was not strong enough to hold either Rosty or us.

In America, unlike most other societies, left-right polarization has ordinarily been rather weak. And ideologically based presidencies have been very rare. But in this case, there was an unusual ideologically based presidency that tended to strengthen the polarization between left and right. The exaggerated polarization stretched the conventional center so thin it seemed to disappear.

On the left, the liberal Democratic Majority Leader of the House, Jim Wright, hardened in his opposition to the Reaganaut wisdom. He refused to go along with the Rostenkowski compromise proposal. Wright offered an alternative of his own, with only a delayed 15 percent rate cut. There was no chance that President Reagan would accept the Jim Wright position, as Wright himself well knew. Wright simply used his proposal to rally the left flank in opposition.

At about the same time, on the right, the Reaganauts demanded that efforts at compromise with the Democratic leadership be rejected. They preferred to challenge the leadership on the House floor. With unusual conservative strength, 192 Republicans and 67 potentially gettable Democrats, that was not a politically unreasonable strategy.

Baker and the others of us who had stepped gingerly toward the middle, and had encouraged a possible compromise with Rostenkowski, were forced to conclude that negotiations could not succeed. Rostenkowski reached the same conclusion. The ground in the middle lacked its ordinary depth and breadth.

When it became clear that only one side could win, both sides marshaled the resources necessary to make sure that the "winning" side was theirs. The determination to "win" led to a seemingly irrational bidding war, with special tax break added to special tax break in a quest for votes. The competition for votes was managed as if it were a life-or-death struggle. Unlike most legislative battles, it grew out of control. In military parlance, it went nuclear. The conventional center was not available. To the extent that it was present at all, it would not hold. With high visibility, high stakes, and high polarization, there could be no moderate solution where both sides might claim victory.

But practical necessity was not the only reason that the pragmatists did not stay with the shrinking middle ground. Forced to choose between two poles, there was little doubt that we favored the work-oriented, investment-oriented philosophy of the President's proposed tax cut, even if not the degree. Further, all of us were mindful of our obligation to the President. He had honored us by selecting us. We had freely agreed to serve. He was elected by the people. We were not.

Beyond these considerations, I felt that, at this particular point in history, America badly needed to see its President succeed. David Gergen, then an assistant to President Reagan, shared this historical perspective. We believed that a successful presidency was a practical public policy interest in its own right. The country had seen too many recent presidential failures. We had several long discussions in which we lamented the decline of confidence in the presidency, and the associated rise of cynicism and defeatism. We felt strongly that this was not healthy for America; that if allowed to persist, it would become self-fulfilling.

So we thought that there was a valuable—indeed, almost essential—public policy virtue in showing that a President could at least get his program enacted. Conversely, we felt that there would be a considerable national loss if yet another President were seen to fail. The country needed the sense that presidential leadership could effect change. We cared not only about economic renewal, but also about a renewal of national self-confidence—including confidence in the institution of the presidency.

And, as I have noted, I personally had an abundance of confidence that if we went too far with the initial program, we could simply marshal our collective skills to force a corrective compromise. Stockman and I discussed this contingency, in detail, on several occasions. To whatever extent might be required, we planned to use what was known as the second budget resolution for any necessary correction. At least on paper, we had available a combination of less vigorous defense spending growth, further restraint on entitlements, and possible tax loophole closing to offset the adverse deficit effects of an excessive tax bill. By law, the second budget resolution was scheduled for congressional action in the fall.

For all these reasons, therefore, I felt I was on satisfactory ground in working to advance the Reagan tax cuts even as it became clear that they were excessive. And for something like these reasons, other pragmatists felt similarly.

Of course, things did not work out exactly as we expected. I repeat: Things did not work out exactly as we expected. For me, that line has been a poignant and persistent echo. It calls to mind a scene from *The Natural.* The hero, Roy Hobbs, was a bright and shining baseball prospect in his youth, a natural with a fantastic future ahead of him. But his career was jolted by a near-fatal wound. Years later, asked to explain the long and mysterious disappearance from his once-promising path, Hobbs looks down a bit and says simply, "My life didn't turn out the way I expected."

The effort to win in 1981 required excessive giveaways in the vote-getting process, the process Stockman referred to as "pigs feeding at the trough." And the effort to right things took many years, not months. We were forced to endure the consequences of our hubris.

This was never more clear than it was to become eight years later when I was to find myself seated alone in the witness chair, in the glare of television lights, facing a bank of inquiring senators. I was challenged to respond to a quote from Stockman's memoir.

I was being interrogated in hearings to determine my fitness for Senate confirmation as President Bush's director of the Office of Management and Budget. The senators were led by the chairman of the Committee on Governmental Affairs, John Glenn. He had been a hero of mine and my generation ever since he had become the first American to circle the earth in space. He'd been diminished a bit by Tom Wolfe's *The Right Stuff*. But he was still a hero. He was even a hero to kids in the next generation. (Our son, Jonathan, then almost eight, asked, "Is he any relation to the astronaut John Glenn in my American history book?") Like a kid myself, I was proud to be in his presence.

The hearing had been going well. Senator Glenn had started it on a favorable note with a very flattering introduction. He then facetiously said, "And, of course, everyone knows of your reputation for humility and a complete lack of ego!" These were qualities I notoriously lacked. Yet even I was embarrassed-when he went on to say, "All kidding aside, let me say that at a time when we don't seem to have enough good role models for our young people, I think it's fair to say that you are a role model for many young people. I congratulate you on that." Coming from one of my own early role models, that meant a lot to me.

But after several senators completed their first round of questioning, Senator Glenn quoted from a *Wall Street Journal* article, which in turn quoted from Stockman's book, *The Triumph of Politics*. He wanted me to comment on what he referred to as Stockman's shenanigans in misleading Congress.

I said that I did not approve of misleading Congress, and that in my years of service had never done so. Before making this point, however, I felt obliged to comment on the quote. It involved a conversation Stockman and I had had in 1981, right after a White House meeting with House Republicans on the tax bill.

Stockman correctly saw the meeting as part of a feeding frenzy. Tax cuts had been added to tax cuts in order to strengthen the administration's side in the bidding war for votes. We were both distressed by what we had seen. The bidding war was getting out of control. On West Executive Avenue, halfway between his office in the Old Executive Office Building and mine in the West Wing of the White House, we stopped to reflect on our plight. We knew that still more bargains would have to be struck in order to secure the necessary alliance with Southern Democrats. The likely bargains would only make the fiscal outlook worse. Since we were in a position to help influence whether those bargains were struck or not, we contemplated the possibility of letting the process come up a few votes short. Stockman reflected aloud that we'd get caught if we tried; and, in effect, that there must be a better alternative.

In recounting our conversation, Stockman attributed the following to me: "I don't know which is worse, winning now and fixing up the budget mess later, or losing now and facing a political mess immediately." The quote may not have been exact. But the choice was as I saw it. It did not seem an attractive choice to either of us. A budget mess was obviously undesirable. And to me, the alternative of a political mess went far beyond personal or partisan politics. It meant the prospect of yet another failed American presidency. We decided, as Stockman's book said, to "win it now, fix it later."

The quote was a bit too neat for ordinary discourse. But there was no escaping the fact that it was a troublesome quote with which to be presented. For unfortunately, the budget problem was still not fixed as I sat there before the senators almost eight years later. And the implication was that we had somehow planned that. Further, the job I was being considered for included fixing the very problem that the quote implied I might have condoned. I tried to clarify that the "later" we were referring to was only months later, back in 1981. I explained as follows:

> He and I were talking at the time not about winning this and causing some large economic problem that would be fixed two administrations later. . . . What he and I were specifically talking about—and, by the way, we were discussing it with some members of the Senate and the House—was going ahead and getting the tax and budget bills enacted; and then, in 1981—1981 [I repeated]— having a second budget resolution that would adjust for what had been the overaction on the tax reduction side and underaction on the spending side. We were planning to have a "fall offensive" in 1981 . . . in what was then almost summer of 1981. The "later" in question was later in 1981 [I repeated one more time]. It was not later, way down the road.

That seemed to me to dispose of the matter compellingly, certainly, and completely. As the hearing moved on, the senators seemed satisfied.

But it didn't really dispose of the matter. I couldn't quite get out of my mind a lingering unease. A twinge of guilt came at the Senate reading of the "fix it later" quote. It came as a shock because the story I had told myself—and believed in all eight years from 1981 to the reading of the quote—was that I had consistently been on the side of truth, right, and justice.

My version of the tale had gone as follows: The 1981 acts had done much good. They had, indeed, helped stop America's evolution toward a European-style mixed economy. Tax rate cuts had been desirable. It was the excess of the overall tax reduction in relation to the politically feasible spending reduction that was the basic problem. But it was I who had argued for responsible compromise in 1981. It was I who had helped enact necessary tax adjustments in 1982, 1983, 1984, and 1986. It was I who endured the wrath of conservatives who consistently sought my firing. It was I who, at some considerable personal cost, struggled to move things along what seemed the responsible path.

In my self-serving version, I thought I was again acting responsibly in 1989 by agreeing to take on the preposterous challenge of trying to right the fiscal imbalance in a context where the President had sworn "no new taxes," and Democrats controlled both houses of Congress. Better than most, I knew how tough this would be. I thought that I had a better chance than most of getting it done. But even so, I suspected I might not be able to survive as OMB director. Somewhat self-righteously, I actually did think of myself as a public servant.

So the twinge I felt when morally challenged came as a jolt. I resisted it. Yet it burned a scar in me. And as the going was to get tougher and tougher toward the end of the Bush presidency, it would begin to tear. I was to be badly bloodied. I would recall my earlier image from the days of the Saturday Night Massacre: bodies falling all over the stage, this time including my own. A sense of gloomy determinism would begin to overtake me. I would wonder whether Stockman and I—and even Baker and President Bush—had each made some sort of Faustian bargain with Mephistopheles back in 1981, for which we were paying a price. I would even reread the *Faust* stories, wanting to know when and how our own story might end.

But that, of course, is not how we felt in August of 1981 at the ranch in the sky. When the big bill signing was over, dressed in cowboy boots and jeans—with a Ronald Reagan buckle that proclaimed "The Buckaroo Stops Here"—I went for a horseback ride on the barren mountain ridges.

Back then, we were all in a kind of cowboy heaven.

5
The Fall Offensive:
The Kingdom for a Mouse

IN THAT AUGUST of 1981, as I rode along the ridges of the Santa Ynez mountains, I felt as if time hadn't moved since I had been a little five-year-old pretend-cowboy taking my first few steps on a pony. The one clear change was that the ring in which I was riding had expanded, out beyond the distant horizon. There wasn't a man-made structure in sight. For that brief while under the August sky, I was again a kid and a cowboy, unconnected with any clock. The open spaces seemed timeless.

I had no illusion of being in control. I let my legs hang loose around the sides of my horse as he picked his way carefully among the rocks—one hoof crossing in front of the other, testing to find the surest footing. Looking forward and upward, I let myself become absorbed in the romantic Western dream.

Only the sun told time. The fall of a hoof-loosened rock sounded an occasional alarm, reminding a rider that missteps could promise a painful plunge. Yet for this short journey in a dreamworld, I ignored the fact that there had been sounds of rocks coming loose. Gazing across the ridges, as I imagined early explorers must have done, I hardly thought that within months we might find ourselves caught in a dangerous slide.

Rocks had in fact begun to loosen before the August bill signing at the ranch in the sky. Among the insiders, Stockman, Anderson, Weidenbaum, Baker, Meese, Gergen, Fuller, and I had all begun to worry about rising deficits well before August. Several Republican senators and congressmen had visited the White House to add their expressions of deep concern before voting for the tax cut that they privately opposed. The President himself was aware that, even assuming adoption of his program, deficit forecasts were becoming increasingly gloomy. Each revision of the forecast was worse than the one before. That was the start of a pattern that was to become a troublesome reality for more than a decade.

But the President tended politely to dismiss such unpleasant intrusions by reality just as one might ignore an unwelcome guest at an otherwise harmonious table. Indeed, at an internal White House luncheon on August 3, 1981, it was clear that one key insider, David Stockman, was on the verge of becoming just such an unwelcome guest. For those interested in keeping the deficit within reasonable bounds, that should have been seen as an unpromising sign.

The luncheon included the President, Vice President Bush, key White House staff, Stockman, and Defense Secretary Weinberger. It was just before the President was to go off to California for his August vacation and the signing at the ranch in the sky.

Stockman was using the occasion to lay a predicate for a project we had termed the "Fall Offensive." Most of us felt that such a legislative offensive would be necessary to make further fiscal policy corrections after the expected tax bill signing. We had in mind a balanced set of corrections. They would have moderated the increase in defense spending and the decrease in revenues, bringing both closer to the levels in candidate Reagan's September 1980 campaign program. They would also have kept domestic spending appropriations in line, while adding a fundamentally important missing element: restraint on burgeoning middle-class entitlement programs.

A precondition for an effective Fall Offensive was a more accurate appreciation of the deficit outlook. That is what Stockman tried to provide. His revised projections suggested deficits that would rise above $60 billion for the year that had originally been forecast at zero. But when he got done with his gloomy numbers, his analysis was peremptorily dismissed by the President. The President remarked, "If these numbers were out, Tip O'Neill would be wearing a halo."

O'Neill was a classic old-style Democrat and ward politician who had risen from humble origins in Cambridge to become a powerful Speaker of the House. As a partisan rival in the power game, he had greeted the new President with a famously derisive "Welcome to the big leagues!" O'Neill and the President shared an Irish delight in storytelling; but they had become principal adversaries in the ideological contest that President Reagan brought to the big time. The President was not about to give the Speaker an easy run. The prospect of an O'Neill halo put an immediate, if temporary, end to serious discussion of balooning deficit estimates.

Meese made a passing attempt to diminish the problem and reassure the President by inquiring about supply-side effects. Stockman tried to explain that his numbers already assumed high economic growth rates; that even with the assumed supply-side growth effect, the deficits would rise. But that line of analysis simply could not connect with the reality several others wished to see. I had the uncomfortable and unpromising sense that, even if there were a disposition to discuss the deficit seriously, that might not be possible.

The luncheon yielded no intellectual progress. Each person left with the same view as he had brought to the table. Weinberger was undoubtedly pleased to have seen both a warning shot and a misfire. Some others of us thought that there had not necessarily been a misfire; that the President was probably just being the sensible politician that he was. He did not need any leaks confirming his program's inadequacy before he had signed it into law. We assumed we could get the President to take the Fall Offensive seriously at a more opportune time, later in the month. That turned out to have been more hopeful than events actually allowed.

Two weeks later, a band of us continued the discussion at meetings in Los Angeles with the President, and in Santa Barbara among ourselves. Those meetings, too, were inconclusive. Our frustration began to mount as we sensed time slipping away. We structured a series of additional meetings with the President starting right after Labor Day, upon his return to Washington. They were intended to produce the definitive deficit reduction program for the Fall Offensive.

They began with a meeting on September 9 to settle the defense contribution. That first meeting was billed as a shoot-out between Stockman and Weinberger. But it was really no contest at all.

Stockman was trying to bring the new defense budget's projected annual growth rate down from about 9 percent (excluding inflation) toward the 5 to 7 percent that candidate Reagan had promised. The defense budget was programmed at the higher level mainly because Weinberger and Deputy Defense Secretary Frank Carlucci had won a rare technical victory in an early negotiation with Stockman. When the full consequences of this had become better understood, Meese undertook the mission to get Weinberger to adjust downward. That was supposed to have been accomplished by June. But by September, there was not only no adjustment; the Defense Department had also fully pocketed and programmed the bonus.

Stockman came to the shoot-out armed with analysis, as usual. But Weinberger came better armed. He brought with him a long-standing trust relationship with the President, which he drew upon subtly. And not so subtly, he suggested that Stockman was merely a draft-dodger in green eyeshades. Weinberger, the graduate of Harvard College and Harvard Law School, wasted no time on serious analysis. Where Stockman brought his command of numbers, Weinberger brought his command of the defense establishment. He was accompanied by the leadership of the national security community.

With this august group as a supportive chorus, he offered a lengthy discourse that consumed most of the available time. His general point was that American strength had declined and that it needed to be restored. The point was valid, as was his abstract emphasis on the importance of American strength. Hardly anyone in the room would have disagreed with him on that. But that was not the issue.

The real issue was not the desirability of American strength, but the resources necessary to secure it. Weinberger spent little time on that question. After gaining the predictable nods on the importance of strength, he simply asserted that only his budget would approach the levels needed to cope with the threat.

The essence of Weinberger's "analytic" presentation was captured in one simple, large chart. The use of such charts was a standard DoD briefing technique. The technique tended to obfuscate through the appearance of clarity. To those of us with an analytic bent, it seemed amazing that important issues could be reduced to caricature in this way. But, routinely, they were.

In this case, as often, the gross simplification achieved its intended result.

The chart was a classic of this particular art form. Indeed, it achieved its own Warholian fame when Stockman later ridiculed it publicly. It featured three cartoon characters representing three defense budgets. One was a tiny soldier without a rifle: the Carter budget. A second was a bespectacled little soldier, which Stockman took to be a cross between Woody Allen and himself. That soldier was holding what looked like a small wooden rifle, and was said to represent the OMB defense plan. The third soldier was a big, square-jawed, fully armed GI Joe. Only that soldier would have met the test of central casting. It represented Weinberger's preference, but was identified as "the President's defense budget"—even though that was exactly what the meeting was called to decide.

With this chart and Weinberger's trust relationship, there was little that Stockman's analysis could do. The internal debate would continue for a while. But the struggle for the President's mind was over.

After a bit more futile back-and-forth in the days that followed, we recognized the inescapable. We decided to formalize the President's decision in order to get on with the rest of the process. Jim Baker and I brought the President a decision paper at Camp David. We interrupted his Saturday afternoon swim. Standing by the pool in his bathing suit, like the lifeguard he had been half a century before, he initialed the option that made it official: Defense would make only a token contribution to a Fall Offensive.

That hurt the math of deficit reduction. More significantly, it hurt the politics and thus compounded the problem with the math. Effectively, it made the politico-mathematical equation impossible to solve.

Political budgeteers, interested in deficit reduction, had come to describe the required formula as a "three-legged stool." The image was meant to suggest a necessary balance among contributions to be made by three basic elements: defense spending, domestic spending, and revenue. Only if all three were adjusted together could balance be achieved.

But if defense were allowed to enjoy very large increases, as the President's decision permitted, Democrats were not about to restrain domestic spending. If spending were not restrained, a heavier burden would have to be placed on taxes. And if too heavy a burden were borne by taxes, Republican support would be too light. A stable coalition for serious action simply could not come together on this basis.

In the first battle of the Fall Offensive, one leg of the stool was cut short. That then meant a shortening of the other legs. This dynamic promised to leave the seat of the stool painfully close to the ground.

Still, those of us who felt that a Fall Offensive was necessary for America's economic strength decided to press on. At that point, we had no idea that we would be pressing on long beyond the fall, and that variations of the leg-shortening dynamic would plague deficit reduction efforts for more than a decade to come. We still thought we could get a fiscal "fix" that fall. For the next two months, we met again and again and again—trying to find our way to an acceptable deficit reduction package and the coalition to enact it.

The economic context was both a help and a hindrance. The big tax cut had been enacted in August and was soon to go into effect. Yet by fall, the optimistic supply-side forecast that critics labeled "Rosy Scenario" had become a mockery. The economic outlook had deteriorated badly. Unemployment was near 10 percent. People were scared. Interest rates remained troublingly high, in double digits. And most financial market experts said the worsening deficit outlook was an important part of the problem. That increased public and political interest in deficit reduction, but decreased the administration's credibility.

Published deficit forecasts continued to rise, beyond the gloomy August projections of more than $60 billion. They were fast approaching the $100 billion mark. That level was disturbing enough, though only half what it was soon to become. For most of the postwar period, deficits had been below 2 percent of GDP. The Reagan plan had originally said the 1983 deficit would be zero. But it was actually on its way to 6.3 percent of GDP—a peacetime record that still stands.

Republican politicians started moving in an initially orderly fashion toward the special form of panic that strikes when economic trouble and election years coincide. Many in the Republican congressional leadership concluded that there should be further action on the deficit. Because this meant unpopular votes, many preferred action in the fall of 1981, not in the coming election year. In principle (so to speak) they favored our notion of a Fall Offensive.

Of course, deficit reduction was almost always favored in principle. The hard part was gaining agreement on the particulars.

Majority Leader Howard Baker arranged secret meetings of Jim Baker, Stockman, and me with his "College of Cardinals" (the Republican chairmen of the major Senate committees). He invited Paul Laxalt, the President's closest friend in the Senate, to join the group. Laxalt, Howard Baker, and the entire College of Cardinals favored adjusting all three legs of the three-legged stool.

But the senators insisted that the domestic spending adjustment must include entitlement restraint. This was substantively correct. However, it complicated the politics even more. At that time, it meant doing something about Social Security. Since Social Security was a major contributer to spending growth, and the Social Security trust funds were then forecast to go bankrupt, it might have seemed reasonable to address the subject. But the President and congressional Republicans had tried to address the subject earlier in the year, and had been badly burned. If Social Security was to be addressed at all, it would have to be done on a bipartisan basis.

Even that, however, was too much for such key House Republican leaders as Dick Cheney and Trent Lott. For political reasons, they didn't want to risk any serious effort on entitlements. And though the President was more than willing to give Social Security another try, his chief political strategist, Jim Baker, agreed with the House Republican point of view. So there was not a unified Republican approach to domestic spending restraint. The closest thing to a consensus seemed to be the possible designation of a bipartisan commission to study the Social Security problem. (That was later established; and in 1983, it produced agreement.) But it did not offer (nor did it, in fact, yield) much near-term deficit reduction.

And, of course, the President didn't really want any part of a tax increase. He was becoming more inclined to argue that the Fall Offensive should involve blaming the Democrats for their failure to act on spending restraint (including Social Security)—and lamenting the lack of an earlier and larger tax cut.

So those of us who were interested in building the three-legged stool found ourselves in a curious position. It was increasingly clear that key carpenters were leaning toward creating a rather odd-looking platform: with one leg pointing up, one pointing sideways, and one pointing down. This was not exactly a stable basis for fiscal balance.

As this unstable prospect started to take shape, Stockman and I were forced to switch metaphors. We started talking in terms of a Ping-Pong game. We imagined that if we could just get the ball in play—serving a proposal over the net from the executive to the legislative branch—we would be at the table, and could make something of the back-and-forth that inevitably would follow.

On September 21, in the Oval Office, the President presented a preview of his vision of a Fall Offensive to the Republican leaders, Howard Baker and Bob Michel. In his smooth radio voice, he read aloud his draft of a television address he proposed to give. He had written it out, in his characteristically neat handwriting, on sheet after sheet of yellow legal paper. It was light on deficit reduction and heavy on the wisdom of his earlier proposals to scale back Social Security.

Baker and Michel sat and listened politely, but seemed to border on a state of shock. When the President finished, they gathered themselves and suggested that he postpone reopening the Social Security debate, and save it for another day. Reluctantly, he concurred.

With this and the other decisions the President had made, it was clear that the Fall Offensive would open with something closer to a whimper than a bang. After discussing this with the President on the twenty-second, Stockman, Jim Baker, and I decided that we would still go ahead and try to manage the Ping-Pong as best we could—even though the President's initial serve would be a weak floating lob.

The lob was served to the Congress and the nation via television at 9:00 P.M. on September 24. It was one of the President's least effective performances. There was something fundamentally incongruous about the whole thing. The proposed remedies were not proportionate to the size of the problem.

Stockman had started the process at the August 3 luncheon with images of "Dunkirk II" and a major Fall Offensive. But in the intervening month and a half, we'd been reduced to a private hope for Ping-Pong.

In its own strange way, the conclusion of the nationally televised address summed it all up. The President recited an anecdote about an American tourist visiting Mount Etna, the volcano, and saying, "We've got a volunteer fire department at home that'd put that thing out in fifteen minutes!" It was surreal.

Baker, Stockman, and I consoled ourselves with the thought that at least the ball was moving, and we might look for something more from the congressional side of the net. To force action—to keep the ball moving—we planned to use the threat of "shutting the government down" (by vetoing the continuing appropriations bill) if we did not get a responsible deficit reduction program by November.

What we failed to imagine was how few players would remain standing at the table when the November deadline arrived.

On October 3, Budget Committee Chairman Domenici reported that he could deliver a reasonably proportioned three-legged stool from his committee. But as Domenici pieced together his support, the President—who was never a whole-hearted enthusiast for this approach—started leaning away. That made the Budget Committee carpenters understandably cautious.

By November 2 and 3, in our internal meetings with the President, it was clear that, though he was coming to accept that the deficit might exceed $100 billion, he was also prepared to give up on the deficit for a while. He said, "Very obviously, we're not going to achieve our deficit goals. But when the time comes, if inflation is down, business is up, jobs are up—if the deficit is bigger, the man on the street will say, 'Okay, things are better.'" (As a matter of politics, this turned out to be exactly correct.)

The option of delaying part of the tax cut had gained support among many of the President's advisers, including some of the Reaganauts. But when it was mentioned, the President said simply, "Oh, Lord, no!" And on defense he said, "A defense spending cut worries me. I don't know how we'd do it without reversing something we've just started worldwide."

These tax and defense positions were, of course, the traditional Reagan positions. But over the years, his commitment to deficit reduction had been similarly firm. In the face of rising deficit forecasts, the President didn't see himself as abandoning deficit reduction but rather as delaying it. Inconsistent with his tax and defense positions as it may have seemed, he still professed a willingness to pursue a deficit reduction package by working with the Senate and using the threat of shutting the government down. Basically, he favored a one-legged stool.

Nonetheless, when the President met with the Senate Republican leadership on November 6, it still seemed that a modest but helpful package might be within reach. The President modified only slightly the talking points I had prepared on behalf of the Legislative Strategy Group. On defense, he made his standard (and correct) points about the Soviets and arms negotiation. But he was not absolutist. He said he wanted to stay "as closely as we can to what we submitted." On the sensitive issue of taxes, he said he'd be willing to consider "revenue enhancement," by which he said he meant "loophole closing and such"—provided this was politically necessary to achieve spending cuts. The gap between the Senate and the President seemed bridgeable.

When later the same day the President met with the House Republican leaders, however, the prospect of a deficit reduction agreement seemed more remote. Several key members— Cheney, Conable, Kemp, and Lott (each for his own reason) —said they wanted to postpone action until the ordinary budget cycle. That meant no Fall Offensive; no Ping-Pong; wait till next year.

It was the *mañana* syndrome. Stockman and I had fallen victim to it in the spring. The congressional moderates adopted it at about the same time. The President assumed his own version in August. The House Republicans reaffirmed their commitment to *mañana* in the fall. And for more than a decade, there were always at least a few essential players who said, when faced with the prospect of political pain, "Not that way; not now; *mañana!*"

Stockman concluded that the only thing left to be salvaged from the Ping-Pong was a few billion dollars of savings in domestic discretionary spending (not entitlements). This amounted to a very short stool with only one leg. Switching metaphors again, Stockman called it a mouse.

He still wanted to go for it by threatening to shut the government down. To me, that hardly seemed worth it. I pictured the President unhorsed like Shakespeare's Richard III, screaming absurdly, "A mouse! A mouse! My kingdom for a *mouse!*" But I favored the threat, as did Baker, still imagining that there might be something more to be salvaged in the "crisis" environment of an impending government shutdown.

We didn't know that we ourselves were about to be shut down.

November 10 was Stockman's birthday. As it turned out, it wasn't a happy day.

A month before, the President had said publicly that he expected a short and mild recession. At the time, that was shockingly negative to many Reagan enthusiasts. On November 10, however, the Council of Economic Advisers revised its economic forecast even further downward for the fourth quarter. Its "optimistic" forecast was for negative real growth—that is, economic *contraction*—of 3.0 to 3.5 percent. As if that weren't bad enough, CEA's "pessimistic" forecast was 8.0 percent negative; and its "probable" forecast was 4.0 to 5.0 percent negative. These negative forecasts were a very long way from the supply-siders' euphoric prediction, less than five months before, that Rosy Scenario would be even rosier.

But the CEA forecast wasn't the really troublesome news of the day. By November, many of us had come to expect something like that. The news that really jolted us started, for me, with a mid-afternoon phone call from Lesley Stahl.

I took her call in my West Wing office. As CBS's White House correspondent, she was working on a story for that evening. It involved Stockman. She knew he and I were close, and asked if I'd seen the new issue of *The Atlantic Monthly*. I hadn't. It wasn't even out yet. But she'd been given an advance copy, and said she thought Stockman might have discussed it with me. I didn't know what she was talking about. Nor was I particularly concerned. People in the media called routinely; and, more often than not, they (and we) took their stories more seriously than they deserved.

Stahl then said that the article was by Bill Greider, the national editor of the *Washington Post*. At that point my ears perked up.

A couple of weeks before, Stockman had told me that he had been talking confidentially to Greider over an extended period of time. This was not entirely surprising. Stockman and Greider represented opposite ends of the political spectrum; but they were, in important ways, closer than they might have seemed. They were both inclined to be intellectual and analytic. They were both skeptical of established power structures. They both enjoyed the interplay of large abstractions and fine details. And they both sought a certain purity in grand, comprehensive, internally consistent theories of policy and politics. From this perspective, it was natural that Stockman might trust Greider's ability to comprehend what Stockman thought he was really about—even though it was evidently a mistake to have let this basis for trust obscure the fact that Greider was a working journalist.

In alerting me, Stockman had said he was having trouble with Greider, who was about to put some things on the record that Stockman had not expected to see so soon. He was annoyed that he could not get the Greider piece postponed. Stockman said he still hoped to get Greider to modify the article, but seemed a bit less confident than he ordinarily did. I didn't make too much of all this until a few days before Stahl's call, when Stockman gave me an elliptical warning that he had failed with Greider—and might have some trouble ahead.

If Stockman had been able to delay the Greider piece, and if its publication were to have followed the President's enactment of a successful Fall Offensive, the article would have seemed much less an act of "betrayal," as his critics termed it. Indeed, it might have been what its title suggested and what Stockman may have had in mind: "The Education of David Stockman," an interesting account of Stockman's intellectual adaptation and his revisionist triumph. But that, of course, is not how things were to work out.

I didn't mention Stockman's Greider worries to Stahl. In a nonchalant way, I simply asked her what the Greider piece had to say.

She said Stockman called the supply-side arguments a "Trojan horse." Stockman had already been plenty controversial, and there had been an abundance of leaks about his efforts to change the President's program. So I had trouble seeing how people could get as worked up about this additional metaphor as Stahl seemed to be. I figured that if Greider had had big news, he would have put it in the *Post*, for which he worked, not the *Atlantic*. But I knew Stahl's instincts for news were outstanding and that, in any case, she wasn't giving me her full story. So, without offering any reaction, I hung up and punched the numbers for Stockman's extension. I was concerned. But I still had no idea that, within a very short time, the Greider story would use Stockman's own words—and the reaction to them— to destroy the credibility of the supply-side argument, the administration, and Stockman himself.

When Stockman got on the phone, I was surprised to hear him say he didn't know that Stahl had the Greider story. He seemed peculiarly subdued. I assumed he must be handling the story in his own way. (I learned later that he was in a state of shock, and was not in a position to handle the story at all.) We decided to talk after the news.

The Stahl-Greider story turned out to be a mighty unpleasant birthday present. The printed version in the *Atlantic* used this quote as its headline: "None of us really understands what's going on with all these numbers." That was from Stockman, the supposed master of numbers. Yet, in some ways, it was the least of the difficulties the article presented.

The article suggested that, for the past several months, Stockman had in fact had fundamental doubts about the administration's program and the process by which it had been developed. This was at the same time that Stockman had seemed publicly to have been the administration's most confident and committed advocate.

Through Greider, Stockman's indictment was comprehensive. He referred to the defense budget as a "swamp of waste." He said, "I've never believed that just cutting taxes alone will cause output and employment to expand." He called supply-siders "naive" and many of his former congressional colleagues greedy and opportunistic "hogs"—adding that "there are no real conservatives in Congress." Stockman's historical account and clinical diagnosis were largely accurate. But their publication, at this point, was awkward to say the least.

After the news, at 7:40, Stockman walked into my office with his deputy, Ed Harper, and his press secretary, Ed Dale. A previous master of control, Stockman had turned himself over to them as if he were no longer able to help himself. For the first time in my experience, he seemed totally defeated.

I got Gergen, Speakes, and Fuller to join the meeting. Stockman's team had drafted guidance for response to press questions. It read:

> The *Atlantic* article details views that have long been known, but offers an interpretation that is wrong. In particular, the President's program is a consistent one and he has not misled anyone. It has always been acknowledged that more would have to be done and that addressing all of the accumulated problems of the past at once would be difficult. The major elements are in place and the task now is to tackle the remaining problems.

Stockman had lined out the word "consistent," and had handwritten "balanced" in its place. But the statement seemed to need a whole lot more work if it was to be of any help. It ignored Stockman! And it ignored the question of whether he had deceived the President and the public.

In point of fact, Stockman had worked harder than anyone to acquaint the President with the worsening deficit outlook and the need to address it. But that fact, while confirming Stockman's private virtue, undermined his and the administration's public posture. The group seemed most concerned about whether or not the administration would seem to stand by its own program. So the guidance was modified to state that Stockman was "convinced that the program set forward by the President is sound."

That was implausible. My concern remained that Stockman was being left very vulnerable, and the revised guidance made him even more so. But Stockman was too weakened to defend his own interests; and the group was in a rush because press deadlines were fast approaching. So with less than satisfactory guidance, the group disbanded.

The next morning's press was bad, but not horrid. The *Washington Post* didn't even run the story on page one. There had not been enough time for the press to develop the negative reactions and tabloid-style quotes that they would treat as real news. The tabloid-style negatives were developed in the course of the day.

In his ten months in office, Stockman had made a lot of enemies. (In subsequent years, I had more than enough opportunity to experience the same phenomenon myself. As defensive consolation, I developed an excessively self-righteous generalization: A strong OMB director, who tries to do his job in times of serious fiscal stress, is bound to have more than his fair share of opponents. That, of course, was not the whole explanation for the superabundance of adversaries; but it was a part.) Stockman's opponents, like mine, ranged widely: from congressional adversaries, to mistreated cabinet officers, to people offended by his intellectual arrogance, to Reaganauts who resented his "betrayal" of the President. When he was strong, his adversaries sniped anonymously. But when he seemed vulnerable, his accumulated enemies were emboldened to fire more directly.

By the morning of November 12, their work was evident. It was reflected in the press. And one could feel it in the halls around the Oval Office. It seemed as if Stockman's fate was hanging in the balance.

In the anteroom to the Oval Office, the President's longtime assistant and loyal protector, Helene von Damm, expressed her outrage in no uncertain terms. That was an unpromising sign, given her closeness to the President. Regan, Meese, and Deaver wanted "to throw Stockman over the side," according to Baker. I argued with him that there was a need to be fair; that Stockman had worked harder than anyone to give the Reagan Revolution concrete meaning; that other people had failed in one way or another and had not been fired; and that it would be difficult to go forward without Stockman. Baker had reached the same conclusions independently. I then made the arguments to Regan and von Damm.

I also gave the President a copy of the *Atlantic* article. He, like others who actually read it, found it to be not nearly as bad as advertised.

The famous "woodshed" luncheon of Stockman alone with the President was arranged for 12:45. By the time of the meeting, Baker, Meese, and Deaver had scripted the outcome. The President was to lead off by expressing his disappointment. He was to let Stockman make his case, and then "decide" to allow Stockman to continue in office. An appropriate public apology would follow.

At 12:30, Baker coached Stockman that his role was to "eat humble pie." Stockman then went in and did an even better job of acting than he imagined he would. Upon leaving the Oval Office, at 1:30, he returned to Baker's. Deaver, Baker, Stockman, and I then met for half an hour to go over what should be said by Stockman in an afternoon press conference, and what should be said in a related written statement representing the President's position. After we settled on the substance, Deaver emphasized to Stockman that the best thing would be for people to see "a subdued David Stockman." I was designated to draft the White House statement and to assure that Stockman's fit with it.

As we left Baker's office, Stockman told me privately that his story had brought tears to the President's eyes. I thought to myself that there was still a way to go to see the subdued David Stockman. But I felt relieved that Stockman was staying. We both went off to do our tasks.

Preparing the White House statement was easy. I wrote it out on a yellow legal pad. My draft included a set of reasons why the President kept Stockman. The President found these acceptable, but changed their order. Deaver, however, did not want to bolster Stockman. He argued that the reasons should be used only for background; so they were dropped from the final text. But that didn't make any significant difference. The statement was brief and to the point. It ended with the crucial operative statement: "The President decided not to accept Mr. Stockman's resignation."

Working out Stockman's opening statement was a little trickier. I went over to his office to look at his draft. It referred to his own "poor judgment and loose talk," defended the President's personal integrity and commitment, affirmed Stockman's belief in him, and expressed deep regret for "any harm that has been done." It ended as follows:

> I am staying on because even more deeply I believe that
> the President has charted a sound, constructive course. I
> am grateful for the chance to play a continued part in

getting on with the job the American people sent us here to do.

I edited his draft slightly and took it over to the President in the Oval Office. He read it carefully at his desk. Then he looked up. I wasn't sure what his reaction was going to be.

Referring to Stockman, the President said with a mixture of wonder and appreciation, "He'll do all this?" I nodded yes. The President seemed touched. A consistently gracious man, he was like a grateful father accepting an errant son's confession and apology. Of the person about to be publicly described as a woodshed victim, he said simply, "God bless him!"

But Deaver wasn't as satisfied as the President. He insisted on changing Stockman's last line to read, "I am grateful *to the President* for this *second* chance." This changed the tone. It shifted the emphasis from Stockman's gratefulness to the precariousness of his position. It suggested that Stockman was still on trial, and that there would not be a third chance. The President saw the effect immediately, and seemed hesitant about demanding the change. But Deaver was insistent. So I was commissioned to go over to Stockman's and get his concurrence.

When I told him of the intended change, he was furious. But he agreed, and went ahead with the press conference as scripted. Indeed, he improved on Deaver's script by inventing his story of having been taken to the woodshed.

He also met with the President and the Republican leadership. He apologized to all, explaining that he had been "shafted by a journalist." The President was sympathetic and understanding. He volunteered a story about how that had happened to him. Stockman seemed weakened, but back in the fold.

On Saturday, he and I went to lunch in the White House mess. We reviewed the overall situation aloud for about three hours. It was clear that his normal combativeness was returning: He expressed determination to get even with Deaver. And he was again set to get something out of the threat to shut the government down. But at the same time, having been allowed to stay in office, he had become ambivalent about doing so. He reflected again and again upon the possibility of his resigning then and there.

Years later, in his memoir, he tried to explain why he decided to stay. His answer was diametrically opposed to the "sound course" answer he had drafted and recited in his woodshed press conference. Though I think he partly believed in both answers, I suspect the second version was closer to what animated him. He said:

> I resolved to clear my name by doing everything I could
> to help correct the enormous fiscal error that I had done
> so much to bring about. That was the main reason I
> stayed on. . . . There was no longer any revolution to be-
> tray, only a shambles to repair.

Whether Stockman was right to have stayed on is a matter one might debate. (Years later, in somewhat similar circumstances, I myself decided to stay.) He worked assiduously for four more years to try to right the fiscal balance. But his wins were small in relation to the growing problem. And at the time of his leaving (as with me, at mine) he had not successfully restored either the personal credibility with which he had started or the fiscal balance he sought to correct.

The problem that we were to have again and again was immediately evident in the end-play of the Fall Offensive. We ended up doing too little, too late.

Weakened by the *Atlantic* affair, we lost whatever chance we might have had to use a threatened government shutdown to force the enactment of a sensible deficit reduction package. Many thought that chance had independently fallen toward zero. Be that as it may, we were reduced to a minimalist approach to saving face.

The President went through with the threat. The government was briefly put through a near-meaningless shutdown drill. On November 23, within twelve hours of his first veto "shutting the government down," the President received a token spending compromise. It purported to save a few billion dollars, but failed to address any of the underlying budgetary problems. Congressional Republicans, using Senator Laxalt as an intermediary, urged the President to sign it. He did.

The Fall Offensive was officially over. Metaphors converged. The Ping-Pong ball lay battered on the floor like a flattened white mouse.

In the years ahead, we were to return to the table countless times to try to close the widening deficit gap. We were to work within the conventional congressional process and around it. We would form special bipartisan negotiating groups from the "Gang of 17," to a secret offshoot of the Social Security Commission, to highly visible "summits." And we were to spend thousands and thousands of thankless hours at the difficult and tedious task of getting reluctant political officials to reach agreement on deficit reduction measures. We were able to do some useful piecework—from Social Security restructuring and tax reform to enforceable budgetary caps, pay-as-you-go lawmaking, and "down payments on the deficit." Yet we were never quite able to get the whole job done.

Our problem was not, as many thought, that President Reagan refused to raise taxes. He didn't refuse. As part of a larger compromise, he was willing to raise taxes in the fall of 1981. (He was spared when the Fall Offensive collapsed.) And after 1981, he actually did raise taxes in five of the seven remaining years of his presidency (1982, 1983, 1984, 1986, and 1987)—sometimes more than once a year!

Our problems were more basic and systemic. They were partly rooted in what are ordinarily strengths of the American political system: its tendency to change in modest increments; and its attentiveness to the short-term interests of the broad middle class.

As an academic matter, the problem might be put abstractly. The roots of the deficit problem went back to the expansion of entitlements in the 1960s and 1970s, compounded by the hyperinflation of the 1970s. But what drove the deficit to new heights in the 1980s was an atypical deviation from American incrementalism. It was the product of a bold double shock to the monetary and tax systems. The subsequent effort to correct for this unusual deviation, however, took place within the normal incremental framework of American politics and government. To put the matter more plainly (and mix metaphors still further): The red ink came in an unconventional flood; but the process of correction used conventional measuring spoons for bailing.

As a practical matter, incremental adjustment might have sufficed if we had been able to make the first adjustment in the fall of 1981. But with the *Atlantic* affair and the flattened mouse, we missed that chance.

From then on, the problem kept growing faster than the incremental remedies the political system would support. Middle-class entitlements were left uncontrolled. Tax revenues no longer grew automatically with inflation. Significant adjustments in either spending or taxes required a willingness to take from the voting middle class, one way or another. Yet that, of course, the American representative democracy was not eager to do. So the gap between spending and revenue was left to grow exponentially.

We lost the ability to catch up with the growing deficit problem. We kept on trying. But as the deficit gap grew larger, modest increments of correction became increasingly inadequate. To the many incrementalist politicians who were reluctant to advance a bold correction, even modest corrections began to lose their appeal. The gain didn't seem worth the political pain.

At the same time, larger corrections were just not feasible. In the post-*Atlantic* executive branch, there was neither the firm conviction nor the credibility to lead an effective deficit reduction effort. In the House of Representatives (among both Republicans and Democrats), there was an abundance of posturing, but practically no natural disposition to address seriously the spending side of the problem. The Senate was occasionally more conscientious, as in 1985 when it passed a serious deficit reduction package. But it couldn't legislate without the executive branch and the House. In the political system generally, there was a confounding tendency to focus more on the small and the immediate—leaving courage and the future to fall victim to the *mañana* syndrome.

It was all highly frustrating. Many of us who had hoped to help build a city on a hill were left scrounging around in the uninspiring rubble, struggling to shore up the fiscal foundation. Our once-grand visions of shining cities, or even the simple image of flowers blooming, seemed at best a distant hope as we crawled around in the muck. And as things were to turn out, we were stuck there not just for one unproductive fall, but for more than a decade to come.

If that sounds too self-pitying, the thought should be dismissed. For the sadder truth is that it could fairly be said—it has been said!—that we were simply getting our due. In the spring of 1981, we decided to "fix it later," thinking that "later" would be a matter of months. Throughout that year, others made a similar choice, as the political system would do again and again and again in the years to come. Having ourselves once opted to defer political pain, we became victims of the larger *mañana* syndrome. Our brighter tomorrow remained ahead of us, and ahead of us, and ahead of us. Always ahead of us, we were never quite able to get there.

The *mañana* syndrome held most of us captive for years. We were bound to our fate by the political system's inertia, its tendency to move in modest increments and defer difficult decisions. Our struggle with deficits came toward its end only slowly and painfully.

But for the Reagan revolutionary fiscal policy, the end came much more quickly and definitively. The same system that slowed our efforts at correction also prevented any further lurches in the supply-side direction. In January 1983, a little over a year after the Fall Offensive's anticlimax, a dramatic denouement followed. It marked a return to power by the forces of moderation, a belated victory for "the system." This anti-Reaganaut victory was heralded, live and in color, by none other than President Reagan as he delivered his State of the Union address.

The months leading up to this had not been friendly to the Reagan Revolution. On September 3, 1982, to reassure financial markets, the President had signed the largest tax increase in the history of the country. It did not raise personal tax rates; but it eliminated a host of narrowly focused personal and corporate tax incentives and loopholes. As counterbalance, the President promptly said his real objective was the complete elimination of the corporate income tax. That remarkable non sequitur created a minor firestorm, which the President defused with humor and the implication that he was not really serious.

In October, George Stigler, the distinguished conservative economist, was asked to meet with the President and then the press. As a Nobel laureate, he was thought capable of instilling confidence. It didn't quite work out that way. The news he made was for saying, "You know we're in a depression now"— and for describing supply-side economics as "a gimmick" and "a slogan."

On November 2, the midterm elections reflected the deep recession. The results effectively eliminated the conservative majority in the House.

By mid-November, the *Washington Post* headlined, "GOP Governors Strongly Criticize Reagan's Policies." The critics ranged across the spectrum from Thomas Kean of New Jersey and Robert Ray of Iowa to John Sununu of New Hampshire and Robert Orr of Indiana. The Republican governors' complaints included high deficits, excessive defense spending, and favoring the rich. The tone was suggested by conservative South Dakotan William Janklow, who said administration policies were "scaring people to death." He was particularly critical of the President's proposals for scaling back Social Security, which he dismissed as "screwball ideas."

On November 20, the President was caught joking through an open microphone as he prepared for his customary Saturday radio talk to the nation. Listeners were surprised to hear him refer to the economic situation by saying, "We're in a helluva mess!" Since this was the fourth such technical mix-up, Craig Fuller said the technicians should be fired. Less sympathetic observers focused more on the President.

At Thanksgiving, from the comfort of the Santa Barbara White House, the administration leaked and then withdrew, under fire, an idea that came to be known as the "Thanksgiving turkey": taxing unemployment insurance benefits.

Upon returning to Washington, the President was treated to budget appeals from his own cabinet. Most of the requests from this supposedly conservative group sought to increase government. The appeals ranged from proposed increases in categorical job training programs to increases in IRS personnel. In general, the President responded with split-the-difference compromises. Then he went on to fight successfully for a federal gasoline tax increase (having previously proposed to return the gas tax to the states). He did so by defeating a Senate filibuster that was led by conservative Senator Jesse Helms.

There was no small amount of irony in this pattern. Yet it reflected a serious practical problem. Between the dictates of uncompromising ideology and the imperatives of practical politics, Republicans were being torn apart. At the slightest sign of compromise, ideological activists like Richard Viguerie and Howard Phillips became alienated. By January 1983, they were insisting that President Reagan should not run for reelection. Phillips confidently predicted "an all-out effort to persuade him not to run in 1984"—while expressing the hope that the President would perhaps save himself by firing compromisers like Baker, Deaver, and me. At the same time, the absence of coherent compromise alienated a broad center. In the midst of economic difficulties, the country wanted a basis for confidence. But the administration's policy confusion failed to provide it.

A *Wall Street Journal* poll of business executives revealed a sharp fall in confidence in the President's economic policy. More generally, Gallup polls of the electorate showed the President losing badly in trial heats with both former Vice President Walter Mondale (40 to 52 percent) and Senator John Glenn (39 to 54 percent).

At midterm, the *Post*'s David Broder reviewed the evidence and concluded:

> What we are witnessing this January [1983] is not the midpoint in the Reagan presidency, but its phase-out. "Reaganism," it is becoming increasingly clear, was a one-year phenomenon, lasting from his nomination in the summer of 1980 to the passage of his first budget and tax bills in the summer of 1981. What has been occurring ever since is an accelerating retreat from Reaganism, a process in which he is more spectator than leader.

I had reached a similar conclusion. But I attributed more conscious choice to the President. From the inside it seemed increasingly clear that, when forced to choose, the President was willing to risk alienating his right flank in order to strengthen his political viability in the broad American middle. He would sacrifice the purity of his ideology for the practical necessities of governance. That is, he was prepared to abandon the purists' version of the Reagan Revolution in order to assure a popular Reagan presidency.

Never was this more compellingly clear than on that evening of January 25, 1983, when the President took center stage for what was becoming a Reaganesque theatrical ritual, the annual State of the Union performance.

The President had spent a lifetime as an ideologically committed outsider. But he led off by celebrating compromise, cooperation, and bipartisanship. He had long argued that Social

Security should be voluntary. But that night he sought (and was soon to get) the prompt enactment of an agreement he had reached with the bipartisan commission on Social Security. The agreement promised to preserve the integrity of the governmental Social Security system for generations to come. It was a roughly half-and-half mixture of benefit reductions and tax increases (referred to euphemistically as tax "acceleration"). Considered politically explosive if mishandled, it had been simultaneously announced and accepted ten days before by the President, the commission, Senate Majority Leader Baker, and the President's frequent ideological adversary, House Speaker O'Neill—all of whom the President saluted.

Years later, after the stock market crash in 1987, Senator Moynihan was to cite the process that had produced the 1983 bipartisan Social Security agreement as an inspirational model for addressing the larger deficit problem:

> If you really want to do these things they are not that hard. Early in this decade, Social Security was having troubles. It took us three years to decide to fix them. But when we did, it took Bob Dole, Jim Baker, Barber Conable, David Stockman, Dick Darman, and me exactly twelve days . . . to do it.

I didn't see this bit of history as quite as easy as Moynihan suggested. I remembered commission chairman Alan Greenspan's early calls saying the commission was in stalemate, and asking for help. Prior to the November 1982 election, we set up secret meetings with him and the President to lay the groundwork for compromise. I was authorized to open a back channel with the Democratic dean of Social Security, Bob Ball. He was the Speaker's man on the commission. We had worked together a decade before in the old HEW department. (I had earned his trust by refusing an order from the Nixon White House delivered "on behalf of the President." The order was to include a political advertisement in the envelopes with Social Security checks.) Approaching seventy in 1982, Ball was still active, and found himself sneaking out the back of his house and across a neighbor's yard to avoid being seen by the press as he entered a White House limo for one of many secret meetings. Gradually, Stockman, Baker, Ken Duberstein (then the President's extraordinarily capable assistant for legislative affairs), and I drew on every such relationship we had—one-by-one, two-by-two, with one secret meeting after another—to build the nucleus of a core group and a potential compromise.

The process of coalition building was at all times precarious. Agreement was in doubt until the very moment it was seized and announced. The process took months of hard work, not days.

But my sense that the process was harder than Moynihan later suggested was only a quibble. On the larger point, I agreed wholeheartedly that the bipartisan leadership model was desirable for addressing supposedly intractable political and policy problems. That Moynihan and I might have agreed on this is perhaps to have been expected. What was surprising for many in 1983, however, was to find President Reagan leading the cheers for bipartisan leadership and cooperation.

In point of fact, the President did not mind direct negotiations among bipartisan leaders. He used them, at times, for budget negotiations (with mixed results, in 1982 and again in 1987). But, for understandable reasons, he did not really like the bipartisan commission model. It was almost a guaranteed formula for the type of split-the-difference solution that he tended to dislike. He accepted such solutions only as the end-play of difficult negotiations, and correctly thought that delegating authority to a balanced commission gave up too much leverage at the start. In the case of Social Security, he had been forced into using a commission by the political explosion that had greeted his earlier unilateral proposals. He had no intention of delegating tax and defense issues to a commission. But recognizing that he could make little progress on deficit reduction with unilateral proposals to the Congress, he made a conciliatory nod to bipartisanship.

Citing President Franklin Delano Roosevelt, he said:

> He also reminded us that "the future lies with those wise political leaders who realize that the great public is interested more in government than in politics."
>
> So let us, in these next two years—men and women of both parties, every political shade—concentrate on the long-range bipartisan responsibilities of government. . . .

Having thus opened his State of the Union performance by praising bipartisanship and reversing his long commitment to a more voluntary Social Security system, the President moved on to another remarkable turn. About a third of the way into his speech, he uttered a single sentence which resolved the debate about deficits and taxes that had been argued intensely within the administration.

In anticipation of the State of the Union, one faction had favored accelerating the final stage of the phased-in tax cut that had been enacted in 1981. But that option was strongly opposed by several key advisers including Marty Feldstein, the chairman of the Council of Economic Advisers. Another faction favored proposing radical tax reform, replacing the progressive income tax with either a flat tax or a consumed income tax that would exempt net savings and investment from any tax at all. But detailed work on radical reform had not been done; and many felt that it would be too unsettling in an economic environment that desperately sought a basis for renewed confidence.

Still, the President felt that he had to propose something. On January 3, he had looked at the results of his own budget decision making with horror. To the group of us who comprised the Budget Review Board, he exclaimed, "We can't live with out-year deficits. I don't care if we have to blow up the Capitol, we have to restore the economy. How can we come out with that string of figures without driving interest rates right back up? How can we put this out without creating a public panic?"

It was in that frame of mind that he came to accept the unusual compromise captured by a single sentence in the State of the Union. To help restore confidence in the administration's fiscal sanity, he formally abandoned the supply-side principle that lowering taxes was the way to reduce the huge projected deficits. He said: "Because we must ensure reduction and eventual elimination of deficits over the next several years, I will propose a stand-by tax. . . ."

This might have seemed like the coup de grâce for the Reagan revolutionary fiscal policy. But there was a moment of even greater symbolic import that was still to come. As the President moved toward the end of his speech, he mouthed a line I had inserted, reflecting one of my favorite thoughts, "Right now, we need both realism and idealism." Understandably, that got no response. Then the President went on to a line he had written in his own handwriting. It got the biggest ovation of the night.

He said, quite simply: "We who are in government must take the lead in restoring the economy."

Senator Moynihan had read ahead and seen the line. Sensing the extraordinary irony, he stood up as the President read it. Like the first violinist of a symphony orchestra, with a shock of bright white hair atop his ruddy face, Moynihan started to applaud the master conductor. He was followed by all other Democratic senators and members of the House. Faced with all the Democrats standing and applauding their President, the Republicans were then forced to stand. It was a bit like the moment in the movie *Casablanca* when both the Germans and the French stand to sing their competing anthems. But in this case, the Republicans had no choice but to appear to be joining the Democrats. As the nation watched, the entire Congress stood and paid apparent homage to the maestro's dictum that, in restoring the economy, "*government* must take the lead."

With that, it was evident that the power of the Reagan Revolution's official fiscal policy was spent. The President tried to make fun of the moment by ad-libbing, "And here all that time, I thought you were reading the paper." But the reality was there for all to see.

The longtime advocate of voluntary Social Security was proposing to make *governmental* Social Security secure for generations to come. The supply-side President, who in recent months had signed two significant tax increases into law, was proposing two more: a *tax "acceleration" to fund the Social Security system* and *a stand-by tax to reduce the deficit*. The committed anti-government activist was arguing that, to restore the economy, *government* must take the lead. And the most ideologically rooted of America's Presidents was framing all this by singing the praises of *compromising bipartisanship*.

I couldn't help thinking that, in much of domestic policy, the President had become a mere resultant—a vector pointed toward the center, by the center, for the center. The abortive Fall Offensive was long since forgotten. Yet clearly, the purists' form of Reaganism was in full retreat. On budgetary matters, the system had taken command.

6

Symbols and Substance:

"You Ain't Seen Nothin' Yet"

As THE REAGAN ADMINISTRATION continued its coming of age, evidence accumulated that the system, more than the President, controlled the fate of much of the Reagan Revolution. Yet most people gave the President credit for being a powerful force for change. For a while, this puzzled me. I saw the forces of moderation and inertia as having greater power than the forces of radical change. Events proved me partly right about this. But I seriously underestimated one dimension of the President's power: his capacity to affect the nation's spirit through the use of symbols and populist communication.

For a time, I had been blinded to this dimension of power. The disappointments of the 1960s and 1970s had moved me away from the days of Camelot's inspiration. By the time President Reagan had taken office, I had become contemptuous of the contrived use of symbols, rhetoric, and illusion. I tended to dismiss Hollywood, media hype, and oversimplification. And my professional training led me to concentrate less on romance than on hard evidence and returns on investment. Like many moderates, I was, to a degree, culturally disadvantaged when it came to communication through the mass media. I understood intellectually that in governance, as in life, illusion is itself a fundamental part of reality. But it took me some time—and a strong dose of political reality therapy—to grasp the fundamental importance of this point, and to accept its legitimacy.

President Reagan did not have to learn this. From the moment he was elected, he used his command of illusion—and the language of populist iconography—to revive the American spirit. Gradually I came to appreciate what many Americans must have known intuitively: that this spiritual reawakening was an achievement of far greater force and favorable effect than any actually produced by the Reagan revolutionary program. And, as it happened, notwithstanding the fate of his legislative program, the President's continued personal popularity was assured by his mastery of populist communication and spiritual revival. That dynamic was new to me.

There was probably no American who had risen to the presidency who was better prepared than Ronald Reagan for the splicing together of illusion and reality. In the television era, that splicing had become a special requirement for effective performance in the Washington wonderland. For Ronald Reagan, it had been his life. He had done this splicing again and again as boy dramatist, radio announcer, movie star, television personality, promoter, and politician. He had made a successful life out of fictionalizing, turning unattractive realities into one or another version of the mythic American dream. He himself personified the splicing together of Hollywood West, cowboy hero, citizen-statesman, and Hollywood East.

Better than most, he understood the connection between illusion, reality, and governance. Intuitively, he seemed to grasp three important points. These had become essential for governing the television-centered democracy that had arisen in the latter part of the twentieth century.

The first point was basic: Whatever influences the perception of reality will also influence reality itself; therefore, the systematic management of illusion must be part of the effort to manage reality. The second point seemed obvious—except for the fact that several modern Presidents missed it. To maintain the capacity to govern, a President must maintain audience appeal. In the television era, that meant that a presidency's perceived entertainment value had to be positive. It could not be negative. It could not be boring. It could not be uninspiring. It certainly could not be debilitating. And the third point that President Reagan understood was important for success with the first two: In the television era, symbolic communication had become key.

The best symbols with which to be associated were American icons. Traditionally, these icons included: the Flag, the Colors, the Patriot, the Pioneer, the Underdog, the Commoner, the Defender of Fair Play, the Cowboy, the Bold and the Brave. Whether in fact or in fiction, Ronald Reagan had the advantage of having long been associated with all of these. So his effort to identify with them was credible. Indeed, he had become an American icon in his own right.

Television communicated through icons. It was more like poetry than prose. President Kennedy had successfully pioneered its use, starting with Robert Frost at his inaugural. And President Reagan was the first since President Kennedy to use the medium effectively. He was fully conscious of the parallel. In fact, he actually linked himself with the romanticized version of President Kennedy in over a hundred speeches and prepared remarks. In the years since Kennedy, American icons had been shattered. President Reagan set out to restore them. He used symbolic communication—the icons themselves—for the task.

In his first outdoor ceremony at the White House, he celebrated the release of fifty-two American hostages with a formal backdrop of fifty-two large American flags. Throughout his presidency he was proudly wrapped in the flag. He relegitimized traditional respect for the military. America's post-Vietnam attitude toward the use of military force was at best ambivalent. But President Reagan reminded Americans that some wars could be fought for what the nation took to be noble purposes. He visited the beaches and battlefields of Normandy. In poignant ceremonies, he celebrated the fortieth anniversary of D-Day. He visited the oft-forgotten soldiers of an oft-forgotten war, the Freedom Brigade at the edge of Korea's demilitarized zone. Closer to home, he helped heal the wounds of the Vietnam era with a moving dedication of the Vietnam War Memorial. In these and countless other ways, President Reagan not only renewed respect for the military but he also helped reawaken a traditional sense of patriotism. He renewed a spiritual appreciation of the virtue of shared sacrifice on behalf of the precious values our nation represents.

None of this symbolic communication was programmatic in the ordinary governmental sense. There was no change of law, no new spending program or regulation. But there was clear intent and undeniable effect. By the artful use of iconography, President Reagan strengthened himself, the presidency, and America's traditional sense of itself. The mood of the country was lifted.

Even folk music showed the change. It turned to country, grew more confident and unashamedly patriotic. Bruce Springsteen rose to the cover of *Time* with a theme song that balanced its post-Vietnam resentment with a proud refrain, "Born in the U.S.A." Lee Greenwood became the number one country and western vocalist with an unequivocal "God Bless the USA." The television advertising culture itself was permeated with the new national spirit. Chrysler-Plymouth echoed Springsteen-Greenwood with a highly successful theme for its ads, "The Pride Is Back—Born in America." Chevrolet then echoed with its own refrain, "The Heartbeat of America." The pride may have seemed a bit shallow. But the restored confidence soon seemed to run deep.

President Reagan's use of symbols helped reconnect America with her own mythology. This was not all that most Reaganauts had in mind for a Reagan Revolution. It was nonetheless essential if America were to retain her greatness. A great power must believe in its favored place, and its mission, if it is to sustain the energy to build a shining city upon a hill. President Reagan restored that belief. In this sense, his achievement was a triumph of spirit. It was what I came to think of as the Reagan *Restoration*. Had the mislabeled Reagan Revolution accomplished no more, this restoration of spirit would still have been of fundamental importance. And as the reelection year of 1984 approached, the country seemed to understand and appreciate that.

It took me a while, however, to realize just how powerful the revival of spirit really was—and how significant it was politically. I tended to focus more on conventional substantive matters. I was concerned that, after the Social Security compromise of early 1983, little was being accomplished on the programmatic front. The deficit problem had been alleviated some by the action on Social Security and by the tax increases of 1982. Yet the deficit required serious further attention. Left as it was, it promised to be above $200 billion per year, well into the future. To reduce it required restraint on growing entitlements and either a slowdown in planned defense growth or a further adjustment of taxes. The Congress and the public did not like touching middle-class entitlements. The President did not like a defense "cut." And no one was enthusiastic about proposing a tax increase. So there was an unstated political agreement between the executive and legislative branches: Go easy on deficit reduction until after the 1984 election.

But while this was cause for concern, the President's political advisers could take comfort from the fact that the economy had returned to growth, and was forecast to grow still more strongly. The "misery index" was coming down. At least equally important, the American spirit was being renewed in a host of ways. And the combination of economic and spiritual renewal seemed a firm basis on which to build a campaign strategy. Attention to programmatic needs—what some referred to as "pain"—promised to be somewhere between unpleasant and foolhardy. So it was avoided.

Still, the needs for further deficit reduction and program reform were real. And it was not entirely natural for me to appreciate that attention to them could be postponed. Initially, I didn't imagine that a conscious strategy of ignoring the unattractive could produce the largest electoral college win in American history. Obviously, when it came to electioneering, I had a lot to learn.

I knew, of course, that presidential elections do not ordinarily conform to the image of organized, issue-oriented rationality suggested by generations of civics teachers or such civic-minded groups as the League of Women Voters. I knew, too, that up close campaigns are not pretty to behold. What I did not fully understand, however, was that they are often a celebration of collective populism, American-style. And it took me a while to reach the unnatural conclusion that, in the words of many, that ain't all bad.

My first close-up view of a presidential election did not come until 1984. I had been an interested observer of elections since early childhood. Yet this was the first election in which I participated actively near the center of a campaign. From my vantage point in the White House, I had the good fortune to be associated with a historic win. But what I experienced was not entirely uplifting.

At an abstract level, the campaign was painted in broad strokes of red, white, and blue. It celebrated American values, pride, and patriotism. It communicated mainly through symbols. As symbolic communication, it was genuinely inspirational. At the more concrete and operational level, however, it was less than noble. Far less attention was paid to serious substance than to cynical ploys. These were the principal domain of the rising breed of political professionals, trained primarily in campaigning. The new professionals tended to move from campaign to campaign, guided less by principle than by a compass seeking some happy combination of victory, visibility, credit, and cash.

I had heard and thought I understood the famous aphorism "Politics ain't bean bag." Yet as things were to develop, some of the pros might well have said to me what they had the President say to campaign crowds, "You ain't seen nothin' yet." For someone who had been schooled primarily in substantive analysis and bureaucratic power, there was much to learn about people power and populist politics. What became increasingly clear was that political management was mainly about populist communication, not substance as I had been trained to understand it.

The mechanics of populist political management intrigued me some, but did not naturally interest me much. I gravitated more toward things like preparations for presidential debates. These were, after all, intentionally designed to focus on substantive issues (my area of possible comparative advantage). Yet even here, I was forced to learn that excessive attention to substance could be seen as actively harmful. Symbolic communication, demeanor, and one-liners were evidently more important. To a degree, of course, I knew that. But the conscious submergence of substance seemed more extensive than I would have thought necessary or proper.

I might have indulged this high-minded reflection at greater length if the presidential debate process, of which I had become a part, had not taken an unexpected turn. Immediately after the first debate, my mind was suddenly forced to focus on three inescapable practical facts. The first was a surprise. Uncharacteristically, President Reagan had failed a populist communication test. Second, professional political managers had reacted by turning toward the finer arts of throat cutting. And third—from my personal standpoint, most compelling—the throat targeted for cutting was mine. The forced refocusing of my mind promised to expand opportunities for learning. But to enjoy the luxury of that academic perspective, I had to handle the more immediate challenge of avoiding the long knives.

I became aware of my little problem on October 11, 1984, four days after the disastrous first presidential debate between President Reagan and former Vice President Walter Mondale. It was less than a month before election day. Several of us were about to begin a meeting of the Campaign Strategy Group. We were in the White House chief of staff's office waiting for the general campaign chairman, Senator Paul Laxalt. He was a regular member of our group and usually on time.

Before we started, as we all waited for Laxalt to arrive, we were handed a wire service report. A rare silence fell over the group. "The President was brutalized," said the wire.

I couldn't believe my eyes. But that's what the wire report said: "The President was brutalized . . . by his staff." It was a line that would stick in one's mind. It seemed preposterous. We lived in a democracy. This sounded more like the kind of wire report one would expect from some primitive island dictatorship—as if the presidential guard had taken over, and had physically beaten the titular head of the republic.

"The man was absolutely smothered," the report went on. We stared at the wire report in a state of mildly stunned amazement.

But there was no doubt about it. "The President was brutalized. . . . He was brutalized by a briefing process that didn't make sense . . . loaded with briefing books . . . smothered with numbers and forced to endure six dress rehearsals that would have been totally unfair for a twenty-one-year-old. . . ." That at least was what the President's close friend, the one and the same Paul Laxalt who was the missing member of our little group, was said to have said at a full-blown press conference.

It was easy enough to sense that trouble must be brewing behind this curious message, so publicly delivered. It did not take much to appreciate that the staff being criticized presumably included me. But I wasn't sure what the charge of "brutality" was meant to refer to. It seemed to me absurd, both factually and tactically.

When Laxalt finally did walk in, he lacked his normal easygoing smile. He looked, as always, as if he'd been sent from central casting, with his solid athletic frame mounted on fancy cowboy boots, and his leathery Western face capped by silver hair. But he seemed much more stern and tense than I'd seen him before. Still, he couldn't have been more matter-of-fact as he said, "I just had a press conference. I had to take the pressure off the man. I took the blame. I blamed myself and the process for what went wrong."

What went wrong was clear enough: The Great Communicator—the accepted master of television and of political debates—was judged to have blown the first nationally televised debate with his underdog challenger. What was not yet so clear was why the debate had been blown. Laxalt's "brutalization" hypothesis was new.

As general chairman and "First Friend," Laxalt had been involved thoroughly in the briefing process. But though he told us he'd taken the blame for it, nothing in the wire story suggested that. In the next day's *Post*, Lou Cannon was to write that "though Laxalt mentioned no names, his comments were seen by several administration and campaign officials as directed largely at White House chief of staff James A. Baker, who negotiated arrangements for the two debates, at presidential assistant Richard G. Darman, who directed preparations, and at OMB Director David A. Stockman, who impersonated Mondale in the debate rehearsals." That was how most interpreted Laxalt. With us, however, Laxalt emphasized that he was simply trying to deflect blame away from the President.

Deflecting blame away from the candidate was a natural and reasonable objective. But the issue of the President's performance had seemed to be in the process of passing. I thought it foolish to bring it back front and center. Further, the notion that the President could be "brutalized" by his staff seemed less than helpful in the context of opponents' suggestions that the President was not in charge. One senator took to the Senate floor immediately and commented on Laxalt's "damaging admissions." Referring to the President, he asked, "Does he have no mind of his own? Is he an old-time movie actor who is sent on stage and told what to do? The notion that the President can be brutalized in the briefing process by his own staff is a stunning admission."

Four days before in Louisville, on the night of the debate, those of us who were the alleged brutalizers had watched on television monitors backstage. We felt that the President had done passably for the first three quarters of the debate. Campaign pollster Dick Wirthlin's moment-to-moment electronic tracking of the viewing audience supported that judgment.

There were, of course, presidential pauses and bits of seeming disconnection here and there. But these were thoroughly familiar phenomena for those who had watched the President in press conferences over the years. His winning way with television depended more on his smile and themes than on factual accuracy or the structure of his argument. We regretted that the President didn't use any of our prepared one-liners in the first debate, and that he rarely seized the offensive. The major disappointment, however, was with the President's closing statement. I had scored the debate as if it were a prizefight. And though the President might have deserved a draw on points, he'd in fact been victim of a self-inflicted technical knockout in the closing round.

Having been given unclear guidance by the moderator, Barbara Walters, the President prefaced his final statement by saying, "I'm all confused now." Combining rebuttal and a close, he went on to deliver a statement that seemed to confirm his confession of confusion. It failed to provide the uplifting themes and emotion that people were accustomed to expect of Ronald Reagan. It was uncharacteristically defensive and mired in bits and pieces of fact. And worse, based largely on notes the President had made during the debate, it seemed to wander. When combined with the conventional Reaganesque disconnections, it seemed to border on incoherence, which the press then analyzed as "possible senility."

At the Strategy Group meeting on the eleventh, Wirthlin provided poll results on the extent of the damage. It wasn't as bad as some had expected. The President had lost seven points on the "leadership" issue; but on that indicator, he was still twenty-seven points up. He was similarly up on "effectiveness." And although he had lost twelve points on "the future," the President's head-to-head lead over Mondale was holding steady. It was 55 to 37 percent on the day before the debate; 53 to 39 percent on the day after. And for the second through fourth day after the debate, the President's numbers had been stable at 52 or 53 percent. "People are in effect saying, 'Walter Mondale won the debate; so what?'" Wirthlin observed.

The one problem Wirthlin identified was a worry about the

age issue. On this, he was strongly seconded by two tough and seasoned campaign pros, Stu Spencer and Lee Atwater. Atwater reinforced the group's tendency toward mild panic by dismissing the stability of the head-to-head numbers and worrying about a lag effect. He said, "We've got to shift the focus of the campaign."

Having anticipated mild panic, I had placed "strategic perspective" as the next item on the agenda after "polling data." I argued that the fundamentals were on our side; and the immediate problem would pass with just a half-decent performance on the next debate. The senility discussion was being carried so far by the press that it seemed to me that all the President had to do in the second debate was to survive physically, in a standing position, and show he was capable of speaking intelligibly at the close. That modest achievement would be enough to rebut the senility critique. And with the senility issue thus neutralized, the strategic basics would then dominate. I said that there was no reason to panic. We needed to show confidence in our strategic position; stick to our plan; and unify in support of its execution. That plan called for moving on at this stage to a thematic emphasis on "taking command of the future."

I had prepared a one-pager which noted that this theme was "the most needed—and the least natural for many key players." And it pointed out that "as the going gets rough, there is a tendency to fall excessively into Mondale-bashing." I was well aware that the campaign organization was inclined in exactly that direction. And I was prepared to admit that it might have some short-term tactical merit. But it seemed to me to be strategically wrong, a carryover from years of being in opposition on the outside. I argued that the President had a chance for a very big win; that our mood would change dramatically once we got by the second debate; and that if we let a negative tactic grow into a negative strategy, we might actually make the election close.

Nonetheless, the group decided to go heavily into Mondale-bashing. The next day we were scheduled to mimic "Give-'em-Hell" Harry Truman, whistle-stopping through Ohio aboard the old *Heartland Special*. The professional politicians decided that the President should bellow puffs of anti-Mondale rhetorical smoke, and conclude each whistle-stop rally with a ringing, "You ain't seen nothin' yet." I had to restrain myself from observing that this vacuous cry had an ironic double meaning.

In the context of fixing blame for the failure of the first debate, I was aware that my emphasis on a strategic perspective must have seemed like a defensive effort to change the subject. Still, I was surprised by the vehemence of Laxalt's reaction to my comments. Ordinarily, he was jovial, solicitous, or quiet in our meetings. But this time he nearly exploded. "I'm not panicking," he said angrily from the chair next to mine.

"This is reality," he went on. "This is the end of the ivory tower. It's time to take the gloves off. We're in a streetfight. We've got to let Reagan be Reagan. We've got to hit Mondale on hypocrisy. . . . We're going to have a different process."

I suddenly realized that my position was a bit more risky than I had thought. Since I was the one member of the group with evident academic proclivities, Laxalt's reference to "the end of the ivory tower" seemed to be aimed at me. The expressed intention to have a different process suggested that he may actually have believed what he said publicly; and that, whether he did or didn't, I might be displaced.

As I listened to Laxalt's unusually pointed comments, something reporters for the newsmagazines had told me suddenly seemed relevant. I was receiving a great deal of credit from members of the administration and the campaign for being the President's "chief debate coach." Getting credit for adversity was not surprising. I was sure that if things had gone well, there would have been many more claimants of responsibility (as indeed there were after the more successful second debate). What was surprising was that a few reporter-friends felt that I was in serious danger of being fired. They were hearing reliably that the First Lady was incensed with me for the way in which the President had been prepared. And I knew that an incensed First Lady generally got her man.

I wasn't really worried about what would happen to me if I were fired. It seemed to me that it would be transparent that I was just being used as a scapegoat. And I could think of worse epitaphs than the one I imagined my critics were providing for a cartoonist to put on my gravestone: "He gave his President the facts." But I didn't think being used as a fall guy would be fair to me or the President. I concluded that I'd better take a little preventive action.

I had to let Laxalt know that there was a limit to how far he could go in blaming me. After the campaign group meeting, I walked with him down the West Wing stairs and out to West Executive Avenue. We stopped on the sidewalk by his car. I looked him squarely in the eyes and said, "Paul, you know perfectly well what really happened. We didn't overload the President. It was he who kept asking for rebuttals and facts. We had to keep refining things down. And it was the First Lady who kept Baker and me from getting him to rehearse his closing statement. She wouldn't let us go over it even once. She stopped our final briefing at Camp David so she and the President could have a leisurely lunch and an afternoon ride. And on the day of the debate, she kept him hermetically sealed away. She wouldn't let any of us near him."

I then went on, "I understand the need to get the focus off the President. I'm happy to take some blame to help. But it's beginning to look as if some people may want me to take all the blame, and then some. You need to know," I said slowly and clearly, "there is a limit to how much I'll take. I will take a reasonable amount. But it's got to be at least halfway reasonable."

I didn't say what I would do if it weren't halfway reasonable. I just looked Laxalt coldly in the eyes, without blinking, and let him imagine.

Laxalt's normally very direct gaze seemed to weaken a bit. He protested that he had meant to focus blame on all of us. I said fine. He got in his car, and I walked back into the West Wing thinking that that little preventive action had been well worth taking.

Another bit of prevention that I took was straightforward. I decided that the better part of valor was to stay low—both inside and outside—until the second debate was over. With this little program for temporary self-preservation, I felt increasingly secure as the second debate approached. I assumed the preventives must be working when no one formally asked for my scalp. And I looked forward with an anticipatory sigh of relief to that moment when we might think that the second debate had been won.

That moment came about a third of the way through the

second debate on October 21. The President's substantive performance that night was mediocre at best. He began inauspiciously by speaking of a "CIA agency head in Nicaragua," and then saying that he had "misspoken." He later ended the debate by misjudging the timing of his close. He was still standing and talking. But he had to be cut off by the moderator at a point where his critics said he left them wandering aimlessly down the California coast thinking about a time capsule! None of that was to matter, however. It was rendered irrelevant by a single exchange that took place in between the misspeaking and the wandering.

The moderator had moved things along tediously enough: "Mr. [Henry] Trewhitt, your question to President Reagan." Then came this, the stuff of which defining moments in presidential debates are made:

> TREWHITT: "Mr. President. . . . You already are the oldest President in history. And some of your staff say you were tired after your most recent encounter with Mr. Mondale. I recall that President Kennedy had to go for days on end with very little sleep during the Cuban missile crisis. Is there any doubt in your mind that you would be able to function in such circumstances?"

> THE PRESIDENT: "Not at all, Mr. Trewhitt. And I want you to know that I also will not make age an issue of this campaign. I am not going to exploit for political purposes my opponent's youth and inexperience." This was followed by audience laughter and applause. The President went on, "If I still have time I might add, Mr. Trewhitt—I might add that it was Seneca or it was Cicero, I don't know which, that said, 'If it was not for the elders correcting the mistakes of the young, there would be no state.'"

> TREWHITT (unintentionally suggesting that the President had just hit a home run): "Mr. President, I'd like to head for the fence and try to catch that one before it goes over. But I'll go on to another question."

He didn't really have to. The President's quip had cleared the bases, and the game was essentially over.

The press declared this debate a Reagan victory by virtue of the President's having recovered to achieve a draw. Again, substance was largely ignored. *Newsweek*'s treatment was characteristic. After the first debate, it headlined, "Reagan and the Age Issue." After the second it proclaimed, "Reagan Wins a Draw"— explaining that "the President deftly defused the age issue with a well-timed vintage Reagan quip."

The morning after the debate, the Campaign Strategy Group met at 7:00 in our Kansas City hotel. Confidence seemed to be returning. The President had squeaked by. Later, on *Air Force One*, Laxalt seemed in great spirits. He was gracious and jovial with me. And floating along at thirty thousand feet, with the President's "victory" an accepted fact, it seemed to me that all was well.

But I was wrong.

Back in Washington later that week, Stu Spencer stopped by my office at around 4:00 one afternoon. Spencer was a troubleshooter who had been invited to ride shotgun on three consecutive Republican presidential campaigns. He had managed the first Reagan campaign for governor of California almost two decades before. Savvy, earthy, unpretentious, and irreverent, he was one of the few people to enjoy the near-complete personal confidence of both the President and the First Lady. This was true in spite of his having helped President Ford defeat candidate Reagan in 1976. That was excused as entirely consistent with Spencer's persona as a hired gun with an instinct for winning.

As it happened, I wasn't in when Spencer stopped by. He waited for a while, and then left just before I returned at 4:30. When told he had been waiting for me, I figured he was perhaps socializing next door in the office of my friend and colleague Craig Fuller. But when I looked in Fuller's office, Spencer was not to be found. I trusted that he would call if he really needed something.

At around 5:00, I drifted into Baker's office, as I tended to do routinely, pushing open the unlatched door while running my knuckles across it in a light knock. Instead of his normal welcoming look, Baker seemed to turn away and look out the window. "What's up?" I asked, in exactly the offhand manner I often used to put that question.

"Well," he started hesitantly. "What's your reaction?" He

had an evident uncomfortableness that I couldn't quite figure out.

"My reaction to what?"

"Didn't Stu talk to you?" he said with a note of puzzlement.

"No," I said. "He stopped by my office. But I wasn't there. And when I came back, I couldn't find him."

Baker was gazing through the window overlooking the patio. He seemed to be looking for birds at his feeder. That's what he did to get his mind away from the conventional world of human struggle. Whether wild turkeys in the dry Texas scrub, or doves near the green White House lawns, he'd watch for them as if, perhaps, they bore some special message.

"What did Spencer want?" I asked innocently.

Baker turned and looked me in the eyes. "He was going to tell you that you had to resign." I felt as if I'd been hit in the stomach with a good-sized medicine ball. When Spencer was commissioned as the angel of death, there weren't many victims who survived.

"Well," I said slowly, managing to keep a degree of balance, "I'm glad I wasn't there. I hate to think what my reaction would have been." I paused, then asked, "What is the supposed reason I'm to resign?"

"The First Lady wants you out."

"Uh, huh . . . Have you talked with her?" I didn't doubt that the First Lady wanted me out. I was just trying to get a sense of how far along things were.

"No. But a job's been done on you. Spencer says she's dead serious. I argued with him. And I want you to know I told Spencer that I would have to get the message from the President," Baker said.

He was a friend, and was ultimately to become a much closer friend. But he had a tendency to be careful when it came to putting his interests at risk. I understood and appreciated that. "You mean you didn't say, 'If he goes, I go'?" I half-joked.

Baker took this a bit more seriously than I intended. He reminded me that I had always said that if I ever became an undesirable burden for him, I would go—grateful for having had the opportunity to serve. I had often volunteered that pledge and stood by it. "But," I said, "I'd want to hear from the President myself. I don't believe he'd fire me. I'd ask for an explanation; and I don't believe he'd think he had one that could justify it."

Baker agreed that I should have a discussion with the President if it had to come to that. But he wasn't sure whether or not the President had been cut in on the First Lady and Spencer's machinations. In any case, he seemed relieved that he wouldn't have to carry the burden of the argument. And I was relieved that I was free to handle my own case. I hoped and guessed that Spencer was acting on the basis of conversations with the First Lady, but not with the President.

I asked Baker not to do anything until I had a chance to think over what I should do next. I went back to my office and checked my call sheet. Spencer had not called. I decided I would duck him for a while if he did. I needed time to find out more about what was really up, and to decide how to handle it. In the circumstance, Mike Deaver was my most promising source of information, notwithstanding his possible participation in the plot. I went to his office. He had left for the evening. I decided not to tell anyone anything, and to see Deaver in the morning.

Early the next morning, I asked Deaver for his advice as a friend. I told him that Spencer had tried to see me, but had missed, and that Baker had filled me in on what I understood to be the First Lady's desire that I go. I said that if anybody wanted me to go, I would have to hear from the President that he himself wanted that; and I would wish to discuss the matter with him. But before getting to that, I needed to know what was really up.

By the sheer luck of my having been out when Spencer came to call, Deaver was put in an awkward position: To verify the Spencer message was to be the actual hit man. Face-to-face, he had to choose between being a friend and being the hit man.

"The First Lady does want you out of the White House," he said. That bit of confirmation was unsurprising, but still unwelcome. I felt a little gulp somewhere deep inside. I didn't know of anyone who'd survived in the Reagan White House when a problem had gotten this far. Several had fallen when they were the focus of the First Lady's ire, just as several more would fall later.

Deaver went on: "Laxalt gave her an earful after the first debate. She was very angry and upset. You became the main target. I think Maureen may have really worked on her in the residence . . ." (Maureen Reagan, the President's daughter, thought I was responsible for *Time*'s reference to her as a six-hundred-pound gorilla.) "Still, I don't think you should do anything until after the election," Deaver continued. That led me to think the President was still not in on the plot. And I worked for him, not the First Lady.

I emphasized once more that if there were a decision that I should go, I would insist that it be the President's decision; and I would of course want to discuss it with him. The reason I kept emphasizing this point was straightforward: I did not think the President would feel comfortable firing me. And I wanted whoever was involved to get the message that they would have to deal with this problem. They surely knew that the President would believe that the merits did not justify my removal.

After all, I had been providing the President with his written briefings for virtually every meeting and countless decisions for four years. And I had coordinated the White House staff work, in one way or another, for most of what the President did—as well as what was done in his name. The President and I were linked directly by an almost constant exchange of information and requests for action, an exchange that went back and forth well into most evenings and virtually every weekend.

Better than anyone, I knew that the President was a harder worker than the public was led to understand. Similarly, the President knew better than most that when he needed staff work done, at whatever time of day or night, he could count on my being promptly responsive. He knew, too, that while I failed to meet the ideological purity test, I had a partially redeeming virtue: I could be counted on to present the relevant facts and competing considerations, the pluses and the minuses, in a relatively neutral and direct manner.

As for the alleged brutalization, the President provided his own perspective months later in a private interview with Jack Germond and Jules Witcover for their book *Wake Me When It's Over.*

"Well, let me say that there were, by that time, so many things in which I thought there'd actually been mis-

statements of fact about figures and so forth, and what
had been accomplished, that I set out to cram. I thought
that the debate might then offer me an opportunity to
rebut a great many of these things. . . .

"I wanted to make sure I had everything at my fin-
gertips. . . . I just crammed myself. . . . The main factor
was myself. I brutalized myself with my cramming."

As I sat in Deaver's office discussing the First Lady's desire
for my resignation, I assumed that something like the account
later given to Germond and Witcover was the President's perspective. But I couldn't know for sure. What I did know, of
course, was that the First Lady was not quite as charitable as the
President. So when Deaver said I shouldn't do anything until
the election, I wasn't quite sure what he was up to. Nor did I
quite see how the First Lady's wrath was to be better directed toward the public good. Yet Deaver pressed on. "Let me handle
this with her—but not right away. I think I can take care of it. I
think the whole situation will be better after the election."

I couldn't be certain that Deaver was really going to help.
It was possible that he was just trying to keep me cool until after
the election. But I got the feeling he meant what he said. Getting up to go, I thanked him. And I added one final thought. "I
think I'd best not pursue the matter with Spencer." This was an
obvious understatement. Unlike most people, Spencer would
have had no problem at all reconciling his roles as both friend
and hit man. Indeed, as a self-respecting hit man, he would not
have wished to shoot and miss. So I decided not to be an available target for a little while longer. And when Spencer and I finally did get together for a little chat, things took an amazing
turn.

By some means or other, Deaver worked his magic with the
First Lady. Indeed, he proved to be a Houdini. For just as
strangely as I had come to be visited by Spencer, a would-be angel of death, I found myself visited again by Spencer and
Deaver in the guise of angels of mercy.

On November 4, two days before the election, *Air Force One*
had landed in California. We were just about to complete what
was billed as the last presidential campaign swing of the President's career. I was still a member of the traveling party. We
were spending the night in Sacramento's Red Lion Inn. Rather

ironically, I was assigned the room next to the President and First Lady's.

As I was settling in, there was a knock on the door. It was Mike Deaver. He wanted to talk. I invited him in. In the all-American-rustic comfort of the Red Lion, we sat down.

"Stu and I spent an hour and a half talking with the First Lady on the plane," he said. "We broke through." His manner suggested that I should be glad, so I gathered that the breakthrough involved me. We had not discussed my problem with the First Lady since the day in his office when he had offered to help. "Stu and I managed to get across how essential, how vital you are to Ronald Reagan's success," Deaver continued. "We made an enormous amount of progress. We've got it all agreed. You can be the head of the OMB within six months."

This was indeed a curious reversal of fortunes. Suddenly—within less than two weeks—the very people who had been arranging my ouster were now promising me one of the most powerful positions in the cabinet.

It crossed my mind that perhaps they didn't know how significant the Office of Management and Budget job was. Or perhaps they just wanted to use me to displace my good friend Dave Stockman, one of the few people who may have ranked higher than I did on the hit list. Or perhaps Deaver was planning to become chief of staff and he wanted someone he could work with at OMB. Or perhaps they were focused literally on getting me out of the White House, and OMB qualified, because although it was located in the White House complex, it was in a separate building. The speed and degree of the reversal seemed so irrational that my mind was doing a quick random search for possible explanations. None seemed satisfactorily logical.

"You've got to be kidding," I said. "That seems a rather substantial switch." Recognizing this full well, Deaver had a self-satisfied look on his face, as if he'd accomplished no small feat. I asked for more of a flavor of the conversation, but Deaver didn't offer much, and told me, in effect, just to be happy with the result. He had to go off to dinner.

The next morning, before breakfast, Spencer stopped by my room. He had never actually delivered or mentioned the message seeking my resignation. The combination of luck and my preventive actions had thwarted him. Though we had traveled together in the meanwhile, I had never brought the subject up with him, or with anyone else. He had continued to act as if we were good friends. In that spirit, and in the spirit of someone who might later want a return favor or two, he seemed pleased to be what he thought was the first to inform me that I might be joining the cabinet. He and Deaver had discussed the second term with the President and the First Lady—and he was happy to be able to say that he was sure I would be head of OMB within six months.

Perhaps I should have been pleased. Yet when Spencer left, I made a note of our conversation and scrawled across it: "What a business!"

I couldn't figure out what these people were trying to do with me. But I decided that I had had enough. The OMB job was something to be taken seriously. Yet it seemed to me that both the job and I were being trifled with. I suddenly realized that I wanted out of the White House at least as much as the First Lady or anyone else had ever wanted me out. I was sick of living in an environment where people and issues were so often treated as if they were part of some fickle Hollywood world, where agents manipulated characters and scripts for the sole purpose of advancing their star. I had learned a bit about the world of populist communication. But I wanted to get away from the games of posturing and promoting, and back into a world of substance.

When we got back to Washington, just after the election, I checked with my friend Stockman to see what he was going to do. Rather than take his job, I thought we both should go. But he told me that he was going to stay through one more budget cycle, another eight months. To me, the thought of inhabiting the White House for that long—the very house the First Lady had so recently wanted me thrown out of—seemed an extraordinarily unattractive prospect.

At just that moment, chance worked its curious will. Don Regan had an angry reaction to a press story. As a form of protest, he told Jim Baker that he would resign. When Baker talked him out of that, Regan mentioned in passing the idea of switching jobs. At a private lunch with me a few weeks before,

Regan had asked about Baker's interest in Treasury. So I wasn't entirely surprised when Baker told me of Regan's suggested swap, and I leapt at the prospect.

The Regan idea opened up the possibility not only of getting out of the White House fast, but also of doing something valuable. Baker had long wanted to get into something more substantive, having originally committed to be chief of staff for only two years; and Treasury was high on his list of desirable new challenges. I had written a memo for Baker and the President on major accomplishments the President might reasonably seek in his second term. Tax reform was high on the President's agenda, and I had put it at the top of the domestic list. It made Treasury an exciting and attractive opportunity for me as well as Baker. So, with Deaver's help, the Regan-Baker swap was arranged. In early January, the President nominated us to be Secretary and Deputy Secretary of the Treasury.

After four years, we were fortunate enough to be able to leave the White House with a degree of respect in the outside community, and a degree of pride within. Many of our predecessors (and some of our successors) were not so fortunate. Some left after electoral defeat. We had been associated with a historic forty-nine-state electoral win. Some left in legal disgrace, or amidst a widespread perception of policy failure. We were not associated with either. And we were able to tell ourselves that confidence in the institution of the presidency was being restored. So, on the whole, we did not leave with bad feelings; quite the contrary.

Yet I could not help reflecting on what I'd learned from the election experience. Some of what I learned simply reinforced with direct experience what I had already known intellectually. Yes, politics was not bean bag. It could, indeed, be thoroughly cutthroat—a fact never more clear to an observer than when it is his or her throat that might be cut. And yes, televised presidential debates turned less on substance than on style and one-liners—a fact already well established by the pattern from Nixon's problems with makeup to Carter's problems with the winning Reagan refrain, "There you go again." These points were hardly new.

What was new to me, however, was suggested by reflecting upon just what it was that had constituted my offense in the eyes of the political tacticians. I was, in effect, accused of being excessively attentive to the President's need to be substantively prepared. The tacticians knew what I did not suspect: Too much attention to substance could be harmful. My whole career had been built on the notion that a superior command of substance was a key to success. So the insight did not exactly come naturally that, in debates, substance could actually be a negative if it came at the expense of style or poetry. Still, the threat of being fired over the issue did bring the point home.

More interesting, the lesson applied far beyond the structured frames of televised debates. Debates were obviously not the specialized context I had tended to think they were, in which substance was more important. The debates were like the election as a whole.

The public and the press were interested in human foibles and failings, whether a superficial lack of humor or a more fundamental "senility." They cared about values, whether private ethics or larger orientations toward the public good. They had a gossip page interest in the secret side of celebrity; and a sports page interest in trial runs of the horse race—who "won," who "lost," and why. Together, the press and the public were like impressionist artists, creating a powerful picture with one lively stroke added to another. But on the large impressionist canvas, the finer details of substantive argument had little place. And just as the debates were reduced to simple tests of senility and humor, the election was reduced to a referendum on the restoration of American pride and strength—painted in bright, simple strokes.

Perhaps more than any modern presidential campaign, the 1984 Reagan campaign—the forty-nine-state win—managed to bypass conventional substance altogether. It highlighted American flags and American heroes; Western rodeos and the Grand Ol' Opry; the simple repetitive chant of the Los Angeles Olympics, "U. S. A., U. S. A.," and the more melodious Lee Greenwood theme song, "God Bless the USA."

The Reagan campaign offered no new programmatic initiatives. Like most campaigns, it provided little serious or detailed analysis. It was helped, of course, when former Vice President Mondale tried to dismiss the tax issue by saying the only difference between the candidates was that he would admit his intention to raise taxes and President Reagan wouldn't. But by academic or League of Women Voters' standards, the campaign was close to substance-free. In the unintended sense, the President was almost literally correct when he rallied crowds with the tacticians' favorite line, "You ain't seen nothin' yet!"

I understood the political value of this substance-free approach, and in some significant respects contributed to it. But initially, I felt that it seemed somewhat cynical, treating the public a bit like fools. Gradually, however, I came to a different realization. In ways not applauded in the ivory tower, the public was in fact being given a meaningful basis for choice.

There was an element of rationality to the public's failure to insist on a conventional, issue-oriented, substantive dialogue. After all, President Reagan was extremely well known; and more reliably so than most politicians. His performance for eight years as governor and four as President was a matter of public record. His character, values, operating style, and ideological preferences were clear and predictable. And to a considerable degree, the same could be said of his opponent, a former senator and Vice President who himself had been highly visible, consistent, and predictable.

But more fundamentally, the reality is that some of the most important substantive issues to command a President's attention are not known during an election. Tax cuts, the Cuban missile crisis, and the decision to go to the moon were not central to the Kennedy election in 1960. Vietnam was hardly on the screen for the 1964 Johnson election. The abuse of executive power (Watergate) was not thought significant in the two Nixon presidential victories. No major public figure predicted the Arab oil embargo, the energy crisis, and the recession that were to doom the Ford reelection bid; or the Iranian hostage crisis that was to dominate the end of the Carter presidency. And yet, these unpredicted, undiscussed matters became the defining issues of their respective presidencies.

Politicians, professional analysts, and the media all have less than clear crystal balls when it comes to predicting what substantive matters will prove highly relevant. Given this, the public can be seen as rational when it attends more to the nonrational measures of values and style than to the substance of debates or position papers. For it is values and style that more reliably suggest how a President will approach the host of unpredicted issues he or she may face.

The language through which values and style are communicated is not generally taught in respected academic institutions. It is not the language of formal argument. It is largely a language of symbolic communication. Much of it is not even verbal. It is found in body movements and facial expressions; in bits of empathy, anger, or humor; in apparent attractions and repulsions; in assumed postures and accidental gestures; in poetry at least as much as prose. And it is all given a degree of coherence through themes and iconography more than through organized analysis.

It is a language that is meant for populist communication. And in an age of mass communication, burgeoning complexity, and information overload, its emphasis on the visual and the symbolic makes it all the more effective, perhaps even essential.

The public has an uncanny capacity to decipher this language, to separate the true from the phony, and to intuit conclusions about character and predilections that are more reliable in their predictive power than any cold verbal statements of policy. Indeed, in the process of interpretation, the public does not treat statements about policy as of much importance for their literal predictive power. Rather, policy statements are treated as neither more nor less than additional bits of symbolic communication to be synthesized along with the rest.

The American political system is, in a sense, a running dialogue with the people. To understand or participate in that dialogue effectively, one needs at least to know the language of populism and to accept its inescapable importance.

My early childhood in a New England mill town had left me with a populist commitment to fairness and traditional American values, along with a share of populist resentments. These were in some respects deeper in me than the Harvard-elitist patina I had later acquired. But my style, analytic bent, and approach to problem solving were not naturally those of a populist. In gaining respect for the language and legitimacy of populist communication, I was learning as I went along. And by the time the election was won, my intellectual orientation had grown to include a special appreciation for the legitimate power of populist thinking.

One might well ask how it happened to take so long to

learn the obvious. But speculating about that seems less relevant now—since it turned out later that the learning did not exactly stick.

It did stay with me for at least a few years, however. And as I moved to Treasury, I went armed with my newfound appreciation for populism. I didn't kid myself that I personally might be much of a populist messenger. Still, I did try to link my new appreciation for the dynamics of populist power with the substantive challenge at hand: reforming a tax system that populist America had come to hate.

There was, of course, a negative taste left from my encounter with the anti-substantive school of political management—and the related interest in firing me. But that was largely left behind. The lessons about populist communication were well worth the experience. And looking forward, it seemed that we might even put populist communication to constructive substantive use. If we could get meaningful tax reform enacted, we might actually give the refrain "You ain't seen nothin' yet!" its positive meaning: The best was yet to come.

7

The Levelers' Mandate:

Tax Reform—Dead or Alive

WHEN THE NEW CONGRESS convened at the start of 1985, Baker and I were confirmed as Secretary and Deputy Secretary of the Treasury.

Stockman stayed on for a while at OMB. He was making one last valiant attempt to build the three-legged stool. In due course, after yet another round of difficult negotiations, he was to get close to a significant victory on a deficit reduction package. For the first time, it was to include restraint on the growth of Social Security. In a late-night session of the Senate, under the courageous and effective leadership of Bob Dole, Senator Pete Wilson was wheeled into the Senate chamber straight from a hospital bed to cast the unpopular tying vote in favor. And Vice President George Bush cast the necessary tie-breaker. But then the House and the President lost some combination of trust and nerve. One leg of the stool was sawed off, and another. The support for a package deal collapsed. This time, Stockman left in disappointment. And the remaining deficit problem was left for the future.

In accord with the Regan-Baker swap, Don Regan had taken over management of the White House. After Stockman's departure, Regan relied on his successor, Jim Miller, for the management of deficit reduction. In time, they were to become enamored with a simple deficit reduction system, a kind of fail-safe automatic pilot. Named for its Senate sponsors, Phil Gramm, Warren Rudman and Fritz Hollings, it was intended to have a self-executing enforcement system to ensure that declining deficit targets were met. Unfortunately, though the growing economy helped turn the deficit down, fiscal balance was to remain elusive. Federal spending stayed above 22 percent of GDP; tax receipts stayed near 19 percent. And the automatic pilot's course had to be reset, and reset, and reset.

In the continuing struggle for fiscal control, Regan did not seek much help from those of us at Treasury. That was understandable, and in some ways welcome. At Treasury, there were useful things to accomplish without getting bogged down again in the debilitating politics of deficit reduction.

Our top domestic priority was one of the President's highest: tax reform. And internationally, our agenda included several interesting and important challenges: the pressing problem of developing country debt; a need for greater currency stabilization; and an opportunity to build an improved system for international economic policy making. This set of interests was more than enough to keep us occupied without any lingering yearning for daily involvement in the affairs of the White House.

Indeed, life was a good deal more pleasant at Treasury. The daily management of the international issues for which we were responsible was largely ignored by the domestic press and politicians. Externally, these issues were followed mainly by a community of experts, interested in the merits. And though tax reform was inescapably entangled with politics—and most observers considered it a long shot—it gave us a chance to do something we had not done for several years: We got to work on a substantive issue that was actually popular with a large number of frustrated Americans.

In the 1984 campaign, President Reagan had referred to tax reform only in the most general way—promising to reduce tax rates, and make the tax system simpler and fairer. The Treasury Department, under Don Regan's leadership, had then produced a major tax reform study that was released after the election. With modest adjustments recommended by the new Baker Treasury, that study provided the basis for the President's reform proposals in the spring of 1985. And with further congressional adjustment, the Reagan-proposed comprehensive tax reform was to become the most significant domestic victory of the President's second term. It was enacted a year and three quarters after Baker and I set our new course at Treasury.

Tax reform became the most visible domestic victory for the President since the heyday of 1981. And it deserved the attention it received. The 1986 tax reform was one of the largest ever legislated in the United States. It affected every sector of the economy. It modified hundreds of billions of dollars in special tax preferences—for real estate, entertainment, passive investment losses, capital gains, and a long list of others that had worked their way into the complex American tax code. It touched every American taxpayer. And it surprised many, because on its up-down path toward enactment, it had often been declared dead.

As in 1981, it gained its political force from the power of populist dissatisfaction with the tax system. But in this case, the center was able to play a stronger role; and the ultimate legislative outcome was widely viewed as responsible.

In two important ways, the 1986 tax reform was unlike most large-scale federal reform efforts. First, it actually became law. Previous efforts—not just tax reform initiatives, but large-scale reforms of all kinds—had typically amounted to little more than bold talk. They were normally followed by either legislative stalemate or the conventional mush of half-baked compromise. Tax reform had had a particularly unpromising history. All prior efforts at comprehensive tax reform had failed. But in 1986, tax reform not only was achieved. It was actually enacted on the same comprehensive scale as proposed, and with a fair degree of intellectual integrity. That was extraordinary.

Second, tax reform was a significant substantive success. It was not only viewed as such at the time; it also fared well in a host of later analyses. It flattened and simplified the personal income tax rate structure, reducing the number of tax brackets from fourteen to two. It raised the personal exemption, and took millions of the working poor off the income tax rolls. It lowered the top tax rate from 50 to 28 percent (with an additional 5 percent "bubble" for some higher income taxpayers). In so doing, it increased incentives for work and dramatically reduced incentives for the use of special tax preferences. It made the effective rate of corporate taxation more nearly uniform, reducing the bias in favor of the old industrial sector and improving the competitive position of the large new service sector. It made the use of tax shelters, with excessive paper "losses," far less attractive. It thus reduced artificial distortions in the allocation of capital, making the economy more efficient. Its alternative minimum tax made it almost impossible for substantial earners to escape taxation. And, perhaps most important, it reduced what had been the growing and corrosive public perception that the American tax system was unfair.

Like the tax cut of 1981, the tax reform of 1986 was a case of going for the bold—and getting it. Admittedly, tax reform was not as bold as some felt it should have been. Many thoughtful analysts, concerned about America's low savings rate, wanted to replace the income tax system with a system that penalized consumption more than income. But a pure consumption tax system was not politically feasible; and a hybrid threatened to be even more complicated and confounding than the system it was meant to reform. So the effort of 1985–86 rejected this alternative. It also rejected the oversimplification that appealed to more populist advocates. It did not eliminate all deductions, apply a uniform flat tax, and allow tax filing by postcard. In its extreme form, that was a pipe dream. What tax reform did do, however, was flatten rates considerably, and at the same time increase fairness. That is what made it bold.

It did this while staying within the income tax system. It thus kept just within the bounds of American incrementalism. Yet to the hundreds of special interests and their thousands of lobbyists, tax reform seemed more than bold enough.

Indeed, just as with the 1981 act, it is a wonder that such a bold initiative was actually enacted. It was opposed by much of the establishment. Leaders of heavy industry did not warm to the idea of reducing taxes on the service sector if that meant rising rates for them. Similarly, leaders of high-tax states did not want to risk any reduction of the deductibility of state taxes to finance someone else's tax reduction. And leaders of distinguished private universities, foundations, and churches didn't want to see tax rates reduced if incentives for charitable giving would be hurt. But opposition was hardly confined to the establishment.

Opposition to one reform element or another stretched across a wide swath of American culture and geography. It ranged from concerned protectors of employee benefits to legitimate critics of the high cost of capital to sleazy masters of tax avoidance. Reform was as fervently opposed by oil drillers in the Southwest as by peddlers of tax shelters on Wall Street; by rough-and-tumble wildcatters as by urban sophisticates claiming to be worried about dependence on Mideast oil. It triggered the wrath of much of the real estate industry, even as excessive tax incentives created an unsustainable development boom. Reform was no more popular among the hundreds of thousands of insurance agents, worried about the possibility of reduced preferences for life insurance. Big professional sports moguls and small owners of restaurants found common cause in the effort to preserve deductions for meals and entertainment. Similarly, big banks and smaller credit unions shared an interest in preserving their respective accounting advantages. These and hundreds of other groups—from drug companies to manufacturers of luxury yachts—organized to protect their particular preferences.

The opposition was as deep in its financial backing as it was broad in its political reach. Further, many of the key congressional leaders were less than enthusiastic about tax reform.

That was especially clear in the powerful Senate Finance Committee. As a practical matter, tax reform was simply not going to be possible without the support of Finance. But its members offered almost no hope as we started out in 1985. Senator Bob Packwood, later a crucial and effective champion of reform, was openly discouraging as he assumed the committee's chairmanship. "On taxes," he was widely quoted as saying, "I'm as predictable as the sun rising. . . . I sort of like the tax code the way it is." In our early private meetings with individual members of the committee, Baker and I found a large majority ready to express polite interest in reform, but active support for something else.

Given the attitude in Finance, it was probably just as well that the Constitution required tax measures to start in the House. That is where Baker and I allocated most of our early effort. We wanted to build some momentum on the House side before getting serious with Finance.

By mid-July of 1985, however, momentum in the House was modest at best. Most conventional Democrats and Republicans were reluctant to reduce the tax benefits that special interests enjoyed. And the reform spirit had not exactly bloomed in Senate Finance. Pundits were declaring tax reform "dead"—as they did again and again throughout the process. In order to prevent its death, we needed to suggest that tax reform would not go quietly. We had to remind key players that reform was not just a Treasury priority, but that it would remain a top White House priority as well. The politicians had to feel that they might be held accountable if they failed to produce reform.

With that objective in mind, we arranged for chief of staff Regan and Vice President Bush to host two meetings with the members of Finance. (The President was recovering from surgery for colon cancer.) At eight o'clock on July 17, we had breakfast with the Republican members in the old family dining room of the White House. On July 18, we repeated the ritual for lunch with the Democrats. Don Regan led off by referring to a Paul Harvey commentary titled "Spare My 'But'"— using it to tweak those who were adopting the "Yes, but" approach to tax reform.

The committee responded with a lengthy equivalent of "No thanks." They weren't much interested in increased fairness, and had mixed views about lower rates. We had promised to reject tax reform if it increased the deficit. But several senators wanted to go one step further: to use "reform" to raise taxes. Senator John Danforth said that the "twin deficits" (budget and trade) were the key problems, and they were going unattended. Senator David Boren proposed to add a new oil import fee. Former chairman Russell Long termed the deficit a grave national problem, and noted casually, "You could pick up twenty billion like lookin' at it." Senator Steve Symms preferred to decrease revenues. He favored a flat tax, and liked to admonish us with his folksy Western wisdom, "Don't jump halfway over the ditch." Senator William Roth went yet another way. He opposed our approach and favored a "business transfer tax." Senator Moynihan facetiously identified himself as a representative of "the Northern bloc of socialist states." He noted the "iron law of incrementalism" and cited this quotation: "When Dr. Johnson said, 'Patriotism is the last refuge of the scoundrel,' he underestimated the potential of reform."

And so it went. One by one, almost every member volunteered words of discouragement.

As the second meeting ended, Senator Spark Matsunaga somewhat plaintively offered, "Maybe now that the President has had his operation, he would be willing to consider a revenue increase." One of our White House hosts provided a quick rejoinder: "The President didn't have a lobotomy!" The meeting broke with a good-spirited ring of laughter.

Still, I had the clear impression that our White House colleagues and most of the senators thought Baker and I were engaged in a losing enterprise. Reasonable observers would certainly have put very long odds on the possibility that Senate Finance would pass any serious tax reform. The senators themselves would surely have bet against.

And yet, the unlikely is exactly what happened. Ten months later, after weeks of daily meetings in Senator Packwood's office and a final flurry in the proverbial back room, we reached agreement.

On May 7, 1986, shortly after midnight, our intense behind-the-scenes negotiating stopped. The press and cameras were summoned. Spotlights came on in the Senate Finance Committee's hearing room. Every member of the committee took his assigned seat. Most of the administration's top economic officials were in Asia. They were announcing a new system of international economic policy coordination at the Tokyo summit. Having done a lot to help develop that system, I had hoped to be in Tokyo, too. But anticipating the possibility of a breakthrough on tax reform, I had stayed behind in Washington. I was asked to sit at the witness table, alone.

On my recommendation via telephone, Baker, Regan, and the President took a long-distance leap of faith. They authorized me to support officially the compromise we had just struck. On behalf of the administration, I offered a brief public endorsement and congratulated the committee.

Then the roll was called. The very same senators who were negative in July voted, one by one, to pass historic tax reform. They did so in a form even bolder than we had proposed—with lower tax rates, greater limitations on the use of passive paper losses to avoid taxes, and fewer ways to beat the system. And they did it by a unanimous vote, twenty to zero!

A month and a half later, on June 24, the full Senate passed the bill, 97–3. Having emerged from the House at the end of 1985, by voice vote without objection, tax reform had made it through both houses of Congress with a grand total of three votes against. It was approved by the House-Senate conference on August 16, passsed again by the House and Senate, and signed into law on October 22, 1986. The ceremony was held on the South Lawn of the White House. It was too large for the Rose Garden.

As with the 1981 tax act, one might well wonder what brought about this remarkable turn. The tale was like *The Perils of Pauline*. Tax reform's brushes with death were countless. But reform seemed somehow to have been meant for heroic rescue.

There was no lack of available heroes. Bill Bradley, Dick Gephardt, Jack Kemp, Bob Kasten, and Don Regan each had the courage to author and advance bold reform plans, and then continue to work the system to get a reasonable approximation of their ideal enacted. Dan Rostenkowski used his extraordinary legislative skill and magic to get tax reform through the House. Bill Diefenderfer, David Brockway, and Bob Packwood invented the conceptual plan and political strategy that were the key to both tax reform's revival in the Senate and its ultimate enactment. The staff of Treasury's Office of Tax Policy—under the leadership of a series of first-class assistant secretaries, Don and John Chapoton, Ron Pearlman, Roger Mentz, and Ken Gideon—exhibited not only their well-respected professionalism, but a work ethic that should make critics of government "bureaucrats" think twice, and twice again. Jim Baker demonstrated his distinctive combination of substantive seriousness, political acumen, interpersonal skill, and strategic insight to pull together a coalition that hardly anyone thought would prove to be manageable. President Reagan once again showed the courage to go for the bold, along with the skills of both a populist public communicator and a centrist political manager to achieve what lesser leaders would have failed to grasp. And there were, of course, many others.

The story of these heroic people is well chronicled by the *Wall Street Journal*'s Alan Murray and Jeffrey Birnbaum in *Showdown at Gucci Gulch*. Murray and Birnbaum also generously included me among the good guys in their telling of the tale. I must note, however, that in doing so they dismissed the argument I had made to them: that talk of heroes made entertaining reading, but more abstract forces actually made history.

For me, this was not merely a matter of posturing. I genuinely believed that tax reform was made both necessary and possible by historical forces that were larger than the contributions of various supposed heroes. I had given this serious thought back when Baker and I first moved to Treasury and were setting our top priorities. Though conventional wisdom did not take tax reform seriously, it seemed to me that forces were arrayed to give it a pretty good chance.

When we started on tax reform in 1985, much was as it had been in 1981. We had a popular President. He had just come off a forty-nine-state electoral win, and could claim tax reform as part of his "mandate." Key players from his legislative and campaign strategy group had moved to Treasury, bringing credible legislative management skills to the challenge. With fourteen tax brackets, a top rate of 50 percent, and continuing dissatisfaction with government, the public's appetite for lower tax rates had not abated.

And though a plurality of voters still identified themselves as Democrats, many Democratic members of Congress continued to fear the possibility of party realignment. They had to worry about the potentially transforming appeal of a President who called for both lower tax rates and a fairer tax system. Among those with this concern was one absolutely essential congressional Democrat, Dan Rostenkowski, the chairman of the Ways and Means Committee.

Further, Rosty had seen the centrist leadership bowled over by a populist wave—and pushed out of the way—when the tax bill was enacted in 1981. He was not likely to wish to repeat the experience. Yet he had to worry. Just as there had been a rare political alliance of ideologues and pragmatists to make the 1981 economic acts possible, an unusual and promising political combination was also attracted to tax reform. In Congress, neoliberals and neoconservatives converged to support relatively similar tax reform proposals (named for their sponsors, Bradley-Gephardt and Kemp-Kasten). This time, the early absence of a strong political middle didn't trouble me. Having learned a bit from the first Reagan term, I judged that the missing middle could be brought along by the force of populist spirit—and might even be inspired to "lead."

Indeed, I concluded that the populist force would be irresistible if we could just make the political system face a simple, binary choice: "Are you for tax reform to lower rates and increase fairness, or do you favor the status quo?" At crucial moments in the public debate, that is exactly the question that President Reagan was to put to the Congress and the American people. And given the breadth of populist anger at the tax system, the answer to that question had to be reform.

Fortunately, there were many substantive ways to produce lower rates and increase fairness. That gave us important room to negotiate without losing the essential characteristics of reform. The harder part was procedural. We agreed early—I agreed at my confirmation hearing—that an acceptable bill must be "revenue neutral." That assured we would not repeat the bidding war of 1981, and increase the deficit. It also bolstered support for measures that would increase fairness in order to pay for lower rates. The key requirement, however, was to make tax reform the only alternative to a defense of the status quo, and to force politicians to choose.

In order to force the choice, Baker and I had to keep the legislative process moving, as Stockman and our White House team had done with the tax and spending bills in 1981. That was not always easy. Indeed, keeping tax reform alive, not to mention moving, was at some points highly controversial. But it seemed to me that in the end—faced with a credible reform alternative that would lower rates and increase fairness—it would be a rare politician who would vote to defend the tax system as it was. Most Americans felt that the tax system, as it was, was indefensible.

In several speeches, I tried to underline that fact by sounding some populist themes. It was not my intention to educate the general public. They already knew what I was saying. Nor was I personally pretending to be a populist. That was implausible. What I sought to do was use the public media to communicate with insiders. I was trying to impress two basic points upon the observing press, commentators, and politicians. These were points that they would know President Reagan, in his own more popular way, could—and ultimately would—make to a wider national audience.

First, I wanted observers to appreciate what was unquestionably a fact: that there was a strong populist force driving tax reform—a force that had to be reckoned with. To the extent that they acknowledged this, it increased the chances that the status quo would be treated as unacceptable. Second, I wanted to carry the point a bit further and suggest that there was an inexorable political logic to tax reform. The forces of reform not only had to be reckoned with; they also had to win. That was arguable. But asserting it was so helped make it so.

As a Republican deputy secretary of the Treasury, I thus became a somewhat incongruous voice, attempting to explain the virtues of tax reform as a necessary populist corrective. I started with a speech that I knew might get attention because I scheduled it for tax day, April 15, 1985. The title suggested the line of argument: "Historic Tax Reform: The Populist Correction." For the academically oriented in the audience, I intellectualized a bit. I talked about the rise of "market-oriented populism," "white-collar populism," and "flat tax populism"—describing each as a significant historical development with powerful sociopolitical underpinnings. And I theorized about "a natural politico-economic law that excessively progressive tax systems must degenerate." Then I got down to the basics that were of general interest:

> There are obvious unsettling aspects in the current system. The overwhelming majority of taxpayers eat lunch without being able to deduct their meals as business expenses. They buy baseball or hockey tickets without being able to enjoy the luxury of business-related sky boxes. They talk on fishing boats, but don't take the tax deduction for ocean cruise seminars. They strain to pay interest on their home mortgages and may take the tax deduction for their payments, but they can't quite figure out how others can invest in real estate shelters and get more back in tax benefits than is put at risk. They read that of those with gross incomes of over $250,000 before "loss," more than a fifth pay less than 10 percent in taxes; and of those with gross incomes over $1 million before "loss," a quarter pay 10 percent or less in taxes. From this perspective, it is little wonder that flatter would seem fairer.

I went on to conclude with a summary of my perspective and a genuine expression of confidence:

> In a democracy, large-scale, nonincremental reform requires a broadly based, emotionally driven, popular ap-

peal. Populist resentment, the new populist appreciation
of market-oriented growth, and the populist quest for
fairness are the basis for just such an appeal. Their con-
vergence with "supply-side" and "neoliberal" ideology is
fortuitous. I doubt that they—and the historic reform
movement of which they are a part—can be denied.

The press response and commentary were as I hoped and
imagined they would be. On the morning after most Americans
had to file their tax returns, the *Wall Street Journal* headlined,
"Reagan Is Planning Populist Proposal for Tax Reform." The
Baltimore Sun was even more direct: "Reagan Aide Cites Anger
at Tax System." Its subhead was right from my speech: "Populist
resentment and the quest for fairness are powerful motive
forces for reform." Other papers gave the speech similar
play. Having thus framed the issue in populist terms at the start,
we were able to keep the quest for reform framed as: the people vs. an unacceptable status quo. And when the going got
tougher, I was able to refer to my historical perspective, and
argue with some credibility that tax reform should not be
counted out.

For example, in that period in July 1985, when progress in
the House was stalled and the Senate Finance Committee was
privately discouraging, I spoke to a large group of lobbyists and
congressional staff. After the speech, in order to give it a bit of
an echo, I discussed it in a briefing for out-of-town economic
editors and broadcasters. The speech led off somewhat dismis-
sively with regard to the naysayers:

> We're at that stage in the process of "revolution" when,
> upon hearing shots fired, many presume there must be
> fatalities—when, in some quarters, the crowd begins to
> run; and when, among instant historians, debate begins
> to rage as to how key battles were lost. . . . But to my ears
> at least . . . the sounds I've heard seem to be more like
> the pops of a shooting arcade. And tax reform is like the
> target bear. It gets "hit." It rises, pauses, turns a bit—and
> then it keeps on going.

I proceeded to rebut the prevailing criticisms of tax reform
and its progress. Then I returned to my basic perspective. I argued that tax reform was part of a longer-running movement

than assumed by those who thought of it as having been launched with the President's proposals. It arose, in part, as a response to people's dissatisfaction with the growth of government and inflation in the 1970s. That dissatisfaction was met in part by the 1981 tax bill. But, I argued, the movement arose also out of dissatisfaction with the perceived unfairness of the system; and the response to this cause of dissatisfaction had yet to be enacted. Again I expressed confidence:

> Yet a response is bound to come. The dissatisfaction with the present system is unsustainably high and will demand a remedy from our democracy. . . . Fortunately, the American political system does not allow self-destruction. It just operates like a melodrama and heightens the suspense before finding its way out of the latest trial or tribulation. . . . So the bear will keep on coming in its relentless pursuit of progress.

Notwithstanding my confident assertions, doubters seemed to remain in the majority. Indeed, even after the unanimous vote in the Senate Finance Committee in May of 1986, I had to continue to argue publicly that tax reform was actually going to be enacted. On May 30, I spoke to the National Association of Manufacturers. They were not natural enthusiasts for reform. But they were realists. And if persuaded of tax reform's inevitability, they (like other practical interest groups) were likely to be more cooperative.

The manufacturers were also sports fans. At the time, not only was tax reform riding an apparent high; so, too, were the Boston Red Sox. I planted an obvious suggestion by citing two important sources of wisdom:

> The fever of hope has even reached my nine-year-old and five-year-old sons—not the hope for tax reform, but hope for the Red Sox. They've temporarily swapped their orange, black, and white Orioles hats for the distinctive Boston blue with the red B. They think they know a winner when they see one.

To make my join-the-winning-team suggestion credible, however, I had to make an important distinction. I acknowledged a thought that I knew would run through the minds of many in the audience.

We all know that the Red Sox have a tragic flaw: a chronic habit of entrapping their fans with a strong start, only to leave them with a broken heart. . . . Occasionally it doesn't come until the seventh game of the World Series. But every year since 1918, sooner or later, the fall has come.

I then went on to try to demonstrate that tax reform would not go the habitual way of the Red Sox.

Thanks to the effective leadership of Assistant Secretary Margaret Tutwiler at Treasury, a broad-based coalition had been organized in support of tax reform. Tutwiler was a first-class professional with outstanding political sense and organizational skill. She had been Baker's right-hand person in the White House, and had assembled an able staff at Treasury led by CeCe Kramer. I had great confidence in their work, and reminded the manufacturers of the size of the coalition that had been pulled together.

But I still had a major worry. It was that the various self-interested opposition groups might themselves unite and become a single "killer coalition." We had, of course, worked to keep the groups divided—showing a willingness to compromise selectively. And we were aided, in no small measure, by the essential narrowness of the opposition groups' individual interests and perspective. Still, I wasn't comfortable relying on this alone.

So, after reciting a number of technical and inside-Washington points, I tried to prevent my major worry from materializing. One more time, I got back to the populist basics. I warned: "Kill-the-bill strategists will have to justify their approach on national television. They will have to be prepared to defend the preservation of the current tax system—in the face of its overwhelming unpopularity with the American people."

I concluded by switching to a more consistently successful sports metaphor, "The Golden Bear," Jack Nicklaus. Nicklaus had just thrilled millions by winning the Masters golf tournament in middle age. As he walked up the fairway toward the eighteenth green, the crowd and much of the nation responded emotionally. I suggested that tax reform was working its way toward a similar finish. "Now, as tax reform starts its charge up the back nine, waves of people are beginning to sense that they may witness, encourage, and even participate in a historic American victory." (Unfortunately, to preserve my own legitimacy as a realist, I had to add: "As for the Red Sox, it's best just to hope.")

It is true, of course, that much of this public posturing was a matter of tactics. Tactical considerations were inescapably involved with every dimension of the effort to advance tax reform. Indeed, there were literally thousands and thousands of individual tactical decisions that were made to help move reform along. One had to attend to what seemed a zillion things that might make a difference: hundreds of small-group negotiating sessions, the timely invention of compromises, and a host of more mundane tasks.

In addition, one had to take a few risks. These took a toll in terms of personal popularity, but helped build the necessary momentum for reform. In developing the surprise breakthrough in Senate Finance, to cite a pleasant example, we decided to risk alienating some supporters of reform by passing up an available 11–9 victory and making additional compromises. We did so in order to gain the force of a unanimous, 20–0, vote. Before we had that luxury, however, we had to make many less pleasant calls.

When tax reform was near death in the House, for example, I decided to meet secretly with Chairman Rostenkowski and his key staff. I told them I was speaking without the administration's authorization. Then I suggested elements of a bill that I said was unacceptable to the administration, but which could at least get out of Ways and Means without provoking an irreversible rupture. I hinted that, for House purposes, we might have to accept a slightly higher top tax rate than we had previously been willing to consider, and said we would have to take our chances on improving the bill in the Senate. I made clear that we would need some accommodation from the House in the ultimate House-Senate conference (which Rostenkowski was to chair). But at least the bill would not die a premature death—before the system had given it a fair chance for improvement.

At 10:00 on the evening of the expected Ways and Means vote, Baker and I got grudging White House approval to support a defective bill procedurally, not substantively. Midnight came and went, however, and the committee still did not vote out a bill. Obliged to get up very early that same morning, Baker went home to get a few hours' sleep. At 1:30 A.M., Rosty temporarily lost control of the committee. He then broke for a caucus among Democrats. When a revised bill finally emerged from the caucus, it was worse than we had anticipated or I had ever suggested. It was clear to me that I could not indicate support for it in any way.

But I still did not want reform to die in the House. So, rather than expose the extent of Republican opposition to the bill, I agreed privately to a sudden voice vote—at 3:30 in the morning!—to get the bill out of committee. I did so knowing that members who felt disenfranchised by a procedural device would also be understandably outraged (to understate the matter).

At times, these processes of procedural maneuver and necessary compromise left Baker and me somewhat alone. This was true even at what many took to be the crucial moment of victory—August 16, 1986, at 11:10 P.M.—when the House-Senate conference voted to approve historic tax reform.

Right up until that moment, the outcome remained uncertain. The day itself, like so many before it, had been long. For me, it had started at twenty-five before one in the morning, with Senator Bill Bradley calling me at home. He offered some final tactical suggestions. A few hours of sleep later, at 6:00 A.M., Bill Diefenderfer—Senate Finance's extraordinarily able staff director, strategist, and negotiator—called with a tactical review of his own. He alluded to our having passed the hundredth near-death experience in the *Perils of Pauline*. But there were still a few more to come in the course of the day.

By midday, the debate within the Senate Finance caucus was getting emotional. End-stage compromises had been struck. It was becoming absolutely clear that some members would not get what they wanted. On one contentious issue, Chairman Packwood reported that the compromise produced 80 percent winners and 20 percent losers. Senator Dole quipped, "Where do the losers live—Iowa and New Hampshire?" The group broke into laughter. But not all conflict was so easily defused.

Senator John Danforth was most upset. He tried to postpone a vote by arguing, "It is a revolutionary tax bill and we haven't seen it. . . . It's not fair to people to ram it through after long nights on the last day." Bradley asserted, "We know what's in the bill." Long said both sides were right. There needed to be an opportunity to see crucial language; but the bill couldn't be left hanging. Moynihan observed, "We put at risk the most important tax bill in forty to fifty years." Danforth could not be mollified. Sensing defeat for his point of view, he pleaded, "I ask you, I ask you, give us to Labor Day."

Moynihan then made a telling point about the group's responsibility to vote without having to refer everything back for immediate popular reaction. Emphasizing individual syllables as if each were a word, he intoned, "There comes a time when you say, 'We are a Rep-Ree-Sent-Ta-Tive Government.'" Whereupon, Packwood said he would call for a vote: "I think the bill will die if we don't sign the conference report today."

But neither the votes nor the conference agreement was yet quite there. The Senate caucus recessed. In early evening, Packwood, Bradley, Rosty, Baker, and I worked out one last crucial compromise on the rate structure. (It was relatively technical, a slight upward adjustment of the so-called bubble rate for higher income taxpayers.) It squared the final circle, and made conference agreement possible. At 7:30, the Senate conferees reconvened to consider the agreement. Packwood called for a voice vote. Danforth demanded a show of hands. It came out 6–4 in favor of the conference report. Senators Long and Bentsen then switched to join the majority, making it 8–2.

At 9:05, the group joined their House counterparts for the official House-Senate conference committee vote. Just prior to that vote, members offered closing remarks. For tax reform's supporters, they were words of celebration. Among the most poignant were those by Chairman Rostenkowski and Russell Long.

In calling on former Chairman Long, Rosty referred to him as an idol, and noted, "This might be the last big conference that we'll have the privilege of serving with him on." Everyone stood and applauded. Long's perspective was that of one who had known the Senate for half a century:

> As all of you know, my father served in the Senate about fifty years ago. He died when I was sixteen. . . . I'm one who has served on the Finance Committee for more

than thirty years. . . . I didn't feel this way in the beginning. But I do now. This is the best revenue bill in fifty
years!

The conference then voted to approve the historic reform
that it had negotiated. Right after the vote, before adjourning,
Rosty expressed the pride that many felt. "They said out there
that it couldn't be done. Well, we've done it!" He then read a
brief prepared statement and concluded: "Ladies and Gentlemen, the political process worked. The center held."

There was a little irony in this, I thought, since the centrists
in the Congress had managed the process of reform partly out
of reactive fear of losing power to a combination of the populist
left and right. But that didn't change the essential facts: Populist forces had not only provided an impetus for reform. The
center had also risen to the challenge and done its job, delivering reform that was responsible.

Baker and I were as proud to have reached that point as
anyone there. But we were in a slightly awkward position. We
had helped negotiate and pass the conference report. But in
the long and fast-moving day, we had not yet secured the full
support of the White House staff and the President. At the moment of apparent triumph, our celebration was necessarily
modest. We went back to the Treasury by ourselves. At 11:45
P.M., Baker and I clinked two cans of soda, shook hands, walked
to our cars, and went home.

The President's unequivocal support was secured the next
day. The victory we had all worked for was at hand.

Having expected that victory would one day arrive, I had
saved a sample of negative headlines from tax reform's more
difficult days: "Rosty's Bill Ends in Limbo" (*USA Today*); "Hopes
for Tax Reform Bleak" (*Washington Times*); "Tax Reform on the
Ropes" (*U.S. News & World Report*); "Tax Overhaul Foundering"
(*Christian Science Monitor*); "Sharks Waylay Tax Reform" (*Wall
Street Journal*); "Tax Reform Down for the Count" (*Chicago Tri-
bune*); and only months before, "Tax Reform: Mission Impossible?" (*Time*). I thought I would be able to look back at them with
at least a mild sense of pleasure in the irony.

I was not disappointed. With no small amount of pleasure,
I read *Time*'s answer to its "mission impossible" question in big

bold print, "THE MAKING OF A MIRACLE: Against all odds, Congress hammers out a radical tax reform plan." *Newsweek's* special report on tax reform used the identical characterization. It was headlined simply, "A CAPITOL MIRACLE." The rest of the press followed suit. And this time they were correct. Tax reform was about to become law.

On the long and bumpy path toward tax reform's "miraculous" enactment, I accumulated volumes of notes and memos which memorialized the bits and pieces of tactics and substance that marked the way. When progress had slowed, and tax reform's death was proclaimed for the umpteenth time, the volumes had threatened to become a paper monument to some god of misguided tactical prowess. But I never lost confidence in the larger strategic view. The tactics were sometimes clever and often tedious, frequently necessary and occasionally bold. But ultimately, they were of little significance. The volumes of tactical maneuvers were no more the essential story than were the triumphs of supposed heroes.

Strategy was, as it generally is, far more important than tactics. And the basic strategy was to align with the forces of populism, encourage the center to assume responsible leadership, force a simple choice upon the political system, and let the system work its will.

It did.

8

Buckner's Bobble—

And the Cowboys' Farewell

THOUGH 1986 WAS A GOOD YEAR for tax reform, things didn't turn out so well for the Red Sox. In May, when I had used the Red Sox to make a point to the National Association of Manufacturers, I had suggested that tax reform would probably fare better than the Sox. Being a lifelong fan, I knew what to expect. And, as I feared, the seemingly inevitable collapse came in the fall. It was, perhaps, the most dramatic and disappointing demise in the Red Sox' long and troubled history.

At the risk of treating symbols too seriously, one might suggest that the end-play for the Red Sox was an unfortunate harbinger of things to come—not only for the baseball club, but also for the Reagan administration. Our highs were not to last.

In the months ahead, I personally was to flirt with a new populist agenda. But it was soon to be clear that that agenda could go nowhere at the time. With Iran-contra, the administration was to seem to have lost its way. And I was to take a temporary leave from government. But before getting to that, a brief Red Sox replay is in order.

In October, the Red Sox found themselves in the World Series against the New York Mets. Hopes had been raised and frustrated again and again since the Sox won the Series in 1918 and then committed the seemingly unforgivable sin of trading Babe Ruth to the Yankees. The annual cycle of disappointment was understood as a matter of near-metaphysical necessity. It was accepted wisdom—even by such loyal fans as Dan Shaughnessy, the Boston sportswriter, who elaborated the explanation in *The*

164

Curse of the Bambino. Nonetheless, hopes soared one more time.

Amazingly, at the end of the fifth game of the Series, the Sox were up, three games to two. Having spent many days in the Fenway bleachers, I knew what was likely to happen. Yet the fact—the possibility—remained: One more win, and the curse of the Bambino would be lifted.

By this point, our two young sons had become committed Red Sox fans. I felt I could not let them miss what might be the baseball triumph of the century, a once-in-a-lifetime Red Sox win. My wife, Kath, has many virtues; but she is not a lover of baseball. Still, she let me talk her into my taking Willy (then age ten) and Jonathan (then five) to the sixth game of the World Series. It was at Shea Stadium, not Fenway. But we knew we had to go. This might be the final, winning game.

I warned Willy and Jonathan that they should not let their hopes get too high. I reminded them of the Red Sox tendency to do to their fans what Lucy did to Charlie Brown. Lucy promised she wouldn't; but each year, she did. She set the football up for Charlie's kick and, at the last minute, pulled the ball away—leaving him fallen and disappointed every time. Yet even such dire warnings underestimated what was to befall us.

At Fenway, baseball had always been a well-appreciated sporting event, meant for families and baseball-lovers. That is what we were accustomed to. But at Shea, the World Series was treated more like a cross between a binge and a war. As we walked through the stadium parking lot, smoke from grills with flaming red coals swirled about. It gave the evening a sinister cast, as if we had entered the home of the devil. Boom boxes blared, beer cans rolled, and restless natives screamed intimidating chants at two scared young kids, who had made the innocent mistake of wearing Red Sox shirts and hats. The kids felt lucky to escape with their lives. And that was just the start.

When we got inside the stadium, things didn't settle down easily. A daring fan interrupted the opening ceremonies by dropping out of a plane, illegally, and parachuting toward home plate. If ever there was a sign that this was not to be an ordinary night, that was it. Even Mets fans were shocked into oohs and aahs before returning to their more habitual raucous rudeness. They were quieted only by the Red Sox' early strength. Roger Clemens, a future Hall-of-Famer, had a shutout and a no-hitter going into the fifth inning. He and the Sox were ahead, three to two, in the seventh. Willy, Jonathan, and I looked at one another without daring to say what we actually let ourselves think. Two little innings to go—it looked like the Sox would really do it at last. And we were there to see it!

Unfortunately, Clemens developed a blister on the middle finger of his pitching hand. Johnny McNamara pulled him for a pinch-hitter in the eighth, and the Mets tied it up. The game had to go into extra innings.

Then, miraculously, the Sox actually did it. At midnight—could it have been any better—in the top of the tenth, they took the lead with a home run off the *Newsday* billboard in left. Red Sox fans went wild. Twenty cases of champagne were delivered to the Sox clubhouse.

Alas, the game was not over. The home team was, of course, entitled to last at-bats. The first two Mets who came to the plate in the bottom of the tenth flied out. The Sox were one out away from their first World Series win in sixty-eight years. Calvin Schiraldi, the Sox reliever, got two strikes on the next batter. The Sox were one strike away—a single strike. But Schiraldi lost that batter, and the next, and the next. Bob Stanley, "the Steamer," was brought in to relieve with the Sox still up, five to four. He quickly got two strikes on Mookie Wilson. It was approaching one o'clock in the morning. And again, the Sox were one out—one strike—away from baseball's version of heaven.

Then came the fall. The Steamer threw a rare wild pitch, and the game was suddenly tied. Wilson was still up. There was a chance to get him out, and go on to win in the eleventh. Wilson hit a chopper down the first base line toward Billy Buckner. Buckner was a seasoned pro, playing gamely on bad ankles. The ball was coming right at him. It looked for sure like an easy play to end the inning. But amazingly, the ball just kept on going. It bounced right through Buckner's legs. That was it. The Mets won. Buckner had had a long and respectable professional career. But from that moment on, he was to be remembered in Red Sox lore for one, most visible, failure.

The Mets fans were triumphant and merciless—even to two young kids who were up way past their bedtime. Jonathan and Willy had been on a roller coaster they might have preferred to have missed. But they wouldn't say so. They hardly said anything. Willy, the older, felt the disappointment more deeply. He stood in dazed silence. Tears rolled down his face. His younger brother stared up at him. Tugging at his brother's shirt, he tried to be consoling by borrowing a parent's refrain. "Willy," said Jonathan, "it's only a game." That was easier to think if you were five, perhaps, than if you were twice that age. It was probably impossible to think if you'd waited sixty-eight years—or if you were Billy Buckner.

As with the Red Sox, the fortunes of the Reagan administration went down from the high achieved at tax reform's signing. The end of the Reagan presidency was not so cataclysmic as the Red Sox sixth and seventh games. Yet it was certainly far less positive than the euphoric moments of victory in October 1986.

With my newfound interest in populism, I had looked beyond tax reform and given some thought to an agenda for the future. It involved addressing populist concerns with corporate accountability, education reform, and traditional American values. If these concerns were not attended to, I feared, populist forces might become more alienated. And, in response, policies might ultimately be adopted that would destabilize the balance between sensible government and our market-oriented system.

President Reagan had held together an extraordinarily broad political coalition. Halfway through his second term, he still appealed to blue-collar Democrats, and both rural and white-collar populists, in addition to the traditional Republican base. But it was not at all clear that the broad Reagan coalition could be consolidated and passed on to a post-Reagan generation of leadership. The traditional Republican base was not large enough or committed enough to serve as a protector of sensible market-oriented policies by itself. For sensible market-oriented policies to survive in a post-Reagan political world, I thought, such policies and their advocates would somehow have to be made more broadly attractive to the wide base of ordinary American populists.

I couldn't quite explain what I thought should be done in a way that captured people's imagination and interest within the administration. So I thought I might show what I meant. I decided that, after tax reform was enacted, I would give a series of three speeches to help frame an agenda with a somewhat populist cast. The speeches were to deal with corporate behavior, education reform, and values. I scheduled the first speech for November 7, right after the 1986 midterm elections.

It definitely captured some people's interest. It became known as "the 'corpocracy' speech." In it, I argued that tax reform had special value in the American culture but that it was not sufficient to ensure U.S. competitiveness, inspirational power, and fulfillment of the romantic conception of "America." That conception, I noted, was rooted deeply in the traditions of the Pilgrims, the Revolutionaries, and the pioneers. Yet the modern American culture was at risk of straying from it. The establishment appropriately identified the deficit as a problem in need of attention. But important though it was, I observed, identifying the deficit as the primary target was too facile. My theme was broader: "I believe we have deeper *cultural* problems that demand our attention. And for clues as to what they are, I suggest we look again to the forces of populist correction."

I warned against the destructive populist attraction to isolationism and protectionism; and urged attention to more constructive populist interests. Among these, I cited the widespread interest in improving education. I underlined its importance with what was then an increasingly worrisome observation, "The once-envied American universal public education system is itself becoming noncompetitive on the world scene." Then I raised the voltage a bit, using a rhetorical formula that was meant to make a respectable point, but with a slight populist edge:

> While the children of some societies are now in disciplined learning environments for 240 days of the year, the children of America's urban ghettos are being schooled in the ways of their street culture. And the children of America's boom generation of yuppies and yumpies are being liberated to learn karate, or gourmet cooking, or river rafting—worthy activities, but not exactly a sign of overwhelming commitment to the intellectual capital development on which future generations must depend.

I used the same rhetorical formula in talking about America's need to improve corporate vision and productivity. None too subtly, I placed much of the blame on management, with observations like these:

> As a general matter, we pride ourselves on our pioneering traditions; but outside the publicly funded defense area, we underinvest in R&D. Some high-priced private managers seem to spend less time developing R&D budgets than they spend reviewing golf scores.

As expected, this got some press play. The *New York Times* not only ran a story on the speech, it also did a special two-page follow-up, the title of which captured the mixture of reactions, "Flak After Darman's Speech, But Some Hail His Criticism." Several business leaders were outraged; others were supportive. But the speech was not meant for business leaders alone. My intended audience was a larger public. It was also a much narrower group at the top of our own administration.

Initially, Commerce Secretary Malcolm Baldrige, a well-liked and respected member of the business establishment, was disturbed. But he saw the merit of a more visible push for improved productivity, and got into the news cycle with themes that were consistent with mine—without the edge. What I really hoped our own little establishment might see, however, was that the populist tinge could help us achieve our policy objectives by broadening the base of our appeal. I was counting on editorial reaction and commentary to make this clearer. And I was not disappointed.

The favorable reaction stretched from the liberal *New York Times* to the conservative *Washington Times*. The former concluded an editorial on my speech with as warm an endorsement of the Reagan administration as it was ever able to muster: "The administration's new willingness to encourage bold business deserves a cheer." That alone was not likely to influence any Reaganauts. But it was at least something to think about when combined with a piece by Stephen Green that filled the Commentary section's cover page in the *Washington Times*. It said:

> [I]t is evident that Mr. Darman's remarks were a logical extension of President Reagan's populist philosophy. The same populism that can find waste and inefficiency in government also can uncover similar problems plaguing America's biggest corporations. . . .

Taking on the giant corporations could reinvigorate the last two years of the Reagan Presidency. Furthermore, it could broaden the populist base of the GOP and thereby increase the party's chances of retaining the White House and regaining the Senate in 1988.

Unfortunately, however, there was not to be much high-level thinking about the populist framing of a sensible market-oriented agenda—or anything else that I may have stimulated in the way of future-oriented debate. The President, the White House staff, and key administration officials were about to be consumed by an entirely different line of interest that was developing in the press. It had started in a paper far removed from either *Times*. On November 3, *Al Shiraa*, an Arabic magazine published in Lebanon, had begun to outline the arms-for-Iranian-hostages story.

By the time press reaction to my first speech was beginning to create interest in my next one, the arms-for-hostages story was starting to explode. Speculation about high-level resignations mounted. It was clear that the administration was soon to be under siege.

I decided that I should not complicate matters by causing any new conflict with my second speech. It was scheduled for November 24 at Harvard Business School. It was part of an eminent speakers series, and I could not cancel. So I just rounded off the sharp edges, and took the sting out of the speech. Network television cameras covered the event, having anticipated a lively expansion of my initial critique. They were disappointed. Though I used Muhammad Ali as a metaphor, and his famous "rope-a-dope" as my subtitle, I pulled my punches.

As it turned out, it wouldn't have made much difference what I had said. On the very next day, at five past noon, the President announced that he had accepted the resignation of his National Security Adviser, Admiral John Poindexter; and that Lieutenant Colonel Oliver North had been relieved of his duties. The exposure and investigation of Iran-contra was about to command central attention within and without the administration. For a while, it was to prove spectacular.

I had respected Poindexter's intelligence and commitment to public service, and would not have expected him to take foolish risks. Ollie North, however, was a bit different case.

I had thought that he might be a cause for concern, "in need of adult supervision," as some said.

Having served in four administrations, I had seen a fair sample of risk-taking troupers in extraordinary acts. I was nonetheless surprised to learn that this one cocky performer had been allowed to strut on a very high wire, with the presidential command structure somehow floating above him like the Flying Wallendas. It turned out that he, a mere lieutenant colonel, had run not only a hostage release operation in the Mideast, but also an off-budget insurgency movement in Central America. And he had done so without any identifiable civilian control. His motives were largely patriotic. But when the spotlights exposed his unusual feat, the tightrope began to sway; and the long-popular Reagan act was effectively sent tumbling.

The sinking feeling that the administration was effectively over struck me from the moment I watched the initial press briefing by the President and the follow-up by then-Attorney General Meese. I had been through things like this before. They inevitably proved all-consuming for those involved and for the press. It was obvious that until this cleared, no positive agenda would have much chance; and it was going to take some time for this to clear.

I had been thinking of leaving the administration after tax reform's enactment. With the exposure of Iran-contra, I told myself that I definitely should depart. But I thought it would have been unseemly to do so at such a vulnerable point. So I waited until the spring.

Things grew difficult and painful, as I suspected they would, for those enmeshed in Iran-contra. One especially unfortunate victim was Don Regan. As White House chief of staff, he had to expect some of the criticism for what went wrong. But he got more than his fair share.

In early December, I represented Treasury at a cabinet meeting and passed Regan a note. Though he was better suited for executive positions than for a job like chief of staff, I liked and respected him. Recalling his heroic service in some of the most difficult battles of World War II, I suggested he had survived tougher tests than he was then undergoing. On a White House pad, in his distinctively neat penmanship, he wrote this poignant note, and passed it back to me:

I find some amazing similarities between surviving in WWII jungle battles, and surviving in Wash. political circles. The one big difference—guys on one side didn't shoot at the leader. Here in Wash. apparently you get shot at if you *don't* shoot at your own leader.

Loyalty in Wash. is something that is found primarily as a word carved in marble on statues, and applies only to a bygone era. . . .

Or do I sound as tho' I'm getting battle fatigue?

He *was* suffering from battle fatigue. And not long thereafter, on February 27, 1987, he was unceremoniously relieved. His departure was accelerated by unseemly leaks that were said to have flowed from Stu Spencer and First Lady Nancy Reagan, the duo who had once tried to get me.

Fortunately, I was able to leave on my own terms in April, shortly after helping Jim Baker reach an international agreement known as the Louvre Accord. It was the product of two years of work aimed at strengthening the Group of Seven industrialized countries and the system by which they developed international economic policy—an extension of our earlier work on the Plaza Agreement of 1985 and the 1986 Tokyo Summit Communiqué. Though far less visible, this was in many ways the international equivalent of success with tax reform, and another good note on which to depart.

I read polite compliments for my service in the press, and was pleasantly surprised to find myself in the unusual position of receiving little criticism. It was a bit odd, like getting a chance to read one's own obituary. Among the letters I received, one was especially surprising. It was a handwritten note from President Nixon. Given my resignation from his administration, at the time of the Saturday Night Massacre, I had thought I might be on his enemies list. But he was warm and flattering. He concluded in characteristic style:

Incidentally, you were right in criticizing the inefficiency of many American business executives. They needed to be shaken up.

Sincerely,
RN

I imagined he would have understood what I was trying to do had I been able to finish my series of speeches on corpocracy, bureaucracy, and American culture. But that was academic. I was moving to the outside. Iran-contra was drawing down the administration's energy and its reservoir of trust. The Senate had shifted to Democratic control, joining the House. The administration's capacity to advance bold legislative initiatives was obviously limited—and, for all intents and purposes, there were to be no more. The economy continued to grow; but fiscal policy remained on autopilot. Even the stock market crash in the fall of 1987 was insufficient to prod the divided government to enact major structural reforms. The system seemed to be suffering from a general battle fatigue.

Toward the end of that year, I looked forward with interest to the annual rites of renewal and the coming State of the Union message. Though an outsider, then, I hoped to see President Reagan finish his presidency with some of the romantic freshness he had brought to it when his newly minted belt buckle first proclaimed, "The Buckaroo Stops Here." I tried to persuade my old friends in the White House that the President had one last chance to define an agenda that could lift up his presidency in its final stage. But my former colleagues did not seem interested.

So I put a condensed agenda, without any populist edge, in a column I wrote for *U.S. News & World Report*. I asked whether the President was "reduced to the role of master of ceremonies for a political opera in which the proverbial fat lady is about to sing?" And I tried to suggest that it need not be so. I offered a sample of possible initiatives. In foreign policy, they ranged from a North American accord and a mini–Marshall Plan for Central American democracies to a Pacific Rim initiative. In domestic policy they ranged from welfare reform and a technological revolution in education to the development of outer space. These were all to be capped by a series of farewell addresses from a President who could look forward to the twenty-first century as one who had seen most of the twentieth.

Unfortunately, however, the State of the Union speech was unoriginal and uninspiring. It had no bold initiatives. President Reagan, who had once combined nostalgic conservatism with hopeful populism and future-oriented boldness, was obviously looking backward more than forward. The nostalgic brand of American conservatism had taken solitary hold. Clearly, the fat lady had already sung.

"Big government" had been at 22.9 percent of GDP when the new bronc-busters had come to town in 1981. It was "shrunk" to 22.1 percent as the cowboy hero readied himself for a westward return into the sunset.

The challenge of framing a new agenda, dealing with populist dissatisfaction, and building a new governing coalition would fall to a successor.

9

The Reagan Restoration:

Who's in Control?
(Revisited)

IN THE COURSE of his presidency, Ronald Reagan's progress in reducing the size of government was obviously limited. In seeking to end "big government," he rose in popularity, but fell in effective power. It made me wonder. The question that had been the nation's focus when the President was shot and Haig seized the podium lingered in my mind: Who was in control?

Back in August 1981, a trivial event served both to mock and to highlight the who's-in-control question. It suggested a more serious point that I thought about, from time to time, throughout the Reagan years.

The event took place one evening in Los Angeles, beneath the famous hills of Hollywood. That night I happened to be the ranking aide accompanying the presidential party to a private social dinner. The dinner was held at Chasen's. It was the supposedly posh, and for some reason fashionable, restaurant from which aficionados had shipped chili to Washington to spice up their inaugural dinner.

In fairness, I should note that although I developed no special taste for Chasen's, I did come to appreciate not only chili, but also presidential excursions to California. I was forced to admit that much of California was, in fact, beautiful.

Those of us who were senior White House staff stayed in oceanside villas in Santa Barbara. We were invited to parties where, for example, I got a chance to meet one of my boyhood heroes, Davey Crockett (aka Fess Parker). To his surprise, I asked him for his autograph—not for my kids, but for myself.

He signed, "Ol' Davey." To my amazement, he asked me for my autograph. I guessed that must be the polite thing to do in California.

For a Northeasterner, Santa Barbara required a little adjustment. I wasn't used to walking along the beach with Rolls-Royces bearing mink-clad ladies passing on one side, while topless female joggers passed on the other. It seemed just as odd, but less pleasant, to encounter tar on the beach; and to look out at the expanse of the Pacific and see oil rigs on the horizon.

The natural environment had much to recommend it, however. The White House press corps, previously stationed in Plains, Georgia, was fully prepared to document this point. I myself acquired a special taste for riding horses along the sharp stony ridges of the Santa Ynez Mountains (accompanied, occasionally, by one of my young sons). In those beautiful mountains, kids of all ages could pretend to be cowboys in the familiar dry dust of the once Wild West.

The night of that private dinner, however, wasn't so Western or wild. In fact, it was rather boring.

Part of the problem may have been generational. The President and the First Lady were young looking for their years, almost two generations above my own. They enjoyed old-style dinner dancing, which is certainly unobjectionable. But there was something about the ambiance, the people, and the action that seemed like a movie version of a 1920s ocean cruise. Or maybe it was just that I was still operating on Eastern time. Whatever the reason, I was prematurely tired. So I left early, and went outside to the presidential motorcade.

Such motorcades were not casually arranged. There was a specified sequence of cars and Secret Service vehicles. They included such oddities as a decoy presidential limousine, a SWAT team van with machine guns ready, an ambulance, and helicopter cover hovering overhead. These were all connected with one another and a communications base by radio. There was a well-rehearsed discipline to the management of any presidential movement.

As the senior aide for this event, I was in what was called the "Control" car. "Control" was, in effect, the upper nerve center in the spine of a moving presidency. In addition to a senior White House aide, it carried the President's physician, with his black doctor's bag. It also carried the President's military aide, with a rather different black bag of his own, to be used for the management of U.S. nuclear forces.

If one was not in one's place when the President was ready to move, the motorcade would move regardless. There was no threat of being left to fend for oneself like an ordinary citizen. Cars were assigned to pick up stragglers. But the threat of embarrassment encouraged promptness. I had been through this drill many times. But I still felt uneasy with it, and was happy to find my way to the Control car early. I got in and sat down next to a two-way dispatch radio. Promptly, I fell asleep.

Some time later, the communications trip officer announced over all radios, in standard fashion, "Be advised: We have a departure. All cars and stations, signal depart. Signal depart."

But I didn't hear him. As the motorcade began to move, my head nodded uncontrollably. I strained to hold it upright, but did not have the power.

Then, cracking over the radio airwaves, came this: "Who's in Control? Who's in Control?" A concerned advance man was checking on my location. I could half-hear. But I couldn't quite respond. "Who's in Control? Who's in Control?" the radio demanded again. A colleague responded for me. And I nodded off.

So there I was: a relative newcomer, at the center of supposed power. I was moving through traffic that was parting like the Red Sea. We were protected by a flotilla of security; fully prepared for any emergency; able to engage worldwide communications instantaneously—in "Control." And I was sound asleep!

Did it make any difference that a person in Control was sound asleep? Not a bit. The system functioned satisfactorily with me as a sleeping passenger along for the ride. The motorcade proceeded uneventfully. I was awakened upon arrival at our hotel. I went up to our assigned floor, past the Secret Service guards, and into my room—where I continued my sleep.

But the question that cracked the local radio airwaves harmlessly for a few seconds that night was resonant. It was not only the question months before when Haig seized the global networks to declare, "I am in control here, in the White House." It was the question that occurred to many when U.S. fighters shot down Libyan aircraft, and presidential counselor

Edwin Meese did not wake the President. It was the same question several years later when then–Attorney General Meese announced that the Iran-contra affair had been uncovered, and the President had no knowledge of the diversion of funds to the contras.

These cases were ideal for cartoonists. One portrayed President Reagan speaking into a phone, "World War III? Six hours ago? No kidding? Well, gee, thanks for calling, Ed." Another showed Ollie North, the folk hero of Iran-contra, sitting at a witness table saying, "No, sir. To my knowledge the President was never directly involved in the presidency."

The theme was a consistent focus of ridicule. When President Reagan was still in his second term, the *Wall Street Journal* ran a lead editorial titled "Reagan for President." It was not suggesting a third term. Indeed, when things seemed to be falling apart toward the end of the Reagan presidency, it was common to joke, "None of this would have happened if Ronald Reagan were still President."

The jokes were funny. But the underlying question was serious. It came back again and again. "Who's in control? Who's in control?"

As the Reagan presidency progressed, it seemed increasingly clear that individuals who thought they were in control were deluding themselves. That applied to both "pragmatists" and "revolutionaries." More than any single individual, including even the popular President of the United States, inertial forces seemed to be "in control." And although President Reagan was one of our stronger Presidents, there really wasn't anywhere near as much of a Reagan Revolution as the hard-core revolutionaries had expected or hoped.

This is not to suggest that President Reagan was historically insignificant—far from it. His achievements were of major proportions. And there surely would have been important differences had he not served.

President Reagan helped bring back American pride and confidence about the future. He helped reduce post-Vietnam trepidation about the possible projection of American force through symbolically significant military forays in the Gulf of Sidra and Grenada. He helped reorient thinking about strategic weapons, beginning to emphasize defense more than offense and nuclear arms reductions more than escalating arms agreements. He went on to tilt the federal judicial system back toward traditional values and judicial restraint. He flattened tax rates. And he helped preserve America's distinctive, market-oriented, entrepreneurial society—slowing the trend toward a European-style mixed economy.

Every bit of this was of significant value. All of it was of substantial historical importance. Indeed, its value should be viewed as all the greater for the historical context in which it was achieved. And much of it might not have occurred without Ronald Reagan. The record of extraordinary achievement was, on the whole, a mark of the distinctive Reagan contribution: a triumph of the traditional American spirit.

But in the programmatic terms intended by hard-right conservatives, this did not amount to a Reagan Revolution. It was more of a corrective restoration than a revolution. In January 1984, the President himself said, in his most resonant State of the Union address, "America is back"—not revolutionized, but back. Until the disappointment of the Iran-contra affair, the Reagan presidency was widely accepted and welcomed as this kind of corrective. America seemed almost to demand it.

Yet in spite of this widespread sentiment, and well before Iran-contra, this was clear: With the exception of the 1981 tax act, the more radical elements of the Reagan revolutionary program were unequivocally rejected. Though President Reagan made contributions of enormous importance, the point is simply this: Neither the President nor his administration—nor the more radical external enthusiasts of a Reagan Revolution—was capable of forcing a revolution upon the remarkably stable American political system.

Reagan revolutionaries sought to shrink the federal government. But during the Reagan administration, government grew to a scale larger than it had ever reached before. As a share of gross domestic product, federal spending reached 24.4 percent, a new (and still unsurpassed) peacetime high. A newscaster in a 1986 *New Yorker* cartoon made the formal announcement, "Big government today officially changed its name to *humongous* government!"

Reagan revolutionaries sought to balance the budget and begin to retire the federal debt. But in the Reagan presidency, the deficit rose to a new (still unsurpassed) peacetime record,

6.3 percent of GDP. More debt was added than in all prior presidencies combined. Indeed, total federal debt soon tripled; and the United States became the world's largest foreign debtor.

Reagan revolutionaries sought to increase the savings rate and the real economic growth rate. But in the two Reagan terms, the savings rate actually declined. And the real growth rate averaged only one tenth of a percentage point better than in the Carter administration—substantially less than in the 1960s.

Reagan revolutionaries sought to make Social Security voluntary, and railed against Medicare as a step toward socialized medicine. But President Reagan helped enact reforms that expanded the mandatory Social Security system and assured its survival well into the twenty-first century. The President also enacted a more comprehensive Medicare regulatory scheme than ever before and the most dramatic expansion of Medicare coverage since its inception.

Reagan revolutionaries sought to avoid government interference with the private marketplace. And some gains were made in restoring a degree of regulatory balance. But President Reagan signed legislation that allowed a massive growth of farm subsidies. And he approved additional intervention throughout the economy—ranging from the largest bank bailouts in U.S. history to import quota arrangements for autos, textiles, steel, machine tools, and semiconductors.

Reagan revolutionaries sought Constitutional amendments to ban abortions, permit organized prayer in public schools, and require balanced budgets. But during the Reagan presidency, no such amendments were advanced for ratification.

Reagan revolutionaries sought to return powers to the states that had been "usurped" by the federal government. But the President's New Federalism went nowhere. And in several areas, his policies actually sought to increase centralized regulatory power: supporting federal product liability rules; threatening to cut state highway funds as a means to raise the minimum drinking age; and so on.

Hard-core Reagan revolutionaries denied federal responsibility for addressing the problem of acid rain. Yet, the President and his conservative Canadian counterpart, Brian Mulroney, assumed such responsibility—as they supported an acid rain agreement to celebrate a "Shamrock Summit," one happy Saint Patrick's Day. Similarly, President Reagan himself vowed to limit the Superfund program for the remediation of toxic waste dumps, and to veto any new broad-based Superfund tax. Then, as he campaigned to preserve control of the Senate in 1986, he said he would sign the exact legislation he had opposed.

Republicans then lost control of the Senate, and became an even smaller minority in the House. After six Reagan years, the earlier talk of party realignment and a new conservative majority seemed hollow in the face of voters' evident reluctance to form any stable majority coalition.

Looking back, one of the fathers of modern Republican conservatism, Barry Goldwater, said of President Reagan's domestic record:

> Once in office, he never really cut down spending. Didn't stop welfare. Didn't diminish the bureaucracy. . . . Had I been in Reagan's place, this country never would have gone three trillion dollars in debt.

Reflecting similarly on the Reagan years from the perspective of the early 1990s (before the electoral revolution of 1994), David Frum, conservative analyst and author of *Dead Right*, summarized as follows:

> The great conservative revival of the 1980s is over. Government is bigger, taxes are higher, family values are weaker, and the Democrats are in power. . . .
>
> Conservatives who had breathed animosity against overbearing government out of office, found themselves, once elected, making extraordinarily rapid and happy peace with the beast.

Even in foreign policy, the pattern was somewhat similar.

Hard-core Reagan revolutionaries sought to displace communist China and restore Taiwanese control of the mainland. But President Reagan visited the mainland, embraced Deng Xiaoping, and with instant revisionism deemed the China of the 1980s "so-called communist."

Reagan revolutionaries sought to ostracize the Soviets as an "evil empire." But in practice, the President's summitry legitimized Soviet leaders and alienated several prominent American conservatives. Though all of them were delighted by the collapse of the Soviet Union during the subsequent Bush presidency, many felt more betrayed than delighted in the Reagan years. Richard Viguerie said President Reagan had become an "apologist for Gorbachev." George Will accused him of accelerating America's "intellectual disarmament" and "succumbing fully to the arms control chimera." And Howard Phillips termed President Reagan a "useful idiot for Soviet propaganda."

As a final symbol of the hard-right revolutionaries' failure to assume control, there was this: When his presidency seemed most threatened, at the height of the Iran-contra affair, President Reagan chose Senator Howard Baker to be his chief of staff. Howard Baker was quintessentially a government man. He had led the fight for the ratification of the Panama Canal treaty during the Carter administration. He supported the Equal Rights Amendment to the Constitution. He favored substantial tax increases to reduce the deficit. He was an anti-confrontational compromiser, not an ideologue. He was chronically moderate. And he had contemptuously referred to the revolutionaries' economic program as a "riverboat gamble." Yet, in time of need, he was the President's choice.

In this, as in most other matters of governance, it seemed clear to me that the hard-core Reagan revolutionaries turned out to be little match for the dominant forces of moderation in the American political system.

The Reagan record amounted to a striking anomaly. The revolutionary forces were formidable: a unique combination of strongly held ideology, seemingly invulnerable presidential popularity, and powerful charisma. Together, these forces moved against the system. Yet, though they enjoyed some significant victories, in the end the system won.

President Reagan was unrivaled as a modern political communicator, able to move the public through the artful use of personal style and television. With only two notable exceptions (the recession and Iran-contra), he seemed invulnerable to adverse reactions to his policies. He was equally invulnerable to reactions to the errant ways of some of his appointees. He was said to be protected by Teflon. He ran for reelection against what should have been a tough opponent. Walter Mondale was an experienced and successful politician, who had served as Vice President of the United States, and who was the nominee of the majority party. Nonetheless, President Reagan won a landslide forty-nine-state reelection victory.

And yet, there was this inescapable, unyielding reality: President Reagan had only limited success in advancing the hard-core Reagan revolutionaries' agenda. In many areas, he had no success at all. Indeed, in the areas where the President did succeed, it was only by allying himself with popular sentiment and working within the system. In this sense, the Reagan experience was less a revolution than an affirmation of the power of the American political system.

Understandably, this left many Reagan revolutionaries upset. David Stockman decried the inability to impose his preferred policies. He lamented more than he praised *The Triumph of Politics* (the title of his best-selling book). He and many others regretted the limits that the system imposed upon their ability to effect change.

Toward the end of the Reagan presidency, with the trials of Iran-contra and increasing political stalemate, it became fashionable again to ask hard-edged questions about "the system." Proponents of executive activism questioned congressional intrusiveness. Proponents of democratic restraint questioned the adequacy of checks on a "rogue" executive. And proponents of legislative-executive cooperation questioned its evident breakdown.

In the quarter century that had followed President Kennedy's assassination, the variety of forms of questioning "the system" had become striking to me. And the variety of proposed remedies seemed close to exhaustive: a weaker executive, a stronger executive, a weaker Congress, a stronger Congress, a weaker White House staff, a stronger White House staff, Constitutional literalism, Constitutional revisionism, and the perennial "power to the people."

Yet even more striking was this: The system endured. Change took place within it. But the system itself was not fundamentally changed. From this perspective, the answer to the who's-in-control question came to seem compellingly clear. In some important sense, the system was "in control."

PART TWO

RESTORING THE BALANCE—

Of Prudence and the Future

10
Read My Lips:
Back to the Future

BY THE SUMMER OF 1988, as many Reaganauts were planning their departure, the Republican party was about to nominate Vice President George Bush to be the successor to President Reagan. But it was not at all clear that the Vice President would, in fact, succeed to the presidency.

In July, the Democratic convention nominated Massachusetts governor Michael Dukakis. Amidst a Reaganesque display of American flags, he declared, "The Reagan era is over." Public opinion surveys seemed to agree. With the boost from his convention performance, head-to-head polls had Dukakis beating the Vice President by seventeen points. Going into the Republican convention in August, Dukakis was still up by about ten points.

Vice President Bush's strengths were many. He was a decorated hero of World War II who had come back from the war and made his way as a Texas risk-taker—independent, courageous, and unpretentious. He was also attractive, gregarious, highly intelligent, and thoroughly decent. By experience and character, he was as well qualified for the President's job as anyone who had ever contended for it.

But he had a practical dilemma. To gain the nomination, he had to present himself as the natural heir to the Reagan mantle; while to lay claim to the future, he also had to separate himself from the past. The challenge was complicated by the fact that his strengths did not naturally include either populist style or the inclination to present a future-oriented vision. It was not that he did not care about Americans' future; he certainly did. Rather, he hesitated to commit prematurely or simplistically to objectives and strategies for what he knew to be a complex, changing, and unpredictable world.

In this context, some looked to the selection of the vice presidential nominee as a means to add a degree of populist appeal or future-oriented vision. A few longtime Bush advisers were so concerned about the need to add populist strength that they considered recommending Clint Eastwood for the ticket. They dropped him quickly when polling in California showed he had a surprisingly negative effect. The two front-runners in most people's minds were Senator Bob Dole and Congressman Jack Kemp. Dole added a degree of populism. But as a fellow veteran of World War II, he did not complement the Vice President by adding a reach for the future. Kemp added both. But his personality was that of a starting quarterback, not a backup. The ultimate choice, Senator Dan Quayle, exhibited an obviously contrasting willingness to assume a junior position. Further, he combined a populist conservatism with a youthful image, which might have suggested a reach across the generations, forward to the future—if he had not been the victim of his own launching.

On Monday, August 15, the first night of the Republican convention, the Vice President invited a small group of friends and staff to dinner at his residence in Washington. I was there as an outside economic adviser. After leaving Treasury in April of 1987, I had become a managing director of Shearson Lehman Brothers, where I was still working. But the Vice President had asked me to join his team of outside economic advisers in May of 1988. And with Baker's subsequent decision to leave Treasury to head the Bush campaign, I had become an informal member of the campaign core group.

Over soup, Reubens, and subs, we watched President Reagan's speech and the TV coverage of it. Our host, with characteristic humility, crawled around on the floor to adjust the three television sets we were watching. When we left at midnight, none of us knew who his selection for Veep would be. Nor did we imagine that the choice would be announced in the middle of the next day at a riverboat landing in New Orleans.

I had not expected anything consequential to happen that Tuesday, and didn't leave for New Orleans until later that day.

After a late dinner, I found a note at the Marriott hotel from Margaret Tutwiler. In addition to being Jim Baker's trusted right-hand person, she was a longtime Bush supporter, and a skillful intuitive analyst of politics and public relations. "Dick," her note said, "you MUST come to 3820 for JAB [Baker] ASAP—MDT, 11:25 p.m."

So I went to room 3820, Baker's suite, and found the top echelon of the campaign gathered there. It was not a happy group. Reactions to the Quayle announcement and his subsequent press performances were not good. Neither the new candidate nor the campaign had been properly prepared for the surprise launch. They were on the defensive.

Unsubstantiated rumors were running wild: that Quayle's family had used money and influence to get him out of the draft; that he had had sex with Paula Parkinson, a buxom blonde who had been linked with several congressmen; and that he was nothing but a spoiled lightweight. The campaign group was telling itself not to panic, and to suppress any talk of dumping Quayle. That in itself was an indication of how badly things were going.

Baker wanted me to help him get command of the facts. He called Quayle and told him I would be coming over with Bob Kimmitt to interview him. Kimmitt was then Treasury's general counsel and an informal legal adviser to Vice President Bush. Baker told Quayle that we all needed to prepare for the morning's press assault. It seemed obvious that if—if—there were to be any change of candidate, it would have to be done by Thursday, before the acceptance speeches. Any switch thereafter would be devastating for the campaign. So I concluded that our interrogation of Quayle had better produce a correct assessment, and was glad Kimmitt was going with me. We had worked well together at Treasury and the White House. He had organized the background checks on the potential vice presidential candidates. And notwithstanding the flap of the moment, I had very high regard for him.

At a little after midnight, Kimmitt and I snuck our way to Quayle's hotel room. He had obviously been awakened by Baker's call, and was wearing only his underwear. His wife, Marilyn, was in bed. We decided not to interview her until morning. Quayle's father was up, however, and joined us. He seemed a nice man; and I couldn't help feeling sorry for him. What should have been a moment of great pride was turning into a nightmare.

I had similar feelings for Dan Quayle, whom I had known for several years. We had been sideline parents together at our kids' soccer games and basketball practices. I knew he was not a spoiled lightweight, as the press were suggesting. He was more the victim of his youthful looks and manner. I hoped he could put the other accusations to rest. But I had a job to do. I had to gather and assess the facts as best I could. He and I both knew we had to endure the awkwardness and get on with it.

Kimmitt and I did not leave Quayle's room until after 2:00 in the morning. We had names and notes to check on—a task that kept us busy for most of the next twenty-four hours. But first we went back to Baker's suite to report on our initial reaction. The campaign group was still there, waiting anxiously. I reported what Quayle had said, and gave them my assessment that, though there was much he could not remember, he was most probably being honest. At three o'clock in the morning, I offered my preliminary judgment: Quayle was not hiding some unexploded bombshell.

That judgment turned out to be correct. With time, Quayle's answers stood up far better than the exaggerated press reports. None of the harmful rumors was supported by facts. But the damage done by the first few days of reaction did permanent harm. Though Quayle was kept on the ticket, the previously planned campaign role of the vice presidential nominee was radically reduced. Even Quayle's name was shrunk by a less-than-respectful staff, who referred to him as "Q." More important, Quayle's unfortunate introduction to the American public left him fundamentally weakened as both a messenger and a symbol. The reach to the future, across the generations, was not then to be made through Q.

Without a symbolic bridge to the future, the burden fell more heavily on the explicit articulation of a vision. But since that was not a natural strength of the presidential nominee, the campaign staff tended to fall back upon the proven techniques of driving up the opponent's negatives.

In this, the Bush campaign was aided and encouraged, in

no small measure, by the extraordinary extent to which the Dukakis campaign made itself vulnerable. I had known Dukakis when we both taught at Harvard, and had not expected him to make so many mistakes. At the Democratic convention, "the Duke" had entered the hall like a championship fighter, surrounded himself with American flags, sounded populist themes, and looked confidently toward the future. But instead of sticking with that approach, he reverted to form as a legalistic debater. He insistently responded to attacks, and thus found himself playing on his opponent's ground. At one point, he got so far from his own turf that he was mimicked for riding around in a tank, wearing an absurd-seeming helmet—looking like a cross between a whirling dervish and an earthbound version of Snoopy's adversary, the Red Baron.

Beyond such blunders, Dukakis had two special vulnerabilities when it came to populist symbolic communication. One was his opposition to a requirement that teachers lead students in the Pledge of Allegiance to the flag. The second was his association with what was then known as the state of "Taxachusetts."

Candidate Bush took advantage of both these vulnerabilities in his convention acceptance speech. He asked the audience to join him in reciting the pledge. And he delivered the line that mimicked Clint Eastwood, "Read my lips . . ." The acceptance speech was generally more subtle and sensitive in tone than these bits of populist posturing. It talked of "the better angels," "reliable love," "a thousand points of light," "a new harmony," "a greater tolerance," leaving old baggage behind on a "journey to a new century." But the most lasting impression was left by the powerful Eastwood imitation, "Read my lips, no new taxes."

I had actively opposed using the read-my-lips line in the speech. The speech was drafted by Peggy Noonan, who had worked for me in the Reagan White House. She had previously worked for Dan Rather, and her hiring had been opposed by Nancy Reagan. But I had helped marshal the case for hiring her. She was a wonderful impressionist poet. President Reagan was well rewarded by her work. And Vice President Bush was right to seek her magic. Of course, at the time of the convention, she no longer worked for me. She worked directly with the

Vice President. I couldn't just scratch out the line that seemed to me unwise. I could only draw on our past relationship of mutual respect to try to influence the result. Obviously, I failed.

As the draft speech was working its way toward final form, I had tried to enlist the campaign's few policy people. I argued that, with the commitment to a strong defense and the requirements of the Gramm-Rudman-Hollings deficit reduction law, it would be impossible to make ends meet without a major reform of entitlements. Entitlement reform was substantively appropriate. But the political system didn't have much stomach for serious restraint of entitlements. Some future compromise might be necessary in order to get a desirable result. It was fine, I said, to be against raising taxes. But it was imprudent to be absolutist. I made the obvious point that a President should never lock himself in a box—not knowing, then, that the box would also be my own!

I was told that the no-new-taxes commitment had been made before. I noted it had not been etched in the public mind via prime-time television. From the perspective of the campaign, however—down by ten points—I was indulging in the fantasy of governing without attending to the prior imperative of winning.

With Noonan I had tried a different approach. The political and media advisers thought her draft too mushy. I came to her defense, and helped fend off some rough criticism of phrases like "a thousand points of light." I expected she might return the favor as I argued that the read-my-lips line didn't ring true, and therefore might not work. I noted the obvious: George Bush was not Clint Eastwood. Unfortunately, that was exactly the wrong tack to take. Those who thought that the candidate was not an Eastwood felt that was all the more reason to include the line. Roger Ailes, who said the read-my-lips line was one of the few strong lines in the speech, vowed he'd rehearse it so it would work. No one doubted he could do that. The line stayed in the draft as we all moved to New Orleans.

In New Orleans, I got consumed with the Quayle problem, and missed the chance to argue further. I doubt it would have made any difference, however. At that time, I had no special relationship with the candidate to draw upon; and I had no support for scratching the line. It stayed in until the end. And it was well delivered.

"Read my lips, no new taxes." Once said, there was no escaping it. For me and for President Bush, the line was to prove as haunting as it was memorable. But from the perspective of the campaign, the line worked brilliantly. Clint Eastwood wasn't on the ticket. Yet for a defining moment, before a huge national television audience, the presidential nominee exuded Eastwood's power, directness, and absolute firmness.

A couple of years before, I had been asked to appear as a panelist at the New Populist Forum. It was a more natural habitat for my co-panelists (including a then-obscure congressman named Gingrich) than it was for me. But I was indulging in the luxury of reflecting on the dynamics of populism. As part of my boringly nonpopulist presentation, I offered the following:

> It may be useful to distinguish between negative and positive populist orientations. . . . Negatively oriented populism will arise from time to time to do its work as a valuable corrective force against the abuses of excessively concentrated power, privilege, and pretense. But, having done its reactive work, the populist wave will then subside unless it moves to a more positive and creative orientation.

As the 1988 election developed, it became clear that the reactive populist wave had not fully subsided. The election was yet another in which populist symbolic communication was dominating. The read-my-lips approach proved more effective than any future-oriented vision. A creative and forward-looking populism had not yet taken hold. And the impression was created that all that was needed was some happy combination of a strong defense, the private personal virtues of a kinder and gentler past, and Reaganite anti-tax policy.

While clearly attractive politically, this combination was hardly sufficient for effective governing. It did not take into account either the fiscal realities or the social complexities of a rapidly changing America. It was a nostalgic version of Back to the Future. The job of advancing a more complete and forward-looking agenda—along with a coalition to support it—still lay ahead.

On November 8, 1988—election day—I took an early flight from Washington to Houston. I had been invited to join

Vice President Bush at his Houston home, which was then the Houstonian Hotel and Conference Center. With victory in sight, I was glad to be going.

In the weeks before, I had played the Duke in practice debates with candidate Bush. I knew I might be risking my own uncertain relationship with the Vice President, but had decided I should be as tough on him as Dukakis could possibly be. I had clowned around a little—standing on a riser, wearing a tank helmet, holding up an ACLU card. But basically, I had combined rough populist attacks with merciless policy critiques. After the first trial debate, observers congratulated me on my effectiveness. After the second trial, however, it seemed that I might have gone too far. The Vice President was so upset that he walked off the set angrily without rehearsing his closing statement, and without saying a word to me. He was normally courteous under all circumstances, but he didn't even give me the ritual handshake. I left that rehearsal thinking I might have guaranteed I would never be asked to serve in a Bush administration.

I had hoped the Vice President might understand, and perhaps even appreciate what I had done. But given my excessive performance, that was asking a lot. Further, as it turned out, the real Dukakis was a mild opponent. In the most memorable moment of the 1988 debates, Bernard Shaw asked, "Governor, if Kitty Dukakis were raped and murdered, would you favor an irrevocable death penalty for the killer?" Dukakis self-destructed with a coldly clinical response. He showed neither passionate concern for his wife nor populist anger toward crime and criminals. The debate was over with this self-inflicted TKO. My roughness in rehearsals was thus rendered unnecessary, in addition to its having been rude. So I felt lucky indeed to have been invited to Houston.

Shortly after arriving at the Houstonian, I ran into the Vice President in the hall. Dressed in his jogging attire, he stopped to talk. My mind drifted back to the sensitive subject of our debate rehearsals. I asked if he'd seen the *Saturday Night Live* version of the Bush-Dukakis debates. He had not. Bob Teeter, the respected pollster and campaign strategist, was with me. He had a taped copy in his room. The Vice President said to get it, and to come to his suite to watch it. With Barbara Bush and a few friends, we all roared in laughter. Then the Bushes invited us all to lunch at the health club. I concluded that the Vice President's natural generosity of spirit had overridden whatever anger he might have felt at my excesses in the debate preparations.

While we were at lunch, candidate Bush received a private telephone call, which filled him in on the networks' exit polls. He took notes, and gave the tally to me. At the top of a lined yellow sheet, he had penned "NATL 52–47." Then, neatly down the left side of the page he had recorded, line by line, state by state, the consistent pattern. Next to four states, he put an asterisk: New Jersey, 57–43; Ohio, 54–46; Texas, 57–43; and Florida, 58–42. He then ran a vertical line down the page, dividing it in half. On the right side of the page, he wrote just three little words, which stared at me all by themselves. They read: "sure to win."

The Vice President was no longer the candidate. He was the President-elect. But none of us acknowledged the change. Conversation remained completely casual as we finished our lunch.

As I was finishing mine, "sure to win" began to sink in in a ridiculous way. Given the Vice President's evident friendliness toward me, I now thought that, in spite of my debate performance, I might be considered for a job in the new administration. I knew from experience how much pressure high-level government jobs entailed, and how demanding they could be physically. Sitting in the health club, I thought to myself that I might have to eat a lot more of these unsatisfying salads to get in shape to survive. At that moment, the obvious point did not intrude: That would be the least of my problems.

Eleven days later, at 1:30 on November 19, I returned home from a Saturday soccer game with our son Jonathan, whose team had just completed an undefeated season. As we walked from the car toward our house, I noticed a small scrap of paper on the ground. It looked unimportant. With a bit of laziness, I hesitated. But I had to set a good example. So I bent over and picked it up.

The scrap was torn from the bottom of a calendar. As I started to crumple it up, I noticed a penciled note on the back. It said simply, "Dad call V.P." The handwriting was Willy's. I found him and asked what was up. Wanting to be sure I would see it, he had left the note on the door sill. Apparently the wind had blown it away from its intended spot. I called the Vice President right away.

He got on the line immediately. "Dick, can you come over at about five tomorrow? I want to get this thing all wrapped up. As far as I'm concerned, all signals are go on this." The conversation lasted barely a minute.

The President-elect didn't actually say what "this thing" was. But I had been kept informed by Jim Baker, and by the newly designated co-chairmen of the Bush transition, Bob Teeter and Craig Fuller. They had said that the President-elect was close to nominating me to be director of the Office of Management and Budget and a member of his cabinet.

By 6:00 on Sunday, it was settled. When I got home from the Vice President's, I found Jonathan watching TV. I gave him the news: "Jonathan, I'm going to do that job." He responded, "Thanks very much." I assumed he was distracted by the television.

I said with a tone of underscored puzzlement, "Thanks?" He repeated firmly, "Thanks." Kath explained that he thought I was agreeing to do the job of helping him draw an equator on a globe he had made. He had his own good sense of what job was important. I clarified that I would do the equator-drawing job and also the OMB job. He gave me a big smile, and returned to his television program.

At 8:00, I picked up Willy, who had been at dinner with his geography teacher and class. He, too, seemed pleased. Then I wrote an outline of my remarks for the press announcement on a three-by-five card.

At 9:30 the next day, November 21, 1988, the President-elect made the public announcement about the OMB job. (He didn't know about the equator-drawing job.) My statement at the press conference included what many may have thought was a ritual line: "Mr. President-elect, like you I feel that public service is not only an obligation and responsibility, but also a privilege." I meant that—one hundred percent.

I had looked forward to the possibility of serving in a President's cabinet since first inspired by President Kennedy. By chance, it was almost exactly twenty-five years since his assassination. The obligation to serve—and the privilege of service—seemed all the more special to me.

In time, however, there were to be days when I would think it might have been better if Willy's note had blown farther away in the wind. Given my years of experience, and knowing of my appreciation of Ted Williams, a colleague generously suggested that I might be able to be to executive branch service what Williams was to baseball. I knew that was an impossibly high standard. But I certainly didn't expect that I might end up feeling like Billy Buckner.

II

An Awkward Two-Step:

From Now-Now to New Balance

On November 21, 1988, Dan Rather led the evening news with President-elect Bush's announcement of his intention to nominate me. All the networks treated the announcement favorably. Bob Teeter called me and observed, "It's rare that someone leads the CBS evening news and the story is favorable!" He and I were both experienced enough to know there would not be many more days like that. Indeed, I knew the budget numbers and politics well enough to recognize that the job I was taking on could well be my undoing.

The Reagan administration was leaving office with federal spending still at a little over 22 percent of GDP. That happened to be just about where the new buckaroos had found it when they first rode into town in 1980. The problem wasn't simply that spending was about 3 percent of GDP higher than federal receipts (with that gap being the deficit), and that the Gramm-Rudman-Hollings law required that the budget be brought into balance. It was that most of the easier spending reduction and loophole closing had already been done in the Reagan years. Doing more on either the spending or revenue side of the balance was going to be a great deal harder politically than what the Reaganauts had already done. Further, since there had been little restraint on the popular middle-class entitlement programs (Medicare, Social Security, student aid, veterans benefits, farm programs, etc.), a time bomb was left ready to explode.

In the campaign, candidate Bush had been encouraged to propose a "flexible freeze" as his approach to balancing the budget. Some critics had ridiculed it as oxymoronic. But the concept worked on paper. The actual mathematics of the flexible freeze allowed overall spending to go up at the inflation rate (hence, a "freeze" in inflation-adjusted terms). And with the natural growth of revenues from a growing economy (at a rate higher than the inflation rate), the deficit would be brought into balance. The math could work.

The concept also worked politically for the period of the campaign. It allowed the candidate to suggest that he would "freeze" overall spending, while being "flexible" in deciding which programs should go up and which down in order to achieve the overall freeze. That is, it allowed him to support a popular abstraction, the freeze, while postponing the decisions on the less attractive particulars.

Unfortunately, however, with the election having been won, the time for decision on the particulars had come. And that meant a big problem. The President was conservatively inclined in that he disliked inefficiency and excessive debt. But he was not inclined to cut overall funding for defense, crime fighting, drug interdiction, transportation, and a number of other functions that he thought to be legitimate for the federal government. And of course, he had unequivocally refused to raise taxes. So the particulars could only be made to work with a major attack on entitlements. They were the biggest part of the budget, and growing much faster than the inflation rate.

This may sound like technical gobbledygook. But it had an inescapable political meaning that was very straightforward. Democrats (and many Republicans) were opposed to any significant restraint on entitlements. Republicans did not control either the House or the Senate. Privately, they indicated they would run from a unilateral reform initiative by President Bush unless they had Democratic cover. But the Democrats' price for negotiating entitlement reform was almost certain to be a tax increase. Thus, at the intersection of politics and the numbers, there was an inescapable dilemma.

Yet, partly because I did know the politics and the budget, and partly because I had had favorable experience with difficult legislative challenges, I thought I had a better chance of succeeding than most people did. And I felt a strong obligation to try to do the job. In the end, I might become the victim of my own hubris. But I would not fail for having been naive about the difficulty of the task.

Right after the announcement of my nomination, at 11:00 in the morning, President-elect Bush and I met with former Presidents Ford and Carter. They both congratulated me—and offered their sympathies. They informed us that, "based on definitive analysis, it would be very difficult to balance the budget without some considerable increase in revenues," and there was "no likely way to increase defense." They supported increased taxes as part of a proposed bipartisan deficit reduction package.

So, roughly thirty minutes into my new job, we had two former Presidents recommending a tax increase. They represented a group that included not only themselves, but also a bipartisan selection of notables that ranged from the Democratic former head of the Congressional Budget Office, Alice Rivlin, to such Republicans as Alcoa chairman Paul O'Neill and former Tennessee governor Lamar Alexander. This was not an entirely auspicious beginning for proponents of the no-new-taxes pledge.

Later that day, President Nixon put out a public statement on taxes and the deficit. He sent me a copy by fax, along with a handwritten note of congratulations. The note was warm, and concluded with a thought that left me with mixed reactions: "You have the toughness & political skill to handle the most difficult job in government—RN." If President Nixon said a job was "the most difficult job in government"—given his experience—one could be sure the job was challenging. His public statement neatly straddled the no-new-taxes problem:

> I don't know whether the flexible freeze will work or not. But in view of the election results, we should give President Bush a chance to see if it will work. If it doesn't, then, and only then, is it appropriate to debate a tax increase.

That sounded thoroughly reasonable. But in practical effect, the Nixon approach was likely to yield one failure in order to get to a second—a rather unattractive two-step process. A no-new-taxes deficit reduction plan was not invalid substantively; it could be made to work on paper. But without Republican control of Congress, it was likely to prove unworkable politically. Its restraint upon entitlements had to be stringent, so it was almost certain to be declared "dead" in its encounter with the Democratic Congress. Without a tax concession, the flexible freeze was likely to prove non-negotiable, and thus a failure. Yet any tax concession would itself be declared a failure—whatever the other substantive benefits of a deal with which it might be associated. Again, the dilemma was obvious.

Still, President-elect Bush agreed with President Nixon that the alternative of just throwing away the campaign promise without trying to negotiate something like the flexible freeze was a nonstarter. It would seem cynical. And it could undermine the new President's credibility across the board. So the dilemma had to be faced. We had made our bed, and would have to lie in it—even though we might have short-sheeted ourselves.

Later on my first day, the ranking Republican on the budget committee, Senator Pete Domenici, called. We had worked together in the Reagan years, and I valued his informed and conscientious counsel. I suggested an approach for the revision of the Reagan budget that would give the flexible freeze an initial test, making changes selectively and then capping broad categories of expenditure. He thought it "terrific." Beyond that he wondered, as I did, whether we should formalize a budget summit process. I asked a favor in jest: "Please vote no on the Darman nomination. Get me out of this!"

Senator Phil Gramm then called. It was clear I would have no lack of interesting advisers. A smart, tough-minded thinker and populist, Gramm was a sometime rival of Domenici's for primacy on the budget. I was not surprised to hear that he had a plan of his own. Though a hard-liner, Gramm was also a political realist. He knew that with Democratic control of Congress there might have to be a concession on taxes down the road. He suggested we increase our leverage by highlighting the natural growth of revenue and how it was to be allocated. What he really wanted was major spending restraint and no increase in the tax *rates* we had lowered in 1981 and 1986. I agreed, and looked forward to working with both him and Domenici.

Alan Greenspan then called. He opened with flattery: "When your appointment was uncertain, I was thinking about tearing up my tickets to the inaugural." I said, "You probably think the less of my intelligence for my taking the job." Greenspan replied, "No, you see a big mountain there to climb." He invited me to lunch, at which he made it clear he wanted a major deficit reduction package. His polite implication was that he would not allow higher money supply growth or higher real economic growth without our first achieving a legislative solution to the deficit problem. As a central banker should be, he was worried about risks of inflation. He knew, however, that slow-growth monetary policy could risk recession and widen the deficit. He treated that risk as all the more reason to push toward a bipartisan legislative compromise. He knew the politics well enough to know that this would likely have to mean some concession on taxes. But if the tax concession were part of a serious spending reduction package, he seemed to think it a price worth paying.

Then Jack Kemp called. Without knowing of my conversation with Greenspan, he argued specifically against Greenspan's hawkishness on the deficit, and in favor of supply-side wisdom. The dividing lines among Republicans were beginning to show before serious negotiating even began. They were just as they had been since 1980.

Kemp and I had known each other even longer than that, since the Ford administration. We had become friends in the Reagan years. I told him I hoped he would join the cabinet. He protested that he couldn't. I said, "If the President asks, you'll have to." I sided with those who were urging the President to make Kemp an offer. He had a combination of positive vision, idealism, and inclusiveness that I thought would be a valuable complement to others in the new administration. I knew, of course, that we might end up differing on some future possible tax compromise. But I thought it would still be better to have him as a member of the team. What I failed to imagine was the extent to which future differences would put a strain on this and many other friendships.

I did know, however, that the going would only get tougher. The conflicting points of view among Republicans—not to mention the differences with Democrats—were bound to be hard to reconcile. I imagined that in trying to help force a compromise to fix the fiscal problem, I might be forced to resign. But the job clearly needed doing. It was imprudent, at best, to allow federal debt to continue to mount as a share of GDP. And there would be little creative policy until the fiscal house was put in order. I saw the job as extremely tough, but not impossible; and felt a special responsibility to give it a try.

For those not schooled in the curious ways of the Washington Wonderland, it may be natural to say, "What was the big dilemma here?" Why not have just sent Congress the budget the President wanted; and then have vetoed whatever the President had to, until he got what he wanted? It would certainly have been simpler if things could have been that easy. But they could not.

Two of the reasons are technical, but necessary to note. First, more than half of all federal spending was "mandatory," the result of standing law that didn't come up for annual renewal. This automatic spending (largely, but not exclusively, the middle-class entitlement programs) was the fastest growing part of the budget. It was not presented to the President each year for him to sign or veto. And even when it was presented to the President, a veto would ordinarily result in a reversion to the standing law. Automatic spending would then continue to grow.

The only way the automatic spending growth could be restrained—an essential requirement for the flexible freeze to work—was by legislated reform. That is, it required affirmative legislative action, signed by the President after passage by both houses of Congress. But, of course, the government was divided. The President was Republican; and the House and Senate were controlled by Democrats. So while a veto strategy would not produce the necessary deficit reduction, a strategy for affirmative legislative action would have to involve compromise. The former couldn't work substantively; and the latter was hard politically.

The second reason things were not so easy was that the Gramm-Rudman-Hollings law required a balanced budget, but without a viable means of delivering it. It had been meant to enforce discipline upon federal spending. It established annual deficit targets, which declined to zero over several years. If in any year a target was exceeded, it provided for automatic spending cuts to meet the target. When enacted, it had seemed an attractive fail-safe system to some. But it was flawed.

Its formula for automatic cuts fell too heavily on defense to suit Republicans (including the new President and his national security team); and too heavily on domestic spending to suit Democrats. That meant it was really a formula to force the parties to negotiate. Yet the unfortunate history was clear: When the targets were about to be exceeded, the politicians got together and raised them. They did that even in the aftershock of the stock market crash of 1987, when spotlights shone on a bipartisan negotiating group established to reduce the deficit. That group produced only trivial "savings," and a big increase in the deficit targets. To expect that financial markets might welcome such sleight of hand again would have been imprudent at best.

Given the divided government, any serious examination of strategic options had to lead to bipartisan negotiations in the end. That was true whether one chose a veto strategy, a Gramm-Rudman game of chicken, or any other strategy. The practical issues were when to enter the bipartisan negotiations, and how to get there with maximum leverage.

One approach was to rely on good will, statesmanship, and respectful argument on the merits. It might seem naive to have hoped for that, but I had occasionally been party to negotiations where that formula had worked. Political leaders often had better selves than they displayed in their partisan posturing; and it was possible to appeal to these better selves if the right context could be arranged. Though difficult to do, my preferred choice was to give that a try. I knew that as a matter of style the President would be comfortable with this approach if it could be made to work. But to work politically, it had to reach across the full range of the bipartisan leadership.

As a first step, I started on the right. At 8:50 in the morning on the day after the announcement of my appointment, I walked over to the office of Vice President–elect Quayle. He was temporarily ensconced in the offices ordinarily reserved for visiting former Presidents, on Lafayette Square. A CBS camera crew was outside seeking an interview. I declined. Inside, I walked up the three flights of narrow stairs where I found Quayle, alone. He laughed as he greeted me, remarking how far we'd come since I had interviewed him in his undershorts at 2:00 in the morning in New Orleans. We then talked for an hour and a half.

I especially wanted Quayle's reaction to the idea of skipping the ordinary budget process and initiating bipartisan leadership meetings quickly. He was not only a new leader, whose support could be important; he was also a former member of the Senate Budget Committee. He understood the players and the difficulties that Gramm-Rudman presented for defense. He said he was attracted to my approach. It would avoid our budget being declared "dead on arrival" (as all Reagan budgets had been). It would override the congressional budget process, which was contentious and unproductive. It would get us off the hook that called for us to present a budget which simultaneously had to meet campaign commitments, deficit reduction targets, and the test of political viability. "The main reason I'm attracted," he said, "is it represents a unique twist in dealing with the problem of divided government." He added, "It gets the Democrats off a hook, too. But I bet they won't let us do it. I bet they'll just sit back and demand a Bush budget."

With this half-encouraging response, I initiated a series of one-on-one meetings with key congressional leaders. The Republican leaders, Bob Dole and Bob Michel, were highly receptive to the idea of bipartisan negotiations (as were most of their colleagues). Dole and Michel were the kind of old-school leaders who could be highly partisan, but who would rise to the occasion when the public interest demanded bipartisan action. Dole recommended negotiations commence right after the swearing-in. Michel went a step further. In his open Midwestern style, he soon said publicly what most Republican leaders were saying privately, "I suspect down the road a piece that a tax increase may be part of the answer."

In talking with the Democrats, however, it became clear right away that Quayle was right about their reaction. Majority Leader George Mitchell of Maine, Finance chairman Lloyd Bentsen of Texas, and Budget chairman Jim Sasser of Tennessee weren't going to let the new President off the hook by heading straight to negotiations. Nor were House Budget chairman Leon Panetta and the House leadership. Several Democrats argued that candidate Bush had known he could not keep his tax pledge and meet the deficit targets. They were determined to force him to embarrass himself, and insisted that we must submit our budget before any negotiations could begin. Clearly, any approach that would rely on bipartisan statesmanship would have to wait.

I started an internal process to review our strategic options. On December 4, I met with President-elect Bush and a core group of key advisers. They were: the Vice President–elect, Treasury Secretary Nick Brady, Secretary of State–designate Jim Baker, Bob Teeter (on the verge of deciding to return to Michigan), and John Sununu, the newly designated White House chief of staff. We had all known each other before.

Only Sununu might have been viewed as an outsider. But by virtue of his new position, he was immediately treated as an insider. A conservative former governor of New Hampshire, he had been instrumental in turning the Bush campaign toward its primary victories after a disappointing start in the Iowa caucuses. Sununu had a reputation for arrogance and abrasiveness, which I welcomed for a selfish reason. I hoped his reputation might make mine less notable. Unfortunately, it didn't. Soon, we were *both* said to be arrogant and abrasive. It was assumed that we would clash. We never did. I respected Sununu's quick and inventive intelligence. I also appreciated the warm and generous personality that he showed in private much more than in public. Notwithstanding his public persona, he was in fact funny, kindly, family-oriented, and seriously interested in public-policy problem solving.

From 5:00 until 8:00, at the Vice President's residence, I led the group through a memo I had prepared. Its title, "Thinking About Budget Strategy as of Early December," suggested this would be a continuing and evolving subject. The memo was intended to give the new leadership team a common base from which to start. Slowly but surely, I did what the campaign policy staff had evidently been unable to do in any detailed and systematic way. I forced the group to focus on the hard budget realities. For several members, the experience was not pleasant.

The memo started by showing how much the deficit had to be cut to meet the Gramm-Rudman targets. It noted what was well known: that the Reagan forecast of the economy's future performance was more optimistic than others. Then it pointed out that if interest rates were merely 1 percent higher than forecast, and real growth 1 percent lower, the deficit would be about $135 billion higher in the year it was supposed to be balanced. The picture got worse, not better, from there.

Even with the optimistic Reagan economic forecast, total spending growth had to be limited to 2.8 percent in order to meet the Gramm-Rudman target. That was less than the rate of inflation, the growth rate that the flexible freeze had called for. And that was before exempting Social Security from restraint, as had been promised in the campaign. "It's exactly because the budget is this hard that the Democrats are demanding (and will continue to demand) that President-elect Bush go first—that he submit his own plan," the memo said. In cold text it went on:

> The practical problem is that putting social security and interest aside, the amount by which all other spending (including defense) can go up is on the order of only 5–15 billion dollars. . . . A zero real growth rate for defense would use up about 10 of that 5–15 billion. . . . That's how the problem looks before one considers the issue of how to treat campaign program initiatives. . . . That's also before one considers such unavoidable expenditures as the costs of straightening out the S&L problem. . . .

For those who, at this point, might have wanted to put the whole deficit problem aside, the memo noted that temporary Social Security surpluses masked an even deeper long-term problem. Then it made a basic point:

> More fundamentally, our deficits are disproportionately financing current consumption rather than investment in future productive capacity. Our savings and investment rate is relatively low. And unless this is corrected, our long-term economic future cannot be what Americans have traditionally hoped for and expected.

The memo argued further that regardless of one's personal view of the deficit, markets at home and abroad perceived it to be a problem. And if that perception was not taken seriously, there would be a price to pay in terms of rising interest rates, lower investment, and a falling dollar.

In any case, the memo pointed out, if the deficit was not addressed, the Gramm-Rudman "sequester" provisions (for the automatic withholding of spending) would enforce "surprisingly deep percentage cuts in sensitive areas" (as in defense, for example). This was a matter of law. Sequester could only be avoided by enacting the necessary deficit reduction or by changing Gramm-Rudman. Either approach required a mechanism to make divided government produce legislative change. "If we want to reach agreement, we will have to deal with the Democratic leadership."

The memo went on to outline a way the President could get off the hook on which the Democrats wanted him impaled. He could take the offensive procedurally: extend his hand and call for early bipartisan negotiations; ask to address a joint session of Congress shortly after being inaugurated; present a limited set of revisions to his predecessor's budget (as other incoming Presidents had done); frame these revisions as an application of the flexible freeze, without any tax increase; commit to meet the deficit targets; make it clear that the next step required *Congress* to produce a budget resolution by April 15; and offer "to work with the Congress—to negotiate day and night if necessary—in order to help the *Congress* reach bipartisan agreement on a budget resolution."

Without yet knowing exactly how an acceptable set of budget revisions could be put together (my problem), the group was inclined to adopt this approach. If it could be done, it would neatly seem to fulfill the campaign commitments while shifting the burden back toward the Congress. Negotiations could then commence without any loss of leverage.

Baker and I almost always understood each other's thinking quickly and naturally. This was no exception. Addressing the group, he captured what I was up to in two sentences. "You need to deal with the budget early on. Once you're in negotiations, you let it play out." The first step was to start the negotiations. Judgments about succeeding steps could better be made later, with an informed sense of what might actually be negotiable.

In pursuing this approach, I recommended a tactical posture that involved "simultaneously moving down two seemingly contrary paths":

> (i) the essence of reasonableness and good-spiritedness—visibly attending to bipartisanship, flexibility, good-faith negotiating; and
> (ii) the essence of firmness—less visibly, but surely, preparing to take the sequester if necessary and to veto anything that is not consistent with the deficit-reduction strategy.

Apart from the follow-up work that was to be done—which was left to me—there was one last matter the memo addressed. After the 1987 stock market crash, a bipartisan National Economic Commission had been established to address the problem of the deficit. The incoming President could add two members to the existing group, which was scheduled to report by March 1, 1989. The general issue was what posture to take toward the commission. The memo simply outlined the alternatives without making a recommendation.

As it was to turn out, the issue was largely moot. The commission was split along partisan lines. Much of what it was prepared to recommend was conventional establishment wisdom. Its co-chairmen, Republican Drew Lewis and Democrat Bob Strauss, had informed us that the only way they could produce a bipartisan majority was with a substantial tax increase. That presented the obvious political problem. In trade, the tax increase would get only modest reform on the spending side. The commission was ready to restrain Social Security increases, but offered little reform of the larger entitlement structure. Nor did it offer much in the way of serious budget process reform. The main thing the commission did offer was cover.

But the President-elect did not want cover for a tax increase at this stage. Before I joined the core group meeting, Brady and Teeter had raised the tax issue, and suggested that the President-elect should work with the commission. Quayle later reported that Teeter said the President would have no choice but to raise taxes; whereupon Baker responded he couldn't do it in his first year. The President-elect seemed strongly inclined toward a not-in-the-first-year formulation.

On December 6, he met alone for lunch with his old friend from the Ways and Means Committee, Chairman Dan Rostenkowski. Out of respect for their friendship, Rosty allowed as how he could avoid embarrassing the new President on taxes for one year—but for only one year, in Rostenkowski's version of the conversation. Given the no-new-taxes pledge, even a one-year reprieve seemed better than none. It had obvious appeal for the President-elect compared with an immediate reversal with bipartisan cover. The commission was thus rendered largely irrelevant.

In the next ten days, establishment pressure to ditch the tax pledge rose to what President Nixon termed a "propaganda offensive" of "almost ludicrous proportions." In a private memorandum, he expanded upon his earlier two-step approach. He faxed copies to the President-elect and to six top business leaders who were strong Bush supporters, but who were apparently wavering on the tax issue. In characteristic style, the new President sent the former President a self-typed return fax—typos and all. It read in part:

> Dear Dick,
>   My fax machine spit out that good letter you sent to those "six mutual friends." I agree with it. To roll over on the Read My Lips pleadge [sic] would guarantee oblivion. . . .

The President-elect sent copies to the members of our core group before a meeting we were all to have on December 21. I had prepared a memo for the group, titled "Hard Choices Ahead." Just before the meeting, the President-elect invited me to lunch in his Executive Office Building office. For the first half hour, we were alone. I had suggested that I could produce a budget that would get us by the first year, if that were what was wanted. But after that, the choices were going to be very hard indeed. I knew the President-elect cared about deficit reduction. And I knew he understood better than most that, given Democratic control of Congress, it was going to be close to impossible to negotiate a workable long-term program without some concession on taxes. With the not-in-the-first-year formulation in mind, I wanted to know what end-play the new President might have in mind, or be willing to consider.

So, over tuna salad sandwiches, I raised the question. The President-elect responded with his own variation of the Nixon two-step, "Only if it's after we have tried our best—and then only if it's into a trust fund to reduce the debt, with no loopholes, if possible." It seemed obvious that he felt conflicted, and hoped we could somehow avoid "it" altogether.

I was sympathetic. At the moment, I didn't know exactly how to square the circle. I started thinking seriously in terms of a two-step negotiating process—with emphasis on the first step, first; and then, letting the negotiations play out.

It was easy to develop some ordinary human feeling for George Bush and his read-my-lips dilemma, and to want to help him. The feeling came not just from a sense of official responsibility, but out of a bond of personal loyalty that he naturally engendered. It is true that the dilemma was partly his own doing. But he was intelligent, decent, sensible, public-spirited, and thoroughly well meaning. And on a personal basis, he was extraordinarily considerate. A thousand little vignettes come to mind to illustrate the point. But this early one will do.

On Friday, December 30, 1988, I was in my office, getting ready for my confirmation hearings and trying to put together a workable budget for the new President. The phone rang. I had thought that, among the new officials-to-be, I might be the only one in Washington working. It turned out there was another. He was on the phone. It was the President-elect.

"Dick, let me try something on you. Are you going to be around over the weekend?" I said I would. "Now, you may just want to reject this altogether; and if so, just do. How'd you and Kath like to come out to Camp David? Bring your boys. They could all find something to do. And you and I could talk. I need to know more about FSLIC [the agency dealing with the savings and loan crisis] and these other problems. Could you drive out first thing tomorrow morning, get to Camp David by ten, say? Or come for lunch. Or come on Sunday."

After checking with Kath, I agreed we'd all be at Camp David at 10:00, on Saturday morning, the day of New Year's Eve.

When Kath, Willy, Jonathan, and I got there, I was surprised to learn that we were the only guests. Barbara Bush greeted us. The twinkle in her eyes reflected a spirit that was always as refreshingly young (and occasionally irreverent) as her hair was silver. She took Kath and the boys on a walk and then bowling. She beat them, though Willy said he'd win the next time.

Meanwhile, the President-elect and I sat in his small office in Laurel Lodge and talked about the S&L crisis. The subject was complicated, technical, and boring. I kept asking if he might wish to switch subjects. He insisted we continue. After two hours and twenty minutes, he finally said, "Let's go for a walk." He wanted to talk about nuclear weapons production, tritium, and the costs of environmental cleanup. All of these were serious problems that complicated our budget problem still further. The President-elect had inherited these problems from his predecessor. But it was the contrast between the two Presidents that struck me.

Unlike his predecessor, the new President was not waiting for staff to bring things to him. He had initiated our conversation in an effort to get on top of his job substantively. He was far from passive. Indeed, he often seemed hyperactive. But the difference was even more extreme on a personal level.

Before lunch, the President-elect watched part of a televised football game with the boys. Then we all had a late lunch at a table for six. We discussed everything from favorite sports, children's books, Kath's work, and World War II to the comparative merits of different fast-food franchises' fried chicken. On the latter, the President-elect expressed a strong preference for Popeyes over Jonathan's choice of Roy Rogers. He seemed as interested in the kids as in any head of state. In this and a thousand other ways—throughout the Bush presidency, and beyond—George and Barbara Bush made us all feel like part of a family.

More abstractly, what struck me about our host was what I termed the "new balance" he was bringing to the presidency. New Balance happened to be the name of a running shoe, which was in some ways appropriate. But I had the ordinary meaning in mind. George Bush was a balanced personality in almost every respect. Culturally, he was an American mixture of Greenwich and Maine and Texas; of lobster and Tex-Mex. He was conservatively inclined, but not an ideologue. He rarely saw things in terms of only black and white. He saw the many grays, and wanted to understand them. He was capable of firmness, but was not rigid. Although prepared to fight for principle, his preference was to find solutions that could somehow satisfy all factions. He liked jokes, but was unquestionably serious. He was intellectually sophisticated, but not inclined to flaunt it. Where some politicians preached the virtues of private generosity, family values, and military heroism, he actually practiced these—with grace and humility. His résumé read a bit like Superman's, but his manner was more like that of Clark Kent.

This chronic tendency toward balance was a plus for all the obvious reasons. But it was not entirely a blessing for the new President. In an era of populist correction, with a premium on the ability to communicate through the mass media, balance was often a disadvantage. Balanced formulations were rarely likely to seem as visionary and inspirational as statements that were stark, simple, polarizing, or bold. Yet the new President was not inclined to polarize; and the patterns of his thinking did not often yield simple declaratory statements. Nor did visionary statements come naturally to him. In a way, defining a future required an arrogance and presumptuousness that he did not have, or wish to exhibit. And he was uncomfortable being programmed.

It was rare that he would fully accept the necessities for theater and posturing that had become the hallmarks of political management in the television era. Of course, when he did so, it could also be a mixed blessing—as in the case of the rehearsed read-my-lips line.

It was later to strike me as ironic that he was criticized for reversing himself on the tax pledge, when the real reversal was in so visibly adopting the absolutist line in the first place. Ordinarily more cautious and qualifying, his dramatic rendering of the read-my-lips line was atypical—which is partly why it was so striking, and why some advisers thought it so necessary. It became larger than I suspect he thought it would when he was rehearsing to meet the standard set by the press: "the speech of his life." For better and for worse, the line was a highlight of the speech. We had to work with that reality—and all the complications it presented.

Further, we had to work with the reality that the President-elect was still the balanced human being he had always been. He wanted to keep the broad Republican coalition together even though its "moderate" and "conservative" wings were pulling apart. He wanted to do what was right, and did not want to resist compromise among reasonable people with honest differences. He wanted to honor his commitments. And he wanted me somehow to find a solution that everyone could live with.

I was worried that there probably was no politically available solution that could meet all these tests. Yet, in addition to the desire to succeed in professional terms, I had developed a personal feeling: I didn't want to let the new President down. He may have wanted the impossible. Yet I wanted to see if we could grasp victory from what looked an awful lot like the opening jaws of defeat.

Five days after the Bush inauguration, the Senate voted 99–0 to confirm me as director of OMB. On the next day, the

214 / <small>RICHARD DARMAN</small>

President presided in the Oval Office as I was sworn in. Being uncomfortable with large ceremonies, I asked that this be small, for one last bit of privacy. It was a proud moment. Yet I wanted only my immediate family to join me. This little plan actually worked—almost. Jonathan held the Bible. Willy read the oath for me to repeat. The President and Kath stood witness. There were only two interlopers, National Security Adviser Brent Scowcroft (whom I had known since the Ford administration) and my friend and mentor Jim Baker. I was surprised, but happy they were there.

Two weeks later, with the special help of OMB deputy director John Cogan, presidential assistant Roger Porter, OMB associate director Bob Grady, and OMB's extraordinary professional staff, the larger plan I had outlined in my December 4 memo was also implemented. We revised the Reagan budget in record time, under the ambitious title *Building a Better America.* The Bush revisions were delivered in a well-received address to Congress on February 9.

The groundwork for bipartisan negotiations was laid. Commentators from both right and left seemed to approve. Messrs. Evans and Novak expressed appreciation for my willingness to endure a sequester if necessary. They complimented the new President, "While Ronald Reagan's steel in dealing with Congress often did not match his rhetoric, George Bush uses soft words and a hard strategy." At the same time, the lead *New York Times* editorial headlined, "The Bush Budget: Alive on Arrival." That was a phrase that had not been seen for a decade.

The net effect was to get the President off the hook the Democrats thought he would be caught on. We produced a moderately credible budget and adopted a posture of sweet reasonableness, while holding to the no-new-taxes line. In so doing, we increased our leverage, shifted the burden to the Congress, and made negotiations impossible for them to refuse.

I testified before the Congress on February 21 and 22. The opening statement I prepared was organized under four headings that said most of what I had to say: "Changing a Habit of Mind—From Wonderland Budgeting to Common Sense Budgeting"; "Shifting Perspective—From Preoccupation with the Present to Investment in the Future"; "But How Do We Pay?— Growth, Priorities, and Balanced Restraint"; and "The Need to Negotiate—We Cannot Settle for Business as Usual."

Our approach was met with some of the conventional partisan posturing. Yet on the whole, our reasonable tone was well received. The President had extended his hand in his inaugural address:

> We need a new engagement between the Executive and the Congress. . . . We need to compromise; we've had dissention. We need harmony; we've had a chorus of discordant voices. . . . To my friends, and yes I do mean friends, in the loyal opposition—and yes I mean loyal—I put out my hand. I am putting out my hand to you, Mr. Speaker. I am putting out my hand to you, Mr. Majority Leader. . . .
>
> [W]e don't wish to turn back time, but when our mothers were young, Mr. Majority Leader, the Congress and the Executive were capable of working together to produce a budget on which this nation could live. Let us negotiate soon and hard. But in the end, let us produce. The American people await action. They ask us to rise above the merely partisan. "In crucial things, unity"— and this, my friends, is crucial.

In public and private, I did my best to suppress my reputed arrogance and combativeness. When testifying, I endured the ritual criticism of the opposition with a mixture of politeness and silence. Differing genuinely with the new breed of polarizers, I stated, "The key is to get on to negotiations. If people take positions that are too sharp, too partisan, too publicly, it tends to prevent the system from coming together."

As expected, the Democrats soon agreed to convert my informal private consultations into formal bipartisan negotiations. Under the general direction of the bipartisan leadership and key committee chairmen, the negotiations began on February 24. The day-to-day negotiating was delegated to a group chaired by House Majority Leader (and soon to become Speaker) Tom Foley. It included the four budget committee leaders, with Brady and me representing the administration.

Prior to entering the negotiations, Brady, Sununu, and I had lunch with the President and Vice President to discuss strategy. As usual, I had prepared a discussion memo. It outlined four options: (1) Muddle Through; (2) Muddle Through, from a Distance; (3) Head for Sequester; and (4) Big Fix.

As often happens, the group tended toward a combination option. Influenced by Sununu, and by the President's not-in-the-first-year inclination, we tentatively adopted both options 1 and 4. This amounted to a revised two-step process. We would first try to conclude a one-year budget deal, quickly, with no new taxes for the first fiscal year. Then, as a second step, we would try to build on the initial process, reconvening the negotiations later in the year in order to pursue a more ambitious long-term deficit reduction agreement.

The first step would be consistent with the campaign pledge, buy some time, and allow us to explore what else might be negotiable. For the second step, we would try to gain leverage by threatening to live with the Gramm-Rudman sequester if no agreement were reached. And if the second-stage realities were to dictate some tax increase as part of a negotiated settlement, we could offset conservative criticism somewhat by negotiating a decrease in capital gains and restraining the growth of "mandatory" spending. I knew, of course, that if things worked out this way—even with a capital gains cut, significant entitlement restraint, and a dedicated deficit reduction fund—there would still be a political price to pay for any deviation from read-my-lips.

But it seemed to me that if the second-stage negotiation included some hard-core conservatives, if the ultimate agreement were supported by the bipartisan leadership, if it were enacted late in the first year of the Bush presidency (as opposed to the second year), and if the Federal Reserve let the economy return to strong growth in the third and fourth years, then the President's reelection prospects would not be jeopardized. Unfortunately, those were four very big ifs. And not everything turned out quite the way I hoped.

The first stage of the negotiations proved to be tedious and barely productive. The daily negotiating was uninteresting, and went rather slowly at the start, with each side feeling out the other.

The most exciting event of this period happened at home, not at work. On Saturday afternoon, March 18, I was at the office when Kath called to say that a sudden windstorm had blown a big tree down on our house. It had knocked off part of the roof, poked branches through in several places, and scared young Jonathan, who was upstairs when it hit.

I picked up Willy at a basketball team party and drove home. As we came down our drive, we suddenly saw that a giant tree had indeed enveloped our house. It was a scene of considerable destruction. Speaking for teenagers everywhere, in a world that had not yet experienced the wireless revolution, Willy exclaimed, "WOW! Does the phone still work?" Nothing at the negotiating table matched that.

When the negotiations stalled, I reviewed our basic options again with the President and Sununu. For a meeting on March 30, I also invited Scowcroft and Defense Secretary Dick Cheney. The subject of my memo, "Mapping Backward from Possible Sequester," affected defense especially. In the privacy of the White House residence, from 5:00 until after 6:00 in the evening, I took the group through the sequester scenario in some detail. It was clear that the national security team had little stomach for the deep defense cuts that might be involved. They were nervous about a game of chicken. Expecting this, I raised the possibility of going for a big fix early, along with a half-dozen other options.

The next day the President called me back from meetings on the Hill to discuss the March 30 memo's options further with him and Sununu. He asked what I would recommend. All things considered—including both read-my-lips and the security team's reluctance to play chicken with sequester—I said I thought option 4 would be best: "Staged Compromise—Small Now; Big in August." The President agreed.

This affirmed the earlier two-step approach, with a timetable for the second step. The President wanted to declare victory after step one. I said we couldn't oversell it, and emphasized the importance of getting to stage two by July or August, not later. There was some understandable hesitance to set a fixed time for stage two. The political risk of the tax issue was obviously unattractive. So, too, was the risk of opening up the volatile issues of serious entitlement restraint. Trying to alleviate the sense of risk, I volunteered to explore stage two on a deniable basis, and be fired if I were exposed. Sununu said, "You can't get out of your job that easily!"

Before having the luxury of thinking about that, we had to get step one accomplished. With a decision to accept a modest step one, that was done quickly. Late in the evening of April 13, our negotiating group reached agreement. The agreed deficit reduction program was indeed modest. But it did at least meet the Gramm-Rudman target (as estimated by both OMB and the Congressional Budget Office). And though this wasn't really saying much, the intended deficit reduction was actually larger than what came out of the summit negotiations after the 1987 crash.

After midnight, in the early morning of April 14, I drafted talking points for the President to use in a meeting with the bipartisan leadership. He and I went over them at 8:00 in the Oval Office. The leadership group assembled in the cabinet room at 9:30 and endorsed the agreement. Then all went out to the Rose Garden steps for the ritual announcement and photos.

Near-identical versions of the ceremonial photo appeared in both *Newsweek* and *Time,* but over rather different headlines. Emphasizing step one, *Newsweek*'s read, "A Budget Deal in Record Time." Emphasizing the crucial step two that was yet to come, *Time*'s read, "Wait Till Next Year."

I, of course, did not want to wait until the next year. Nor did I want market-watchers and deficit hawks to think that we would rest on our laurels with only a modest step one. With the intention of implementing the "Small-now; Big-in-August" option, I got the bipartisan leadership to include in the April 14 agreement this language:

> The President and the Congressional Leadership will continue to consult closely to seek opportunities for further deficit reduction . . . to balance the federal budget by fiscal year 1993. . . . In order to facilitate progress toward that objective, the bipartisan Budget Committee Leadership, the Secretary of the Treasury, and the Director of the Office of Management and Budget shall continue discussions in consultation with the bipartisan leadership of the appropriate committees of the House and Senate.

On Sunday, I went on ABC's *This Week with David Brinkley* and defended the modesty of the agreement in answer to a question from George Will. Responding as one baseball fan to another, I reminded the viewing audience that not every hit had to be a homer to bring runs home. Among the viewers was Newt Gingrich, who had a habit of sending me handwritten epistles with advice and commentary. The next day, another in the running series of Newt-grams arrived. It read as follows:

> Dear Dick:
>
> Your baseball analogy on Brinkley was excellent. The budget agreement gets us on first, capital gains advances the runner to second, an appropriations veto strategy fills the bases, and agreement in August, on our values, would be a bases clearing home run.
>
> I look forward to working with you.
>
> Your friend
> Newt

Gingrich wanted to get on to step two every bit as much and as fast as I did. I looked forward to working with him. But I knew the second part of the two-step would be a lot more difficult to manage than the first.

Though I testified often, I gave formal public speeches very rarely. Since I wrote my own, they took precious time. I gave them only when I thought I had an important purpose. Step two was obviously sufficiently important. So, with the August timetable in mind, I decided to begin to prepare the way. Months in advance, I scheduled a speech for July 20 at the National Press Club. I felt that if we were going to persuade the public that serious deficit reduction was worth the price, we had to frame the problem more broadly. We had to get beyond accountancy to a larger understanding of our cultural problem; and beyond the target of mere budgetary balance to a more idealistic vision of an American future.

I titled the speech "Beyond the Deficit Problem: 'Now-Now-ism' and the New Balance." The speech was more than merely tactical. It touched on public policy themes that had been important to me since I'd first been inspired by the Kennedy inaugural. "Now-now-ism," however, was a word I coined for the specific occasion. To me, it seemed to merit at least as much attention as the popular political entertainment of the time, attack politics:

> For every minute devoted to political mau-mau-ism, I'd like to see another devoted to what I would term cultural "now-now-ism"—a shorthand label for our collective

short-sightedness, our obsession with the here and now, our reluctance adequately to address the future.

I noted that America has long been an impatient culture, and that that has been part of our distinctive strength. But it is one thing to be impatient about such forward-looking challenges as opening new frontiers. It is something entirely different to be impatient about consuming the fruit of overplowed ground.

> Our current impatience is that of the consumer not the builder, the self-indulgent not the pioneer. It borders dangerously on imprudence. . . . Collectively, we are engaged in a massive backward Robin Hood transaction— robbing the future to give to the present. . . . In the public domain, this self-indulgent theft from the future borders on public policy wilding.

The implication was obvious that, notwithstanding the success with step one, I was still being critical of deficits and mounting debt. The debt was merely feeding consumption, not investment in the future. I said it was like a second mortgage without the house. But I tried to go further and argued that the deficit should be seen as "a kind of silent now-now scream"—a symptom of a larger problem of "cultural values" that was crying for attention. Now-now-ism could be seen in the failure to reform a lagging education system, the tax system's bias toward consumption over investment and debt over equity, an unproductive drug culture, underinvestment in R&D, and a lack of attention to the problems of a baby-boom generation moving toward older age.

I provided a flurry of references to popular culture to try to connect with the public through the media. The speech was being given on the twentieth anniversary of man's first landing on the moon, fulfilling the Kennedy promise. So I contrasted that with the then-current fad of Michael Jackson's moonwalking.

> There is a fundamental difference between the two types of moonwalking. One is a symbol of pioneering spirit; the other a symbol of entertainment. One is a set of steps, the benefit of which is for all mankind. The other is a set of steps that give the appearance of forward movement, when they are really a backward slide.

I then worked my way toward the would-be wow finish. In one final clash of symbols, I tried to underline the importance of moving beyond the concerns of mere budgetary accountancy and the values of Tom Wolfe's best-selling *Bonfire of the Vanities* to a more ennobling image from Isaiah. "The American Dream is not meant to be filtered through green eyeshades. Nor is the human spirit meant to crawl on the floor like a dachshund. It is meant to rise up with wings like eagles."

I used three popular movies to end on a hopeful note, suggesting that a reawakening might be under way:

> A few years ago, the most popular youth movie was *Ferris Bueller's Day Off*. Ferris was a forward-looking kid in only a limited sense. He was brilliant at plans to play hooky from school—entertaining, but hardly constructive. Now the three most popular movies are more positive morality plays, wrapped in healthy romance. *Indiana Jones and the Last Crusade* is a quest that binds two generations in search of the Holy Grail. *Batman* has returned to rid the world of Gotham's greed. And in the very heart of America, a *Field of Dreams* is built out of a barely self-sustaining farm in response to a guiding voice, "If you build it, he will come." Lost generations are reborn, future generations are inspired, in a seamless game of catch that stretches across the generations. One senses the spirit being renewed.

My hopeful reach was stretching things a bit. But I didn't want just to blame American culture. In a way, I agreed with a point often stressed by Jack Kemp: You can't sell pain. It wouldn't do simply to moralize against current consumption, and argue for one form or another of self-denial. I wanted to remind people of America's remarkable capacities to renew the spirit and build for the future. It was that perspective I felt we needed if we were really going to reconstruct the budget—and public policy—to build a better America.

The public wanted to get rid of the deficit, but showed no serious inclination to deny itself in order to do that. For near-term restraint to be made acceptable, it had to be linked to something more inspiring than merely the abstract tidiness of fiscal balance. It had to promise a better future for the very Americans who might be asked to deny themselves now. Contrary to what had long been the defining American spirit, Americans were increasingly uneasy about the future. So I tried to suggest that a better American future could, indeed, be built. To do so, we had first to recognize that not just our budget, but also our *values* were out of balance. We needed a new balance—giving somewhat greater weight to the future and somewhat less to the present. We needed both bold vision and prudence. In my own mind, I converted the pragmatic two-step into a larger transition: from Now-Now-ism to a New Balance.

Public reaction to the speech was generally favorable. C-SPAN played it again and again. Letters from viewers were supportive. And on the whole, reaction through the media was positive. However, inside the administration, the speech had no resonance. I thought that by beginning to sketch a larger vision I might help show the way. That was not to be. Brady called to object that I had not run the speech by him before giving it. Kemp objected that I was trying to sell pain. Among the White House senior staff, only Bill Kristol volunteered an enthusiastic positive reaction. I gave the President a copy. He offered no reaction. I took that as a polite negative, and abandoned cultural commentary for a while.

But I soon realized that a more basic internal problem had developed. Some on our side had come to take our initial political success with step one too seriously. Because many assumed that I could pull another rabbit out of the hat, the idea seemed to develop that we could somehow avoid a painful step two altogether—or certainly for a while. There was, therefore, no significant interest in laying a predicate for the next stage, which I had hoped to conclude in August. The *mañana* syndrome had begun to slip step two toward some much more distant tomorrow.

At the same time, however, I knew that our troubles were mounting. Indeed, the superficial success with step one masked several problems that were right beneath the surface. They had been eroding our overall chances of success right from the start.

One of these problems was the Greenspan monetary policy. Concerned about long-term interest rates, Greenspan had been unwilling to give us a tiny bit of slack, even though inflation seemed to be under control. The chairman of the President's Council of Economic Advisers, Michael Boskin, was particularly concerned. On March 3, he wrote a memo to the President noting that "inflation-adjusted money growth has been negative for the last six months," and many private economists forecast a "slow-down or a recession in late '89 or '90." "Further Fed tightening since these forecasts increases the recession risk," he warned. "We should begin to see the effect of past Fed tightening in the next six to nine months." I said publicly that Fed policy "should be an additional prod for action once we are in negotiations." But Greenspan was forcing upon us a slow-growth economy that was to be tipped into recession in mid-1990.

Another problem was that our threat of taking a big sequester, if necessary, wasn't made believable. The threat had to be credible if we were to win a game of chicken on the budget. But in private and public conversations, our national security team made it clear that they did not intend to endure the defense cuts that would go with a big sequester. Here, too, the signs of trouble were evident from the start.

On February 2, 1989, as I was forcing decisions on the first Bush budget, Scowcroft and I brought two competing positions to the President for his decision. I argued that defense should be held to zero real growth. Scowcroft argued for 2 percent real growth (beyond inflation) for each of the next four years. The President sided with me: zero real growth for four years. Two days later, on Saturday morning, Scowcroft and I were at Camp David. He reopened the issue with me and the President, saying the military chiefs were very disturbed and wanted to talk with the President about the budget.

The President commissioned us to meet that afternoon with the chairman of the Joint Chiefs of Staff, Admiral Bill Crowe. We met in Scowcroft's office from 4:15 until 6:15. Crowe was surprisingly emotional. I was under enormous pressure to get our budget done if we were to be ready for the President's address to the Congress. So, after the meeting, when I bumped into Sununu in the driveway, I said, "You're chief of staff. I want to take an order to go to print right now at zero, zero, two, two." That was the obvious compromise. I wanted to lock in at least two years of zero real growth without risking an emotional performance by the chiefs with the President. One step ahead of me, Sununu responded, "Go ahead. I already confirmed it with the President."

But the issue wouldn't stay settled. On Sunday I was informed that the chiefs still wanted to meet with the President. A meeting was set for 9:00 on Monday, February 6.

When I got to the Oval Office, it was clear that Scowcroft had done the inviting. The crowd was bigger than for any normal Oval Office meeting. I alone represented OMB. Brady and Sununu were there. But Scowcroft had come with the entire national security establishment. The pro-defense Vice President was seated beside the President. Crowe and the four service chiefs were there in full military uniform. As if that were not enough, the chiefs were joined by the Secretary of State, Defense Secretary–designate John Tower, acting Secretary of Defense Will Taft, CIA Director Bill Webster, and Deputy National Security Adviser Bob Gates. At the top of my penned notes from the meeting I recorded this calculation: "Votes appear to be at least 12 against as we start!" The meeting was so obviously rigged that I thought (or hoped) that might actually work in my favor with the President.

I was wrong. Each of the chiefs made a lengthy speech, with the conventional dire warnings. The security chorus chimed in with support. I waited politely, thinking we were fast running out of time. When the President finally asked me to rebut, I had only a few minutes in which to put on a respectable show and make it easier for him to do what I thought he was inclined to do: side with me. So I quickly touched on everything from the facts that in real terms defense was higher than at the Vietnam War peak and I was not proposing a cut, to the legal requirement of meeting the Gramm-Rudman target, to the risk for the President's credibility if he were forced to reverse himself on "no new taxes."

After the meeting broke up, I walked back to my office feeling uneasy and alone. Within minutes, the phone rang. It was the President. He had done what I had seen President Reagan do again and again when faced directly with a budget appeal. He split the difference; and then split it once more. He decided that defense should have zero, one, one, two percent real growth (above and beyond inflation) over the next four years. The budgetary future was beginning to look even more bleak. Taxes and Social Security had been ruled off the table in the campaign. There was understandable nervousness about trying to restrain entitlements without Democratic cover. Now, with defense apparently off limits, too, the only thing reduced to zero-zero-zero-zero was room for maneuver.

We were left with a modest one-year "freeze," and a defense budget going up. It was "cut" only in relation to the higher levels the defense establishment had wanted. We made the most of this "cut" publicly. I still threatened to take a sequester, if necessary, because that was essential to give us any chance of leverage. But I knew inside that if push came to shove, there were at least twelve strong voices, with easy access to the Oval Office, that would argue for calling off the game of chicken.

The defense establishment was not satisfied with their private victory. They leaked it to the press, and reinforced it with public arguments in favor of a defense buildup. Their public position might have been used for bargaining, except that the national security team made clear to all that they would vigorously oppose letting defense become a chip in a deficit reduction game. The political community correctly concluded that the Bush administration would have little stomach for a defense sequester.

In addition to this problem, we had yet another. In the aftermath of step one, we allowed our "victory" to be overplayed, and unintentionally alienated some of the very Democrats we would have to negotiate with in step two. Headlines like this from a Germond and Witcover column made the problem clear: "Democrats Roll Over for Bush on the Budget." No self-respecting Democratic political leader wanted to be left in that position. Many of them felt that the Bush election win had been, in a sense, illegitimate. In their eyes, it had been gained by the improper use of racist imagery (Willie Horton), by unjustified questioning of the Democratic nominee's patriotism (the flag), and by a knowingly cynical use of an impossible pledge (read-my-lips). They were bitter about that. To then have their noses rubbed, however politely, in a budget deal that did not give them their pound of flesh only deepened their bitterness.

That problem was compounded by a misunderstanding with one particularly important Democrat, Senate Majority

Leader George Mitchell. Mitchell shared the resentment that other Democrats felt. Beneath his judicious surface demeanor, he was an extremely tough partisan. But in the pursuit of the initial budget agreement, he had in fact been quite helpful— expecting that the first step would be part of a larger process that would ultimately do the job that needed doing. At the start of the process, Mitchell had told Brady and me privately that he could not accept a cut in the capital gains tax rate and that he could only accept preferential treatment of capital gains in the context of an increase in ordinary income tax rates. He made absolutely clear that this was his position. But I still did not understand fully what he meant.

I had known Mitchell's substantive view since we worked together on tax reform in 1986, and had no doubt that he held his position strongly. I happened to have a different position. I favored a capital gains tax cut. It was not fair to tax "gains" that were merely the result of inflation. They weren't really gains. Further, consistent with my critiques of corpocracy and now-now-ism, I felt there needed to be greater incentives for long-term investment. These were not peculiarly the views of "the party of the rich." Most farmers and middle-class homeowners opposed a tax on inflated gains. And a bipartisan majority of both houses of Congress favored one form or another of capital gains incentive. I understood Mitchell to say that he would do everything in his power to resist a capital gains cut. But I took that as merely a statement of how strongly he felt. I treated our difference as one that would have to be resolved in negotiations and the political process. Someone would win; someone would lose. That was how democratic politics worked. What I failed to understand was that Mitchell meant he would treat any attempt to fight this battle on the Senate floor as a personal affront— and grounds for terminating cooperation on the larger deficit reduction negotiations.

It was not our original intention to challenge Mitchell on the Senate floor anyhow. We had planned to win the fight for capital gains within the context of the negotiations and through the related implementing work of the tax committees. In the Senate, we expected to have the support of Finance chairman Bentsen, who had long favored a capital gains incentive. When things did not work out quite as planned in step one, I thought we would eventually succeed in step two, as part of the larger settlement.

But in between, we lost what influence we had on the process. Many congressional Republicans, especially the more conservative members, did not want to wait for a step two to get a capital gains tax cut. We cooperated with them in successfully pushing a cut through the House. On the Senate side, however, Mitchell organized to prevent capital gains from moving forward. He persuaded Chairman Bentsen to resist it in committee. Some Republicans then determined that Mitchell should be challenged on the Senate floor. We in the administration did not think that was a good tactic. We did not expect it to succeed. And we feared its likely adverse effect on the step-two negotiations that might ultimately have produced a capital gains cut as part of a larger settlement. But forced to choose between confronting our right flank and confronting Mitchell, we chose to confront Mitchell.

Mitchell made sure that we lost doubly. He used his position as Majority Leader, and his control of the parliamentary process, to deny us a straight up-down vote on capital gains. Then, offended by what he took to be our violation of his intended understanding, he made it impossible to reconvene the negotiating group at any point in 1989. He decided that before he would allow Senate Democratic negotiators to return to negotiations, he would force the President into a politically weakened position.

Knowing that the performance of the economy was making the deficit problem worse, Mitchell determined that further negotiations should wait at least until the President had submitted a full budget in early 1990. That would force the administration either to go first with large and unpopular entitlement cuts, or unilaterally to cut defense, or raise taxes, or produce an evidently noncredible budget. Any one of these would strengthen the Democrats politically. Further, Mitchell decided he would insist upon an explicit presidential commitment to put taxes on the table before negotiations could resume. He seemed to be after at least two pounds of flesh. And there was no moving him.

As the legislative season of 1989 worked its way into its increasingly contentious fall session, I personally was in unusually good favor with conservatives. Though the President, Sununu, Brady, Boskin, and I had all suggested at one point or another that taxes might be subject for discussion, there had been no concession on read-my-lips. Supply-siders were happy with the push for capital gains (though it was misguidedly undertaken outside the negotiating context). Some deficit reduction measures were moving forward, and we were ready to take a minor sequester to assure their progress. On monetary policy, in answer to a question from Andrea Mitchell in an August appearance on *Meet the Press,* I had offered some rare public criticism of the Fed's excessive tightness. That elicited two big felt-tip-penned notes from Jack Kemp:

> D.D.   You are the 1st ever to take them on! You're right & I (we) thank you—   J.K.

> Dick—You're the Q.B. who can lead us to victory! Don't give up—

> > > Your "right tackle" Jack

Even my Newt-grams remained supportive:

> > > 9/6/89

> Dear Dick
>   As we start the Fall session, I want to thank you for all the help and support you gave the Whip Team during the Spring and Summer—
>   We won some good ones together and we can do it again this Fall

> > > Thank you
> > > Your friend
> > > Newt

I knew this could not last. Time, the economy, and the budget numbers were moving against us. So as the unpleasant fall legislative session moved toward its close, I made a last-ditch effort to reconvene the negotiating group.

I wanted desperately to avoid the predictable problems of waiting until 1990. I had the feeling that some of the other negotiators with whom I talked thought I was pathetically unrealistic for even trying, and were indulging me only because I happened to be the OMB director. At that point, I felt like the director of nothing. I did get Tom Foley (who by then had become Speaker of the House) to try to get the negotiations restarted by talking to Mitchell. He did not succeed. Brady and I then appealed to Mitchell personally. But it was all to no avail. I flailed around helplessly, and then concluded I had failed.

We had to wait until 1990. And that was bound to make a big difference. The Greenspan-constrained economy was weakening. That was widening the deficit gap. The size of the forecast sequester was growing; but the credibility of our threat to take it was shrinking. The elections of both 1990 and 1992 were getting closer. The political context was becoming still more adversarial. We would not be able to continue the negotiations in a spirit of collegial good will. And I was obliged to produce a balanced budget without touching Social Security, risking significant political damage on other entitlements, cutting defense, or raising taxes! The chance of producing a credible budget, under these constraints, was close to nil.

Clearly, the transition from Now-Now to New Balance was not going to be an easy two-step.

12

Ted Williams and BUBBA:

"Read My Lips Is History"

NINETEEN EIGHTY-NINE may not sound as if it was a terrific year in which to have been director of OMB. It certainly did not end with a promising prospect. And by some people's reckoning, things went downhill from there. Yet 1989 did have one high-light worth noting before moving on to what many conservatives came to see as the sinful fall of 1990.

When things were still in their happier phase, as we were about to conclude the step-one budget agreement, the President decided to go to the opening baseball game at Baltimore's old Memorial Stadium. The Orioles were playing the Red Sox. So the President invited his friend and campaign supporter, the last of the .400 hitters, Ted Williams. Knowing that Williams was a childhood hero of mine, the President invited me along to join Williams and him in the owner's box. He also invited a visiting head of state, Egypt's President Hosni Mubarak.

Naturally enough, President Mubarak didn't understand the game. President Bush tried to explain it to him. But Roger Clemens was pitching for the Red Sox and having a good day. So for a while, there wasn't much action to explain. It looked like a bunch of guys in uniforms spread about the field, standing around watching two others throw the ball back and forth, back and forth.

Sensing a bit of boredom, Williams said, "Let's get some balls to sign." Williams was then almost seventy-one, no longer the Kid or the Splendid Splinter, but still the greatest hitter of all time. He was an impressive and imposing presence. Base-balls were delivered almost immediately. I struggled to maintain decorum as Williams reached for a brand-new white ball right next to me, and started to sign it. I had been waiting forty years for my chance to get a baseball autographed directly by Ted Williams and thought this was the moment. The baseball I'd wanted since I was a kid was about to be mine. But instead of handing it to me, Williams handed it to his left. He gave it to President Bush.

Disappointed, I thought I'd just have to wait my turn. But then Williams did something that astounded me. He asked the President to sign it. For a moment, as the President readied his left hand with a pen, I considered stopping him. I thought absurdly: What's he doing? Doesn't he realize that ball's just been signed by Ted Williams? I corrected myself with the consoling notion that I might soon have an interesting rarity, a baseball autographed by both Ted Williams and the President of the United States. But then, an even more astounding thing happened. Always polite, the President felt obliged to give the ball to President Mubarak. With only two signatures on it, the ball still had quite a bit of white space. The President of Egypt gave it a puzzled look. President Bush explained that people signed these things. So President Mubarak took out a pen. My expectations were changing quickly. But soon enough, I became the proud owner of my very own Ted Williams baseball. It just happened also to bear the signature of a former Yale baseball captain and, in bold black ink, some distinctive Arabic script.

That, however, was not my most memorable recollection of the day. The President had kindly arranged for me to have breakfast with Williams earlier that morning. We met in the White House mess. Though we talked mainly about baseball, Williams was also interested in the federal budget debate. I outlined the budget dilemma to him, and asked for his reaction. A strong conservative, Williams had no favorable inclination toward either big government or taxes. He didn't want the President to have to break his pledge. But, like most Americans, he wanted a balanced budget. After reflecting a bit, he volunteered, "People would understand if the President just stepped forward, right out on the front porch, and said he'd have to raise taxes to get the deficit down." His attitude seemed to be: If you've really got to do it, just explain yourself directly, and do it.

I told the President what Williams said. But we had just decided to go for step one of the two-step approach—the single, before the big swing. It was not yet fully demonstrated that the politicians would reject serious spending reduction, and that taxes would have to be raised. The President wanted to get step one done before there was any consideration of that. Even so, Williams's advice lingered with me for a long time.

From time to time, I brought it back up for consideration. I raised it, for example, on August 15, 1989, when I met for lunch with the President, Brady, and Sununu to discuss our approach to the next year's budget.

As usual, I handed out a memo with options. Our negotiations were in abeyance at the time. But the memo served to frame issues related to them as well as to the budget for year two. After noting that we seemed to be doing the impossible in year one, the memo warned, "The string has just about run out. . . . The task for [fiscal year] '91 will be more 'impossible' than for '90." The memo went on:

> We are still operating under a set of *major constraints:* "no new taxes"; grow defense at inflation plus 1%-1%-2%; don't touch Social Security; and meet the G-R-H [Gramm-Rudman-Hollings] targets. But for FY'91 the G-R-H deficit target is much lower. Many of the one-time savings used in [fiscal year] 1990 are no longer available. And the economic outlook is not quite so rosy. . . . If an FY'91 budget is to be presented without relaxing any of the key constraints, it will have to be a *genuinely radical* budget.

In the memo, I pointed out that radical budget cutting could not get through the Democratic Congress. It could produce stalemate until the 1990 elections. And if debated in the context of election politics, it could make it even harder to restrain entitlements. I argued there were interest rate risks with a stalemate, as there would be if the Gramm-Rudman deficit target were relaxed. The memo then raised again the possibility of a "big fix"—with "all the virtues and vices noted in our previous discussions of this approach." (It included budget process reforms; entitlement caps and means testing; a defense freeze; selective investments in the future; a debt buy-down fund; along with gas and sin taxes.)

As for getting to the big fix, I outlined four choices labeled "The Bipartisan," "The Fudge," "The Combination Platter," and "The Ted Williams." The memo noted that the tell-it-like-it-is Ted Williams approach "could be used in either January with a unilateral presentation of a big fix budget, or in October with a call for Camp David negotiations."

On issues of basic strategy such as these, I knew I was not the decision-maker. In this case, as I had always done, I tried to present the facts and options fairly for consideration by the President and his other key advisers. I didn't really need a decision, and didn't push for one. All I needed was a sense of people's preferred direction.

Sununu and the President each responded characteristically. Sununu was philosophically inclined toward radical spending reduction. The President was willing to consider the Ted Williams approach. But both Sununu and the President were sensitive political animals. Political skill helped get them where they were. They each added a fundamental constraint to their inclination. Sununu wanted me to flesh out a radical budget "in a politically acceptable way." With Democrats in firm control of the Congress, and conflict guaranteed over popular middle-class entitlements, a "politically acceptable" radical budget seemed to me to be a contradiction in terms. The President said he'd be willing to consider the Ted Williams—but only if I tried the options on various Republicans, "and if enough would be with us." "Otherwise," he said, "we'd be accused of being the ultimate pragmatists."

Here, too, there seemed to be a contradiction, or at least a chicken-and-egg problem. There were not likely to be enough key Republicans willing to follow unless there were enough key Republicans in the lead. And there were not likely to be enough in the lead unless there were enough committed to follow.

I left the meeting with a feeling I had had before. I was asked to square a circle. And impossible though it seemed, I was going to give it a try. Until I could work things out privately—if they could be worked out at all—the Ted Williams was not going to be brought up to bat.

As it happened, it was not possible to work things out privately in 1989. Most of the key Republicans supported a big fix in private, but not enough of them. Nor was I able to come up with a radical budget that was politically viable. The concept was attractive; but the detail was not. So as 1990 started, we were back on the hook. We had to present a budget under the same difficult constraints. The Ted Williams approach was in abeyance.

Among the Bush cabinet, there was close to zero serious interest in a radical reduction of spending—or any reduction at all when it came to cabinet officers' own departments. After a year in office, almost every member of the cabinet concluded that he or she needed a budget increase, not decrease. Several said privately that a tax increase was necessary to fund what was needed and balance the budget. The most adamant of the big spenders were the supposed conservatives: Housing Secretary Jack Kemp for federal spending on housing and drug "czar" Bill Bennett for federal spending on a war on drugs. As expected, the moderates also demanded more spending, not less: Transportation Secretary Sam Skinner for transportation investment, Energy Secretary Jim Watkins for nuclear waste cleanup, and so on.

Even the President found himself acting, at times, a bit like a congressional appropriator. He urged me to protect funds for interests that ranged from domestic fishing to Radio Martí. He had a host of worthy ideas for which funds were just not available: from serious health reform at home to a more ambitious reform agenda abroad. The extent to which he felt strapped is suggested by this handwritten note he greeted me with early one morning:

FROM THE PRESIDENT

> To: Dick—
> Money for
> Salvador
> Andeans
> E. Europe ? ?
> But where from ?
> Salv. must succeed!
> Big "Marshall Plan $$"
> any in hiding ? ?

The competing internal claims for resources were not easy to settle. But all things considered, they were resolved relatively amicably (with only occasional exceptions). The external contest promised to be much more difficult, however. The political cry was for a balanced budget. But the internal reluctance to reduce spending was mild compared with that of the democratically controlled Congress. And we were still committed to increase defense, protect Social Security, avoid taxes, eschew the unpopular, meet the Gramm-Rudman targets, and prevent sequester.

As I looked toward presenting the first full Bush budget in January of 1990, I struggled to find a way to preserve a degree of intellectual integrity and credibility. The President had decided to preserve all the substantive and political constraints. So I decided to shift the focus, attack the budget structure and process, introduce new dimensions of the budgetary problem, and indirectly lay a predicate for serious action.

We were not following the Williams advice to step right out on the porch and lay it all out. But I still wanted to find a way to communicate the problem to the general public. I concluded I might better do this in my own voice than in the President's. So, for the first time, I included a "Director's Introduction to the Budget." This would not ordinarily have been thought of as fun-filled reading. To get it some general attention, I linked serious points to metaphors from popular culture. For example, to underline the budget's "excessive tendencies toward consumption," I termed it the "Ultimate Cookie Monster." I argued that we needed to get beyond the primitive system of cash budgeting, and on to a system that better reflected assets, liabilities, and a more dynamic view of the future. With regard to future liabilities, I highlighted rising costs of health care, unfunded retirement programs, contingent risks of credit and insurance programs, and the enormous growth of so-called mandatory programs—referring to these as "Hidden PACMEN, waiting to spring forward and consume another line of resource dots in the budget maze." Beyond the introduction, also for the first time, the budget's supporting analysis provided extensive detail on the size and character of these "hidden liabilities."

To a degree, the effort to popularize worked. My use of the Cookie Monster and Pac-Men was highlighted in a box on the front page of the *New York Times*. It called attention to a full page within, which reprinted selections from my Introduction. The *Wall Street Journal* picked up on my critique of Alice in Wonderland budget games in a supportive lead editorial headlined, "Wonders in Darmanland." Later in the year, and for many years thereafter, that same space was to be used to lambaste me rather than praise me. But that was later. The column right beside was also to be used routinely for criticism in the future. (Most often it was from Paul Gigot, whom I had recommended for his prior job with Baker at Treasury, and whose work I respected on subjects other than me.) But for the moment, I was pleasantly surprised to find the op-ed space filled with another selection of excerpts from my introduction to the budget.

Within days, however, the attention to serious points disappeared as congressional hearings reframed the issues in conventional partisan terms. In my introduction, I had pointed to the gross hypocrisy of the annual ritual of partisan criticism. But, of course, that did not stop it.

When the lights went on for my testimony before Congress, Democrats unloaded their most colorful and extreme criticism to try to get TV coverage—later offering me private apologies or congratulations when the cameras were safely gone. Partisans from both sides tried to outdo each other in their public protestation of concern about the deficit. But privately, Republicans urged me to be very, very careful with entitlements. They wanted us to force the Democrats to go first on Medicare; not to touch "the third rail of American politics," Social Security; to remember the political importance of farmers and veterans and all-too-numerous others. Well-known deficit "hawks" from both parties pleaded for seriousness about deficit reduction in public, and privately pleaded even more to fund their special interests. I'm sure they thought they were just doing their job.

The conventional political posturing was tiresome, but predictable. It was complicated, however, by an imaginative distraction thrown up by a less predictable source. Senator Moynihan, who had previously been seriously concerned about deficit reduction, was frustrated by supply-side politics. In late 1989 and early 1990, as I was trying to frame the budget problem in a way that might lead to bipartisan action, Moynihan used the existence of temporary surpluses in the Social Security trust fund as an excuse to call for removing Social Security from the budget and for reducing the Social Security tax. This would have made the challenge of balancing the rest of the budget impossible without a substantial tax increase. In the poker game of deficit politics, Moynihan said, in effect, "See you, and raise you a trillion." To me, this was a disappointing turn.

I had hoped to see Moynihan among the bipartisan problem-solvers, as he had been in 1983 and 1986 with Social Security and tax reform. His initiative was politically clever but, from my point of view, unhelpful. The federal budget had serious accounting problems, but the treatment of Social Security was not high among them. Further, Moynihan knew better than most that, with the coming retirement of the baby-boomers, Social Security was projected to be revenue-short in the twenty-first century. And the politically attractive offer of a tax cut was not what the fiscal situation really called for. Conservative commentator Charles Krauthammer termed Moynihan's proposal "a candidate for most irresponsible idea of the decade."

Moynihan's fellow Democrats resisted his temptation, and rejected it. But the distraction cost time and energy. And, as Moynihan undoubtedly knew it would, his modest proposal sowed seeds of dissention among Republicans. It whetted the appetite of supply-siders for yet another across-the-board tax cut. This did not make my job any easier.

While this was being played out, each new release of economic statistics made it clear that the earlier tightening by the Greenspan Fed was slowing the economy. Boskin and other economists increased their assessment of the odds that we would soon be tipped into recession. This made the looming deficit problem larger. And it made impossibly large the legally mandated sequester that would be triggered in October if the necessary deficit reduction were not enacted.

I knew for a certainty that neither the President and his national security team nor the congressional politicians would accept the cuts associated with a large sequester. It was obvious: Negotiations were inevitable. I was impatient to get on with them. But I knew we still had a way to go.

On February 25, I addressed the National Governors Association. The governors must have been somewhat surprised to hear me express a degree of frustration by referring to the quest for deficit reduction as like the exchange between Vladimir and Estragon, waiting to be saved, at the end of

Samuel Beckett's play *Waiting for Godot*: "At the end of the long wait, one says, 'Well? Shall we go?' The other responds, 'Yes, let's go.' *And nothing happens. They do not move.*"

As usual, my similes and metaphors jumped around. After referring bleakly to Melville's Captain Ahab, I switched to baseball for an image of hope. I distinguished between the unfortunate Billy Buckner in the Red Sox' 1986 loss and such well-known heroes of the fall as Roy Hobbs, "the Natural," Carlton Fisk, and Reggie Jackson, "Mr. October." Knowing that necessity would eventually force action in the fall, I said, "For baseball, the prospects of playoffs and the World Series focus the mind. For local budgeteers, the less romantic prospects of a large sequester and the need to avoid default will serve the same purpose. . . . The season for seriousness will come. And when it does, we will not be bound by inertia."

I treated action as inevitable. But seeking to encourage would-be heroes to step up to the plate, I added, "What remains to be determined is who will prove to be the local equivalent of Mr. October."

At about the same time, Newt Gingrich was becoming even more active in providing me with criticism and advice about communications. His suggestions were consistently of interest, even though I was often unable to accommodate them.

On one late-February day, I received a double dose of Gingrich's advice. He sent me two long, handwritten notes. One invited me to join the House Republicans for a weekend retreat. In the style of someone writing from and for history books, the note was signed: *"Your devoted servant, and your friend, Newt."*

Gingrich's suggestion was sound. But one of my failings was that I was not gregarious. I was uncomfortable in large social settings. My discomfort led me to decline invitations such as these, and I declined this one. In this and other ways, my social unease was often translated into aloofness or arrogance. Clearly it might have been better, especially when the going got rough, if I had been able to be a more conventional political animal. Unfortunately, I just wasn't.

The second Gingrich note seemed to address what I suppose he took to be my large ego and grand ambition. It opened, "You are too intelligent for most of us in the House." It went on to define the challenge in historic terms: "You are being asked to play Alexander Hamilton." Gingrich recommended a

"Hamilton quality macro-proposal (e.g. First Report on Manufactures)." That was not exactly catchy. But he translated the notion into oversimplified popular terms. He said we needed a title like "The Balanced Budget, Safe Security System and Maximum Economic Growth Act of 1990." That was not exactly catchy either. But I appreciated Gingrich's point. He then added, "I know it's hokey but it's the right tone."

Again, Gingrich's tactical concern was valid. Obviously, I lacked the knack for communication with a wide popular audience. (That was, indeed, a more general problem for our administration.) I used popular images; but when it came to concepts and analysis, I was too much of a complexifier. I badly needed to simplify the presentation of a solution, and make it popular.

That said, it was also the case that the realities we were facing were complicated. Our substantive problems and the necessary solutions were, in fact, complex. Yet worse, there was deep-seated conflict among Republicans about one of the most basic elements of a fiscal plan. "No new taxes" had been simple and popular as a campaign slogan. But faced with the responsibility of governing—and with Democratic control of both houses of Congress—the Republican party, the Republican leadership, and even the President himself were each of conflicting minds about what we should be prepared to do on the difficult issue of taxes.

To me, it had become increasingly clear that the crop of Washington politicians we were dealing with—with vintages mainly from the 1960s through the 1980s—were not about to undertake a serious reform of federal spending. I had guessed that would be the case at the start of the Reagan years. The Reagan experience served to confirm it. And my own daily experience as OMB director in the Bush administration only deepened my skepticism that the fiscal problem could soon be solved on the spending side alone.

At the start of the 1990s, Washington had few serious advocates for major spending reform. The Democrats who controlled Congress had no philosophical interest in reducing spending. And quite understandably, most Republicans questioned the wisdom of taking the lead, along with the political consequences, in a losing battle with the Democratic Congress.

Polls showed that the public wanted to reduce government only in the abstract, not in the fundamental particulars. So, though sometimes discouraging, it was not surprising when again and again—in countless letters, phone calls, and private meetings—the overwhelming majority of congressmen, senators, interest group representatives, and cabinet officers pleaded with me privately for at most a moderate approach to spending reform.

Unfortunately, however, moderate spending reform alone would not do. The gap between spending and revenue was approaching 5 percent of GDP. That gap was far easier to explain than to close. It grew out of a policy shift that had been under way for three decades. To close the gap with spending restraint alone would have required a major policy reversal.

From 1960 to 1990, the top income tax rate had come down from 91 percent to 28. But that was not the problem. Federal revenues as a percent of GDP had really not changed much in thirty years. Total revenues were within 1 percent of what they had been when President Kennedy took office. It was spending that had steadily grown. The pattern was a secular trend—clear during both Republican and Democratic presidencies. By 1990, spending levels were 5 percent of GDP higher than in 1960. That growth was accounted for primarily by one phenomenon. In the thirty years since 1960, the middle class entitlement structure had exploded.

That structure cried out for reform. It was inefficient, went far beyond a humane safety net, and undermined incentives for saving. Yet even the modest reform proposals of the Reagan and Bush administrations had been rejected unequivocally by the Congress. The practical political fact was that the American middle class had become addicted to its "entitlements." Politicians on both sides of the aisle resisted serious reform. In this respect, the stalemate on the budget was not merely partisan. It derived from the reluctance of politicians on both sides to face the internal contradictions of their own positions.

Republicans wanted to reduce the deficit. Most of them publicly (and some privately) opposed tax increases. Several entertained the notion that a further tax cut might stimulate enough economic growth to close the 5 percent deficit gap. But it was a straightforward matter to calculate the real growth rate needed to close that gap. To close the gap with tax incentives alone required a sustained long-term real growth rate that was considerably more than double the postwar average. Unfortunately, that was viewed as absurd by most informed analysts. It was not consistent with demographic trends and productivity forecasts, even allowing for significant improvements. Major spending restraint—including entitlement reform—had to be added to the equation. But, having been burned badly by abortive efforts to restrain the growth of Social Security in 1981–82 and 1985, most Republicans were unwilling to lead the fight for serious reform of entitlements.

The inescapable logic of this set of positions was clear: If entitlements were not to be reformed, and taxes were not to be raised, the federal government would necessarily be left overspent and underfinanced.

The logic of the Democrats' position was similarly troubling. Like Republicans, Democrats wanted the deficit reduced. But for both political and philosophical reasons, most Democrats did not favor an approach that would actually have reduced the share of GDP devoted to federal spending. Many wanted to cut defense. A few were enamored with management reforms. Yet most wanted to allocate any budgetary savings to increased investment. "Investment," of course, can be a worthy concept. But what it meant to most Democrats was an updated and repackaged variation of the Great Society. Their approach sought to spend more on education, training, and other forms of direct governmental service delivery; expand the social insurance system's coverage; and add a bit of industrial policy, targeted on chosen industries and technologies. Putting aside the question of its merit, this approach sought more to reallocate than to reduce spending. Yet if spending as a share of GDP was not to be reduced, then the 5 percent deficit gap would have to be closed entirely by revenue increases. Most Democrats dismissed growth-oriented tax incentives as ineffective, unfair "trickle down." That left a straightforward tax increase as their natural solution. But a tax increase amounting to 5 percent of GDP was impossible politically. No matter how much rhetoric might target it on "the rich," its size meant it had to hit the middle class. Further, it was so large as to be counterproductive economically. Even most Democratic economists agreed on that point.

So, by a different route, the set of Democratic positions led to the same conclusion as the Republican set: The federal government would remain overspent and underfinanced.

As a matter of practical fact, neither party was advocating a workable program to eliminate the deficit. Privately, the leaders of both parties admitted that. Most recognized that spending restraint, including significant entitlement reform, had to be linked with a moderate tax increase to break the logjam and get the job done. Since this combination involved substantive compromise and political risk, the leaders agreed it had to be negotiated in private. And since it was bound to be somewhat unpopular, they knew it had to be presented publicly, on a bipartisan basis, as a package solution.

Yet the reality remained that mutual risk-aversion, shared incoherence, and divided government seemed to promise only an extended stalemate. Something was necessary to get the process moving. For better or worse, I felt it was incumbent upon me to be that something.

In January, one of my college roommates, Jeff Forbes, had died of cancer. He had been dedicated to service, was a Vietnam War hero, and was thought by some to have developed his cancer from exposure to chemicals in Vietnam. In reflecting on the difficulty of what I would have to do, I saw the obvious: Compared with Forbes's sacrifice, any price I might have to pay was trivial. I was fortunate to be in the arena where Forbes had meant to be. It struck me, though, that Forbes's grace was sadly missing. I lacked it. And the system seemed to lack it. The ugliness of it all was beginning to get to me.

When, in the weeks following Forbes's funeral, the partisan conflict had heated up, it looked as if most of the year might be spent in angry, unproductive posturing. I believed it when I said that more serious action would eventually have to come with the sequester crisis in October, or with a possible market shock sometime before. But I thought a package solution could not be developed responsibly by simply waiting for the crisis. The elements of the package were bound to be complex. And while a crisis environment helped focus the mind, it did not tend to produce thoughtful solutions. So I decided to try to force the processes of compromise forward, in a more orderly manner, beginning in March.

I was not alone. On March 6, Ways and Means Chairman Rostenkowski came off the bench, where he'd been sitting for most of our first year. He asked to come down to the White House to meet with Sununu and me, saying he wanted to talk about child care. But Rosty wasn't there to talk about child care alone.

We met from 9:30 until 10:45 in Sununu's office, and then the three of us went to the Oval Office to talk with the President. Rosty had given the President his one-year reprieve on taxes, and was now ready to make a big move. He was unilaterally going to put a serious deficit reduction plan forward on March 11. He suggested he would be doing the unpopular, and deserved a medal for valor. He wanted to give us a heads-up; and asked that we not dump all over him for his plan. Without knowing the details, but respecting both their friendship and their interdependence, the President assured Rosty he would not.

At three o'clock on the same day, our small budget working group met with the President. I handed out a memo as usual. But this time it was a bit different, a bit less objective than the memos I'd been writing for Presidents for the past two decades. I had prepared it before I knew of Rosty's intended initiative. That only heightened the need to decide whether we ourselves wanted to get moving. The memo led off with a tie to the President's natural interest:

> Freedom is on the march. The [Berlin] wall has come down. The Soviet empire is collapsing. The new competition for global influence and primacy will be among market-oriented powers. U.S. economic strength and primacy—*if sustained*—hold unprecedented promise for the shaping of a better world order. But at the moment, the U.S. growth agenda is stalled.

The memo ticked off the problems. The economy was soft—"Some recent numbers (durables, factory orders) are the lowest in a long while." Interest rates were going in the wrong direction. Partisan conflict promised to leave the budget process in stalemate. There was a high likelihood of "the appearance of fiscal policy out of control." Market reactions might make interest rates still worse. And we risked losing what leverage we had to either a market crisis or an evidently impossible sequester, the details of which we would be legally obliged to publish in July. I argued (as did my memo) that unless we broke the budgetary stalemate "at a crucial point in the development of a new balance of politico-economic power, the U.S. will be hamstrung by slow growth, continued deficits, and restraints on creative initiatives."

With obviously biased language, I put the question "How and when should negotiations be forced—(a) preemptively; (b) contentiously; or (c) reactively?" After outlining the steps associated with each of these, I added several important notes. The first was tactical: To make negotiations work, it would be necessary "to threaten to veto any bill that would weaken the existing sequester discipline" and later, "to stare down the opposition in the context of a threatened default." The second note was substantive: "For all negotiated settlements, it would be necessary to include additional revenues (though not necessarily income tax increases)." And the concluding note was obviously meant to be telling: "The longer one waits to precipitate negotiations, (a) the larger the market/economic risk; and (b), the less interesting and constructive the ultimate package is likely to be."

I attached a one-page outline of a possible package titled "Elements of a 'Big Fix.'" On the spending side of the balance, it included everything from comprehensive entitlement restructuring to enforceable caps on discretionary spending and limits on the exploding federal credit programs. The revenue side was more difficult. Having worked hard in the Reagan years to help lower income tax rates, I believed strongly that they should not be increased. Low rates encouraged work and removed incentives for tax shelters. I did not propose to change them, and did not want to see them changed. Having also long favored capital gains incentives and a strengthened R&D tax credit, I included these in the "Big Fix." Though their direct effect on the deficit was arguable, they promised to have an important favorable effect on long-term productivity, innovation, and growth. But these alone were not sufficient.

My one-pager suggested some possible taxes on consumption. It raised the issue of trading a mini–Social Security tax rate rollback for offsetting consumption tax increases. And for further deficit reduction, it pointed toward taxes on alcohol and energy. The energy tax had been especially recommended to me by Greenspan. Although politically explosive, these tax measures had one substantive thing in common. They were oriented toward increased savings and investment. In order to gain a larger spending reform and deficit reduction package, I thought they were the better way to go.

Without judging that question directly, the President said of the need to jump-start the negotiation of a Big Fix, "We'll have to go for it." I was instructed to develop and refine the elements of a potential package deal. We scheduled a meeting for March 20 to review the matter.

When Rosty unveiled his package on the eleventh, it did contain unpopular elements: a freeze on all cost-of-living increases, including Social Security, and a fifteen-cent-per-gallon gasoline tax increase. But the President was not the only one to treat the chairman with respect. Sununu gave him credit for "serious and comprehensive proposals." Finance Chairman Bentsen praised his "real leadership." The Senate Republican Leader said, "His proposal could be the wake-up call we've been waiting for." Bill Frenzel, the ranking House Republican on the Budget Committee, went one step further: "For his willingness to take action, even very unpopular action, he deserves commendation. . . . Rostenkowski has shown the way to a presidential-congressional summit."

The Business Roundtable put out a statement that read, in part, "The Roundtable has long held that the budget deficit is the number one economic issue that the nation faces. Chairman Rostenkowski's 'challenge' is a critically needed and positive step in addressing this issue. The Roundtable [is] encouraged by the open nature of the Administration's response." The news coverage and commentary were, on the whole, similarly encouraged. Politicians, commentators, and other observers began to treat as real the possibility of a negotiated Big Fix.

On March 14, I met with Congressman Tim Penny's House Democratic Budget Group. Penny and his group were genuinely concerned about deficit reduction. They had the potential to be an important moderating influence upon other Democrats. I tried to assure them that we were not, as some suggested, laying a trap by treating Rostenkowski with respect. We were unable to support some of Rosty's specific proposals. But we were, I assured Penny's group, genuinely interested in negotiating a big deficit reduction package. After the meeting, Penny told me he appreciated the tone of my visit and looked forward to our working together.

Unfortunately, Senator Mitchell was far less willing to give us the benefit of the doubt. On both domestic and foreign policy, he had become increasingly critical of the President. Speaking to the press on March 20, he offered a blistering attack on the administration. "They have opposed every single position in the Rostenkowski plan, while appearing to be conciliatory. . . . This again demonstrates the President is the cause of the budget deadlock, and only the President can break it." Mitchell seemed determined to make the President take both the lead and the heat.

We, of course, did not agree with Mitchell's finger pointing. But on the same day, we met to follow up our March 6 meeting and discuss what might be our own approach to breaking the deadlock. The meeting included the President, Vice President Quayle, Brady, Sununu, CEA chairman Mike Boskin, presidential assistant Roger Porter, and me. We met in the residence from 5:00 until 7:15 in the evening.

I used as a focal point a memo I had prepared that again described the stalemate, and noted, "At some point, the President will probably have to convene the parties in order to start a serious negotiation. . . ." It presented "Ten Required General Characteristics of a Serious Package," and showed these could only be met by a negotiated settlement. The substantive requirements ranged from "entitlement program savings that automatically extend into the future" to incentives for long-term investment, including a capital gains differential. My ten-point list of requirements for a negotiated package also included the following:

> (8) Its new revenue measures should be weighted heavily toward growth-oriented investment, user fees, and revenue measures that directly promote public goods (e.g., energy conservation, environmental protection, alcohol abuse reduction).
>
> (9) It must be capable of commanding bipartisan Congressional support (from leadership and from a reasonable sample of "followership").
>
> (10) It must be capable of earning the Federal Reserve's respect and cooperation.

Based on earlier discussions, I was not surprised to find that the group agreed with the "Ten Required Characteristics."

The only significant argument came in response to the President's questions concerning a value added tax (or VAT), which is like a sales tax applied at each level of production or distribution. He had raised the issue of a VAT's merit before, and seemed attracted to it. For purposes of discussion, he asked, "Why not just put it on for seven years and clean this whole thing up?"

The VAT had several virtues. It tilted the tax system more toward savings and investment. It was relatively hard to evade. Its discretionary character was popular. It could be designed to replace the highly unpopular income tax (though this would not be consistent with a "temporary" VAT). And if combined with the Ted Williams approach, it could conceivably have had a chance of being appreciated for its boldness of purpose. But the Vice President objected strongly. Like many conservatives, he seemed worried about the revenue-raising power of a broad-based hidden tax. To me, the issue seemed moot. I knew from tax reform that a VAT was able to muster some respectable intellectual support, but that it lacked a sufficient political base. Senate Republicans split down the middle on the VAT, while Rosty and most liberal Democrats were opposed. It was likely to slow things down and go nowhere. Among our would-be negotiating team, Brady was nonetheless attracted to the VAT; while Sununu and I were more disposed toward a broad-based energy tax. No agreement was reached on this. The significant point to me, however, was not that we disagreed on the type of consumption tax to include. Rather, it was the fact that not a single word was raised against the "general requirement" that some consumption-based revenue measure be part of the negotiated package.

After reviewing other elements of a possible package, we adjourned without formally changing our approach to negotiations. It seemed clear, however, that read-my-lips would not necessarily be an obstacle to a worthwhile deal, if one could be negotiated. The question that still remained was how and when we would get on to serious negotiations.

On March 28, the President met with the Republican leaders in the cabinet room to discuss the issue. The Senate Republicans had long been interested in convening a "summit." The House Republicans had been more cautious. But frustration with the conventional process was mounting. When Bob Michel and Newt Gingrich deferred to the respected ranking Republican on the Budget Committee, Bill Frenzel, it became clear that the House Republicans, too, had opted for a summit. Frenzel explained that the Democratic budgets were unacceptable, the Bush budget was "not strong enough for the problem," and what was needed was "a more heroic product, from a summit." Frenzel went on, "There is some nervousness about walking the plank through the budget resolution process. We would prefer summitry now—by presidential request if necessary."

A month later, our private efforts still had not managed to get serious negotiations under way. It seemed clear they would not start unless there were visible presidential engagement. So on Sunday, April 29, Brady, Sununu, and I met to present a plan to the President. We met in the residence from 5:00 until almost 7:00 in the evening.

The memo I had drafted for the meeting was titled simply "BUBBA." BUBBA was an acronym with obvious populist connections. I had strained to derive it from "Budget: Big Bipartisan Agreement." This was not quite Hamiltonian; but it did have a certain Gingrichian quality. It was arguably absurd, but it was convenient.

The BUBBA memo noted that the Congress was not producing serious deficit reduction; and the projected sequester had grown to a size that "would not prove sustainable politically." It went on, "A danger is that without BUBBA, all would be postponed until a lame duck session; and that a lame duck session would produce a lame duck." It warned that long-term interest rates were inching up, and that "pressure on capital markets may keep inching rates up—unless there is either an economic downturn or BUBBA." And it concluded: "It's time to start the process moving seriously toward BUBBA. Delay would not be good in terms of political risks, economic risks, or opportunity costs."

Sununu, Brady, and I recommended that the President and we meet with the four congressional leaders, Mitchell, Dole, Foley, and Michel, to get things started procedurally. We recommended, further, that the President seek agreement from the four to convene a larger group of twenty-four congressional leaders for a one-day Camp David retreat. In addition to the bipartisan leaders and key committee chairmen, we proposed to

WHO'S IN CONTROL? / 249

include four "leadership selections," in order to get Senator Gramm and House Whip Gingrich included. We wanted them there not only for their substantive skills, but also for their strong connection with the Republican right.

The purpose of the first two meetings would be to agree on procedural and substantive parameters within which BUBBA would be developed, and to commission subgroups for the necessary further negotiation—with a planned return to Camp David thirty days later. The hope was to reach a comprehensive agreement at the second Camp David retreat. With this in view, the BUBBA memo observed: "It could be introduced with bipartisan fanfare for prompt Senate action. The House could then recede to the Senate in conference. The implementing legislation could then move with the debt limit."

The President was in general agreement. But he had two changes in the recommended procedure. He did not want to use Camp David. He preferred to convene the group of twenty-four at the White House. And he wanted to meet alone, secretly, with each of the four leaders before we convened as a group of eight.

As our meeting ended, the President said, "Well, fellas, we're on the right track." He then paused and added conspicuously under his breath, "From a good-government standpoint, that is!" Always quick with a rejoinder, Sununu offered a facetiously consoling thought: "Remember, there have been lots of great one-term Presidents!" The four of us laughed. The President responded, "I can assure you that is not in any way on my mind." He was only half-facetious. He was well aware of the risk he was taking on behalf of good government.

After our meeting, the President scheduled his one-on-one meetings with each of the four leaders. They took place on May 1 and 2, and the President said they went well. Unlike many such meetings, they remained secret.

Not long before, the President had had a "secret" lunch with his friend Rosty. I learned about it the same night at the annual Gridiron Club dinner, an enjoyably sophomoric event at which Washington's would-be power elite attempts to poke fun at itself. (In a typical press skit, a character posing as Moynihan sang to the tune of "Stout-Hearted Men," "Give us a man like New York's Moynihan who can stick it to Bush with finesse. . . . I'm much more charmin' than Richard G. Darman. . . ." It was hard to argue with either point.) At about 1:00 in the morning, Rosty draped an arm around my shoulder. At some length, he told me of his lunch with the President. I noticed many people watching our encounter with obvious interest, but I'm not sure Rosty did. In what might be described as a booming whisper, he declared that, based on his lunch, he was now sure we could put the big deal together. That was how Washington normally handled secrets.

On Sunday, May 6, however, the President's efforts at secrecy were a bit more successful. In mid-afternoon, he hosted the Presidential Lecture Series on the Presidency. David McCullough, the historian and gifted raconteur, was the lecturer. Among the many invited guests were the four congressional leaders, along with Brady, Sununu, and me. By prior arrangement, we seven took the President's private elevator to his study in the residence when the event concluded. No one noticed.

From 6:15 until 8:00, over popcorn and shrimp with hot sauce, we met with the President. At the President's direction, I briefed the group on the worsening sequester outlook and the costs of stalemate. I then handed out a modified version of the "Required General Characteristics of a Meaningful Bipartisan Budget Agreement." One of these was, "The growth of 'mandatory' programs (now half the budget) should be slowed with significant, multi-year program reforms." Others dealt with a host of necessary improvements in mechanisms to assure budgetary discipline. The language on revenue was intentionally shifted to emphasize the importance of attention to effects on economic growth.

But naturally, perhaps, the group spent more time on process than on substance. It was agreed that, after consulting with others, an expanded group of twenty-six would be convened promptly at the White House; and that meeting would be followed by intensive negotiations. It was also agreed that the President would chair any meetings of the eight or twenty-six; House Majority Leader Dick Gephardt would coordinate meetings when the President was not present; and the process would formally begin with a publicly announced meeting of our group of eight on May 9, which it did.

At that meeting, as we knew he would, Mitchell demanded

that all agree there must be "no preconditions" and no negotiating through the press. The former was obvious code language that undid the in-your-face absolutism of read-my-lips without necessarily agreeing to increased taxes. The group agreed, and the process started amicably.

So on May 10, my birthday, I received what I thought was a welcome present. It was a picture in most newspapers of our group of eight, the President, Speaker Foley, Majority Leader Mitchell, Republican Leaders Dole and Michel, Sununu, Brady, and me. We were meeting at long last in the Oval Office to start serious negotiations. And we were smiling.

Unfortunately, the smiles captured in the morning newspaper did not last the day. On behalf of the leadership group, a press release had been issued by Marlin Fitzwater after the May 9 meeting. It set out the charter for the bipartisan negotiating group and codified the understanding that there were to be "no preconditions for negotiation" and "no negotiations through the public." At Fitzwater's White House press briefing on the tenth, he was questioned heatedly about an Ann Devroy and John Yang story in the *Washington Post*. It seemed to undo the understanding.

The story was attributed to "a senior White House official traveling on a plane from Costa Rica to Washington." Sununu was the only such official. Devroy and Yang wrote that "no preconditions" meant that "Democrats could propose tax increases, but the White House would veto them." Because the story seemed to come from Sununu, it was given serious attention.

In response to the first question on this, Fitzwater said, "I've just talked to the President this morning at great length about this matter. And I assure you that there are no preconditions and that our interest is in reaching agreement." Asked specifically about the veto threat, Fitzwater responded, "Well, that's crazy. There's no such thing as a veto. You're going into a negotiating situation where you either come out with an agreement or you don't."

In difficult negotiations, it is generally important to build a reservoir of trust. In this case, suspicions were high at the outset. Resentments lingered from the 1988 campaign and the 1989 capital gains fight. The reservoir of trust started low. And only one day into the summitry, it was almost emptied. The Democratic leadership group (not only the Senate and House leaders, but also the six key committee chairmen) issued a statement of righteous indignation:

> We reject the statements made yesterday by the President's Chief of Staff. They were unfair, untrue, and ill-timed. In our meetings with the President, he repeatedly stated that there would be no preconditions to budget negotiations. . . . Governor Sununu's remarks directly contradict the President's assurances to us and the statement issued yesterday by the White House.
>
> This is not solely a question of the budget deficit, and how best to reduce it. It is a question of trust, of whether or not agreements are to be honored, of whether or not the Administration is prepared to negotiate in good faith on this important matter. If these negotiations are to be successful the terms for their conduct must be observed by all participants.

There was a degree of studied hyperbole in this. And, in the long course of the negotiations, the Democrats were themselves to violate the basic understanding many times. But by the end of my birthday it was clear: Starting the negotiations was the least of the problems.

The next morning, the President boarded *Air Force One* at Andrews, headed for Texas. Before taking off, he went to the back of the plane to talk to the press, with the obvious intention of keeping the negotiations moving forward in good faith. Talking informally to the pool reporters, he said:

> My position is I make this offer to sit down in good faith and talk with no conditions. And that's exactly the way it's going to be. . . . So I'd respectfully suggest you take your guidance from me on this one. . . . And I think everyone realizes something might be done. So let's see if we can get something done. I don't contribute to it if . . . I try to dictate to anybody. I'll be there with no preconditions.

Then, he offered a personal perspective on the turbulence of the moment:

So tomorrow there'll be another tidal wave. So keep your snorkel above the water level, and do what you think is right. That's exactly what my Mom told me when I was about six. "Do your best. Do your best." I'm trying hard. Stay calm.

Four days later, the first meeting of the expanded group took place under the President's direction. Twenty-six chairs were crammed awkwardly around the cabinet table, which ordinarily seated a maximum of twenty-one. That allowed all parties to feel like equal participants, even if those at the end of the table had to stretch some distance to reach it. On the whole, the meeting went well for an initial meeting. The President did an excellent job of framing the challenge and the obligation. Other leaders congratulated him. Their tone was formal, but promising.

As was to prove characteristic, many of the players seemed like character actors, drawing on familiar bits from their distinctive repertoires. Not all were ponderous. Two of the more colorful characters were House appropriators. Jamie Whitten, the chairman, was from Mississippi and well on his way toward his record fifty-three consecutive years of service in the House. On budgetary matters, he tended to deny the legitimacy of most authority other than that of the Appropriations Committee. But he was unfailingly courteous. So, seated at the President's cabinet table, he confined his remarks to his well-known arguments for "real production" (agriculture) and his standard critique of "paper money."

Silvio Conte, from Massachusetts, was the ranking Republican appropriator and chronically entertaining. He told a joke about numbers. It involved a guy on a trip who called home only to be told his wife was having an affair. The guy called a hit man, arranged to pay him to kill his wife and her lover, and gave the hit man a phone number. The next day, the guy called the number and was told by a policeman that the woman of the house and a stranger were both dead, floating in the pool. "In the pool?" he questioned, with a sudden sense that something was terribly wrong. "Is this 695-4847?" "No," said the policeman, "It's 695-484-*eight*." Everyone laughed. Conte's point was relevant. Concern about numbers was important, but also subject to error.

The only substantive presentation in the meeting was an introductory briefing I provided at the request of the President. It was humorless, but still of evident interest. Gingrich passed me a note when I finished:

Dick, You weren't boring enough. Too many people were alert when you got done with your briefing. Dull, Dull, Dull. Only desperation to escape from the room will lead to breakthroughs. . . .

With admiration
Newt

Little did either of us realize how dull things would soon get.

On May 17, the meetings continued, but without the President. The site of the negotiations switched to the Capitol. With the President not present, the chairmanship switched to House Majority Leader Gephardt, as had been agreed. Although Gephardt exhibited considerable fairness as a chairman, there was a rapid return to partisan paranoia and tactics. Democrats demanded that the President go on national television immediately to explain the "crisis."

In response, the President said he would address the nation, but only when agreement was reached. The Democrats went into slow motion. The schedule was set so that day after day was spent examining the problem. Congressional staff wandered in and out of the "negotiating" room. Press roamed relatively freely through the halls. Neither side was willing to go first with any serious proposal for fear that the other would leak it. And as a result, another month went by without any serious negotiating.

It was so "dull, dull, dull" that Gingrich started coming to meetings with magazines to read. But though the process met his dullness test, there was no breakthrough. It seemed to many Republicans that the Democrats were engaged in an intentional stall. And many Democrats thought the whole thing was just a Republican trick to blame them for the stalemate, or for insisting on a tax increase. Cartoonists rightly ridiculed the process. The *Post*'s Herblock had an administration mouse push a "Dems" mouse toward a cat. The "Dems" mouse carried a bell labeled "taxes." The administration mouse said, "You can be sure I'll be right behind you." More neutrally, Carlson of the *Milwaukee Sentinel* showed a plane going down with the President and Congress aboard. Each wore a parachute labeled "taxes." And each insisted that the other go first. "After you! No, after you! No, you first! No, no, you first." So it went.

As summer approached, the "negotiations" seemed to be going nowhere. They had degenerated into a polite, partisan seminar. My pen pal Gingrich relieved his boredom by passing me handwritten notes as one after another of his colleagues piqued his fancy. On June 13, for example, after Phil Gramm gave a characteristically hard-line talk on spending control, Gingrich scribbled in jest:

> Dick
>
> Is this where I sell out and call Gramm a destructive Neanderthal or do I still indicate I am tough?
>
> Newt

A week later, on June 20, the "negotiations" still seemed to be going nowhere. Gephardt asked all staff to leave the room, and gave the negotiating group a welcome pep talk. Sununu followed by emphasizing that the President wanted results, saying, "We will work our damnedest to get a quick solution." Senator Wyche Fowler of Georgia intervened. He was Mitchell's selection to counterbalance Dole's inclusion of Gramm. Trying again to get the President to go first, he argued, "Somehow we've got to bring people along with us." Sununu responded, "The President is willing to use the bully pulpit."

Gramm then added, "If people here agree, I don't have a doubt in the world we can sell it. I know that in any agreement we work out, there'll be stuff in it I don't like. But it's important that we think big." Coming from Gramm, this signaled a real possibility of compromise that might include the Republican right. Minutes later, Gingrich added, "I can imagine a five-year package where I try to sell taxes."

It suddenly began to look as if the logjam might be broken. Rosty, who was still the only one with a politically courageous proposal on the table, took special note of Gingrich's statement. Rosty then promised to be constructive, and not to criticize other proposals publicly. The group was on the verge of agreeing to negotiate without staff and to designate a single spokesman to deal with the press. But Budget Committee Chairman Jim Sasser objected strongly.

He, like Fowler, was a close ally of Mitchell's, and was seen as such. He refused to allow the proceedings "to be kept under wraps," insisted on including staff, and declared his intention to report to the press. "We're going to have to open this up. If we think there's going to be some immaculate conception [the very premise of the negotiations], that's just not going to happen." In a thinly veiled slap at the President, like Fowler's, he added, "The reason we're trying to do this brick by brick from the bottom is because there's no leadership from the top." As if in a coordinated effort to make sure there was not much progress, Fowler quickly added, "I might note that the only staff that's in the room is the President's." He was referring to Brady, Sununu, and me —and to the absence of the President.

Ranking Ways and Means Republican Bill Archer of Texas tried to get things back on track. He was promptly supported by Finance Chairman Bentsen (who was more independent of Mitchell than were Fowler and Sasser) and by House Republican Leader Michel. But then all of a sudden Chairman Whitten intervened. It was not clear whether or not he had heard the prior discussion. He launched into his standard speech on the importance of agriculture and real production, emphasizing that "the idea of taking in each other's laundry" wouldn't do.

Ranking Budget Republican Domenici made yet another try at getting the positive momentum back. He said, "Every one of you has an opportunity to be a hero here. It's not going to get done by being shifted over to regular committees or the President." Domenici said he would be offering a comprehensive proposal of his own for the group to consider.

But then, Whitten intervened again. He thought we were all on the wrong subject. "A balanced budget and wealth are entirely different," he lectured. "This paper money's not anything. It ain't worth a damn." Gingrich, again using his pen as a release valve, handed me a note:

Dick,

Whitten has convinced me.

Can I offer a high tariff as a revenue raiser?

Newt

The meeting had reverted to form.

The positive momentum that had started to develop was lost to a combination of coordinated opposition and Whitten's random intervention. But Whitten was not the real problem. Rather, it seemed to be Mitchell, who did not attend because the President did not attend, but who was represented by Fowler and Sasser. Their point of view was inconsistent with what the rest of the group agreed was the only workable approach.

I concluded that things had to be straightened out among the small group of leaders, including Mitchell and the President, before any progress could be made in the larger negotiating framework. And if I had any doubt on that point, it was eliminated the next day. At the meeting on the twentieth, I had tried to move things a bit further forward by advancing a new proposal, with the President's approval. It still met the no-new-taxes test, but would have reduced the deficit by $450 billion over five years. In response, on the twenty-first, Sasser put out a report for the press titled "Still No Leadership: The Bush Budget Summit Proposal."

The whole process seemed on the verge of becoming a Big Bipartisan Embarrassment. It threatened not only to fail to address the fiscal and economic problem, but also to deepen the public's cynicism about government. There was neither a Ted Williams nor a BUBBA. There was only an increasingly puerile version of Alfonse and Gaston.

And while the vaunted "negotiators" were sitting around the table in evidently unproductive chatter, interest rates had headed up. And economic growth had weakened. As it was to turn out, we were only a month away from the further interest rate run-up that came with the Iraqi move against Kuwait, tipping the weakened economy into the official start of recession. Yet Greenspan was continuing to cut things close with monetary policy, running the risk of recession, while insisting on a budget agreement before he would provide even a modest cushion of monetary relaxation.

On June 22, Brady, Sununu, and I reviewed the situation with the President. We met from 8:45 until 10:00 in the Oval Office. My memo for the meeting led off by reporting, "A satisfactory deal cannot be put together for announcement before the July [congressional] recess. . . . The big negotiating group is insufficient to do the job. A top leadership group will also have to get in the act." The memo noted, "If no deal is done by the August recess, we're headed for a lame duck—which no member seems to think will be productive."

The day before, Brady and I had had lunch with Bentsen and Rostenkowski in the Treasury Secretary's private dining room, where Baker and I had done so much business years before. That was followed by a private meeting in Bentsen's hideaway office in the Capitol. We reported to the President that, based on those meetings, we felt Bentsen and Rostenkowski were prepared to negotiate a private deal with us, help sell it to the leadership, and try to deliver its enactment before the August break.

They seemed willing to accept a broad-based energy tax as the only new tax, and assumed that both entitlement reform and a capital gains cut would have to be part of the mix. But they emphasized that the way needed to be prepared with their respective leaders, Mitchell and Foley. We recommended to the President that he push the process forward with a series of presidential meetings.

The President was initially pessimistic about the prospect of succeeding by July 15, the date we were required to publish details of the prospective sequester. He was inclined "to go to the public with a plan, and blame Congress." But Sununu argued, as we all had before, that we should try to work out a deal by July 15 so that we would not have to go forward unilaterally. The President then decided that he would convene a meeting of the smaller leadership group of eight. To help prepare the way, Brady and I met with Foley that afternoon, Friday, June 22. He agreed to negotiate within the smaller leadership group, using it as a "second track" to help get a deal done by mid-July, with a view toward implementing the agreement before the August recess. He also agreed to try to be helpful with Mitchell.

Before convening the small leadership group, the President wanted to meet with all the Republican negotiators. A meeting was scheduled for Monday, June 25. I had been working almost nonstop for a long time, and guessed that starting Monday I might be up day and night for a couple of months. So I decided to take a weekend break.

On Saturday morning, at her request, I read and commented on Marilyn Quayle's draft of her new novel. On Sunday,

I drove my sons down to King's Dominion amusement park in time to be at the gate when it opened. We rode the Rip Tide, the Berserker, and the Rebel Yell several times, forward and backward. These roller-coaster rides were a real relief compared with what I had been doing. They, too, had their steep ups and downs; but at least they moved fast.

On Monday, I was back at the slow-motion ride. The meeting with the Republican negotiators was in the cabinet room. The press were ushered in for a photo opportunity at the start, and Sara McClendan pleaded, "Can't you give us some news." Sil Conte, who was sitting near her, responded, "I got a new pair of socks!" Everyone laughed, and then got down to business. The President asked me to lead off by framing some issues, which ranged from "the need to accelerate negotiations" to key substantive questions that might make a deal acceptable or unacceptable.

Senator Dole commented first, "If we can't get something by mid-July, Dick's right. We'll be headed toward an unproductive lame duck." Bob Michel said, "I just want to see this darned process speeded up. Boy, it's frustrating." Domenici added, "All hell will break loose if we don't force this as soon as possible." Others all spoke and, in one way or another, favored a big deal soon.

The President seemed particularly interested in what the two most conservative participants, Gramm and Gingrich, would have to say. Gramm spoke unequivocally: "I'm very concerned our Republicans'll panic in sequester. . . . If we can get a deal, we ought to take it. If we've got to do a little bit in taxes to get a deal, do it. . . . Just don't break the pledge until there's a deal. . . . I cannot vote to change marginal rates. But if the deal includes non-incentive-crushing taxes, I'm willing to take it."

By the time Gingrich spoke, everyone else had showed their hand. Not only had Gramm legitimized a tax increase; so had most of the others. Michel made clear he was only holding back on taxes out of respect for the President's public position. Frenzel said he expected the deal to be 50 percent tax increases, but "hoped it could be held to 49." Oregon's Senator Mark Hatfield recognized the practical necessity of entitlement restraint and a tax increase. Packwood recommended freezing the indexing of tax brackets, so that taxes would rise with inflation, along with a consumption tax initiative. Domenici passed out copies of his plan recommending increases in cigarette, alcohol, and energy taxes, along with a host of other possibilities.

Gingrich was conspicuously tepid in response to all this indulgence of taxes. He seemed to make the same distinction as Gramm, saying only, "There's no way you can deal with *income* tax rates." He implied, as he had done clearly with Sununu and me in private, that other tax increases would be acceptable.

Gingrich disagreed "emphatically" with the view that Social Security cost-of-living increases (COLAs) should be restrained. For carefully elaborated political reasons, he opposed this limit on spending. His overriding point, however, was about timing. "We have a better hand now than later. If I were the Democrats, you'd never have an agreement. . . . You have to decide to force the pace."

Not long thereafter the meeting wound down. Gingrich offered a penultimate observation: "In a sense, the political problem is that the country is happy." Conte then concluded on a less joyous note. Addressing the President, he said, "You can see how screwed up we are. We're facing a time bomb. You're going to have to do all these things—taxes, COLAs, everything. . . . If we don't do a deal before August, we'll have another crash."

With that as advice from the Republican leaders, the President entered the smaller bipartisan leadership meeting the next morning, June 26. The meeting started at 7:00 in the family dining room, for breakfast. The President was flanked by Foley and Mitchell to his right, Dole and Michel to his left. Gephardt, Sununu, Brady, and I rounded out the table.

The meeting had been scheduled on very short notice, and there was less time to prepare than there ordinarily would have been. But that didn't seem important at 6:00 A.M. when I wrote out talking points for myself. I imagined, as I suspect the President may have done, that we would all just rely on his interpersonal skills to reestablish trust, rapport, and a shared commitment to get things moving quickly. Our sense of time pressure was great. The Congress was to be gone from June 29 until July 10. The President was leaving for the 4th of July, then on to Europe for a NATO summit and an economic summit. If we were going to get an agreement implemented before the August recess, we had to act fast.

At 6:40 in the morning, Brady, Sununu, and I had walked over to the residence together. We went up to the President's office to get our signals straight before the meeting. We said the purpose of the meeting was to get past the mutual distrust that was inhibiting progress. That required some reassurance on both taxes and blame—but without going so far as to get the President out first publicly. We viewed the meeting as informal, not a negotiating session, and certainly not a session from which a formal press statement would be released. Had we contemplated a release, we would have produced a draft in advance.

At 7:00, when we walked into the dining room, Dole noted the early hour: "My dog wasn't even awake when I left." The President joked in response. Then, somewhat to my surprise, he gave only about a thirty-second introduction. He asked me to summarize where we were.

I first reviewed the substantive areas of agreement and remaining difficulty. I finished this review by observing, "With good will, there is an agreement to be reached here that is good, perhaps essential, for the country." Then I turned to the procedural problems. I noted that all agreed that the seminar stage was over; that it was time to negotiate; and that failure would mean an ugly breakdown and an undesirable lame duck session of Congress. I concluded by observing the obvious: The difficulty was actually getting the negotiations moving. And the problem seemed to involve problems of trust and distrust, which somehow needed to be managed. When I was done with my leading introduction, the discussion went around the table politely. Then the President put a simple question to the three Democrats, "What do you propose?"

Mitchell and Gephardt deferred to Foley. Foley had recently been criticized by some Democrats for being insufficiently partisan. He had responded in his understated way, "Part of the time we have to worry, between elections, about the country's government." Foley was respected for his balance, integrity, and reluctance to engage in attack politics. He was particularly respected for these qualities by the President. Foley responded to the President by saying there needed to be an agreed statement that the size of the problem required a bipartisan solution that would include all of the following: entitle-

ment reform, defense and domestic discretionary spending reduction, budget process reform, and tax increases. Foley said
this simply, graciously, seriously, and with the suggestion that
breaking the stalemate would take no less and no more than
agreement to the general formulation he proposed.

The President had been listening intently. As soon as Foley
finished, the President said, "Okay, if I can say you agreed." The
President seemed to be concentrating more on the need to be
sure that all agreed, and blame was shared, than on the fact that
he would effectively be abandoning read-my-lips. On this latter
issue, I was a bit surprised by the matter-of-factness of the President's agreement. I thought I sensed a trace of fatalistic determination to bite the proverbial bullet and get on with things.
But I wasn't sure I was reading that right. I realized the President and Speaker were talking to each other as trusting friends,
as gentlemen, as the highest Constitutional officers of their respective parties, and as men of natural comity. It was not a context in which to be quarrelsome or petty.

Right after the President's "Okay," the meeting turned toward other issues. It was agreed that negotiations would pro-
ceed promptly on two tracks. The big Gephardt group would
continue to meet. But it would be supplemented by special
meetings of our group—joined by the Ways and Means and Finance committee leaders, as necessary—to handle particularly
tough parts of the deal.

If the meeting had ended at that point, all might have been
somewhat better for us. The mood was good. There seemed to
be procedural agreement. Everything was private. No significant harm had been done. But, as my mentor Elliot Richardson
used to remind me, we all have the defects of our qualities. And
in this case, I'm sorry to say, Brady, Sununu, and I all proved the
point.

Brady had been a successful investment banker, with well-
developed instincts for closing a deal. He had noted that the
group changed the subject after the President's "Okay." Regrettably, he brought the meeting back to Foley's statement. He
asked simply, "Where are we on the Speaker and the President's
statement?" I thought of myself as a closer, too; I'd spent a couple of decades using my pen to take control of situations like
this. Some stupid reflex made me pipe up, "It would be easy to
draft." I didn't really have in mind drafting it then, but Mitchell

seized the moment. "Why don't you start," he said. I looked around. The President and the rest of the group seemed to want me to do it. I quickly scratched out a statement on my ever-present yellow pad. It captured the Speaker-President exchange exactly, but looked like trouble if released. So, before giving it to the group, I stood up and showed it to Sununu.

I was not normally shy in the presence of Presidents. I had a reputation for speaking very directly, though respectfully, to Presidents Reagan and Bush when I wanted them to reconsider an issue or a course of action. But, in this case, I was hesitant to spoil the mood by starting an argument. So, in handing the draft release to Sununu, I left it to him either to share responsibility for what we were about to do, or to be argumentative. I expected he might argue.

Sununu was an extraordinarily quick and intelligent achiever, who loved to solve puzzles. He was also a successful politician, who had well-earned confidence in his own abilities to use language and argument effectively. With Brady looking on from his left, he used these skills to edit my draft. He usefully added "growth incentives" to the Foley package. He explained the nature of the solution not only on the basis of the size of the problem, but also "the need for a package that can be enacted." And he changed Foley's "tax increases" to "tax *revenue* increases." His edits were all helpful. They allowed the interpretation that growth-oriented measures would produce the increased revenue, and that any troublesome elements derived from the necessity of negotiating and legislating with Democrats.

Unfortunately, however, Sununu's edits solved the puzzle without addressing the larger problem. I whispered to him that the agreement would still be read as an abandonment of read-my-lips. He pointed to the word "revenue." Feeling a bit of the weary determinism that I attributed to the President, I said, "I know," and said no more. I showed the draft to the President, who said to have it typed up.

When copies were made and distributed for review, Mitchell asked that we break into Democrat and Republican caucuses. That presented an opportunity to reconsider. We might, for example, have tried to argue that a public statement was ill-advised. It would risk creating a Republican backlash that could jeopardize the chance of enacting the ultimate agreement. It would be better to take the heat when the whole agreement was available—the good along with the bad. In the meanwhile, the leaders could surely trust in the President's assurances to Foley and the group. That is what we might reasonably have argued. But we didn't. Not the President, not Dole or Michel, not Brady or Sununu—not one of us—proposed to change course, or even change a word.

When the Democrats rejoined us, Mitchell proposed to add the words "to me" to "It is clear," tying the President in a bit more tightly. The President accepted the change, and the group agreed that the revised draft should be released to the press. With help from Democratic briefers, the press made much of the Mitchell change. But the problem would have existed with or without it. In Rosty's words, read-my-lips was "history."

At 12:30 on the same day, I drifted into the White House mess for lunch. The statement had been released, and the predictable firestorm was raging. The President, the First Lady, and Fitzwater were seated at the President's regular table. He asked me to join them. I told them of Gingrich's reaction when Sununu tried to persuade him that "tax revenue increase" meant growth initiatives. Gingrich hung up! Fitzwater added that phone calls to the White House were running twelve to one against.

Not all the reaction was negative, however. For partisan reasons, Democrats were ecstatic. But they were not the only ones. Less partisan moderates also applauded the shift. Most business leaders were supportive. The Business Roundtable's press release led, "Roundtable Applauds President Bush's Budget Statement." The more entrepreneurial American Business Conference headlined, "Business Group Supports Bush Budget Initiative." And, as one would have expected, most of the establishment rallied 'round. But that, of course, was not enough to make our action popular.

At 1:30 I had to help brief the President for his upcoming economic summit. Brady and I were taking our places in the cabinet room as the President walked in. He slapped us on the back and said, "You two have any other ideas for today!" Then he added, gently, "This thing's going to be okay." Right after that meeting, another of my mentors, Jim Baker, congratulated me politely on the morning's agreement. I thanked him. He kidded me a bit about Sununu's "revenue" language being too cute. Then, only half-jokingly, this master of timing said, "You've bought yourself about ten days." Unfortunately, his prediction was closer to correct than the President's.

In the years that followed, many were to second-guess the decision to include a tax increase as part of a larger budget compromise. In my view, that was not the mistake. If there was to be an agreement with a Democratically controlled Congress, it had to include a tax increase. That was a practical fact. The mistake we made was tactical. It was important, highly significant, but still tactical. It was a matter of timing and presentation. We should not have allowed the press release to go out when we did, the way it did.

We had not originally planned to do so. We had not prepared the way with the public or even with our own negotiating team. We allowed the President to make his biggest possible concession publicly without, at the same time, announcing a complete substantive compromise.

The President was bound to pay a political price sooner or later. But it would have been far more understandable and acceptable if the public could have seen clearly that the price was paid in order to achieve things that were good for the country. We should have insisted that our general agreement would remain private until we could announce all the details—and the Democratic concessions on entitlement cuts, spending caps, credit limits, and growth incentives—to go with it. If Mitchell were still distrusting, we could even have signed the statement and put it in a safe.

When we entered the meeting on June 26, we had intended only to improve the basis for trust and get agreement to accelerate the negotiating process. Halfway through the meeting, we had accomplished that without even talking about a public release. And, one way or another, we should have found a way either to stop at that, or to get back to that. Our failure to do so was costly. We weakened the President politically. And we reduced our leverage considerably for the negotiations that were to follow. I regret that deeply.

But on the larger issue of including carefully selected tax increases as part of a comprehensive budget compromise, I have no regrets. In the historical context in which we found ourselves, for all the reasons I've suggested, that was an inescapable strategic necessity if we were to do what had to be done for the economy.

On June 29, President Nixon expressed this view in a thoughtful letter that President Bush shared with me. It read in part:

> You are taking heat on the tax issue, but you had no choice but to do exactly what you did. . . . As you know, I had to burn a lot of my own speeches and eat a lot of words when I went to China in 1972. What mattered most was not that I had changed my mind, but that I had done what I thought was best for the country and for the cause of peace in the world.

Writing in her diary on the same general point, Barbara Bush expressed a view that seemed to me to be her husband's as well as her own:

> Everyone wants to pile on, but I don't worry. George IS doing the right thing. We just have to get the deficit down. I find myself in the funniest mood. I truly feel that George is doing what is responsible and right for the country and to heck with politics. There is a life after the White House and both of us are looking forward to it.

PART THREE

THE VISION THING—

Struggling to Be Reborn

13

Neo-Media-Pop-ism:

Trashing the 1990 Budget Deal

THE SUMMIT NEGOTIATION that followed the breakfast agreement on June 26 played out like a tragicomedy, and at times looked like a farce. Critics later panned the performance. Leaders of the populist rebellion scorned the summiteers as an elitist band of mandarins out of touch with their audience. But that was not the problem. It is true that the summit negotiating group was isolated physically for a time. Like a jury, we were sequestered at Andrews Air Force Base. But that was not exactly a playground for the elite. And the members of the group were hardly out of touch with ordinary American culture. Indeed, in two very basic respects, the summiteers were true representatives of mainstream America.

One of these was social origin. Though they had come to enjoy the perquisites of high office and the life before cameras, almost every summiteer continued to have a deeply felt connection with both humble origins and the American romance.

On the first day of negotiations after the breakfast agreement, the theme was struck by West Virginia's senior senator, Robert Byrd. He commanded the group's attention by insisting, "I want you all to know where I'm coming from."

"I had to start at the bottom," Byrd began. "My father was a coal miner. He earned two dollars a day. I wore sneakers in the snow, and ate scraps that were meant for pigs. The first 'refrigerator' we had was half of an orange crate nailed up on a window." Referring to the days of violence around the mines, Byrd said, "Fortunately I wasn't a good marksman or I wouldn't be here today. I'll let you guess what that means." Byrd spoke emotionally about the plight of Appalachia, and of "going back home and facing the wrinkled, worn faces." Addressing those interested in foreign aid, he intoned, "Talk to some of my people. Charity begins at home." Sounding a theme that was increasingly familiar among cultural critics, he lamented the state of American education, and argued, "We've got to get back to basic values. We're turning out a mediocre generation, fed on junk movies and junk television." And he concluded, "We can't turn our back on the people who built this country. . . . The laborers who've given their sweat and blood to make this great country will be looking over our shoulders." Behind Byrd's studied senatorial manner, the passionate populist was still very much alive and well.

And Byrd was not alone. Bob Dole had one of the most compelling stories of personal triumph over adversity that could ever be told. He did not have to tell it with words. The pen placed in his clenched right fist was an ever-present reminder. Phil Gramm liked to cite his humble Texas origins and note that he was the first in his family to be able to go to college. He wore his populism on his sleeve with pride. Even Texas's senior senator, Lloyd Bentsen, who had acquired the smooth manner of a monied aristocrat, still connected with his more humble lineage.

Bentsen took a private moment to tell the story of his Danish grandfather's immigration to America. He labored for a landowner whom his son, Bentsen's father, was able to buy out years later. Upon seeing this reported in the local paper, Bentsen's then-disabled grandfather exclaimed with pride, "Vhat a country!"

In the strange cloistered confessional of the summit, almost every participant, Republican and Democrat, had a classic American tale to tell. This group had not lost connection with its roots.

There was a second way in which the negotiators were connected with mainstream America. Though sequestered, they were not without telephones. The lines to the press seemed especially good. In spite of the group's preachments about secrecy, its deliberations often showed up in the newspapers. This, in turn, generated reactions from interest groups and constituents. The feedback effect was immediate. On one occasion, the summiteers tentatively reached a bold late-night agreement on Medicare. Its effect would have been to subject Medicare to a form of means testing. But the next morning's papers reported what was up, and political panic took over. The approach to Medicare was changed from an important philosophical reform, reducing subsidies for higher-income beneficiaries, to a conventional dose of across-the-board cost controls. Each day, the summiteers were similarly torn between the calling to be statesmen and the howls to be politicians. Often—especially among the representatives from the House—the howls prevailed.

Of course, this was the American system at work. The House members acted as if they were in a constant reelection campaign. In their low-tech way, they tended to approximate the Perotista-Gingrichian ideal of continuous town meetings, teleconferencing, and polling. Far from being out of touch with their constituents, a case might be made that they remained too close, unwilling to take the political risks that responsible representative democracy required. At times, a parliamentary system's capacity to deliver a majority in support of the head of government might have seemed to offer greater freedom for statesmanship. But then, of course, one would have to recall: In the end, it was a parliamentary revolt that sullied the work of the 1990 summit.

The process of hammering out the summit agreement was long and hard. It was painful enough to have been memorable. Yet it has often been difficult to find anyone willing to recall having negotiated the agreement. Still, the compromise that twenty-six distinguished summit negotiators eventually produced—though less than it might have been—was an agreement in which all could have taken justifiable pride.

The 1990 act closed spending loopholes in the exploding federal credit programs. It restrained entitlements for veterans, students, farmers, federal employees, and the Medicare population, and reduced subsidies in programs that ranged from public housing to the Postal Service. For the first time in American history, it put an enforceable cap on federal discretionary spending. Also for the first time, it introduced a "pay as you go" system that actually required new entitlement, mandatory spending, and tax initiatives to be paid for at the time they were voted upon. These reforms were admittedly little more than the application of common sense to federal budgeting. But they were nonetheless necessary, valuable, and unprecedented.

The much-decried tax elements of the act were far more modest than the outcry against them tended to suggest. As a share of GDP, the tax increases of 1990 were less than half the size of the tax increases signed by President Reagan in 1982. In the 1990 summit agreement's initially announced form, its tax measures did not increase personal income tax rates at all (and did include incentives for investment in entrepreneurial ventures). And as signed into law, the 1990 act's taxes totaled only 28 percent of a package that saved about two and a half dollars in spending for each additional tax dollar it raised. By the standards of previous budget summits, this was a very, very good deal.

And for a brief period, most of the summit participants were, in fact, proud. There was a formal announcement ceremony. Those who stood together to take credit in the Rose Garden included the President, with Vice President Quayle at his side, the Senate and House Republican leaders, Dole and Michel, and the Democratic leaders, Mitchell, Foley, and Gephardt. They were joined by various matched bipartisan pairs, even including the pair many would have voted least likely to agree: the Senate's specially selected negotiators, liberal Wyche Fowler and conservative Phil Gramm. With only a single exception, every negotiator argued that while the agreed package was not perfect, the summit had done what was politically unpopular, but practically essential.

Within moments of its being announced, however, the 1990 summit agreement came under attack. It was, of course, inherent in the character of any such agreement that it would have unpopular parts. So negative reaction was not surprising. But the leader of the organized opposition was a bit of a surprise because he was a member of the Republican leadership. He had been included among the negotiators at the behest of the Republican President, and had participated cheerfully as a member of the negotiating team in every meeting and preparatory session right through the conclusion of the summit. The theory of the summit had been that if the bipartisan leaders would agree—and if they would stand together to take the heat—the necessary legislation would be enacted, and the public good would be served. But Newt Gingrich, on the advice of close associates, decided to follow a polarizing path and to seize the moment as a defining one for his own advancement.

In a somewhat (but not entirely) shocking move, Gingrich refused to join the bipartisan group of negotiators at the announcement ceremony. He came to the premeeting in the cabinet room, but refused to walk out to the Rose Garden. Gingrich's partner in the Republican leadership, Bob Michel, said that was "the first inkling" he had that Gingrich would abandon the leadership group and disown the agreement he had helped negotiate. Gingrich half-ashamedly explained that, although the agreement met almost every test he had demanded of it along the way, it failed to pass muster with his core group of advisers.

Gingrich then helped organize the extremes of left and right to defeat the middle. As a result, the initial agreement was voted down in the House. Gingrich, at that point, had no intention or capacity to deliver an affirmative majority. So, to pass any deficit reduction bill at all, the President was forced to renegotiate with the Democratically controlled Congress from a weakened position. Some growth incentives were lost. Medicare restraint was relaxed somewhat. And a small increase in the top income tax rate (from 28 percent to 31 percent) was substituted for most of the gasoline tax increase. The revised agreement was, therefore, less strong than the one it replaced. But it was still worth enacting. And at the time of its signing, on November 5, 1990, it became the largest deficit-savings program ever enacted.

At the time (and again years later), the Congressional Budget Office estimated that, over five years, the act made the deficit almost $500 billion less than it otherwise would have been. At this writing, that five-year total—half a trillion 1990 dollars—is still the largest ever. It is larger than the vaunted Clinton deficit reduction program of 1993. And it is larger than the projected savings from the first five years of either the "revolutionary" program passed by the Republican Congress in 1995 or the revised Clinton plan submitted as his proposed budget in early 1996.

In a note to me on a souvenir replica of the bill, President Bush wrote:

This baby will grow up to be as tough and strong as Arnold Schwarzenegger. Tough birth, but it was long overdue.

To some, that may seem absurd in light of the subsequent rhetorical attacks on the 1990 act. But in reality, the President's characterization held up rather well.

The much-maligned budget agreement survived the years of criticism that followed. Its disciplinary measures were challenged at times from both left and right. But they successfully capped discretionary spending and limited the growth of unfunded initiatives. Far from causing a recession, as some critics had predicted, the act actually helped shorten the recession that had started before the agreement was enacted. (The National Bureau of Economic Research officially dated the recession as having begun three months before the 1990 act was signed and five months before its key provisions went into effect.) Indeed, with oil shock fears, high long-term interest rates, and Iraqi war uncertainty, one can imagine that if there had been no budget agreement, reactions in financial markets and the real economy might have been disastrous.

That, of course, is speculation. What is fact—and contrary to the rhetoric of the time—is that, following enactment of the budget agreement, in the final eight quarters of the Bush presidency, the economy turned up, with seven consecutive quarters of positive economic growth. The recovery started in the second quarter of 1991. And in the election year of 1992, which was routinely described as a "recession" year, the quarterly real growth rates were not only positive. They were actually quite respectable: +3.1 percent, +2.4 percent, +3.5 percent, and +5.4 percent.

What did not hold up, however, was any trace of publicly stated political support for the 1990 agreement. BUBBA not only had a tough birth. BUBBA quickly became a half-trillion-dollar orphan.

The unpopularity of the budget agreement was not solely the result of its inherent character and the Gingrichian abandonment. It was also the victim of bad timing. Obviously, things might have been very different if President Bush had succeeded to the presidency at the same time as Republicans took control of both houses of Congress. He might never have had to reverse himself on taxes. But history is not so malleable.

Even with a tax pledge reversal, things might have been very different if the President had compromised much earlier in his presidency (as Ronald Reagan had done upon assuming the governorship of California). But, given the enormous credibility problem that option entailed, it never really had a serious chance. By the time the President did move on taxes, it was halfway through his second year. And though Baker had said the move bought us only ten days, it took more than four months to get from the breakfast agreement on June 26 to the bill signing on November 5. We simply could not force the American political system to a quick closure. In the months that it ended up taking, much changed. And little changed for the better.

In the course of 1990, the economy continued to weaken. By early August, as we were facing yet another congressional recess, the Council of Economic Advisers provided a private report for the President expressing "heightened concern that we may slide into a recession." They argued, "A tighter monetary policy has been a key factor in creating the slowdown during the last one and a half years." They noted, "The most widely used measure of the money supply is at the bottom of the Fed's target range." The council repeated that "deficit reduction remains a high priority," and suggested recession might be avoided "if the Federal Reserve begins to ease soon."

I expressed concern that many statistical indicators suggested we had already been tipped into recession. Gingrich reached the same conclusion and circulated a memo which led, "The *Wall Street Journal* article of August 13 [by Alfred Malabre] makes clear that Washington economic analysts are traditionally slow to recognize recession. Out in the country, however, the story is quite different." Regrettably, the Fed did not see things quite the same way. On August 22, another *Wall Street Journal* piece (by Lindley Clark) criticized the Fed's excessive tightness and headlined, "It may be too late for the Fed to ease."

On the same day, Greenspan called me with a set of reasons not to ease. He professed to be "in the mode to ease." "But," he added, "the CPI [consumer price index] set us back." He mentioned "calls from banks abroad" and expressed "concern about the dollar." He concluded by saying he was "still looking for an opportunity to ease. . . . But as of August, this economy has not turned down." Unfortunately, Gingrich and I, from our differing perspectives, had both reached views about the state of the economy that were later to prove more accurate than Greenspan's.

The Fed's prolonged tightness had, at a minimum, put the economy at serious risk of recession. Whether it alone would have caused the recession is arguable. But in combination with Saddam Hussein's August 1 invasion of Iraq, it made recession certain. Oil prices and interest rates spiked upward. Concerns about a possible recession soon shifted from "when" and "whether" to "how deep." And with the worsening economic outlook came worsening prospects for the deficit.

The deterioration became more and more clear as the summit wore on. The summiteers decided, however, not to change significantly the forecasts that formed the basis of the summit's work. The Congressional Budget Office had an estimating convention that led it to adjust its assumed long-term growth rate, but generally not to predict recessions. The administration, for its part, did not want to predict a recession because doing so could have triggered a legal escape from the Gramm-Rudman discipline. It might also have reinforced negative psychology, thereby deepening the recession. Most important, however, was the thinking of the politician-summiteers. They discussed the need to revise the forecast, and rejected the idea. They did not want to make their deficit reduction job any harder. And they wanted to be able to claim that their work would eliminate the deficit in five years. They felt this last requirement was essential to give fellow members of the House and Senate sufficient incentive to vote for an otherwise unpopular package.

The net effect of this, of course, was to lead the summit to make two serious mistakes. It undersized its deficit reduction "solution." And it created expectations that reality could not meet. It thus contributed to the ultimate discrediting of its own good work.

But the Iraqi invasion in August and the associated economic deterioration were not the only problems that came with the negotiations' stretch beyond Baker's allotted ten days in July. The invasion and the growing deficit forecast also destroyed what little remained of the sequester threat as negotiating leverage.

With the growing deficit, it became evident that the potential sequester was too large to be manageable. This was especially obvious in the case of the Department of Defense, which was readying itself for a possible war. The sequester law did allow special treatment for Defense. The President could choose between an across-the-board sequester and one exempting military personnel (while deepening the cuts for the rest of DoD). On August 9, Cheney wrote me officially recommending the latter. But that did not really solve the DoD problem. In his memo, Cheney stated, "Our existing defense capabilities would be shattered by the implied large sequester with, or without, a military personnel exemption." For emphasis, he added a handwritten note, "Dick, as far as I am concerned there is no way to run the Department under either option!"

There may have been some DoD hyperbole in this. But it was clear to all that in the midst of war preparations, Congress and the President were not about to let a sequester slash through Defense. It was equally clear that, if agreement was not reached by the October sequester deadline, there would be little sustainable interest in a governmental shutdown—which would have had to include parts of Defense. It seemed almost certain that if push were to come to shove, the Congress and the President would follow the line of least resistance, as Presidents and the Congress had done so many times before. They might posture for a little while, and "shut the government down" for a few days. But they would soon continue business as usual under the cover of "continuing resolutions." The summit participants, sophisticated Washington players all, knew that they had this escape. That made efforts to force closure all the more difficult.

I had very much wished that we could use the across-the-board sequester as a means to force a satisfactory resolution of the budget debate; and, if that failed, as the deficit reduction program of last resort. But, as events developed, in the context of Gulf War preparations, it looked to me and to others as if our attempting to use a sequester would simply result in calling our own bluff.

Lacking a credible sequester threat, or a practicable means to shut down the government, or a balanced budget Constitutional amendment, or any other effective forcing mechansim, the American system of divided government took its time. When it did finally produce, it was on the eve of the congressional elections. And, in that context, the divisions that the summit was meant to blur were dramatically heightened by Gingrich's highly visible revolt.

With a prescient sense of the ultimate effect that Gingrich's action would have, some in the administration termed Gingrich the President's "Heseltine." The reference was to Michael Heseltine, the British minister who had undone Prime Minister Margaret Thatcher's government from within—"stabbed her in the back," as some put it.

Years later, in an interview with the *Washington Post,* Gingrich himself showed strong pangs of guilt. Reporting on an encounter that he and his wife had with the President shortly after his revolt, Gingrich said: "We went over and I said, 'I'm really sorry that this is happening,' and he said with as much pain as I've heard from a politician, 'You are killing us, you are just killing us.' Even today it brings tremendous emotion to me. I mean I just want to cry."

So, one might well ask, what was Gingrich really up to? What motivated him to contribute to the undoing of his party's President?

The answer is undoubtedly as complex as Gingrich, a self-described "psycho-drama living out a fantasy." Psychologists will have more than enough to say about a sometimes mercurial Hamlet who helped undo the king; a son and stepson of military men, who saw himself again and again as a conquering "general"; a crusader against the established order, who sought to limit central power while gathering it unto himself. I cannot pretend to explain all that. But I can provide a few direct glimpses of Gingrich's explanation of his revolt.

Though he acted publicly as if he'd been in a fixed position all along, Gingrich had, in fact, been all over the lot in private. After the fact, he criticized the isolation of the summiteers. But he had not only been a part of all the summit meetings. It was he who had specifically insisted on isolation in a meeting in Republican Leader Dole's office on July 27. He claimed he wanted to reduce spending, but he was hesitant about Medicare and adamant that we should not touch Social

Security. Excited about building a coalition in support of "con-crete and high tech," he advocated big increases in spending for infrastructure, research, and space. On taxes, he not only suggested to the summiteers that he might be willing to "sell" a tax increase. He also gave me explicit "bottom-line" guidance on the size and character of the tax increase he would accept.

On July 23, Gingrich called me. Distinguishing himself and Phil Gramm from the "big five" congressional leaders, he said they had joined together as a "critical little two," and were in-sisting on nine "bottom-line conditions." These conditions in-cluded one saying that "marginal tax rates" should not be increased. But they did not insist on no new taxes. Rather, they said, *"Increased taxes and user fees can't be greater than half the pack-age in the first year."*

In June, Gingrich had actually been reported in the press as saying that everything was on the table. But by mid-August, he was again adopting a more visible anti-tax posture publicly. Greenspan, who badly wanted a big budget deal and knew that it must include taxes, asked me what was really up. I told him Gingrich was still being cooperative in private, and was talking about supporting a deal that included taxes if it met his other conditions (which themselves were moving around). Green-span asked if it would help if he talked with Gingrich. I encour-aged him to do so. On August 23, a reassured Greenspan called me to report on his conversation: "Gingrich wants to rattle the cage for a while, but he will support a deal in the end."

The element of consistency in Gingrich's posturing was never a matter of principle. It was purely political. Gingrich's predecessor as House Republican whip was once quoted as say-ing of Gingrich (a former Rockefeller Republican) that he was not a conservative, he was an opportunist. Gingrich's most in-fluential adviser was Vin Weber, then a member of Congress. He offered insight into their calculus in a July 1990 interview with the *Washington Post.* "The issue of taxes is important to us," he said. Yet his elaboration had nothing to do with economic policy. It had entirely to do with House Republican politics. Weber was very direct:

We do not get credit for macro-management of the econ-omy. . . . We need some issues to separate ourselves from the Democrats. What is good for the President may well be good for the country, but it is not necessarily good for congressional Republicans. We need wedge issues to beat incumbent Democrats.

Just before the summit concluded, Gingrich handed Sununu and me a note with a new set of conditions. Unlike most of his other notes to me, this one was typed. I guessed that it did not originate with Gingrich. Its conditions were tougher than he had given us before, and unlikely to be fully met. Gingrich knew that. So I worried he might be laying a predicate for his possible separation from us. He explained that the new conditions were a result of his reviewing the situation with Weber and other personal political advisers. To this limited extent, though we worked hard to prevent it, we were not entirely surprised by Gingrich's last-minute bolt.

But I didn't really feel I understood it until I was treated to an elaboration of Gingrich's perspective in a series of exchanges that started when I picked up my morning newspaper on November 29. On top of page A-20, the *Washington Post* headlined, "Gingrich Calls for Darman to Resign." The lead said he wanted my resignation unless I was willing to "recant" a speech I had given (two weeks before) that was interpreted as an attack on conservatives.

The speech had actually been a nonpartisan lecture sponsored by the Council for Excellence in Government. In reporting on it, the *Post* had headlined, "Darman Asks Careful Use of Policy Ideas." To the extent the lecture involved any attack, its targets were hucksters of faddish "new" ideas that lacked either newness or serious substantiation. It cited examples from both parties. It suggested that the problem of hucksterism was compounded by "today's fast-paced, television-driven, entertainment-oriented world, where there is a high political premium on the sheer volume of 'visibility'"—and where getting on the screen depends upon being controversial in a way that has populist appeal. With a facetious aside, it termed this "Neo-Media-Pop-ism" or "New-Newt-ism."

The November 29 *Post* article quoted Gingrich as demanding, "Darman either must withdraw the speech or leave." After a little gulp of shock, I thought to myself somewhat whimsically: This is no way for a pen pal to communicate, and no way for a "devoted servant and friend" to behave!

I decided to call Gingrich right away. He took the call immediately. Knowing that for this encounter I was dealing with Gingrich the politician, not Gingrich the sometime intellectual, I greeted him with a parody of pol-speak. "Newt, old buddy, how are you? Hope I'm not disturbing your breakfast." I then became slightly more serious. "I was a little surprised to get your message in the paper this morning and thought I'd better talk to you directly to find out what's up. In fact, given our personal relationship, I thought you might have wanted to give me a call before putting your demand in the *Post.*"

When Gingrich stammered a bit, I sensed he was not entirely comfortable with what he had done. Initially, he fumed about wanting to run Sununu and me out of town. But my intuition led me to ask, "Did you read the speech?" He said, with a trace of embarrassment, that he had not read it; he'd been given excerpts. I said, "I bet if you read it, you'll agree with almost all of it." I challenged him to show me specifically what he did not agree with. I appealed to Gingrich the historian and intellectual by asking whether even the small part that angered his provocateurs was not analytically correct. Their "paradigm," he agreed, was not really a paradigm; and their prescriptions for market-oriented decentralization were hardly "new." Indeed, their "revolutionary," "new" prescriptions were exactly what I myself had worked on when I first became involved with policy analysis two decades before.

After a forty-five-minute talk, in a classic Gingrichian turn, he insisted, "There was nothing personal in my attack." With obvious understatement, I said, "The use of the name Darman in the headline certainly could have fooled me!"

Gingrich then suggested that he, Vin Weber, and I should get together and talk. I readily agreed.

Later in the morning, the President called me back into the Oval Office to have a few words alone after we broke from an hour-and-a-quarter meeting on the budget. He termed Gingrich's demand outrageous. But he urged me not to fight through the press. I told the President of my conversation with Gingrich, and of our intended meeting. I mentioned that I had suggested that we bury the hatchet, but not in each other's back.

When I met with Gingrich and Weber, they were friendly and businesslike. They led off by explaining that they had more to gain by being in opposition to the administration than by being supportive. This was not a new posture for Gingrich. Early in his career he declared, "In my lifetime, literally, we have not had a single competent national Republican leader—not ever." When the going got tough politically in the recession of 1982, Gingrich had said, "Really, Reaganomics has failed." In the following year, he observed, "The fact is that President Reagan has lost control of the national agenda." Indeed, he had shown contempt for a number of recent leaders. And, in doing so, he found his way to higher and higher visibility. For him, the formula worked.

With that neatly clarified, Gingrich went on to emphasize that he didn't want to get me fired. He just wanted to get my attention. For two hours we wandered between substance and process. But Gingrich seemed mainly concerned about the latter. He articulated four goals, all of which were procedural. They involved coordinating reform efforts with grassroots organization and media strategy—while treating each other as "partners, with respect." I welcomed the possibility of our working together (again). In the absurd Wonderland way, we parted cheerfully.

A couple of days later, however, on the morning of December 5, Gingrich called. He was back on the adversarial tack. He opened, "My conservative friends say that it's better to have Darman to polarize against, and that I'm getting conned. To solve both our problems," he said, "we need you to do another speech—this one in favor of the reform agenda, and confirming that a pro-growth tax package will be part of it." I considered myself pro-reform and pro-growth. But politely, I declined. I noted that I had agreed that we would work together, "but I'm not going to be coerced or extorted."

Gingrich unloaded, "We're coming after you, then. A group of us got together and decided we're going to make you the Kissinger of '91 and '92." He was referring to the organized conservative attacks on then-Secretary of State Henry Kissinger in 1975–76. I baited Gingrich a bit. "If that's supposed to be a threat, it might actually be fine with me," I said. "Kissinger benefited from conservative attacks. He was fading some until you all helped restore him. The attacks from the right relegitimized him with the middle. I could use a little of that!"

I then turned more serious. "You know, Newt, it wasn't

Kissinger who got hurt. It was President Ford. The conservative attacks helped tip a close election to Jimmy Carter. That's what the conservatives got: Carter." I thought I had made a telling point. But before I could pause to gloat, Gingrich suggested I was making his point. Though I should have been prepared, his response stunned me.

"Exactly," he said, as if lecturing a slow schoolboy. "Conservatives made the Reagan takeover possible. And we will do it again." It seemed he consciously intended to knock off a sitting Republican, President Bush, in order to move the political system to the right—even if it meant putting a Democrat in the White House for a term. I got angry and said he could forget working with me. He quickly switched from the adversarial Newt back to the gracious Newt, and said we should keep our scheduled breakfast for the following morning, at which point we could continue our conversation. At breakfast, however, the scope of Gingrich's ambition became even more startlingly clear.

We met in the House dining room. Gingrich was all smiles. We talked for a little while with his wife, Marianne, before she went about her own business. Our conversation was thoroughly civil. We each had some respect for the other.

I asked if he really thought it was worth defeating President Bush just to pick up a few Republican seats in the House, noting that he was bound to replace Bob Michel as Leader anyhow. I wondered aloud whether he would really find it satisfying to be a Minority Leader with a partisan opponent holding the presidency. He made it absolutely clear that he had no such small thoughts in mind. In his cheerful, confident, radical, professorial way, Gingrich explained that to do what he wanted, government first had to be completely discredited—ethically, programmatically, managerially, philosophically.

While that process of deconstruction was under way, it was better not to have control of the presidency. Once Washington-based government was totally discredited, hard-right conservatives could then sweep to power. I asked Gingrich whether he thought he had the patience to wait for Republicans to get control of the House, allowing him to become Speaker. He answered with a forecast that seemed highly optimistic, but that turned out to be exactly correct, "It will take only four years."

Sitting across the breakfast table, I sensed Gingrich becoming intoxicated by his own vision of shifting power. I realized he would not be satisfied as Minority Leader. I guessed also that he could not be satisfied merely as Speaker of the House. Searching for the limit of his ambition, I asked matter-of-factly, "Then what? Do you yourself want to be President of the United States?"

Here is where he really stunned me. Instead of answering yes, no, or maybe on the question of the presidency, he picked up on the phrase "the United States." He offered a lecture on the changing scope of presidential reach. "With continuous, real-time, global television coverage, and the U.S. a sole superpower, a President who knows how to use the media is in fact *President of the World.*" It seemed almost as if Gingrich saw the presidency of the United States as an outdated concept. I suddenly imagined that my cheerful breakfast companion might actually envision himself, one day, as President, perhaps; but at the same time, as a kind of modern-media-made world ruler.

I should not have been so surprised. As early as 1985, Gingrich had said publicly, "I have an enormous ambition. I want to shift the entire planet." Equating fame with power, he went on, "I am now a famous person. . . . I represent real power." This was not so absurd as it may have seemed. In the world of Neo-Media-Pop-ism, television attention could translate into the perception of power—and the perception could be translated into the reality. Gingrich had recognized this sooner than most, and mastered the art of gaining attention. Still, as I sat before him at our little table for two, I kept a poker face, but marveled inside. I was not someone who lacked hubris. We were surrounded by people with this excess. But in this Wonderland of the ambitious, Gingrich's hubris was still remarkable. Indeed, recalling our mutual interest in the development of space, I supposed that his ambition might know no earthly bounds!

Our breakfast ended amicably. Gingrich seemed to have put his threats aside. Three days later he was a pen pal again, restarting with a five-page handwritten note that began, "Dick, as an act of continued trust building . . ."

Shortly thereafter, on December 14, the President invited me to lunch. Over cheeseburgers and frozen yogurt the two of us discussed the conservative challengers to the Bush presidency, as well as the Gingrich plan to discredit government and advance himself. Generous as always, President Bush volunteered that he would back me no matter how hard the conservatives might make it for him and for me.

Gingrich, meanwhile, was on a two-track course. On one, he sought to work with me—he even included my next budget introduction in his course, treating it favorably as a reform agenda. On another track, however, he allowed his co-conspirators to use me as a foil, the "Kissinger of '91 and '92."

To a degree, the Gingrichian strategy of discrediting the government worked. His decision to attack the budget agreement unquestionably weakened the Bush presidency. The tactic of continuing to focus on me as a symbol of the budget agreement, the nonpopulist order, and the allegedly excessive influence of moderates reinforced the conservative criticism of a Bush presidency. These tactical measures alone did not bring about the Gingrichian congressional takeover of 1994. That was made possible principally by the remarkable Clinton turn to the left—away from the more centrist "New Democrats"—in 1993–94. But the opportunity to campaign against a Democratic regime in 1994 would not have existed if the Bush administration had not been seriously weakened in 1990–92. And to that extent, the adversarial tactics of 1990–92 did help bring about the Gingrichian rise to power.

From the perspective of the Bush administration, of course, those tactics were anything but helpful. If, in dramatic contrast, the budget agreement had been unanimously supported by the leadership, our capacity to govern would have been strengthened, not weakened.

The original agreement would have passed with no increase in income tax rates and with more spending reduction than was enacted in the renegotiated version. Some people would have gagged a bit. But had the Republican leadership moved forward together, attention would soon have turned to other matters. The inevitable second-guessing and infighting would have been kept to a manageable level (as they were after each of the many times that Ronald Reagan raised taxes). Public attitudes toward government and the economy would have been somewhat more confident. The Fed might have been willing to ease more. That and the increased confidence would have meant a stronger economy and a less worried electorate in

1991 and 1992. The price paid by President Bush in the 1992 election would have been somewhat less. And the deficit, though still too high, would have been kept within more manageable bounds. But that, of course, is not what happened.

Many conservative critics, no doubt, would view this perspective as further confirmation that I still don't get it. Some profess to believe that breaking the tax pledge was itself so powerful a sin that no amount of leadership unity could have expiated the offense and saved the administration from the wrath of the electorate. I was not unaware of the wrath, having been a principal focal point for conservatives' anger. But how bad it would have been and how sustained, in a context of leadership unity, is a matter of conjecture. After all, Ronald Reagan had campaigned against taxes, reversed himself in the middle of his first term, and gone on to win a forty-nine-state electoral victory in 1984. That was two years (and three more tax increases) after he signed the largest tax increase in history. The public was capable of forgiving and forgetting—and was typically more concerned about the future than the past.

I am surely a biased observer. But from my perspective, it is mistaken to accept the view that the 1992 election turned mainly on the issue of raising taxes. That explanation is simple and easily remembered. And for some conservative critics it is convenient. But I don't think it is accurate.

The public undoubtedly believed that, as a candidate in 1988, George Bush did not want to raise taxes. He didn't. The public was also sophisticated enough to have recognized well in advance that the tax pledge would be difficult to sustain—especially if Democrats retained control of the Congress. Indeed, polls showed that large portions of the electorate expected the tax pledge to be broken even as they elected George Bush President in 1988.

The subsequent violation of trust was a problem. But unfortunately, trust was a problem for most politicians—not least for candidate Clinton, who had earned the epithet "Slick Willie." In 1992, few viewed him as fundamentally more credible than President Bush. And as for the 1992 candidates' actual policy on taxes, both Bill Clinton and Ross Perot campaigned on programs that advocated larger tax increases than the 1990 act's. And their proposed tax increases were to be *in addition to* the 1990 act's. Together, these advocates of big additional tax increases—Clinton and Perot—got 62 percent of the vote. So it seems hard to defend the proposition that the vote against President Bush was a vote against taxes.

Among political problems, the Gingrichian revolt was at least as serious a problem as the 1990 tax increase. The revolt not only weakened the administration directly. It also complicated the President's problems by indirectly encouraging conflict within the administration, within the party, and in the Republican presidential primaries. Even so, it is no more accurate to blame the 1992 election outcome solely on the Gingrichian revolt than it is to blame it on raising taxes.

A more satisfactory explanation of the Bush loss would also have to give weight to the problem of "the vision thing." The problem was often observed and sometimes ridiculed. But it persisted nonetheless. Simply put, we failed to communicate a vision of the future that was sufficiently relevant and hopeful for the broad middle of the American electorate. In a time of considerable public anxiety, it was this, most fundamentally, that allowed a victory for the "man from Hope."

Our problem with "the vision thing" was partly a function of communications management and style. Beyond political mechanics, however, there were deeper problems that made the basic problem worse. One was that we did not exhibit an empathetic understanding of the unsettling stresses many Americans felt. Middle-aged Americans, for example, were faced with an unprecedented squeeze that threatened three generations simultaneously: widespread job restructuring; children's educational and economic prospects that were not much better than those of their parents; and increased life expectancy for parents and grandparents, but without the resources to make them feel confident. I made this point analytically within the administration and to some of the campaign advisers. But we failed to connect it with policies and people.

A second complication in communicating a hopeful vision was caused by tribal wars among competing Republican factions, compounded by early jockeying for position among future Republican aspirants for the presidency. These prevented agreement on either the merits of what we had done or the substance of what we should do.

From April 1991 on, the economy was turning up. But supply-siders did not want to acknowledge that fact. It weakened their argument against the 1990 act. And some of the pols were afraid to speak well of the economy for fear of seeming insensitive to a worried electorate.

That left us in a politically illogical position. If we were encouraged about economic prospects, we had to talk them up. If we were not, we had to offer significant new proposals. We did neither. We therefore seemed complacent in the face of economic uncertainty. And though initiative was shown by a few members of the administration who were themselves interested in running for President, it was done in a way that advanced their own interests more than the President's. (Often this was seen in their subtly patronizing way of discussing the President's proposals publicly. But there were also more overt breaks. In one classic case, a cabinet officer designed a set of proposals to be maximally popular without any regard for fiscal responsibility. The proposals were put in the form of a memo signed by the cabinet member and several members of Congress, and then delivered to the President via the front page of the *Washington Post.*)

In the end, it did not really help to try to manage these problems better by changing White House chiefs of staff. The President had three in the two years following the budget agreement. Each, naturally, tried to differentiate himself from his predecessor, making it the more difficult to develop and reinforce a consistent vision. The Sam Skinner team rejected much of the Sununu cast. And the Baker team dismissed the policy development that had gone before as insufficient or misguided.

The Baker team correctly recognized that the vision test still had to be met. But they had only seventy-three days in which to frame a message and communicate with the electorate. With the help of the extraordinarily able Bob Zoellick, who came from State to serve as deputy chief of staff, the new team had the President present a domestic policy overview that helped address the problem. Then, after struggling with the tension between new initiatives' costs and fiscal constraints, they considered ideas that ranged from a value added tax to a new Vice President. Yet faced with conflicting Republican political realities, they, too, were stymied.

Underlying all this was a still deeper problem. From start to finish, the administration lacked a viable conception of its intended majority coalition. President Bush was naturally a person of integrity. He wanted to judge individual issues on their merits, hoping that would yield favorable substantive results and, in time, a supportive majority. But he was also politically sensitive. When thinking about sustaining a political majority, he tended to accept the conventional wisdom of his political advisers that he should try to carry the old Reagan coalition forward. That may have been an impossible strategy for him.

Ronald Reagan's natural appeal stretched broadly from traditional conservatives to alienated populists and blue-collar Democrats; and from old-style hard-liners to the newer breed of "opportunity society" advocates. The natural Reagan appeal was relatively thin in the traditional center. The Bush appeal, by contrast, was more naturally in the conventional middle. Trying to stretch simultaneously from the Bush middle to the hard right, the alienated independents, and the populist Democrats was a questionable goal.

Centrists and the successors to the old Reagan coalition were often in disagreement. And though President Bush wanted badly to square the circle, there was often no credible and coherent set of policies that could do so. To do a little for one side and a little for the other looked like waffling. Yet deciding clearly meant alienating one group or another. In this respect, the problem wasn't so much that the President lacked a vision. It was that there was no vision that could satisfy all the competing factions in the unsettled Reagan coalition.

Further, because President Bush was weaker on the right, he and his political advisers were often less willing to risk alienating hard-right conservatives than President Reagan had been. Yet lean right as he might, President Bush was still distrusted by conservative purists. And by seeming to seek their favor, he lost credibility with his natural base. For him, the stretch for the Reagan reach may have been inherently self-defeating.

The President's domestic vision problem was compounded still further by one final bit of irony. Dramatic triumphs in foreign policy were themselves a complication. People wanted at least as much (or more) attention paid to domestic problems. They also were led by the clarity of triumphs abroad to demand equivalent domestic success. The fall of the Berlin Wall set a standard that was hard to meet. Sure, people understood that this was the result of historical forces at work long before the

Bush administration. But still, communism died its official death, live and in color, on President Bush's watch. And then, of course, there was the symbol of symbols: the quick and dramatically impressive victory of Desert Storm.

Just as the success of Project Apollo two decades before had led to insistent hopes for a "domestic moonshot," so demands for a "domestic equivalent of Desert Storm" followed the televised techno-success in the desert. As had the successful moon landing, the U.S. military's success in Desert Storm resulted from a decade of prior public investment. Indeed, Desert Storm also involved a conscious decision to allocate far more than enough resources to meet the challenge—and to actually finance this effort. (This was done partly by assessments levied on foreigners, which some considered a form of tax.)

These characteristics of Desert Storm made the analogy inconsistent with the rising anti-government mood. But that was not noticed. The relevant fact politically was that, one way or another, the public wanted a Domestic Storm. So I tried, at several opportune occasions, to link a set of "Domestic Storm" initiatives to Desert Storm. But the foreign policy leadership didn't want the linkage. And even if they had, the available resources would have been insufficient to meet the standard. Honestly assessed, the vision we were willing to pay for would have come up short.

In the end, the only Domestic Storm we actually did get was the revolt of the electorate, the rising tide of populist frustration that was to sweep us out of office. It was one thing to run as an incumbent, as President Reagan had done, when the public felt that things were getting better. But that was not the mood in 1992. And the challenge of meeting the vision test was simpler for Pat Buchanan, Ross Perot, and Bill Clinton than it was for President Bush. They were not incumbents. They could concentrate on elaborating the problems that concerned the public, much more than on defending their own proposals. They did not have to present their "solutions" in the detail that the administration did when we were summoned to appear before Democrat-controlled committees of the Congress.

Further, they were unusually good at connecting with people who were alienated. Perot and Buchanan, like many populists, were great simplifiers with near-demagogic appeal. And Clinton was a great public empathizer.

The prescriptions of these three populist critics differed radically. But with their mutual interest in highlighting problems, Buchanan, Perot, and Clinton reinforced a single compelling message: Change! After twelve years of Republican control of the presidency, in a context of widespread dissatisfaction with the status quo, "change" was sufficient "vision" to defeat the Republican incumbent.

As an overlay to these problems of vision, there is one additional factor that merits attention. After having long been accustomed to outrunning his Secret Service agents, the President was seen collapsing while jogging. He was found to have a thyroid problem. In the aftermath, there was some temporary difficulty adjusting his medication. For a while, he seemed down, more pensive, less hyperactive. Whether because of the thyroid problem or for some other reason, he appeared to some to be less driven to seek a second term. This may have had a compounding effect.

Be that as it may, I should emphasize that in noting these various possible contributors to the electoral loss, I do not intend to shift blame away from myself. I mean simply to clarify what I do blame myself for, and why. Quite obviously, I have not yet learned what some take to have been the correct lesson about taxes, and do not blame myself for that. I still think that the 1990 budget agreement was the right thing to have done at the time. I am still arrogant enough to think that I could do as well as most in designing a much better agreement on paper. But the agreement we got was pretty nearly the best that could have been negotiated in the actual historical context—and better for the country than no agreement.

I wish, of course, that we had supported it more vigorously, more unitedly, more consistently. And I still believe, even if stupidly or naively, that if we had done so, the public might have forgotten or forgiven the violation of the tax pledge. That is, provided, however, that we had also gone on to present a compelling vision for the future, and tied it to a viable political strategy for building a post-Reagan governing majority. We did not. And for that I certainly deserve a share of the blame.

I sought and was granted influence far beyond what is ordinarily accorded a budget director. I was not only a technician, but also an accepted member of the President's political management team. As such, I shared responsibilities for helping to frame the larger vision, develop a viable majority coalition, connect the two with each other, and communicate effectively with real people. In trying to meet these responsibilities, our group failed. And though the failure was not mine alone, I hold myself accountable. Having sought and gained a larger political role, I should have done more, better, to marshal support for a new, creative, sensible, and viable centrism.

In spite of the lessons I learned in the Reagan years, I remained more prone to intellectualization than to mass communication through simple symbols, much more a policy analyst than a populist. But even as a policy analyst, I was unable to come up with a set of proposals that could amount to a serious "vision" and simultaneously meet the three tests that had to be met. The proposals had to be fiscally responsible in a context of large and rising deficits. They had to be politically acceptable to a workable majority coalition. And they had to have an honest chance of addressing the real problems that mattered to people.

Among these problems, I numbered not only "big government," but also the inadequacies of the health insurance system, the underfunding of the retirement system, the need for improved training and employment opportunities for older Americans, the need for strengthened American competitiveness (through public and private investment in research and an improved education system), and the need to reverse the decomposition and de-civilization of America's inner cities.

I was not at all inclined toward the failed interventionist approach of Great Society programs. But at the same time, it seemed to me that it was naive to pretend that the set of proposals then being bandied about by Republicans were sufficient. Notions such as privatizing many existing governmental functions, reducing the capital gains rate for investment in inner cities, and preaching the virtue of empowerment had (and still have) merit. But all such ideas that were then on the table, taken together, did not have a serious chance of actually meeting the enormous challenges they meant to address. As proposed by their advocates, the "solutions" were not sized to the scale of the problems.

For most large-scale public policy problems, I favored (and still strongly favor) governmental action that incorporates market-oriented incentives in its approach to solutions. But whether through vouchers or tax incentives or competitive pro-

curement from private providers, market-oriented solutions required (and still require) major resource commitments in order to have a realistic chance of working. And, of course, that is
where political strategy and fiscal strategy came into seemingly
hopeless conflict.

In the face of this, my intuition told me, early on, that to
solve our problem we probably had to change our intended
majority coalition. I supposed that the President must choose
between two mutually exclusive, but internally consistent, strategies. One was a hard-right, heavily populist, anti-government
strategy—financing a conservative vision with radical (not just
substantial) reductions in existing government programs. The
other was a centrist strategy. It required abandoning a portion
of the right, building a deeper and wider base in the broad
American middle, and financing market-oriented reforms and
investments with a combination of a politically acceptable form
of consumption tax and a serious, but selective, approach to
spending reduction.

Although there were elements of both strategies that appealed to me, if forced to choose, I favored the latter. Both
strategies would have needed the Ted Williams approach, and
would have entailed major risks. I wasn't sure that either could
work. But I should have forced the choice. In the press of daily
events, however, neither I nor anyone else really made our
group face the essential fact: With the course we were on, our
policy development and our coalition strategy were in seemingly hopeless conflict. Throughout the President's term, I often tended to obscure this point with myself and with others. I
kept telling myself, or going along with others who said, what I
knew to be unlikely: that somehow we could square the circle.
We could not.

This became inescapably clear in the election year of 1992.
By then, however, it was too late to attract and organize a new
majority coalition even if we had decided to try. Our chance of
winning the election turned increasingly on Clinton losing it,
either by moving too far to the left or by failing to pass the
"character" test. He was politically disciplined enough to avoid
an evident turn to the left (while under campaign management). But in examining the question of character, I became
attracted to a notion that was widespread among Republicans:
Clinton's character might, indeed, prove to be our political

salvation. Alleged private vices, a chameleon-like habit of assuming the colors of his surroundings, public vacillation, and a presumed tendency toward prevarication—together, these character flaws seemed a potentially disabling combination. But again, I was wrong.

We tried to link the character issue with the conduct of the presidency. We suggested that Clinton would vacillate in office (as he ended up doing). We asserted that many of his key promises were false and undeliverable. We noted, for example, that Clinton's commitment to balance the budget, while cutting middle-class taxes and providing generous health insurance benefits for all, was essentially impossible. (This, too, was confirmed within his first year.) But the public didn't care. "Character" proved to be at best a distant second to the hopeful Clinton theme of "putting people first." The public wanted "change," and the modest change that we represented did not meet the test.

The end of the Bush term was not pretty. It was painful for us on the inside to watch a decent and able President head down to defeat. It was the more difficult because we believed he was the better person to be President. And it was obviously painful for the President himself. I felt that we—not just some vague "we," but a "we" that included me—were letting a very good man down. That was one powerful reason that the latter part of the Bush presidency was especially uncomfortable for me.

Unfortunately, it was only one of many reasons. Most of what could go wrong did. The Fed did not give us timely help. The challenges from Buchanan and Perot proved distractive and destructive. Tribal wars intensified. In response to his political advisers, the President distanced himself from the budget deal, characterizing the tax increase as a political mistake. The Baker move came too late. A longtime reporter-friend violated both a specific promise and a basic trust with a regrettable public account of the administration's trials. (In my own stupid way, I found myself following in Stockman's footsteps yet again.) More and more, I became a focus of alienated conservatives' wrath.

I saw myself undergo a variation of the up-down transition that I had seen other Washington notables go through, and that I had warned myself I should surely avoid. My coverage in the press described the trajectory. *Business Week,* for example, featured me a decade before as "The White House Team's Rising Star." At the start of the Bush term, the magazine put me on its cover as "The Trillion Dollar Man." Its subtitle read, "Dick Darman wants to do more than cut the deficit. He wants to reshape America. And he's not kidding." (That sounded almost as ridiculously grandiose as Gingrich's intention to "shift the planet.") But after the Gingrich revolt and the decision to make me "the Kissinger of '91 and '92," *Business Week* headlined, "Dangerous Days for Dick Darman."

The subheadline then read, "At worst, conservatives will have his scalp. At best, he is in for a power struggle." The artist's drawing that accompanied the article showed me buffeted by a powerful windstorm, emanating from the trunks of Republican elephants. Having spent the summers of my childhood on the coast of New England, I had weathered many real hurricanes. And I had survived for more than two decades near the eye of countless Washington storms. So I expected that this storm, too, would pass; that one day the sun would shine again.

For a while, it seemed as if the clouds were lifting. My pen pal and sometime adversary became relentlessly friendly. He sent me notes congratulating me on the State of the Union message and the new budget.

He gave me a copy of his first book with this inscription:

To Dick Darman
    a patient friend and a real professor
    in the art of self government
    your friend

                         Newt

That was dated February 13, 1991—three months after he had demanded my resignation. In 1992, Gingrich, arch-foe of the establishmentarian budget deal, took to addressing notes to me as "co-revolutionary Dick Darman." Curiously, he remained friendly right to the end of the administration, and beyond. His anti-"Kissinger" colleagues, however, continued to try to blow me away. Their storming did not subside.

In and of itself, that did not concern me much personally. With the Reagan tax bills of 1982 and 1985–86, I had been through criticism from the right before. I had learned that hard-right vitriol was attended to almost exclusively by the hard right. As the election approached, however, what did concern me was the adverse effect on President Bush. In the Reagan cases, the right really had no place else to go, and the tax bills actually helped the President with the middle. But in the Bush case, the alienated right could move to Buchanan or Perot (or Kemp, if he, too, were to bolt). And the middle wasn't holding.

That did bother me. Several centrist cabinet officers and political operatives became so intimidated by the right that they increasingly supported the critics who argued for renouncing the budget agreement and dumping the Bush economic team. Among the retreating centrists were a few longtime friends who had advocated the tax increase in private, but who in public were seen only when they decided to renounce it. The same weak-kneed tendencies led some of them to give the prime-time opening of the Republican convention to Pat Buchanan. They forgot the general rule that American presidential elections are ultimately fought in the center.

My parents had taught me not to be a quitter. (I had once played the last quarter of a high school football game with a broken arm, fearing my father's reaction if I were to take myself out.) But in these political circumstances, I knew I owed the President the opportunity to accept my resignation easily if he thought that was best for him. I said to him, early and often, "If at any point I am a net burden, please just let me know. I will go with only a 'Thank you for the opportunity to have served.'"

In July 1992, the President asked me to Camp David to consider a range of options that might help with White House and campaign management. Among them was the possible move of Jim Baker from State to the White House. I strongly favored the Baker move, and very much looked forward to the possibility of our being reunited. But I felt obliged to volunteer the specific possibility of the President firing me. I also asked the President seriously to consider the option of dismissing me as part of a larger sweep. The big-sweep option seemed to me to have some obvious merit. Its drawbacks were that it might look opportunistic; and it risked raising questions about the President's own involvement with policies he would be actively condemning. Perhaps for these reasons, but certainly because he was at all times decent and loyal, the President declined to accept my proposal—as he had declined to do before, and would decline to do again.

There were times when, for strictly selfish reasons, I wished that the President might have accepted my resignation. My skin was naturally thin. Yet I was in a position where I had to pretend it was a composite of elephant hide and some modern synthetic laminate. That was hard enough. It seemed harder, at times, on one's family. I wondered if journalists thought to imagine what it might be like, for example, to be a child and find that a gratuitously critical article on one's father was the subject of a classmate's show-and-tell project.

Be that as it may, my family bore up well on the whole. I was determined to stay as long as the President wanted me to. And he seemed to have decided that, having come through a lot together, we would go down together, if go down we must.

On the last full day of the administration, January 19, 1993, few of us were left in the White House complex. The President was still on the job. He called and asked me to help him do a favor for a loyal friend, which I did. I then walked over to his office and delivered a final note of thanks for the opportunity to serve. On the way back to my own office, I stopped by Brent Scowcroft's. Among the senior players, he had been one of the very closest to the President. He, too, was still at work. There was not much we could say. We embraced. With what looked like a tear in his eye, he gave me a final, silent thumbs-up. We had, indeed, gone down; and were, of course, on our way out.

The next day was the new President's inauguration. Our kids asked if we were expected to go. I explained that we were not invited. But for the half-day that remained, I did go to the office. Then, shortly before noon, I walked out, crossed the ellipse, and took a wonderful picture of the American flag blowing in the breeze, with the Washington monument as its backdrop.

In the months that followed, I felt more and more a sense of my own failure. It had obviously been impossible to keep both the moderates and the supply-siders happy. But I felt I let both groups down. The letdown for the supply-siders was clear. But for the moderates, too, I felt I had failed. I helped produce a budget agreement. But the politics had not been managed to produce a sustainable coalition in support of responsible future policy development.

Others undoubtedly shared some responsibility for the failure. But I doubt anyone was disturbed by it more than I. I had been brought up to think of failure as unacceptable. I felt I had let down some terrific professionals at OMB who had sacrificed a great deal in order to serve the public interest—especially the senior group of OMB deputies and associates: Bill Diefenderfer, Frank Hodsoll, Bob Grady, Tom Scully, Bob Howard, Janet Hale, David Taylor, Barry Anderson, and Bob Damus. I also felt I'd let down my mentors and my parents. I was not feeling sorry for myself, just a sense of regret.

My father, who was chronically interested in sports, had used athletic performances (and "choking" nonperformances) as an opportunity to instruct me in various lessons of character and life. So I tended to think about the way I was going out in terms of sports metaphors. Rocky Marciano, the heavyweight boxing champion, had the skill and sense to have retired with a perfect record. That standard was obviously unrealistic in my line of work. Ted Williams had hit a heroic home run in his last at bat. But I felt more like Billy Buckner.

I remembered, of course, the consoling words our son Jonathan had offered at the painful end of the sixth World Series game in 1986, "It's only a game." But though I'd been known for what some people took to be game playing in parts of my public life, public service had always been very much more than a game for me.

Back when the going had begun to get particularly tough on my family, the President had kindly sent a long handwritten note to Kath. Near its conclusion it said:

> The CW song says it best:
> "If we're gonna see a rainbow,
> we'll have to stand a little rain."

I agreed with that. I was almost always ready to hope for the rainbow. But by the end of the Bush administration, the rain had been pretty strong.

14

The Clinton-Gingrich Co-Presidency:

A Field of Stones

WHEN WILLIAM JEFFERSON CLINTON was elected President, I thought he might do what we had not done: form a new centrist coalition that could conceivably hold power for decades. He was well aware of the need and opportunity to do so. With that opportunity in view, he had been a founding member of the Democratic Leadership Council. It reflected the views of more moderate Democrats. He had been a lifelong student of presidential politics, and seemed especially interested in learning from the Kennedy and Reagan successes at inspiring a nation. So I imagined that this self-styled "man from Hope," with the consciously studied JFK gestures, might advance a vision with borrowed elements of Kennedy-Reagan style. He might co-opt the floating center, govern, and renew a sense of hope.

If it were well founded, another renewal of hope would have been good for the country. Yet I personally felt a selfish sense of loss. Just as my generation was taking command of the future, I was relegated to a place on the sidelines. My self-centered lament didn't last very long, however. It soon became clear that I was in fact lucky to be out of government. My guesses that there might be a new centrist governing coalition and a revival of hope were utterly misguided. To my surprise, President Clinton started out by moving to the left, not the center. His presidency was widely viewed as a co-presidency, shared with his pro-government, interventionist wife. For a majority of Americans, this curious team quickly proved to be a source of disappointment, not hope. And the leftward lean was to prove a miscalculation of historic proportions.

By the middle of the first Clinton term, the congressional elections made clear just how completely the Clintons had mismanaged the realignment opportunity. It was predictable, then, that the President might return to the center to regain ground. In time, he might even rebound, as he had done before, to gain reelection. But his party was left wandering hopelessly between defeat and disarray. For the first time in forty years, Republicans took control of both the House and the Senate. That seemed unlikely to change for several years, and possibly much longer. Newt Gingrich was elected Speaker. Under his leadership, the Republican vision was presented as an anti-government manifesto, the Contract with America. Gingrich took unprecedented command of the media and the agenda. He effectively forced President Clinton into a new odd-couple co-presidency—with himself as one of the co-Presidents.

There was suddenly a degree of euphoric interest in the possibility that a Gingrich-led congressional government might actually do what it promised. But the Clinton-Gingrich co-presidency soon proved to be not much more inspiring than the failed co-presidency it replaced. Clinton and Gingrich shared a remarkable number of personal characteristics. But, though each benefited from the existence of the other, they were opposed ideologically and politically. At times, the breadth of the gap between them made divided government seem almost unworkable, even to committed advocates of the system like me. The system did create some opportunities for useful compromises to be struck on spending control and decentralization. But few of the opportunities were seized. And many Americans grew even more frustrated by the excesses of partisan posturing, ugly conflict, and frequent stalemate.

Further, many people found that the actual Clinton and Gingrich programs came up short. Clinton advertised Putting People First. But with initiatives like his health plan, he made it unmistakably clear that he put government first—in a way that was highly visible and widely unappealing. His health plan went nowhere. In contrast, Gingrich earned important credibility early, by moving much of his Contract through the House. But that was not enough. Little of it became law. And in any case, the Contract was largely an agenda for restraining government, which, though appealing to many, had its own inherent limitations. In a curious way, the Contract reflected the insider perspective of a group of conservative Washington legislators: It focused heavily on procedural reforms. Its connection with people's deeper concerns was far from direct or evident. Neither Clinton nor Gingrich really delivered a basis for people to look to the future with confidence—and worry less about health, education, crime, community, job security, retirement, and the other causes of anxiety in their daily lives.

After the first half-year of the Gingrich-Clinton co-presidency, a good portion of the public was looking for change yet again. Many were anxious to dismiss Clinton. But while Newt was an omnipresent media phenom, known by his first name alone, the country was not ready to embrace him. Polls reported disapproval of him more than double his approval. Large numbers of people were dissatisfied with the partisan political leadership of both parties. A broadly disenchanted middle shared an interest in finding a new kind of leader. Whether attracted to a Ross Perot or a Colin Powell (obviously quite different), people wanted the leadership qualities they seemed to embody: strength and integrity, combined with a positive vision and a credible capacity to deliver. That is, the broad American middle seemed to want a responsible basis for hope. And neither Clinton nor Gingrich seemed to provide it.

Politicians had repeatedly failed to deliver on the issues that really mattered to people. So it was not surprising that cynicism about political actors was high. What was interesting to me was that, in spite of one disappointing performance after another, people nonetheless continued to hope. That seemed wondrous. And what was surprising was this: *Both* Clinton and Gingrich—new-generation leaders who understood well the yearning for hope—failed adequately to address it. *Both* missed a chance to build a solid governing coalition, a new national majority.

Historians will someday explain exactly why President Clinton blew his first-term opportunity for realignment. Without having the benefit of future historians' work, the explanation is still a mystery to me. But what is absolutely clear is that he had a historic opportunity. And, for the first two years of his presidency, he clearly did blow it.

When Bill Clinton assumed the presidency, the Reagan coalition had come apart. More than a third of the electorate had no firm party affiliation. A majority was uncomfortable with the failed policies of old-style governmental intervention. At the same time, however, many felt insecure about their prospects in a let-'er-rip "opportunity society." For while some variations of the market-oriented vision were hopeful and inclusive, others had a hard edge that seemed insensitive to those who were left behind, or who feared they might be. The economy continued to recover. Still, large numbers of people seemed again to have lost the traditional American sense of confidence, security, and hope. And additional large numbers of Americans suffered from an even less tangible loss, the loss of a sense of community.

Most of these floating elements of the fluid national constituency were available to form a new coalition—subject to one large proviso. The new coalition had to be inspired, energized, and bound together by a new vision. Such a vision had to cut across the traditional political parties. It had to leave the proverbial old government baggage behind and build on growth- and market-oriented policies, as many Republicans were inclined to do. It had to show active sensitivity to the concerns of those who were at risk, as many Democrats wanted to do. It had to be rooted in traditional American values, which many conservatives, centrists, and populists shared. And it had to offer a credible (not an implausible) basis for hope, which many thought required a new breed of leader.

Candidate Clinton had seemed to understand much of that. And yet as a new President, the man from Hope, who promised future-oriented change, drifted backward. In his first two years, he returned to discredited liberal Democratism. He himself later called this a mistake, while racing back toward the center. But his subsequent centrist moves were not rooted in any new vision. They were politically motivated adjustments that came reactively, in response to countervailing forces in Congress and the electorate. That was neither leadership nor a basis for the inspiration that might energize and bind a new governing coalition.

To me, it seemed particularly curious that President Clinton, a lifelong student of the presidency, was repeating important mistakes made by his predecessors. I saw this failure in both his political strategy and his budget strategy.

Like President Bush, he did not define a new centrist coalition at the start and then manage his presidency on a basis that could build and sustain it. In 1993, he did not adopt the agenda of the moderate New Democrats with whom he had often been associated. Nor did he make any serious effort to include or co-opt the Republican congressional moderates. Many of them, at the outset, would have welcomed the opportunity to join him in governing. Indeed, just as President Bush had led off by tilting to his right, President Clinton led off with offerings for the left, leaving potential centrist allies somewhere between excluded and appalled. This was later to cost him dearly.

And like President Reagan, he submitted an initial budget that could not do the job it pretended to do. He did not use his post-election popularity to take on middle-class entitlements. Instead, he produced an even larger "magic asterisk" than President Reagan had done. Ironically, from one of the early critics of "voodoo," this was a voodoo redo. The Clinton unidentified savings to come were lumped under "health reform." But as in the Reagan case, when it came time to provide the missing details later in the first year, the internal inconsistency of the President's policy was exposed for all to see. Just as there was no workable Reagan plan that could cut tax rates by 30 percent, increase annual defense spending by 7 percent above inflation, and balance the budget, there was also no workable Clinton plan that could simultaneously expand health benefits for all and save hundreds of billions of dollars.

Indeed, the effort to produce such a plan drove Hillary Clinton and her chosen guru, Ira Magaziner, to design a scheme that was widely viewed as embarrassing. It was overtly and actively opposed by the two Democrats who were absolutely essential for enactment of any health reform, Senate Finance Committee chairman Moynihan and House Ways and Means Health Subcommittee chairman Pete Stark. Even the President's own economic team failed to support the scheme.

When the Clinton-Magaziner fiasco had run its course to nowhere, it left only two significant effects. It created a visible and vulnerable symbol of all that was wrong with liberal inclinations toward big, interventionist government. And it failed to produce the entitlement spending reform that, if it had been achieved, might have reduced the midterm appeal of the Republican emphasis on a balanced budget.

As a related aside, I must confess that the Clinton approach to the budget seemed in many ways a marvel. I was undoubtedly more interested in this than many. And at times, the reaction to it was a source of personal envy. For example, the President and every serious budget analyst knew well what I had emphasized again and again: Entitlements demanded major reform. We had almost gained agreement on means-testing Medicare in the budget summit. We did restrain entitlements somewhat in the 1990 act. And we laid the groundwork for capping their growth thereafter. Yet, with reason, that progress was seen as insufficient. But when the initial Clinton budget left entitlements completely alone (except for the magic asterisk), the press gave the President credit for courage.

That was not the only reason to marvel. Right after the 1992 election, I expected the Clinton transition team to use OMB resources to get the quick start that candidate Clinton had promised. When they didn't, I concluded they must be working on a secret plan. I guessed they were getting a surprise announcement ready, with the support of a bipartisan centrist coalition. To my surprise, there was no such surprise.

President Clinton started slowly, working mainly with Democrats. He proposed to abandon the spending caps that we had gained in the 1990 act. Fortunately, Congress insisted on continuing them. Having promised a middle-class tax cut in the campaign, he promptly abandoned it upon being elected. He then ignored the reformist virtue of a low-rate tax system, and raised the top marginal rate by almost 10 percent. (He later said he regretted this, and then regretted his regret!) He thus helped lay the predicate for something else he opposed: a Republican-led movement for flatter tax rates. He seemed almost to be an unwitting jujitsu master. He feigned motion in one direction, then accelerated the movement of his opponents in the opposite direction and often rolled along with them.

When it came to his second budget, he produced what the liberal *New Republic* termed a "budget fudge." He left the projected deficit at Stockman's "two hundred billion dollars as far as the eye can see." The Senate rejected his budget by 99–0. He reconsidered, and promised to balance the budget in ten more years. He then proposed a revised budget that the Congressional Budget Office said would still leave the deficit at two hundred billion dollars as far as the eye could see.

Of course, in spite of all this, the deficit did in fact come down. That was largely thanks to three things. First, the Congress extended the 1990 budget act's caps and pay-as-you go requirements. Second, the congressional Republicans took the lead on serious deficit reduction, including entitlement restraint. And though their efforts were ultimately frustrated, for a while the prospect of possible success helped move long-term interest rates down, reducing federal debt service costs, and contributing to further economic growth. Third, the economic recovery that began in 1991 did, in fact, continue.

It should be noted that President Clinton had nothing to do with any of these. Yet he did, indeed, show a form of political courage: He took the credit.

In watching this disingenuous performance, I suspected that, for some people, it only reinforced cynicism about conventional politicians. But if this was not enough, there was more under other headings.

There was, for example, the subject of ethics. It was obviously awkward for many observers to see President Clinton preach as he did on behalf of traditional values and personal responsibility, while he was the subject of allegations concerning his own possible lack thereof. One Democratic senator publicly described him as "a very good liar"; and another Democratic senator quipped, "If his popularity rises to 60 percent, he can start dating again!"

But even putting unofficial conduct aside, there was an abundance of problems of apparent hypocrisy. Candidate Clinton had criticized ethical lapses in prior administrations. His campaign ads had recited the names of alleged Republican offenders who had been forced to resign. He postured himself and his incoming team as the embodiment of new and higher standards. Soon, however, the Clinton administration was itself the target of ridicule for its ethical failings. Even CBS's friendly commentator, Charles Osgood, chimed in. Strumming his banjo to the tune of "So long, it's been good to know you," he ran through the names of a host of Clintonites who had been forced to depart in disgrace—starting with Associate Attorney General Webb Hubbell and Counsel to the President Bernard Nussbaum, and running on down the long list.

In addition to these officials, there were, by midterm, three members of the Clinton cabinet being investigated by special prosecutors. That was unprecedented. At another level, there was the specter of the imperial White House court gone still further awry, with pictures of the presidential helicopter commandeered by three White House aides. The threesome had borrowed it for an afternoon outing of golf. The golf outing was initially billed as a "training and security mission." And, of course, there was Whitewater (which some said there wasn't). With or without Whitewater, the appearance was hardly one of confidence-inspiring purity.

At midterm, however, the Clinton problem was far more general and fundamental than any such bill of particulars. The *New York Times*'s liberal columnist Anthony Lewis opined:

> Weakness and vacuity are what we see in the Clinton Administration. It moves from day to day, empty of vision, a Government without a design. Mr. Clinton himself seems more and more like Herman Melville's Bartleby the Scrivener, a dwindling, haunting presence in the White House.

At the start of 1995, the man from Hope tried to reinvent himself one more time with a one-hour-and-twenty-two-minute State of the Union message. One wag compared the President to the sometimes tedious O.J. Simpson prosecutor, remarking derisively, "He's no Marcia Clark!" More seriously, the temperate David Broder wrote, "If self-discipline is the requisite of leadership—and it is—then President Clinton . . . dramatized his failure." To Broder's left and right, commentators' reactions to the big Clinton speech were universally negative. Conservative Robert Novak's column was titled "Satisfying Nobody." And worse, the liberal Richard Cohen's column was headlined "All Mush and No Message."

Floundering around in search of his bearings and a broader political base, the President readopted his Republican political adviser, Dick Morris, and tried a few turns to the right. On the widely syndicated *Imus in the Morning* radio show, he was promptly ridiculed by a mimic of Ross Perot saying, "Clinton's done everything but join the NRA and give to GOPAC!" That line of criticism was not sustained, however, because the President soon drifted back to the left. Then, for a while, he seemed almost to disappear. The *New York Times* showed uncharacteristic disdain with this headline for its Sunday commentary: "Peek-aboo: Somewhere There's a President." In the process of wandering to and fro, the man from Hope had become the man from everywhere and, thus, the man from nowhere. President Clinton had become, at best, the junior partner in the Gingrich-Clinton co-presidency. He was reduced to holding a press conference—three of the four networks declined to cover it—at which he argued plaintively, "The President is not irrelevant." In 1995, that point was not entirely clear.

Ironically, this President who had once seemed destined to lead a new centrist majority had become personally responsible for laying the predicate for the Gingrichian takeover. The word "historic" is overused. But the shift—within only two years—from what might have been a Clinton-led governing coalition to a Gingrich-led congressional revolution and a Gingrich-Clinton co-presidency was genuinely historic.

The 1994 midterm election that brought about this historic shift was in some respects unusually ugly. Looking at the process through the eyes of our children, I felt things had degenerated since Kath and I were their age. Negative campaigning was not new. But it had become an omnipresent art form among political "professionals." In Virginia, where we lived, the competing Senate campaign themes amounted to: "You're a liar." "No, you're the liar!" In the neighboring District of Columbia, Marion Barry was working his way back from a jail cell to the mayor's office. Our son Jonathan watched one of the local campaign debates. With a sense of disappointment, not arrogance, he observed that almost every member of his eighth-grade class could do better.

On the national scene, Gingrich's Contract with America was, in some respects, an unusual advance relative to the empty and puerile norm. It was substantive and clear. But still, its substance was largely negative, proposing to stop more than it would start.

Our son Willy was then beginning his freshman year at Harvard. I couldn't help thinking about the world of political possibility that greeted him in comparison with the Kennedy-inspired vision of hope that had greeted me. And I was saddened at the thought of what he and his generation were missing. No serious political leader seemed willing to offer either the challenge or the hope of humankind eradicating disease and war, conquering the deserts and the stars.

The Contract's vision was a stark contrast. It represented a necessary corrective for a government that had grown excessively interventionist and ineffective. The Contract's implied vision was positive insofar as its enactment might enable a market-oriented economy to deliver greater growth and technological advance. But in and of itself, the Contract's best known elements were more a matter of undoing than doing: limiting congressional terms, shrinking welfare, ending unfunded mandates, balancing the budget, restraining regulation, curtailing litigation, and so on. These were more dour than hopeful. They called to mind images of happy accountants more than a city on a hill—for while much of the undoing was needed, it wasn't directly inspiring. It wasn't the stuff of which dreams were made.

Right after the Gingrichian congressional sweep, I had breakfast with a classmate from Harvard Business School with whom I had worked in the "best-and-brightest" days. He reflected upon the shift in national mood. "A whole generation was hurt by infection with the Kennedy-inspired idea that government could take on giant challenges and successfully solve big problems," he observed. "Clinton was a victim of that." I thought to myself that I was still partly "infected" with that notion, notwithstanding the evident shift in mood. Government clearly needed to be reformed. And when it did intervene, it had to do so with much more attention to market-oriented incentives. But I was not about to accept the idea that there were no more big and inspiring challenges for a responsible government to meet. To that extent, I was obviously out of sync with the times.

There was, nonetheless, something inspiring to me about the Gingrich-led populist revolt. It was captured in the reaction of another astute observer and friend, Margaret Tutwiler. "The people," she said, "have reacquainted themselves with their own power."

That was a positive characteristic of the Gingrichian revolution. Clinton had threatened to take the country too far to the left; and the system—the people—were taking it back. As a product of populist reaction, Gingrich was an important agent of correction. In fairness to Gingrich, however, I should note my opinion (and his) that he had the potential to be much more than merely a useful corrective. As he himself put it, he intended "to shift the entire planet." Even after adjusting for the excessive grandiosity of his aspiration, the underlying spirit distinguished him from most of his co-revolutionaries.

Gingrich was not naturally dour or negative. He was a character of much more creative, positive, and hopeful vision than that presented in the Contract with America. Apart from his anger with authority figures, he was naturally a buoyant and cheerful character. Like Ronald Reagan (and Tom Paine), he had the nonconservative notion that "we have it in our power to make the world over again." Unlike most traditionalists, he had an optimistic faith in technology and the forces of change. And whether it was providing laptops for every urban ghetto-dweller, making the District of Columbia into a "jewel," or colonizing outer space, Gingrich was personally ready to embrace futuristic ideas for public policy problem solving. In his heart, though not in his opportunistic calculus, this former Rockefeller Republican was even willing to spend public money on these ideas. In relation to Gingrich's larger vision, the Contract was merely a necessary first step.

In the period of the Clinton-Gingrich co-presidency, however, Gingrich delivered much less than the hopeful, grandiose vision that the dreamer in him entertained. Indeed, though he fulfilled his commitment to advance the Contract through the House, only the most modest portion of it actually became law. Its more ambitious undertakings—from term limits and a balanced budget Constitutional amendment to regulatory reform and spending reduction—all were rejected. As usual, the system forced moderation upon those who single-mindedly wished to impose their agenda upon the nation. But there was more than just the moderating effect of the system that slowed the advance of the larger Gingrichian dreams. Gingrich himself made an important strategic choice that limited his achievement, at least for the initial period of his co-presidency.

Right after his 1994 victory, it was hard to find the right metaphor for Gingrich's enthusiasm. He was flying high. His natural buoyancy was floating him upward on waves of personal euphoria and media frenzy. Jack Kemp said to me, "Gingrich is like Deion Sanders doing a dance in the end zone!" I thought he also seemed a bit like an updated Haig—"I'm in control here at the Capitol!"—except that Gingrich actually was in control of the House. And far from seeming like Strangelove, he seemed more like a giddy Santa Claus, except that he was preaching the virtues of orphanages. The images were a bit confused.

Knowing Gingrich well enough to know of his larger interests, I was curious to see how he would use his newly gained power. Would Gingrich the activist-futurist advance initiatives for large-scale problem solving? Would he seek to build a new coalition that could reach beyond the limited vision of his natural base in the House? Would he thus be able to build a majority coalition in the national electorate and not just in the House Republican caucus? Or would he stick to his narrower base in the House in order to consolidate power and advance only as opportunity might allow?

When the euphoria passed, Gingrich chose the latter. His agenda was the Contract, not something more innovative, futuristic, or hopeful. What was new for him and the country was a Republican majority in both houses of Congress to force action on the Contract. As a down payment on American renewal, that seemed to be enough for Gingrich. Beyond the Contract, he did not go very far. He reached a bit to his Christian right on traditional family values. But family values were not his natural strength. And as for his activist-futurist inclinations, they were put on hold.

Why he did this is a matter of speculation. But at least three explanations suggest themselves. The first, and most obvious, is that the Contract alone was a major undertaking; and assuring success with it was a necessary political priority. Arguably, more could come only after credibility had been earned by fulfilling the Contract's large commitments. That would take time and focused effort. The focus would be blurred if inspirational distractions were added. This consideration, especially when combined with the commitments to reduce taxes and limit the growth of spending, was a thoroughly understandable reason for limiting the agenda. Indeed, it was so reasonable that one might wonder why one would even consider other explanations. But Gingrich was not notorious for his patience. Nor was he well known for a tendency to limit himself. So one might at least wonder what else might have accounted for his self-limiting choice.

A second explanation is related to the first and, perhaps, equally obvious. Gingrich was "leading" by staying close to the predilections of his base. And that base was limited in its interests. The Republican party of 1995 was not nearly as positive, creative, and open-minded as Gingrich was sometimes inclined to be. The moderate wing of the party, which had once been capable of creative influence, had atrophied almost to the point of disappearance. The Kemp wing, with which Gingrich had shared a naturally positive orientation, was also then in abeyance. Its supply-side orientation toward growth was displaced, at the time, by the dominating interest in shrinking government and balancing the budget. And Kemp himself dropped out of the presidential sweepstakes. Thus, the party in 1995 was left, in many ways, to be more negative than positive.

There were several separable strains of the negatively oriented Republican base: anti-liberal, anti-welfare, anti-modern, anti-urban, anti-immigrant, anti-foreign, anti-elite, and generally anti-government. These strains clustered in overlapping (sometimes conflicting) subsets. One was represented by the somewhat libertarian House Majority Leader, Dick Armey. Another was represented by the nativist-traditionalist Pat Buchanan. Neither Armey nor Buchanan—nor many of their followers—had Gingrich's empathy or inclusiveness. Nor did they have Gingrich's naturally optimistic habit of assuming that virtually any problem could be solved with break-the-mold applications of science, technology, and creative organization.

They were not particularly interested in Gingrich-guru Alvin Toffler's Third Wave—not to mention a fourth or fifth or sixth wave. The Armey strain would not have appreciated Toffler's argument that "free-marketism and trickle-downism twisted into rigid theological dogmas are inadequate responses to the Third Wave." And all seemed to treat Gingrich's infatuation with futurist-activism as an acceptable indulgence, provided Gingrich did not get serious about this—and provided that he limited himself to only occasional meetings of the type he enjoyed with Murphy Brown and the Mighty Morphin Power Rangers.

Indeed, for much of the negatively oriented Republican

base, *un*-doing was sufficient inspiration by itself. Gingrich had seized the opportunity to become the House "leader" of this base by using his talents for organization and communication to mobilize its interests in undoing. But this was a marriage of convenience. It was only half-natural to Gingrich. For at least a while, however, it was a tie that would bind.

There was a third explanation why the highly ambitious Gingrich did not add the missing positive elements to his initial agenda. This explanation seemed the most interesting to me. It was less relevant for the short term, and more important for the future of Gingrichism (a work in progress). It was simply: The vintage 1995–96 Gingrich was not yet ready for more than the Contract in any serious substantive way.

For Gingrich to get where he said he wanted—a majority governing coalition—he would, sooner or later, have to get ready for more. The negatively oriented base amounted to only about a third of the electorate. To broaden his reach to a majority, Gingrich could not rely simply on the virtues of undoing the welfare state. He would have to move beyond the undoing, on to a more creative and positive agenda. But his ambition was not only running ahead of his base. As I've suggested, it was also running ahead of his capacity to produce the positive substantive policy that could broaden that base.

Gingrich was inclined to think big. But when it came to initiatives beyond the negativism, he had little more than strong inclinations and bits and pieces of substance that attracted his fancy. He was eclectic. He borrowed some from the Opportunity Society, some from Toffler. And some of his substantive policy came from his own fertile imagination. But little of it was well developed in programmatic terms. Except when absolutely necessary for political reasons, Gingrich did not have much taste for these. He was willing to get intimately involved in the details of political tactics and communications, and in resolving or precipitating policy conflict when his political strategy required. But when it came to policy substance per se, Gingrich's attitude often was: Men of vision don't do windows.

Gingrich, a self-styled man of vision, did concepts and the big picture. He seemed to think, and certainly to prefer, that programmatic details should ordinarily be left for lesser mortals to work out. He liked to talk about the Promised Land, but to leave it to task forces to figure out whether we would all best get there by foot, by spaceship, or via a yet-to-be-invented high-energy inter-temporal transformational system.

That leadership model could work sometimes. It was like the Kennedy decision to go to the moon. President Kennedy provided the clear goal, the vision, without knowing exactly how humans would get there. NASA and the Apollo program then worked out the difficult details and got the job done. The trouble was, of course, that the same leadership model could also produce the Bay of Pigs. And the difference between the landings at the Sea of Tranquility and the Bay of Pigs was not insignificant.

In Gingrich's case, the task forces he drew upon were inadequate to his larger aspirations. They were comprised primarily of conservative members of the House and people from think tanks funded by conservatives. This pattern was reasonable and natural. But if the need was to think "outside the box" (as Gingrich liked to say), Gingrich's many task forces were not likely to meet the challenge. They were the very definition of the narrow, hard-right box. And while he had to accommodate them, he also had to transcend them if he was to reach a broader national majority.

Gingrich, of course, could be quite inventive on his own. He was, for example, with his much-publicized proposals for expanding orphanages, offering laptops to every ghetto youth, and executing anyone caught transporting illegal drugs into the United States. As each of these examples suggested, Gingrich had an ability to cut toward the heart of a difficult problem. Families were not always the best place to bring up children. Technology had enormous untapped potential to help educate and connect otherwise disadvantaged urban youth. Drugs were a mortal enemy of American civilization, and conventional efforts at drug interdiction were an obvious failure. Gingrich's bold ideas had a remarkable ability to force a wide audience to focus on just such important points as these.

But Gingrich himself had neither the time nor the inclination to develop his ideas systematically. They were often untested. So there was little empirical evidence to support them. At one level they had appeal. But typically, they failed to answer the most obvious questions they raised. Were high-quality orphanages to be the new "homes" for all those who were trapped in dysfunctional families? Was the state to decide what families were dysfunctional? What would construction of, and healthy upbringing in, all these new orphanages cost? What would laptops for the poor cost? Who would pay? How would they be distributed? Would death-for-cross-border-drug-traffickers stop drug flow into the country? Or would it simply increase the costs of trafficking (higher bribes, more expensive transportation technology, etc.) and thereby force the further consolidation of organized crime's hold on the drug business?

The absence of satisfactory answers to such questions might have been embarrassing if Gingrich had not moved so quickly on to other things. Yet left as they were, the ideas seemed only half-baked. That was fine for a brainstorming session or a stimulating seminar. But to the people who might have been available to broaden the Gingrich base, public brainstorming was not enough.

With good reason, these people had grown skeptical of politicians' overblown promises and failed programs. Three decades of public policy disappointment had left them distrustful of excessive government, but also unwilling to trust excessive claims that the market alone could cure all ills. They wanted both an inspiring picture of where America was going, and sensible policy proposals that had a serious chance of getting America there.

The various Gingrichian schemes failed to meet this two-part test. It was not clear where his schemes might lead; nor was it credible that they would work. So partly by design and partly by default, Gingrich limited himself to the relative political security of his negatively oriented base.

That was to prove particularly troubling for Gingrich as he tried to bring to successful conclusion his strategy to reach a budget agreement and end big government. He and his House Republican colleagues had persuaded themselves that they could use the threat of shutting the government down, or refusing to increase the federal debt limit, to force the political system to accept something very close to their budget plan.

That plan was relatively bold, though it was certainly not revolutionary. It cut the basic functions of government in real terms. It advanced serious proposals to restrain the growth of Medicare, end welfare as a federal entitlement, and return a large degree of control of welfare and Medicaid to the states. As passed by the House, its projected deficit reduction in the first five years was less than the 1990 budget act's; but that was because it also included a substantial tax cut.

Notwithstanding the plan's boldness, it lent itself to reasonable compromise. It was not a radical plan. It would have left government spending at about 20 percent of GDP. And in that respect, it was not that far from what moderate and conservative Democrats could have accepted. A split-the-difference solution of the type President Reagan would have accepted was clearly within reach—if the two co-Presidents wanted to manage the process to grasp it.

But the House Republicans didn't want just half a loaf. Because they felt a serious shutdown threat gave them extra leverage, and because they thought they could win the battle for public opinion if there was a stalemate, they concluded they should not accept a split-the-difference budget compromise. Yet, as things turned out, the gun they meant to hold to the head of the body politic ended up exploding in their faces.

Gingrich thought of himself as a strategist and tactician not unlike some of the great military generals. From that perspective, he had criticized our strategy and tactics in managing the 1990 budget negotiations. Some of his criticism had merit. So it was somewhat surprising to see the string of tactical mistakes that he and his troops made in managing what was in many ways a similar process in 1995. They snatched a relatively clear defeat from what most had thought would be a far-reaching victory.

First, they made a major miscalculation with respect to President Clinton. Because he had flip-flopped on many policy issues over the years, they assumed they could easily force him to do so again. They told themselves that they were firmly guided by principle, and the President was not. But though largely correct, they missed one crucial point. There was a single thread of consistency that accounted for the President's many flip-flops: He would do whatever he had to do in order to advance his political interest and get himself reelected. On that, he was firm. And given the Republicans' other tactical mistakes, the President concluded that a refusal to roll over to some of the Republican demands could play to his political advantage.

The second major Gingrichian tactical mistake made that

conclusion easy. For a while, the President was all over the lot on the issue of when he would balance the budget: five years, ten years, eight years, nine years, never. He also wanted to be his own scorekeeper. On both these issues, the Republicans had the upper hand with the public. They were for a clear, fixed point at which the budget must be honestly scored as balanced, the year 2002. If negotiations had to break down, this was the kind of issue the Republicans could take to the people and have a chance of winning. Therefore, it was the kind of issue they should have tried not to close early. But they did not see it that way.

The Gingrichians used their shutdown ploy to force a single concession; they got the President to close exactly the issue that they looked best on. They were proud that they had done so on their terms. But in so doing, they took the issue off the table. That allowed President Clinton to say, thereafter, that he and the Republicans had no disagreement on the target for balancing the budget; and they both had plans that the Congressional Budget Office certified would do that. The President said that again and again. In effect, the Republican tactic allowed the President to legitimize himself as an advocate of a balanced budget. And further, the President went on to say, again and again, that the only difference between him and the Republicans was that he was determined to balance the budget without gutting Medicare and Medicaid, without hurting old people and children, or the environment and education. By allowing the President to reduce the difference to that partisan formulation, the Republican tacticians allowed a switch to issues where they were on the unpopular side.

Then, in their next tactical mistake, the Gingrichians overplayed their hand with their threats. Their government shutdown effort seemed to take the wrong hostages: tourists and disabled veterans, for example. And paying government workers not to work seemed to compound the absurdity. When the threat of causing the first federal default in the nation's history was added to the mix, it was clear that, with the American public, the Republicans were mainly discrediting themselves. After taking a protracted and self-inflicted political beating, it was they who rolled over. On January 15, 1996, the *Washington Post*'s front-page headline read, "Republicans Offer to Lift Debt Limit; Government Shutdown Strategy Dropped."

As the 1996 election approached, after a year of aggressively pushing the Contract, Gingrich's strategy had driven public approval of Congress back below 30 percent. It drove favorable views of the Republican party down from 55 percent in January of 1995 to a little over 35 percent in early 1996. And it drove negative views of Gingrich himself up to over 51 percent of the public, compared with only 22 percent who viewed him favorably. Further, in an apparent reversal of the electoral message of 1994, polls suggested that the public actually preferred the once-again-moderately-postured Clinton policies to those of the Republican Congress. By playing mainly to his base, Gingrich had kept himself in firm command of a House majority. But by failing to bridge to a broader coalition, he left himself, and his partisans, a long way from a new national majority.

Gingrich's strategic error was the mirror image of the President's first-year error. He had failed to appeal to the center. But where the President was left with a route back to the middle, the House Republican strategy unintentionally sent the Republican party off in another direction.

The failed strategy yielded neither a victory for Republicans inclined to govern, nor a persuasively hopeful vision for Americans concerned about restoring the Dream. That gave those who had been tied to the House strategy little that was positive to run on. At the same time, it created an opening for those who were less inclined toward budget-cutting pain, and more inclined toward tax incentives for growth and opportunity. Through that opening, Steve Forbes was to enter the Republican presidential race. The failed Gingrich strategy also left a wide opening for someone who would speak directly to the everyday frustrations of ordinary Americans. Through that opening, the Buchanan Brigade was to charge. And that had potential consequences which made even the confident Gingrich fear for the fate of the revolution he had, only recently, thought his leadership could guarantee.

In observing the Clinton-Gingrich co-presidency, I occasionally recalled an image that impressed itself upon me when I was in the Bush administration. Back then, I was often seen carrying two oversized rectangular briefcases to and fro. They were filled with all sorts of briefing papers and analyses. Sometimes, when I was feeling weary, they seemed like two great big granite blocks that I was forced to lug around. Then I would remind myself of a short allegorical tale that a colleague had shared with me.

It was a story about three stonemasons who all worked together. When the stonemasons were asked what they were doing, each had a different answer. The first said, "I'm cutting this stone into big, smooth blocks." The second said, "I'm piling these blocks on top of those." The third seemed to be doing the same sort of things as the first and the second. But his answer soared, where theirs did not. He said, "I am building a cathedral."

The cathedral, of course, is what one might think of as a metaphor for "the vision thing." It is the edifice, or even the first outline of the proverbial shining city, to be built upon a hill—drawing the eye and spirit upward. It is that clear image which gives people a sense of direction, connects one person with another, and gives larger meaning to each person's individual contribution. It is, at once, a symbol of people's higher aspirations and a validation of their collective capacity to move toward them. It is an inspiring and uplifting image, which connects one generation with another, and offers a credible basis for hope.

With the Clinton-Gingrich co-presidency, however, I had the sense—just as some had in observing us in the Bush administration—that each of the co-presidents failed to provide the American people with an image of the cathedral. Co-President Clinton's wanderings left him unable to present any firm image at all, except that he was unwavering in his desire to get himself reelected. He again attended to the political dictum that moving toward the center would help. But it was not clear what he really wanted to build. At the same time, though co-President Gingrich could sketch the images of interesting spires, he failed to build a base broad enough to allow their stable construction. Having tied himself down on his right flank, he was unable to present an image that could sustain itself while reaching outward and upward. He and his colleagues seemed more inclined toward tearing down the old edifice than building the new. They acted like political deconstructionists, not idealists.

There was a large amount of irony in this. Both the President and the Speaker were as close to full-time political strategists as had ever been born. Both understood the importance of a future-oriented vision. Yet they were still mired in the work left over from the past—as we and administrations before us had been also. This was necessary, no doubt. But cleaning the house of remnants from the 1960s and 1970s and shoring up the fiscal foundation weakened in the 1980s were far short of building a cathedral.

Further, both the President and the Speaker understood that a new governing coalition was yet to be stably formed. Both meant to shape and lead it. Both were excellent tacticians. And yet both, at crucial points in their tenure, had underattended to the essential political center. They had thus opened wide the possibility that—unless one or the other was successful in attracting the support of the middle—someone else would restructure the base, and start shaping the new cathedral. At a minimum, each of the co-Presidents postponed for several years—and perhaps missed forever—the chance to lead a new governing majority.

While the co-Presidents were missing their realignment opportunities, it seemed to me that the "vision thing" was still struggling to be reborn. I felt that people in the broad middle of the American electorate had a latent hope for it in their souls. Admittedly, that was not often evident. The quiet majority of political centrists tended to be stylistically moderate. They were not naturally comfortable wearing their bolder aspirations on their sleeves. Their romanticism and idealism typically showed only rarely and indirectly in surprising popular upwellings of a collective yearning. These signs of a latent yearning were diverse: the widespread expression of loss after the Kennedy assassination, not merely at the time, but for a generation thereafter; the revival of evangelical Christianity, in the context of continuing infatuation with the promise of technology; the near-euphoric interest in Colin Powell as a potentially effective and healing leader; or even, amidst the degeneration of popular video fare, the unexpected box-office success of films like *Field of Dreams.*

I believed (and still believe) that the broad, often silent, middle must continue to hope for the cathedral to be built in a field of dreams. In the period of the Gingrich-Clinton co-presidency, however, the middle had no choice but to indulge the political performances of its two somewhat childlike leaders, one with a seemingly insatiable need for attention, the other with an unquenchable thirst for approval. And often, as the nation waited for serious work to be done—hoping for inspiration—it was offered only the unfortunate image of two co-Presidents throwing rocks at each other, creating a field of stones.

That is all the public saw until President Clinton appreciated that the uncompromising stand of the rock-throwing House Republicans had given him a historic second chance. It was with that second chance in view that he borrowed the imagery of President Reagan, assumed the dignity of an adult President, offered the hand of centrist bipartisan reasonableness, and leaned to the right with his memorable declaration, "The era of big government is over."

Still, that was not credible. It alone would probably not have been enough to give him a serious chance of undoing the strategic error he had made with his earlier lean to the left. But then, he got another gift. In the Republican presidential primaries, when the Buchananites stormed the castle, rocks were hurled in every direction. And, through no act of his own, President Clinton was allowed to seem above the fray. Only a band of Republicans was left wounded in the field of stones.

15

Reviving the Sensible Center:

Beyond the Politics of Polarization

THE FIELD OF STONES had come to seem painfully unpromising to many. It was strewn with the wreckage of a political melee.

The political "revolution" of 1994–95 was thought by its supporters to have promised a historic shift, as had the Reagan Revolution before. By early 1996, it seemed threatened with possible reduction to an interesting footnote. Buchananites, Forbesians, Gingrichians, and establishmentarians fought one another to less than the sum of their parts. The wandering Clintonites welcomed the chance to climb atop the rubble and scavenge for opportunity to renew their political strength, as if that alone were sufficient reason for being. Whatever one's politics, the sight was far from uplifting.

I knew that the picture would improve in time. But looking at the field of stones, one might have wondered, as I did: How much lasting damage has been done? How on earth is the cathedral to be built? What ever happened to the field of dreams? And for those inclined toward the politics of the center: What would suggest that we might see the revival of a sensible center—willing to put polarizers aside, stop the false posturing, end the unproductive stalemate, govern, and move America forward?

For me, answers emerged by considering three related subjects, to which I now turn: first, the Colin Powell phenomenon of 1995; second, lessons from the journey from Ronald Reagan through Clinton-Gingrich; and third, steps that might be taken to renew a sensible centrist balance. With these in better focus, one might clarify one's view of the future—where the American system might best go from here, and who should be "in control."

With its charges and countercharges about alleged "extremism," presidential politics grew so ugly in the 1996 primary season that it was easy to forget what many Americans had seen as a shining moment only months before. A large part of the national electorate—bigger than any supporting the actual primary contestants—had been infatuated with the possibility of electing a self-described "sensible centrist" as their President. The phrase was coined by retired four-star general Colin Powell in introducing his political persona to what became a euphorically enthusiastic public.

It is worth pausing for a moment to consider Powell's chosen phrase, the "sensible center." Labels along the American political spectrum often have questionable meaning. Pat Buchanan's anti-corporate and protectionist rhetoric, for example, did not fit a modern "conservative" on the "right." Yet that is what he was routinely said to be (until he was, for a while, relabeled an "extremist" by his opponents and the media). Similarly, the establishment's Steve Forbes was a somewhat unlikely "populist," and Kansas's Bob Dole was hardly a product of the "establishment." In some respects, the application of such labels has seemed absurd. I do not propose to try to straighten out the labels. I'm not even inclined to think it would be good to do so. I mean simply to note that Colin Powell performed a useful linguistic service by adding the adjective "sensible" when referring to the "center."

In America, centrists comprise a larger portion of the American population than in most societies. Their relative importance is underrepresented by the media's attention to the political extremes. Centrists are neither statists nor pure free-marketeers. In policy terms, they occupy the broad and relatively stable American "middle." That is, they are generally pluralistic and market-oriented. At the same time, they are pragmatic when government action is required to advance or protect democratically defined public interests. Yet, the significant characteristic of American centrists is often less a matter of policy than a matter of mental attitude, posture, and tone. As suggested by the adjective "sensible," centrists (or "moderates") are open to persuasion by empirical evidence, respectful of others' rights to hold differing views, and willing to compromise as part of the democratic process in order to avoid unproductive stalemate. They are not ideologues and are ordinarily not angry or alienated. (When they become alienated and angry, they may earn the label "populist.") In a pluralistic democracy, the sensible center's habit of mind is generally necessary to make the system come together and work.

That said, it helps explain one element of the unusual Powell appeal. In the rock-throwing stalemate of the Clinton-Gingrich co-presidency, the public yearned increasingly for the reappearance of a sensible center to help move things forward. People wanted an adult to calm the rock-throwers.

But there was obviously more to the Powell appeal than just that. The sudden upwelling of that appeal was almost unprecedented. As Powell began his twenty-five-city tour in September of 1995, he was reminiscent of only one other similar phenomenon. He appeared to be on the verge of replicating the strategy of another popular former four-star general, Dwight Eisenhower. (I took one of our kids to see the Powell whistle-stop tour as my father had taken me to see Ike's. The only difference was that instead of a train station, Powell's stop was at our local bookstore.) As a possible national leader, it seemed that Powell not only could help mend the most serious tear in America's social fabric, the racial divide. He also could reinforce positive American values. Although opposed by many on the right, he appealed to creative conservatives like Bill Kristol, Jack Kemp, and Bill Bennett, all of whom expressed support for his candidacy. And he had the potential to help build a new governing coalition with a responsible center as an essential contributing part. This was the kind of coalition that had needed building since the end of the Reagan administration, the coalition that President Bush and co-Presidents Clinton and Gingrich had missed their chances to consolidate.

Powell, of course, decided not to run in the 1996 primaries. But the widespread popular reaction to the very possibility of his candidacy was, by itself, significant. It was significant not principally because Powell was a black (who, like Ronald Reagan, simply identified himself as "an American"). In political terms, the significance of the Powell phenomenon went well beyond that. It was a useful reminder of several basic points that had been overlooked for some time.

First, it was possible to be simultaneously "strong" and "moderate," "principled" and "sensible," a "leader" and a "centrist." These were not mutually exclusive. Second, one did not have to be a hard-right conservative to embody and affirm traditional American values. Third, pandering to extremes was not a requirement for popularity. Fourth, there was still a potentially powerful center at the heart of the American political system. Indeed, polls then showed that there were more self-identified "moderates" than "conservatives." And finally, anyone interested in building a stable and creative majority coalition would have to include a large portion of the sensible center within that coalition in order to govern effectively. That is, anyone interested in governing for serious public purposes— not just for personal ego-gratification or a principled journey off a cliff—was well advised to attend to the center.

The system badly needed to remind itself of these basic points. And, for a moment, it had done so.

While the Powell phenomenon was one useful reminder, the lesson about the importance of the center was to be found throughout the journey from Ronald Reagan to Clinton-Gingrich. Indeed, most of the legislative successes of the Reagan years—including the 1981 and 1986 tax rate cuts—were made possible by the center. And the failures in attempting to legislate many of the more radical elements of the Reagan revolutionary program were also a compelling testament to the power of the center. Notwithstanding President Reagan's strong ideological preferences, high personal popularity, and forty-nine-state election win, he was obliged to move to the middle.

The record on that is clear. The evidence ranges from the tax increases of 1982, 1983, 1984, and 1987 to the Social Security compromise; and from the inability to advance Constitutional amendments on school prayer or abortion to the failure to cut the overall size of government. President Reagan clearly understood, as Governor Reagan also had, that in order to govern, he had to compromise with the broad American middle. The identical lesson had been demonstrated again, by negative example, in the Clinton-Gingrich co-presidency. By failing to seize the available middle ground, the two produced little more than unproductive stalemate.

Of course, the importance of the center is not the only significant lesson to be gleaned from the experience of the recent past. Indeed, there is an equally important lesson that may seem to cut against the first. It is, quite simply, that populist anxieties and concerns must be attended to when they represent the views of a substantial portion of the electorate. To put the point more colloquially, when large numbers of people scream "Send 'em a message!" the system must "get it."

The failure to attend to that rule proved costly to us in the Bush administration in the presidential election of 1992. Similarly, it proved costly to the Democratic establishment in the congressional election of 1994, and to the Republican center in the primary contests of early 1996. Conversely, active attention to populist interests helped account for the Reagan-Bush election victories in 1980, 1984, and 1988, just as it did the enactment of the 1981 and 1986 tax rate reductions. One way or another, broadly based populist interests have made it clear that they are forces to be reckoned with.

For a governing coalition to remain effective, a balance must be struck and restruck. Moderates cannot allow their sometimes aloof concern for responsible and orderly governance to blind them to populist grievances. To do so risks provoking an angrier form of populist reaction that may, for a time, make responsible governance impossible. However obvious this point may seem—and it does seem rather obvious—it is one that the centrist establishment periodically tends to overlook.

Of course, even when one recognizes the need for a centrist-populist balance, it is sometimes difficult to move forward effectively. Take, for example, the populist interest in smaller government that has been evident in the past two decades. Since many centrists have also preferred a somewhat smaller government, there may seem to have been an opportunity for an easy populist-centrist consensus. Indeed, both centrists and populists have, from time to time, railed against "big government." The practical problem has shown itself rather quickly, however. It has become visible every time the political system has tried to address the inescapable particulars of shrinking "big government."

Many of the same populists and centrists who might have agreed on the desirability of shrinking government have found they also agree on protecting many of government's core programs. They have not been willing to make substantial cuts in

defense, law enforcement, student aid, transportation infrastructure, public health and safety, biomedical research, Social
Security, Medicare, and a host of other programs. These are
programs for which there is a federal logic and, more to the
point, a relatively direct benefit for the broad American middle.

That brings me to another clear lesson of the journey from
Ronald Reagan to Clinton-Gingrich. Call it "big" or not, government of about the current size seems here to stay for quite a
while. I recognize that is an unwelcome thought for many.
There are, obviously, some politicians who talk simplistically
about cutting government in half, some genuine libertarians
who wish that government would be even smaller, and some
alienated anti-modernists who might be happy to return to the
woods. Such views naturally command media attention, especially when linked with verbal (or actual) bomb throwers. Yet
they are the views of a small minority. They should be afforded
the respect that all ideas deserve in a free society. But there
should be no doubt about what experience has demonstrated:
The specific ideas necessary to make radical cuts in modern
American government consistently fail the test of public ac-
ceptability.

The reality is that the American government is as big as it
is, acting in the areas that it does, primarily because a substantial majority of Americans wants it roughly so. The two Reagan
terms could not shrink "big government." The congressional
revolution of 1994 could not shrink it. And most telling of all,
to my mind, is this one fact: Even among themselves, after their
big victory in 1994, the "revolutionary" House Republicans
could not agree to shrink government to anything remotely like
the level their rhetoric implied. After trying to turn the budget
up, down, and inside out, the most radical spending reduction
plan they could agree upon was a plan that, had it been enacted
and implemented, would still have left the federal government
at almost 20 percent of GDP.

Indeed, after all the huffing and puffing in the great budget battle of 1995 and early '96, the difference between the
plans offered by President Clinton and the Republican Congress was only about 1 percent of GDP. (It would have been
even smaller if, as many thoughtful Republicans would have
done, a slightly higher spending percentage was accepted in
trade for more market-oriented policies guiding that spend-

ing.) Such percentages may not seem meaningful to most people. But it is instructive to know that both the President's plan and the Congress's plan, if fully implemented, would have left the federal government at a higher percentage of the overall economy than it was in the era of President Johnson's Great Society. Clearly, if America had been in an "era of big government," it was nonsense to suggest that it would soon be "over."

There is a final lesson to be drawn from the experience of the recent past, before looking to the future. It is simply this: All the fighting over the size of government often seemed to miss what many Americans took to be more vital concerns. I do not mean to suggest that Americans did not care about foolish and burdensome regulatory intrusions, high tax rates, inefficient and ineffective programs, unresponsive bureaucracies, and other such sins that defined "big government." They certainly did, and still do. But these were often infuriating sources of contemptuous disdain rather than basic causes of human concern. They were easy targets for the expression of a more diffuse frustration.

More fundamentally, people cared—and still care—about the kind of everyday worries that candidate Clinton had recognized with his "I feel your pain" and "putting people first," or that candidate Buchanan recognized with his emphasis on American values and putting "America first." Such worries ranged from the loss of health insurance to the possible loss of a job; from declining opportunities for children to the increasing burdens of old age; from high crime rates to illegal immigration; and from the rise of unconventional life-styles to the risks of rapid change.

For real people, such issues had concrete meaning, whereas the size of government was an abstraction. Getting the fiscal deficit under reasonable control was, and remains, important. For a large number of big problems, it is a precondition to addressing them seriously. But that is very different from actually addressing them.

A variation of this point was well made by Herbert Stein, former chairman of the Council of Economic Advisers and a fellow of the conservative American Enterprise Institute. In the midst of the "revolutionary" debate on the size of government, he said:

I would like the government to be smaller. . . . But would that solve any serious problem? Would there be less crime? Would our children be better educated? Would fewer children be brought up without loving, responsible care? Would there be less racial antagonism? . . . It is the failure to deal with these problems, rather than the size of the federal government, that gives cause for worry about the future of the American society.

Or to put the matter yet another way: With eyes fixed only on the size of the budget, it may be hard to see the way toward fulfillment of the Dream.

With these few lessons in mind, however, one might have some reason to feel a bit more comfortable about what recent history may suggest for the future—and for the possibility of getting beyond the politics of polarization.

At this writing, neither party has officially nominated its candidate for President, although the nominees seem certain. The immoderate polarizers will be out of the Republican race. But it is not yet clear what influence they may have upon the campaign. Who will win the November elections is, of course, undetermined. However, the following seems quite likely. A candidate who will have campaigned in a way that appeals to the center will win the presidency. Polarizing influences will remain strong in the Congress. The issue of how the newly elected leaders will choose to work with one another—and how much influence the polarizers will be allowed to have—will be wide open. And, ridiculous as it may seem, knowing exactly who will be President, Speaker, and Majority Leader should not change very much what recent history suggests will be appropriate in that circumstance.

Whoever fills these high public offices will have to face an early decision: whether to share in governing, or merely to posture in office and continue the politics of polarization. If the choice is to posture and polarize, then we will simply have to wait for the corrective action of yet another election. But if the choice is to build a stable coalition that is capable of governing, then the historical perspective provided here would suggest one general course of action. It is to seize the consensus that is there to be grasped, show the public that their chosen leaders and representatives can act sensibly from time to time, solidify a coalition that includes much of the center, stop the rock throwing, and get about the business of building the cathedral. This course will make sense, in my opinion, whether the newly elected leaders of the executive and legislative branches include a centrist needing to reach outward, or a person from the "extreme" needing the center in order to govern—or, as seems quite possible, both.

Slightly more specifically, my perspective would suggest that the newly elected President should do four things to begin to return a degree of sensibleness to American governance. These four do not amount to a bold agenda. That can and will come in time. These are simply a sensible way to start.

First, the newly elected President should get the debilitating budget dispute settled quickly and out of the way. Second, he should seek quick enactment of a small number of highly visible initiatives that speak more directly to the real problems ordinary Americans are worried about—including, especially, their sense of economic insecurity. Third, he should assume moral leadership in an area where he has a reasonable chance of being credible. And fourth, he should start building the public store of intellectual capital in a way that can inform the larger debate about how best to advance the American Dream. I'll now say a bit about each of these four that may help give them more concrete meaning.

Unfortunately, there is no sensible way around the fact that where the newly elected leaders really must start is with the least attractive issue: the lingering fiscal mess. This is not a place to start because it is exciting or inspiring or even first in the public mind. It isn't. Nor does starting here have much chance of reducing public anxieties about the fears that recent populist candidates have attended to (fears that will also have to be addressed). The newly elected set of leaders should start here for a single practical reason: The fiscal problem will prove inescapable until it is addressed.

The deficit has recently moved back toward a historically acceptable share of GDP, and some people are already putting their heads back in the sand. But the burden of debt is heavy. And the problem is far from over.

With rising entitlement costs and the looming retirement of the baby-boom generation, the long-term fiscal problem promises to get worse, not better, if left unattended. The Federal Reserve and financial markets will not allow it to be ignored. And more attractive issues of public policy will simply not be addressed until this is out of the way. That will be true whether one's policy attraction is toward privatized welfare and Social Security, or universal health insurance coverage, or a wall around the United States, or a flat tax, or any other of the bold proposals recently bandied about. Until the fiscal problem is addressed, it will continue to prevent effective initiative on almost everything else of significant domestic policy interest.

Leaders should start with the fiscal problem for another important reason. The election year is likely to offer only polarized posturing and, perhaps, a few token compromises. But after the election the fiscal problem will again be ripe for a relatively serious intermediate solution. And the country would welcome a sign that its elected officials can come together on something serious.

On the day after his election, at the very start of the honeymoon period, the newly elected President could convene the congressional leadership in a spirit of bipartisanship. He could and should then credibly say to the leaders and the public, "We are unlikely to do anything else constructive until we bring the long-term fiscal deficit under reasonable control. We may not like that, but that is an inescapable practical fact. It is time to act like adults and settle this issue. It has been negotiated and negotiated and negotiated. It should be settled not later than inauguration day, so that we can start the new presidential term by getting on to other important issues on the national agenda."

Whoever is elected President should be able to achieve a multi-year budget agreement in short order. If the newly elected President is Senator Dole, he should simply ask for and sign an updated or improved version of the budget plan that the Republican Congress passed (and President Clinton vetoed) in 1995. And if President Clinton is reelected, he would be well advised to say that if the bipartisan leadership group cannot do better within sixty days, they should simply agree to split the difference between the last Clinton and congressional proposals of early 1996.

The dollar difference between those proposals was almost trivial in relation to both the size of the fiscal problem and the size of the national economy. Over seven years, the major differences in projected savings were: about \$125 vs. \$170 billion for Medicare; and about \$100 vs. \$145 billion for welfare and Medicaid. On an annual basis, each of these differences amounts to less than one thousandth the size of the national product. With good will, and seriousness of purpose, such differences (along with the similarly manageable differences on discretionary spending and tax cuts) could be fairly split without much difficulty. Admittedly, good will is itself a scarce resource. But it is highest in the aftermath of a presidential election. And if good will were drawn upon constructively, the dollar differences could be settled in a matter of days or weeks, not months.

There is, however, one significant difference between the Clinton and Republican plans that went beyond the matter of dollars. Though not entirely a financial issue, it would have to be attended to in order to settle the differences on the numbers. The issue had to do with the nature of the federal welfare responsibility, and the extent to which it should be decentralized to the states. Here, too, there was an available compromise that was not grasped amidst the Clinton-Gingrich stalemate. It was a partial decentralization of welfare and Medicaid, developed and agreed to by a bipartisan majority of the nation's governors.

Again, the newly elected President could credibly set a sixty-day deadline and say that if the federal leaders cannot do better in that time, they should accept the compromise recommended by the governors. The governors' proposal may be as flawed as the average compromise. Yet since the governors would assume lead responsibility under it, they have no reason to recommend an approach they might think would fail. There is no longer a basic value conflict between the national government and the states; and the mood of the country clearly favors decentralization. Like the overall budget compromise, this is one where the Nike motto should prevail: *Just Do It.*

Before leaving the budget stalemate, it is important to note that neither the Clinton budget plan nor the Republican budget plan would fully solve the long-term fiscal problem. Both plans were "back-loaded." That is, they postponed the largest portion of their restraint until years six and seven. This left them subject to future political erosion. And neither plan addressed the looming problem of Social Security finance. At the very start of the term, a split-the-difference solution would be constructive regardless. It would allow the claim legitimately to be made that a reasonable degree of fiscal control had been achieved. It would be of some help economically. At least as important, it would help restore a degree of confidence. And it would free up the process for the serious consideration of other important issues.

With a medium-term budget agreement settled, however, I would not recommend turning immediately to the more contentious issues of big government vs. no government that have led to stalemate in the politics of polarization. I would suggest turning to the second element of the four-part approach to a new sensibleness. That is, enacting a small number of visible initiatives that address problems which are of serious and direct concern to ordinary Americans, but which can attract a working majority quickly.

The small number I would start with is about three. By conventional political standards, that may seem like a very small number. It may seem ridiculously unambitious. But the number has been chosen advisedly. It is just large enough to allow a balanced portfolio of proposals. More important, it is a small enough number to allow the political system to pass the walk-while-chewing-gum test. That is a challenge that has not always been mastered. And if the newly elected President is able to demonstrate early success with two or three of these visible and relevant initiatives, that will provide momentum and political support to help advance the next set of issues that he may wish to put high on the national agenda—initiatives that are far more ambitious, perhaps, than the first set.

With seemingly endless political discussion of budgets and philosophy—without any apparent resolution—it is understandable that many Americans have grown impatient. Some have turned cynical. Others have withdrawn. And some have just wanted to "change," "do something," "do *anything!*" This last reaction stirs a memory of a theme from Andrew Lloyd Webber's hit musical *Joseph and the Amazing Technicolor Dreamcoat.* With a poignant mixture of sadness and hope, a sometimes frustrated Joseph concludes:

> *The world and I, we are still waiting,*
> *Still hesitating. Any dream will do.*

. . .

I would not go so far as to say any dream will do. And I would not pretend that any two or three initiatives could, by themselves, give people a sense that the Dream was closer to fulfillment. But it does seem important to show that the political system can be relevant, attentive, and capable of making a constructive start. What needs to be done now is not so much to propose grandiose "solutions" with grand names. The public is sick of politicians posturing without producing. Before turning to more grandiose schemes, a degree of credibility needs to be restored. What needs doing, in the current historical context, is the quick enactment of focused initiatives that are understood to address directly people's worries about their own economic security and their children's future.

Exactly what few issues are chosen to start with is less important than that the start be perceived as relevant and successful. If it were mine to do (which, of course, it is not), I would begin with at least one issue that is relatively ripe for resolution, not an issue that is likely to keep the political system in unproductive stalemate.

An example of the type I would pick first would be something like the Health Insurance Reform Act sponsored by Republican Senator Nancy Kassebaum of Kansas. (Senator Kassebaum is one of several centrist senators who are retiring, partly out of frustration with the politics of polarization. But on this issue, she has managed to expand a centrist coalition and lead.) The Kassebaum bill, which passed the Senate 100–0, is so ripe for enactment it may have become law by the time this is published. If so, it will be an ironic confirmation of the poverty of polarized politics, and the possible revival of a sensible center. Indeed, one reason for the bill's likely enactment is that polarized politicians, having been locked in unproductive stalemate and looking toward the coming election, will have found an embarrassing need to show they can do *some*thing.

The bill addresses some of the most common causes of worry about the current health insurance system. It forbids exclusion from coverage for those with preexisting health problems. It guarantees renewability of insurance, improves portability from one job to another, and helps people leaving group plans maintain coverage as individuals. It does these important things without increasing federal bureaucracy or adversely affecting the deficit. It is not so extreme as the massively interventionist Clinton-Magaziner health plan on the "left." Nor is it as market-oriented as a voucher-based system proposed by some on the "right." It does not solve the health system's problems of inequity and cost. But it is a sensible and workable advance.

Of course, the bill has not been totally without opposition. It has been opposed, for example, by the original author of the "no new taxes" pledge. He has interpreted the possibility of voluntary private sector premium increases as a "tax increase." But even if there were to be such premium increases for some, most Americans would view them as a price worth paying for increased economic security and peace of mind. That is why most legislators have decided to put this curious definition of a tax aside. They are not letting it gain an absurd tyrannical hold on what would otherwise be sensible governance.

The next issue on my personal list for early action would be somewhat more controversial, but nonetheless doable in the honeymoon aftermath of the presidential election. It would begin to address another element of fear that is widespread among Americans. It is the fear that, in an increasingly competitive world, their children may be left behind by an education system that is not performing as it should. We are all familiar with the troubling statistics. Among American high school students, SAT scores have moved to levels so low that the scoring scale has had to be changed. On international tests in science and math, U.S. students score lower than students from most developed countries. Even the top quintile of American students underperforms in such comparisons. This situation has been widely criticized as intolerable. And, of course, in some schools there is not even the luxury of worrying about academic standards; they present more basic issues of physical survival. Yet, the traditional bureaucracy of the American education system has been chronically resistant to effective change.

Many analysts from both left and right have become convinced that the incentives for necessary change simply will not be sufficient without competitive pressure from a voucher-based system. In a system that includes vouchers, parents and students become more like consumers in a marketplace. They can shop around for the best educational product for their own particular circumstances. And producers of educational products can innovate and compete for clients by providing superior service, results, or value.

A new Republican President would appreciate market-oriented reasoning from the outset. But even if President Clinton were reelected, he might be persuaded to consider this point of view seriously after the election. It would allow him to reverse the strategic error of his first term by starting his second as a New Democrat with a conspicuous move to the center. More important, it would be right on the merits.

There are many ways to introduce voucher-based competition in education: as a mandatory state option in exchange for existing federal assistance; as an allowable option for remedial education programs; as a separate supplement for extra days that school systems may use to increase the foolishly short American school year. Exactly which type of voucher initiative may be negotiable will depend upon the election outcome. But the time has long since come to try some such initiative. The key is to agree on one, and thereby begin to provide a more effective stimulus for creative innovation and accountability.

In the same vein, a related initiative I would recommend for early action would be intended to address another widespread worry: older workers' fear of job restructuring and the inability to get retrained for the new kind of jobs that are to be available. For this problem, too, I would be inclined to introduce a more significant emphasis on vouchers and competition—in this case, by redesigning the existing job training programs, which are largely ineffective.

Both the education and retraining initiatives share an important substantive characteristic beyond those I have mentioned, which would be worth making clear: They shift the focus of debate away from the *size* of government, which, as I have suggested, is an overargued and underproductive focus. And they shift the focus toward the more relevant issue of the *way* in which governmentally financed purposes are best advanced. They accept a governmental financing responsibility; hence, they might be said to tilt to the "left." But they recognize the importance of market-oriented incentives and thus might be said to tilt to the "right." The combination of this left-right tilt is a sensible centrist balance.

Another important issue I would recommend for early

action is the restoration of a basis for confidence in Social Security. Some might consider this too hot to touch. And it certainly would be if it were approached in the spirit of polarized politics. But in a honeymoon spirit of bipartisanship, it might be possible to achieve a modest compromise. Its elements could include the following: a small mandatory set-aside of existing Social Security taxes for private investment (in approved mutual funds or, perhaps, IRA-like accounts) under the direct control of individual contributors; a small reduction in Social Security's wage-replacement rate for higher income earners; a modest increase in "sin taxes" on alcohol and tobacco to help close the remaining financing gap; a further increase in the retirement age; and a heavy dose of moral leadership to stimulate and legitimize new forms of employment for the growing population of healthier and longer-living older Americans.

As with the voucher proposals, this approach would offer something for those on the "right" who are more market-oriented—a privately managed savings pool. At the same time, it would put the publicly managed Social Security system on stronger financial and political footing to assure its long-term survival. And it would give those who are nervous or doubtful about Social Security's future a basis for renewed confidence. Again, it seems a sensible compromise—for a problem that will eventually prove inescapable, and that will certainly be easier to solve if addressed sooner rather than later.

If initiatives such as these do not rank so high with the new leadership, then other attractive and doable initiatives should be selected. The policy-making problem recently facing America has not been a shortage of sensible initiatives that might be taken. The problem has been a lack of seriousness about getting beyond the politics of polarization.

If the new leadership does decide to get serious about governing, however, they will need to organize a process that is intended to produce, not just posture. The leaders themselves should meet to agree on a manageable set of initiatives right after the election. They should set a timetable for legislative consideration and enactment of their chosen early-action initiatives. And they should personally give impetus to whatever negotiations are necessary in order to meet the timetable. But to repeat: The key is that the initiatives chosen must be understood to address people's real concerns directly, affirmatively, sensibly, and in a way that is capable of gaining support in the political middle. If they in fact meet these tests, they will also meet the other important test: They must be enacted relatively quickly.

In addition to quickly negotiating and enacting a budget agreement and a few meaningful programmatic initiatives, the newly elected President would be well advised to attend to the third heading under my four-part approach to renewed sensibleness. He should use the power of rhetoric and personal example to begin to address explicitly an entirely different dimension of America's collective problem: the moral dimension, often termed the issue of values. This may seem to be unrelated to the issues of "big government" that have recently been the focus of polarized politics. But it is clearly high on the public's list of concerns. It is fundamental to both economics and the quality of life. Failure to deal with it adequately has contributed to the general climate of anger, fear, and distrust. And this, in turn, has fed the frustration that has led many to lash out at the current all-purpose target: "government."

Widespread concern about values shows in public polls and private worries. For more than a decade, it has been expressed by Reagan Democrats, New Democrats, traditional conservatives, neoconservatives, and plain, ordinary, conventional, middling moderates. It is elaborated in the book that President Clinton called attention to when he wanted to reestablish his own appearance of concern, *Values Matter Most* by Ben Wattenberg. And it is reflected in the best-selling sales of Bill Bennett's *The Book of Virtues* and *The Moral Compass*. Clearly, a large bipartisan majority would welcome serious presidential attention to some part of the broad values problem. And equally clearly, the problem needs all the constructive attention it can get.

Indeed, this problem may be one of the few that is actually as large as, or even larger than, the expression of alarm it elicits. A serious case can be made that our society is suffering from a corrosive internal threat that is weakening it more fundamentally than its periodic bouts with flawed economic policy. Our value system seems to be in the process of degenerating. Since first publicly expressing concern about cultural problems in speeches on "corpocracy" and "now-now-ism," my own worries have only deepened. I would now put the matter starkly: We are edging toward what one might term de-civilization. While our

economy continues to grow, our civilization threatens to decompose.

By our "civilization" I do not mean fine arts, architecture,
music, and historical artifacts. To a degree, we underattend to
these; and that, as any good elitist would say, is lamentable. But
by "civilization" I mean something more basic, and more widely
relevant. I mean our system of transmitting constructive skills
and values across the generations. This system is every bit as
complex as our economic system, and even less well understood. In addition to our cultural inheritance, it includes
our families, communities, schools, churches, workplaces, peer
groups, role models, media, spiritual beliefs, and technological
links—the overlapping webs that help shape us, support us,
connect us, and give our lives meaning. It is this complex
system that seems, in some ways, on the verge of destructive
decomposition. And just as our economy suffered its Great Depression, if we let our value-transmitting system go unattended,
we could risk a Great De-civilization.

Part of the problem, no doubt, is that the media suggest
an excessively troubled reality by devoting disproportionate
attention to the negative. But even granting that, the facts are
disturbing. The institutions primarily responsible for civilizing
the next generation are in trouble. Among many groups, the
traditional family is becoming an irrelevant anachronism. Di-
vorce rates and single-parent families have risen dramatically.
Out-of-wedlock births among whites, only 2 percent in 1960,
now approach 25 percent. Among blacks the number is almost
70 percent. And no healthy alternative to the once-traditional
family has yet taken its place. The formal education system is
not doing its job. The informal education system features violence on the streets, gangsta rap on videos, and pornography
on the Internet. Howard Stern's and Dennis Rodman's best-
sellers are a modern substitute for Horatio Alger stories. With
apparent reason, America is said to be "dumbing down."

At the same time, America has come to embrace near-term
consumption at the expense of future-oriented saving, invest-
ing, and building. A culture of self-centered hedonism has
been fostered through advertising and the media, supported by
popularized ideologies from both left and right. Yet ours does
not seem a happy civilization. The teenage suicide rate has tripled
since 1960. Depression is common among young and old. The

American violent crime rate has grown to six times what it was in 1960. The percentage of citizens in prison in America is at a record level, higher even than in Russia, and ten times higher than in most Western industrial societies. Among supposedly civilized nations, the United States's murder rate is in a class by itself. Kids are randomly killing kids. Respect for the basic value of individual lives seems threatened. And subtler measures of interpersonal incivility are equally disturbing.

With all that said, it should be clear that presidential rhetoric and example can be but limited tools in a large and complex undertaking. They are tools, however, that must be used—and used constructively. In the television age, America's leaders are almost continuously visible. Their preachments, values, and conduct are under inspection and on display. For better or worse, their service as role models is inescapable. So just as voters should give weight to issues of character, those who are entrusted with office should give more careful thought to their performance as role models.

Indeed, they need to appreciate that, if they are not careful, they may actually do harm. The public has a sensitive eye for hypocrisy. Talk of family values, for example, is not likely to mix well with allegations of infidelity. Condemnation of greed is less effective when complemented by revelations of sharp financial transactions. Homilies on the importance of respect for law may be undermined by the appearance of obstruction of justice. Laments about a decline of civility are taken less seriously when uttered by participants in the politics of polarization. So a President should be careful not to preach what he (or she) cannot reliably practice. It not only risks the obvious political cost. More seriously, it compounds the problems of corrosive distrust and cynicism.

And since practices are often hard to change in adulthood, a President should probably confine his preaching to those good practices he has already made habitual. If he is a hard worker, he may perform a useful service by highlighting the importance of the work ethic. If older, he may usefully highlight the need to increase opportunities for older Americans to continue to contribute. If he is someone whose courage and commitment have allowed him to triumph over personal adversity, he might highlight the triumph of spirit more generally. And so the examples would go, on down the list of virtues.

When the society's basic value structure seems threatened, the public is not comfortable with a loose and uncertain relativism. A majority wants to see their President reaffirm the proposition that there are important American values that are right—whose absence is judged to be wrong. But at the same time, few want to see more political phoniness and empty posturing. The public has seen too much of it. What matters most, at this stage, I suspect, is that virtues be chosen for celebration with an eye toward their being consistently supported by the power of positive example.

All of this, however, is hardly enough to fulfill the public's desire to see further advancement toward the American Dream. Restoring fiscal responsibility, advancing initiatives to reduce the current sense of insecurity, supporting basic American values with considered rhetoric and the power of positive example—these should help restore a degree of confidence and balance. But Americans will clearly want more.

And America's leaders will want to provide that more, whether it be lower tax rates (which are needed), or improved opportunities for older workers (which are needed), or a bold effort to renew America's decomposing urban cores (which is needed), or any of the other issues waiting for a place on the national agenda. Indeed, the quest for the Dream will be a perpetually evolving subject for political debate. What has been suggested here is simply that a few basic things should be attended to early in the next presidency, before risking a return to the unproductive politics of polarization.

With the larger and inevitable debate in view, however, I would turn to the fourth part of the recommended approach to renewed sensibleness: building intellectual capital. That is, learning which governmental policies and programs (along with private sector advances in technology, productivity, and service delivery) are actually likely to help Americans achieve the Dream.

Over the past several decades, it has not really been a lack of dreams or grand schemes that America has suffered from. The frustration has been that with so many grand promises and trials, dreams have gone unfulfilled. If anything, America has jumped too quickly to national trials of bold ideas. We have done so before going through the kind of pilot testing, learning, and engineering that are common in successful efforts by the private sector, military, and technically based government agencies. Whether the Great Society or the supply-side revolution, there has been a tendency to leap before looking. Such grand initiatives have been adopted without anything like the careful buildup associated with such dramatic governmental successes as Project Apollo and Desert Storm.

And the scandal is that so little of positive value has been learned from the trials and the failure. We are almost as ignorant now as we were when Moynihan said of the Community Action Program, "The government did not know what it was doing." Yet this is three decades and several trillion dollars of expenditure later! And it is not just government that does not know, it is also most of government's critics. The scandal of our collective ignorance should not be allowed to continue.

There has, of course, been negative learning. Most Americans have come to recognize that the post-1960s form of the welfare state is not viable. Clumsy governmental intervention of the type associated with the Great Society has proven incapable of solving the problems it was meant to address. Open-ended universal entitlements have proved economically unsustainable. Hopes that a deep supply-side tax cut could be a self-financing panacea have been similarly discredited. But when it comes to the question of what actually does work to solve the problems Americans care about, there is very much less knowledge that is broadly accepted as valid. We have an abundance of conventional wisdom. But most of it is inadequate. That has to change.

Fortunately, amidst the field of stones, there is the making of at least a partial solution to the problem of our public policy ignorance. To learn what are, in fact, effective remedies for America's major problems, alternative trials need to be applied to comparable groups of people. That is, something approaching the experimental model must be roughly approximated in the world of public policy. And, within the limits set by a free society, that is exactly what may soon be possible. In its seemingly bumbling approach to self-correction, our political system is forcing itself to restructure its approach to problem solving. And, whatever may be the system's faults, the direction of its restructuring—capping expenditures, increasing private sector competition, and decentralizing to states—offers great potential for learning.

By capping the growth of federal expenditures, the political system would put a premium on finding new, more cost-effective approaches to problem solving. And it would soon make it evident (as it already should be) that it is impossible to satisfy public demands and expectations unless major technological breakthroughs are achieved. That alone should create some impetus for experimenting, evaluating, and learning. But the restructuring can do more. By creating opportunities for the private sector to compete for the chance to provide publicly subsidized goods and services, it would create powerful additional incentives for privately managed research, reengineering, and innovation. And further still, by decentralizing to states—transferring to them the responsibility for program design and management—a rough experimental framework would be created: "states as laboratories." Whether in educational renewal, crime prevention, retraining and reemployment of the elderly, welfare reform, urban recivilization, the creation of enterprise zones, or any other such important area of policy interest, states could be expected to differ in their approaches to problem solving. And in systematically observing the effects of these differing approaches, there is a wonderful opportunity to learn.

The restructuring alone, however, will not assure that America seizes this wonderful opportunity. Like almost everything else, learning requires the allocation of resources—even learning about the effects of publicly funded or subsidized activities. It requires attention to the design of alternative approaches to problem solving. It requires data gathering and measurement both before and after differing approaches are actually tried. And it requires systematic analysis of information suggesting causes and effects.

So, to help assure that this necessary learning takes place, the newly elected leaders should set aside a portion of the federal research and development budget for the specific purpose of evaluating and learning from "states as laboratories." And if the political tone of the time finds centralized management of such research an offensive concept, it could be turned over to a managing group under the collective control of the governors. What matters is that, one way or the other, a structure is established from which the society can learn.

Further, that structure should take advantage of the opportunity presented not only by states that are innovating, but also by the District of Columbia, which is in seemingly perpetual crisis. The District should be viewed as an opportunity for several reasons. As a decomposing urban core—the sometime "murder capital of the world"—it is symptomatic of a larger national problem. As the home of the federal government, its economy, infrastructure, and land use are, to a considerable degree, under the direct control of the Congress and the executive branch. And as the nation's capital, the District is a source of shame that left, right, and center all would wish to convert into a source of pride—what Newt Gingrich referred to as a "jewel."

It would be relatively easy to take the very best ideas that the new administration wishes to advance and focus discretionary federal resources on these ideas in a large-scale District trial. Such a large-scale trial could bring together an unprecedented combination of innovations in crime fighting, job creation, retraining, education, tax relief, housing, drug abuse prevention, welfare reform, volunteer activity, and so on. A national debate about urban de-civilization is certain to work its way back onto the American agenda sooner or later, by one means or another. The District trial might succeed or fail, in whole or in part. But whatever the results, they could be examined usefully in conjunction with evidence from other state and local experience in order to inform the larger debate.

And that, of course, is the more general point about trying to structure a way to learn. It is not a substitute for debate about what will best advance the Dream. That debate should and will go forward regardless. But it would be sensible if, instead of just the polarized posturing, the debate included a few relevant facts. What is recommended here is a means to ensure that, as the continuing argument about the Dream develops, there is an increasing body of empirical evidence to help inform the debate. The idea, very simply, is to try to increase the odds that America will not only dream, but will actually succeed.

This might be dismissed for its taking too long, or its reflecting too little confidence in the "solutions" that existing advocates already "know" to be right. But the reality is that the American Dream cannot be bought on the cheap. In one way or another, it requires serious investment. Americans will not be in a mood to make such investment until at least these four conditions are met: The existing fiscal imbalance must be brought under reasonable control. Worries about clear and present threats to economic security must be reduced. Confidence in governmental officials must be at least partially restored. And there must be some credible evidence that returns on additional public investment (or tax relief) would produce a positive return.

It is exactly these four conditions that are addressed by the four-part approach recommended here. The weakness and the strength of that approach can be summed up in a single sentence: It is only sensible.

EPILOGUE:

Looking for Heroes

THIS ESSAY BEGAN by noting that, at the start of the 1996 presidential campaign, politics seemed to be polarized. And the sensible center seemed to be missing in action, at least temporarily. I have offered a perspective on how that may have come to be the case. In response to the related question, "Who's in control," I have suggested that the answer is somewhat complicated. In some sense, it is to be found in the workings of the American political system more than in particular individuals, however important they may seem.

But I have suggested, further, that the system itself does not work as intended when the center is missing, or even just weakened. The practical fact is that the system cannot function effectively without the active engagement of the sensible center. The politics of polarization produces only stalemate and rock throwing. So I've outlined a four-part approach for reestablishing a degree of centrist balance at the start of the next presidential term. And I've suggested that adopting this approach would be in the best interest of newly elected leaders (including Newt Gingrich) whether they consider themselves centrists or not. More important, it would be in the best interest of the country.

At the same time, however, I have stayed away from offering an opinion, directly, on who such leaders should be. That is not my subject here. But having lamented the missing in action, I feel obliged to offer one final bit of perspective on the search for sensible centrist leadership.

Just as the size of government is, to a considerable degree, a reflection of the public will, so, too, is the quality of our public officials. For trite as it is to note, we do have the vote. In our democracy, we are all, in some sense, in a continuous process of sharing "control." And if we are dissatisfied, it is especially appropriate that we ask ourselves what types of people we might wish to have "in control"—holding together the big mercury ball.

In America, we are conditioned to look for heroes. As kids, many of us start out with cowboys. My first heroes happened to be TV cowboys like Hopalong Cassidy and the Lone Ranger. They seemed real enough to me. I then moved on to a baseball hero, Ted Williams; and then, in my teens, to a President. By 1980, I had outgrown most of my attraction to heroes. But then, like most Americans, I found myself grateful for the renewal of spirit that was inspired by yet one more confident hero in a white cowboy hat. It seems to be something we are trained to long for.

So it is natural, perhaps, that in seeking to advance a public policy perspective, many of us continue to hope—even if only unconsciously—for the political equivalent of the cowboy hero on a great white horse. It is immature. But we do it. And why not? A cowboy hero would make it all so much easier. He would inspire support of a new consensus without all the dirty work of conventional politics, without the ordinary pain of coalition building. Or so, at least, many of us may be inclined to think.

Yet, whether or not we're inclined toward solutions-by-heroes is probably academic. The reality is that the job that needs doing will have to be done the harder way. Even if there were would-be heroes who might ride into town atop Silver, hardly any of them would be credible. And few would be sensible centrists. Centrists tend to be more reserved in their public posture. Waving pistols or white hats in the air, as a great steed rises on its hind legs, is simply not in the character of most moderate personalities. Nor is it sufficient, in our pluralistic democracy, to accomplish the difficult task of holding a majority together in order to govern and build.

So what does that suggest about a quest for centrist leadership? Let me respond by returning to the American pastime for an elliptical answer.

. . .

As the fall baseball season approached in 1995, the Red Sox again had fans' hopes high. On Labor Day, the Sox were in first place, almost sure to win their division. Talk of getting World Series tickets had already begun in Boston. But the hardest tickets to get in all of baseball were tickets for the September 6 Baltimore Orioles home game.

On that Wednesday, the Orioles shortstop, Cal Ripken, Jr., did not get to sleep until 3:00 A.M. Five hours later, he awoke a little bit late and rushed to drive his daughter to her first day of school. That evening, after she and her younger brother threw out the first balls, Ripken surpassed the Lou Gehrig record he had tied the night before.

Ripken played, and played well, in his 2,131st consecutive major league baseball game. The next closest active major leaguer had played a mere 235 games consecutively. Until Ripken, no one ever had even come close to the Gehrig achievement. Set in 1939, Gehrig's record had been expected to stand forever. And it had gained a place of special poignancy in baseball memories for the words the dying Gehrig had struggled to say upon retiring from baseball, "Today, I'm the luckiest man on the face of the earth."

When Ripken's new record became official, at 9:20 P.M., halfway through the fifth inning, the whole country seemed to be watching. At Fenway Park, the Red Sox game was interrupted by a five-minute ovation when the Ripken news was posted on the scoreboard. In Baltimore, the standing ovation threatened to go on forever. Ripken was forced to take a victory lap around the perimeter of the Orioles' ballpark. The unforgettable scene symbolized yet another triumph of the American spirit.

The Camden Yards crowd was larger than the officially recorded sellout of 46,272. It included celebrities who ranged from Ripken's rookie-year manager, "the Earl of Baltimore" (Earl Weaver), to President Clinton (who was the victim of the night's only boos). But celebrities aside, Ripken attended to the ordinary fans. Instead of just receiving their applause in the way that most athletes would, he interrupted his triumphal lap again and again to stop and shake the hands of young kids and old friends, former teammates and current opponents, ballgirls and policemen, and virtually anyone who made the effort to reach—as if he were congratulating them. Across the nation, the overwhelming popular response seemed to confirm that most Americans were again hungering for something positive to cheer.

My son Jonathan (now called Jon) and I were fortunate to have been in the stands that night. We were not in the owner's box, as we had been when President Bush was in office. We were far from it—happy to be in the upper deck, in line with the left field foul pole, in section 376. Recalling our night at the sixth game of the World Series in 1986, we regretted that Willy (now called Will) couldn't be with us. He was finishing a special course in emergency medicine, before returning to college. Kath also had to miss the Ripken performance. She was preparing for an even bigger family event. Entering her seventh month of pregnancy, she was nurturing a new brother (now called Emmet) for Jon and Will. He was expected (and did in fact arrive) in early December.

With Jon's start of high school set for early the next morning, I had had an uneasy feeling about keeping him out late the night of the game. I had rationalized our going by hoping that the spirit of the evening might itself provide a useful lesson. It did not let me down.

When the game was over, Ripken was escorted back to the field by his father and mother for the postgame ceremonies. And when the conventional speeches were over, Ripken came to the microphone. In his flat, straightforward, understated way, he provided the lesson for the evening: "You are challenged by the game of baseball to do your very best, day in and day out, and that's all I've ever tried to do."

The do-your-best-day-in-and-day-out standard struck me immediately. It joined other echoes from my past. The Ripken standard began to reverberate. It was what President Bush had cited at the start of the budget negotiations, the standard he told the press his mother had pressed upon him since the age of six. It was the standard my parents had drilled into me, just as other dutiful parents, teachers, coaches, and mentors had done across the generations. Most compellingly for me, it was the standard our son Willy had set for himself as a guide for his own heroic recovery from a life-threatening illness.

When I drove Jon to school the next morning, I repeated the Ripken quote to make sure the lesson was not lost. But, of course, that was unnecessary. Ripken's words and performance spoke volumes that no parent could improve upon.

His extraordinary achievement was celebrated throughout the land as a triumph of the values that a majority of ordinary Americans still wished to heroize. Ripken was unlike much of the modern star culture. He was not cheap, sensational, self-promoting, or polarizing. He did not showboat. He was not a TV-created product or some screenwriter's manufactured cowboy. He was genuine. He was not the kind of slugging hero whose every at bat was a swing for the fences. He was steady. Serious, not cynical, he had the toughness and dedication to use his skills, day after day, to fulfill his responsibilities. His was a lesson for all seasons.

Returning now to the issue of our quest for heroes who might assume a degree of responsible control in the political arena, I would simply underline the obvious point: To help revitalize the center on which our political system depends, the Ripken model recommends itself.

Or, switching to another of my favorite metaphors, I would conclude by putting it this way: If we want to build the cathedral—or the city upon a hill—we will have to do it the old-fashioned way. We will need leaders who understand, as we ourselves must understand, the nature of the work that is to be done. It is work that requires clarity of purpose, steadiness of execution, and an ability to work with others. It is not work that is helped by ill-designed schemes, empty posturing, or childish rock throwing. It is work that has large aspirations and lofty purposes, which need to be made clear. But it is not work that seems romantic in its particulars. Visionary preachers and populist motivators have roles to play. But still, there is heavy lifting to be done. Viewed in the small, the job is routinely this: lugging stone after stone, day after day, fitting the pieces together. It is work for dedicated, steady, and sensible builders—whose consistent, cooperative, constructive effort can give shape to the larger mission.

BIBLIOGRAPHIC NOTE

THIS IS NOT a conventional academic-style set of notes. Some important source materials are not cited here. Among these are documents that comprise the public record of federal policy making: presidential speeches, messages, press releases, press conferences, budgets, legislative reports, economic reports, and the like, along with the associated media coverage. Although these are not specifically cited here, they are conveniently indexed in electronic retrieval systems that are readily accessible to the interested public. Source materials for most of the private meetings described here, however, are not yet publicly available. The meetings have been recounted by drawing directly from my own contemporaneous notes and memos. None of the quotations from the meetings has been invented or reconstructed (as has become fashionable in some quarters). Still, I recognize that some researchers may be interested in a more complete view of the context from which these quotes have been drawn. For them, I intend to provide copies of the relevant notes and memos to Harvard University, and to the Reagan and Bush presidential libraries.

The references that are included here represent selected influences upon my thinking and reminders of the context within which thoughts and actions developed. They are grouped in relation to a few key topics that frame the book's narrative and argument.

The American Dream

The book mentions "The American Dream" and "The American Romance" here and there along the way, as if in passing. But these concepts are fundamental. Without them, budgets and policies and political personalities lack both purpose and interest. A romantic conception of America's special mission has been at the core of America's identity from the very founding of the colonies. The Dream and the American Romance have been particularly important to the period and the presiden-

351

cies that are the focus of this book. And the domestic struggles over tax and budgetary policy in the latter part of the twentieth century have, in many respects, been mere proxies for a struggle about whether America remains committed to her larger dreams, and how American government should act to ensure that they may be fulfilled.

As a reminder of this larger perspective, perhaps the most important starting point is the concept of America as a shining "city upon a hill," "a light unto the nations"—for which one should see the original inspirations in Isaiah 42; Matthew 5; and John Winthrop's "A Model of Christian Charity," delivered aboard the *Arbella* (1630).

For America's related interest in the exploration of new frontiers, see: Ted Morgan, *Wilderness at Dawn: The Settling of the North American Continent* (Simon & Schuster, 1993); Frederick Jackson Turner, *The Frontier in American History* (1920); Richard White and Patricia Nelson Limerick, *The Frontier in American Culture* (University of California, 1995); Daniel J. Boorstin's trilogy, *The Americans: The Colonial Experience* (Random House, 1958), *The National Experience* (Random House, 1965), and *The Democratic Experience* (Random House, 1973), with an interesting gloss, for more popular consumption, in his interview with Tad Szulc in *Parade* magazine, July 25, 1993. And for the powerful metaphor of American exploration of space, boldly advanced by President Kennedy, reinforced by Presidents Johnson, Nixon, Reagan, and Bush, but now somewhat out of favor, see: Joseph P. Allen with Russell Martin, *Entering Space: An Astronaut's Odyssey* (Stewart, Tabori & Chang, 1984); Alan Shepard and Deke Slayton with Jay Barbree and Howard Benedict, *Moon Shot* (Turner, 1994); the movie *Apollo 13* (Universal, 1995); "Expeditions of the Human Spirit," *U.S. News & World Report*, July 11, 1994; and Tom Wolfe, *The Right Stuff* (Farrar, Straus & Giroux, 1979).

In addition to the pioneering and expansive conception of America's special mission, a commitment to inclusiveness has been central to the Dream—"Give me your tired, your poor, your huddled masses yearning to breathe free." The classic post–World War II view of America as an inclusive melting pot was reflected in John F. Kennedy's *A Nation of Immigrants* (Harper & Row, revised and enlarged edition, with an introduction by Robert Kennedy, 1964). Unfortunately, the melting pot tradition has also fallen out of favor. In the mid-1990s, it was threatened from the left by a separatist breed of multiculturalists interested in preserving individual ethnic identities, and from various populists of the left, right, and center, who were interested in limiting immigration and exploiting America's periodic tendency toward nativism. Defenders of the melting pot tradition were well represented, however, by: William J. Bennett, "Immigration: Making Americans," *Washington Post*, December 4, 1994; William J. Bennett and Jack Kemp, "The Fortress Party?" *Wall Street Journal*, October 21, 1994; Nathan Glazer, "In Defense of Multiculturalism," *New Republic*, September 2, 1991; Rush Limbaugh, radio broadcast on the state of the American Dream, July 4, 1993; Ned Martel, "I Hear America Assimilating," and Joel Kotkin, "Can We Reheat the Melting Pot?" in the *Washington Post*, July 3, 1994; Frederick Rose, "Muddled Masses: The Growing

Backlash Against Immigration Includes Many Myths," *Wall Street Journal,* April 26, 1995; Arthur M. Schlesinger, Jr., *The Disuniting of America: Reflections on a Multicultural Society* (Norton, 1992); and *Time* magazine, Special Issue, "The New Face of America: How Immigrants Are Shaping the World's First Multicultural Society," Fall 1993. For a view of actual immigrant life in the 1990s, see Sanford Ungar, *Fresh Blood: The New American Immigrants* (Simon & Schuster, 1995).

Among political advocates for the expansive, inclusive, opportunity-oriented version of the American Dream in the 1980s and 1990s, Jack Kemp has been a consistent leader. See his *The American Idea: Ending Limits to Growth* (American Studies Center, 1984), which is even broader in its reach than the related body of speeches by Ronald Reagan. Though Kemp and I have disagreed on the extent to which very large tax cuts would be self-financing, we have agreed on the importance of much else for fulfillment of the Dream: an overarching appreciation of American exceptionalism and the power of the human spirit, fundamental commitments to equal opportunity and political inclusiveness, along with market-oriented economic policies rooted in stable money and low marginal tax rates. Kemp consistently rejected, as I have done, the fashionable literature of the 1970s and 1980s, which spoke in terms of an alleged decline of America. The absurdity (or at least the prematurity) of the declinist perspective became widely evident in the early 1990s, as communism collapsed and America became the world's only superpower.

Still, without jumping to the extreme of American declinism, one would have to acknowledge that the American Dream suffered from a lesser late-twentieth-century letdown. It was not simply that America had failed, as Kemp correctly asserted, to bring the promise of Lincoln to black America. It was also that the Dream proved disappointing for much of middle America. See, for example, Jackie Calmes, "Satisfaction with Today Hides a Fear of Tomorrow," *Wall Street Journal,* March 8, 1996, citing responses from a *Wall Street Journal*/NBC News poll conducted by Peter Hart and Robert Teeter; Stanley B. Greenberg, *Middle Class Dreams: The Politics and Power of the New American Majority* (Times, 1995); Guy Gugliotta, "Scaling Down the American Dream," *Washington Post,* April 19, 1995, and the related public opinion poll performed for the Council for Excellence in Government by Peter Hart and Robert Teeter; *Newsweek*'s cover story, "Bye-Bye, Suburban Dream," May 15, 1995; Robert J. Samuelson, "How Our American Dream Unraveled," *Newsweek,* March 2, 1992, and "Great Expectations," *Newsweek,* January 8, 1996; "Reality Check: The Politics of Mistrust," a five-part series in the *Washington Post* (January 28–February 1, 1996), in which one might see especially Paul Taylor, "Fading American Dream Haunts WWII Generation" (February 1, 1996), and the underlying polling data compiled by Princeton Survey Research Associates for the *Washington Post*/Kaiser Family Foundation/Harvard University survey project (Kaiser Family Foundation, 1996); and David Whitman, "A Bad Case of the Blues," *U.S. News & World Report,* March 4, 1996.

There is a view offered by some traditional conservatives that observations of gloom are often intended to motivate remedial activism by government, and that public disappointment should be dismissed as childish. (See Irving Kristol, "America Dreaming," *Wall Street Journal*, August 31, 1995.) While there is a degree of reasonableness to this anti-romanticism, an underlying premise of this book is that negativism about America's promise should be dismissed. America is getting older, but the Dream is not and should not be. It is the Dream's very nature—and America's—that it must always offer a vision of expanding horizons and future success. This point of view is not merely a matter of romantic illusion. With enormous untapped technological possibility and an indomitable human spirit, the American Dream need not be viewed as beyond reach. It is a further premise of this book that the disappointment of recent years should be understood as a legitimate cause for concern, corrective inspiration, and remedial action.

Antecedents to President Reagan: Disappointing Presidencies from Kennedy Through Carter

This book uses Ronald Reagan's victory in 1980 as the starting point for its history. Though that has its logic, it is somewhat arbitrary. The Reagan presidency and the associated appeal of the Reagan Revolution did not appear out of the ether. While the narrative of the book does not attempt to address the origin of these, except in passing, I would note that my take on this would not give as much emphasis to the intellectual underpinnings of the conservative movement as some are inclined to do. Rather, I see the Reagan accession, in the first instance, as a reaction to the failure of the immediate prior presidency. Similarly, I see the appeal of the optimistic Reagan vision as a reflection of a yearning to return to the confident and hopeful American spirit last seen in the days of Camelot, and lost in the disappointments of the intervening string of presidencies. The references that follow relate only to this perspective.

For somewhat romantic pictures of Kennedy and the making of Camelot, one might see: Philip B. Kunhardt, Jr., ed., *Life in Camelot: The Kennedy Years* (Little Brown, 1988); Robert MacNeil, *The Way We Were: 1963 The Year Kennedy Was Shot* (Carroll & Graf, 1988); Theodore C. Sorensen, *Kennedy* (Harper & Row, 1965); the *U.S. News & World Report* cover story on the thirtieth anniversary of Kennedy's assassination, *"The Lost World of JFK: The America He Left Behind,"* November 15, 1993; and Theodore H. White, *The Making of the President 1960* (Atheneum, 1961). For less romanticized pictures, see: Henry Fairlie, *The Kennedy Promise: The Politics of Expectation* (Doubleday, 1973); Nigel Hamilton, *JFK: Reckless Youth* (Random House, 1992); Richard Reeves, *President Kennedy: Profile of Power* (Simon & Schuster, 1993); and Thomas C. Reeves, *A Question of Character: A Life of John F. Kennedy* (Free Press, 1991).

For the Johnson period's infatuation with government action and rational planning, and the counterpoint provided by the failures of Vietnam and the Great Society, see: Henry J. Aaron, *Politics and the Professors: The Great Society in Perspective* (Brookings, 1978); David Halberstam, *The Best and the Brightest* (Random House, 1972); Charles J. Hitch and Roland N. McKean, *The Economics of Defense in the Nuclear Age* (Harvard, 1961); Joint Economic Committee, Congress of the United States, Subcommittee on Economy in Government, *Economic Analysis and the Efficiency of Government, Hearings* (GPO, September 25 and 30, 1969, and October 6, 1969), and *Report* (GPO, February 9, 1970); Stanley Karnow, *Vietnam: A History* (Viking, 1983); Doris Kearns, *Lyndon Johnson and the American Dream* (Harper & Row, 1976); Robert McNamara, *In Retrospect: The Tragedy and Lessons of Vietnam* (Times, 1995), along with Paul Gigot, "McNamara Reopens the Liberals' War," *Wall Street Journal*, April 21, 1995, for an interesting commentary on the outrage that greeted McNamara's book three decades after the controversial period on which he reflected; Allen J. Matusow, *The Unraveling of America: A History of Liberalism in the 1960s* (Harper & Row, 1984); and Daniel Patrick Moynihan, *Maximum Feasible Misunderstanding* (Free Press, 1970).

For the often-forgotten successes and the much-remembered failures of the Nixon period, see: Jonathan Aitken, *Nixon: A Life* (Regnery, 1993); Stephen E. Ambrose, *Nixon: The Triumph of a Politician, 1962–1972* (Simon & Schuster, 1989), and *Nixon: Ruin and Recovery, 1973–1990* (Simon & Schuster, 1991); Carl Bernstein and Bob Woodward, *All the President's Men* (Simon & Schuster, 1974); Vincent J. and Vee Burke, *Nixon's Good Deed: Welfare Reform* (Columbia, 1974); Richard M. Cohen and Jules Witcover, *A Heartbeat Away* (Viking, 1974); Seymour M. Hersh, *The Price of Power: Kissinger in the Nixon White House* (Summit, 1983); Walter Isaacson, *Kissinger: A Biography* (Simon & Schuster, 1992); Aaron Latham, "Seven Days in October," *New York* magazine, April 1974; Daniel Patrick Moynihan, *The Politics of a Guaranteed Income* (Random House, 1973); Richard Nixon et al., *The Presidential Transcripts* (Dell, 1974); William Safire, *Before the Fall: An Inside View of the Pre-Watergate White House* (Doubleday, 1975); Theodore H. White, *The Making of the President 1968* (Atheneum, 1969), and *The Making of the President 1972* (Atheneum, 1973); Garry Wills, *Nixon Agonistes: The Crisis of the Self-Made Man* (Houghton Mifflin, 1970); and Bob Woodward and Carl Bernstein, *The Final Days* (Simon & Schuster, 1976).

The drama of the breakdown of (or assault on) traditional authority structures in the period from Kennedy's assassination through Johnson and Nixon is captured in Charles R. Morris, *A Time of Passion: America 1960–1980* (Harper & Row, 1984); and, with less intellectualization, in such movies as *Dazed and Confused* (Gramercy, 1993) and Oliver Stone's distorted but dramatically forceful trilogy, *JFK* (Warner Brothers, 1991), *Platoon* (Orion, 1986), and *Nixon* (Disney, 1995).

For the less trying Ford-Carter interlude, see: James Cannon, *Time and Chance: Gerald Ford's Appointment with History* (HarperCollins, 1994); Hamilton Jordan, *Crisis: The Last Year of the Carter Presidency* (Putnam, 1982); Richard Reeves, *A Ford Not a Lincoln* (Harcourt Brace Jovanovich,

1975); and Robert Shogan, *Promises to Keep: Carter's First 100 Days* (Crowell, 1977).

For perspectives on the presidency as an evolving institution in this period, see: Emmet John Hughes, *The Living Presidency* (CM&G, 1973); Richard E. Neustadt, *Presidental Power: The Politics of Leadership, with Reflections on Johnson and Nixon* (Wiley, 1976); Roger B. Porter, *Presidential Decision Making: The Economic Policy Board* (Cambridge, 1980); and Arthur M. Schlesinger, Jr., *The Imperial Presidency* (Houghton Mifflin, 1973).

Reaganomics and the Reagan-Bush Presidencies

The Reagan electoral victories are well reported in: Elizabeth Drew, *Portrait of an Election: The 1980 Presidential Campaign* (Simon & Schuster, 1981); Peter Goldman and Tony Fuller, *The Quest for the Presidency 1984* (Newsweek/Bantam, 1985); Jonathan Moore, ed., *Campaign for President: The Managers Look at '84* (Auburn House, 1986); and John F. Stacks, *Watershed: The Campaign for the Presidency 1980* (Times, 1982). The shifting political idea structure in which Reaganism came to fruition is reflected in: Sidney Blumenthal, *The Rise of the Counter-Establishment: From Conservative Ideology to Political Power* (Times, 1986); Charles Murray, *Losing Ground: American Social Policy, 1950–1980* (Basic, 1984); and Randall Rothenberg, *The Neo-Liberals* (Simon & Schuster, 1984).

As for Reagan the man and his presidency, there is an embarrassment of riches. An illustrative sample of widely differing perspectives (each with its own truth to offer) would include: Lou Cannon, *President Reagan: The Role of a Lifetime* (Simon & Schuster, 1991); Jane Mayer and Doyle McManus, *Landslide: The Unmaking of the President, 1984–1988* (Houghton Mifflin, 1988); Peggy Noonan, *What I Saw at the Revolution* (Random House, 1990); Donald T. Regan, *For the Record* (Harcourt Brace Jovanovich, 1988); Lester M. Salamon and Michael S. Lund, eds., *The Reagan Presidency and the Governing of America* (Urban Institute, 1984); and Garry Wills, *Reagan's America: Innocents at Home* (Doubleday, 1987); along with the presumably excellent, but still-to-be-completed, Reagan biography by Edmund Morris (endorsed, sight unseen, on the strength of Morris's work on Theodore Roosevelt). These are but a few of the many books that have grown out of the Reagan Revolution. If supply-side economics had no other clear effect, it could at least take credit for having spawned a substantial publishing industry among insiders, advocates, and critics.

The following is a selection of some of the more serious work that has focused especially on Reaganomics. It is by both friends and foes of the Reagan Revolution, presented simply in alphabetical order by author: Martin Anderson, *Revolution* (Harcourt Brace Jovanovich, 1988); Laurence I. Barrett, *Gambling with History: Reagan in the White House* (Doubleday, 1983); Robert L. Bartley, *The Seven Fat Years* (Free Press, 1992); Jeffrey H. Birnbaum and Alan S. Murray, *Showdown at Gucci Gulch: Lawmakers, Lobbyists, and the Unlikely Triumph of Tax Reform* (Random House, 1987); Congressional Budget Office, "Assessing the Decline in the National Saving Rate" (GPO, April 1993); Martin Feldstein, ed., *American Economic Policy in the 1980s* (NBER/Chicago, 1994); William Greider, "The Education of David Stockman," *Atlantic Monthly*, December 1981, and *Secrets of the Temple: How the Federal Reserve Runs the Country* (Simon & Schuster, 1987); David Henderson, "Limitations of the Laffer Curve as a Justification for Tax Cuts," *Cato Journal*, Spring 1981; Paul Krugman, "Voodoo Revisited," *International Economy*, November/December 1995; Lawrence B. Lindsey, *The Growth Experiment: How the New Tax Policy Is Transforming the U.S. Economy* (Basic, 1990); Gregory B. Mills and John L. Palmer, *The Deficit Dilemma: Budget Policy in the Reagan Era* (Urban Institute, 1983); Max Moszer, "A Comment on the Laffer Model," *Cato Journal*, Spring 1981; Daniel Patrick Moynihan, "A Political Dunkirk," Address to the Tax Foundation, December 2, 1987, and *Came the Revolution: Argument in the Reagan Era* (Harcourt Brace Jovanovich, 1988); John L. Palmer, ed., *Perspectives on the Reagan Years* (Urban Institute, 1986); John L. Palmer and Isabel V. Sawhill, eds., *The Reagan Experiment* (Urban Institute, 1982), and *The Reagan Record* (Urban Institute, 1984); David G. Raboy, ed., *Essays in Supply Side Economics* (IRET, 1982); David A. Stockman, *The Triumph of Politics: Why the Reagan Revolution Failed* (Harper & Row, 1986); Wm. Craig Stubblebine and Thomas D. Willett, eds., *Reaganomics: A Midterm Report* (ICS, 1983); Jude Wanniski, "Taxes, Revenues, and the 'Laffer Curve,'" *Public Interest*, Winter 1978, and *The Way the World Works: How Economies Fail and Succeed* (Basic, 1979); Joseph White and Aaron Wildavsky, *The Deficit and the Public Interest: The Search for Responsible Budgeting in the 1980s* (University of California, 1989); and Seymour Zucker, "The Fallacy of Slashing Taxes Without Cutting Spending," *Business Week*, August 7, 1978.

At this writing, in the spring of 1996, there is not yet a book on President Bush and his presidency that seems right to me. I expect the President's personal diaries and notes to be an extremely valuable resource, when available. To date, the best personal insights, in my opinion, have been provided indirectly by Barbara Bush, *Barbara Bush: A Memoir* (Scribner, 1994). Contemporaneous evaluations of the early Bush presidency were provided by Colin Campbell and Bert A. Rockman, eds., *The Bush Presidency: First Appraisals* (Chatham, 1991); Michael Duffy and Dan Goodgame, *Marching in Place* (Simon & Schuster, 1992); and Lawrence J. Haas, *Running on Empty: Bush, Congress, and the Politics of a Bankrupt Government* (Business One Irwin, 1990). But these were largely overtaken domestically by the 1990 budget agreement, and internationally by the collapse of communism and the triumph of Desert Storm. The latter are well reported by Rick Atkinson, *Crusade: The Untold Story of the Persian Gulf War* (Houghton Mifflin, 1993); James A. Baker III with Thomas M. DeFrank, *The Politics of Diplomacy: Revolution, War, and Peace, 1989–1993* (Putnam, 1995); Michael R. Beschloss and Strobe Talbott, *At the Highest Levels: The Inside Story of the End of the Cold War* (Little, Brown, 1993); Jack F. Matlock, Jr., *Autopsy on an Empire* (Random House, 1995); and Bob Woodward, *The Commanders* (Simon & Schuster, 1991). Ironically, the extraordinary events abroad set a standard for the subsequent evaluation of Bush domestic policies. That is not necessarily inappropriate. But it is a standard that, in order to be met, requires a very much greater willingness to commit resources (as shown in fighting communism and the Gulf War) than was of interest to Republicans in the 1990s. In addition to this problem, exacerbated by the tax pledge, President Bush also had an inherent problem in trying to hold together the old Reagan coalition on social issues, while also preserving his natural appeal among moderates, as suggested by E.J. Dionne, Jr., "They Shouldn't Blame Bush," *Washington Post*, December 1, 1992, and Garry Wills, "George Bush, Prisoner of the Crazies," *New York Times*, August 16, 1992.

If anyone needs yet another reminder that presidential elections—whether winning or losing—are typically less than inspirational, one should see Jack W. Germond and Jules Witcover, *Whose Broad Stripes and Bright Stars? The Trivial Pursuit of the Presidency 1988* (Warner, 1989), and *Mad as Hell: Revolt at the Ballot Box 1992* (Warner, 1993).

The Clinton-Gingrich Co-Presidency

For the election-inspired domestic policy prescriptions of President Bush's opponents in 1992 (including their proposals for major tax increases), see: Ross Perot, *United We Stand: How We Can Take Back Our Country* (Hyperion, 1992); and Governor Bill Clinton and Senator Al Gore, *Putting People First: How We Can All Change America* (Times, 1992). For the related thinking of Clinton advisers, see also: Senator Al Gore, *Earth in the Balance: Ecology and the Human Spirit* (Houghton Mifflin, 1992); Will Marshall and Martin Schram, eds., *Mandate for Change* (Berkley, 1993); Leon E. Panetta, *Restoring America's Future: Preparing the Nation for the 21st Century* (GPO, 1981); and Robert B. Reich, *The Next American Frontier* (Times, 1983). And for the then-characteristic establishment view, see: Paul Krugman, *Peddling Prosperity: Economic Sense and Nonsense in the Age of Diminished Expectations* (Norton, 1994); and Peter G. Peterson, *Facing Up: How to Rescue the Economy from Crushing Debt and Restore the American Dream*, revised edition (Simon & Schuster, 1993). If nothing else, these references—representing the perspectives of Perotistas, Clintonites, and establishmentarians—underline the point that, in the early 1990s, America was not uniformly marching to the anti-tax right.

Among Clinton biographers, David Maraniss seems to be best to date, with *First in His Class: A Biography of Bill Clinton* (Simon & Schuster, 1995). For additional insight into the crucial first year of the Clinton presidency, see: Elizabeth Drew, *On the Edge: The Clinton Presidency* (Simon & Schuster, 1994); and Bob Woodward, *The Agenda* (Simon & Schuster, 1994). On the absence of a stable Clinton policy core, one might see: Paul A. Gigot, "Why 500 Americans Hold the Budget Key," *Wall Street Journal*, November 17, 1995; Anthony Lewis, "Nobody's at Home," *New York Times*, December 9, 1994; and Leon Wieseltier, "Total Quality Meaning," *New Republic*, July 19 and 26, 1993. And for the presence of an alleged Clinton tendency to prevaricate or cut it close on ethical matters, see David Brock, "Living with the Clintons," *American Spectator*, January 1994; Carl M. Cannon, "Bill Clinton's Pathetic Lies," *Weekly Standard*, October 2, 1995; William Safire, "Blizzard of Lies," *New York Times*, January 8, 1996; and James B. Stewart, *Blood Sport: The President and His Adversaries* (Simon & Schuster, 1996). Whether fair or not, the lines of criticism reflected in these pieces have tended to be recurrent. A related account of Clinton the character and the campaigner, said by insiders to be remarkably accurate though ostensibly fictional, has been provided by Anonymous in *Primary Colors* (Random House, 1996).

Beyond these lines of criticism, the mood contributing to the Republican congressional revolution of 1994 and the rise of Newt Gingrich to the speakership and co-presidency is captured by Robert Hughes, *The Culture of Complaint: The Fraying of America* (Oxford, 1993); and Rush H. Limbaugh III, *The Way Things Ought to Be* (Pocket, 1992), and *See, I Told You So* (Pocket, 1993). For the views of Gingrich himself, there is no shortage of material. In addition to his videos, audiocassettes, and running daily dialogue, one should see: Newt Gingrich, *Window of Opportunity: A Blueprint for the Future* (Doherty, 1984); *Quotations from Speaker Newt* (Workman, 1995); "Address to the Nation" (April 7, 1995); and *To Renew America* (HarperCollins, 1995); along with Newt Gingrich, Dick Armey, and the House Republicans, *Contract with America* (Times/Random House, 1994).

A mainstream sampling of critical mid-1990s perspectives on Gingrich would include: Connie Bruck, "The Politics of Perception," *New Yorker*, October 9, 1995; Vic Gold, "Separated at Birth?" *Washingtonian*, July 1995 (regarding similarities of Gingrich and Clinton); John B. Judis, "Newt's Not-so-Weird Gurus," *New Republic*, October 9, 1995; Charles Krauthammer, "A Critique of Pure Newt," *Weekly Standard*, September 18, 1995; Howard Kurtz, "Loud Speaker: Newt Gingrich Meets the Press," *Washington Post Magazine* cover story, February 26, 1995; Gail Sheehy, "The Inner Quest of Newt Gingrich," *Vanity Fair*, September 1995; Ernest Tollerson, "Scholars Regard Gingrich's Provocative Rhetoric as Brilliant but Polarizing," *New York Times*, December 17, 1995; *Time* magazine cover stories, "Mad as Hell: The G.O.P.'s Newt Gingrich Has Perfected the Politics of Anger," November 7, 1984, and "Man of the Year: Newt Gingrich," December 25,1995/January 1, 1996; and the *Washington Post*'s four-part feature on Gingrich by Dale Russakoff, Dan Balz, Charles R. Babcock, and Serge F. Kovaleski (December 18–21, 1994).

For a reprise on Gingrich's management of the budget battles of 1995–96, see: John Podhoretz, "A Reaganite Reconsiders," *Weekly Standard*, February 5, 1996; Thomas Rosensteil, "So if Hardball Doesn't Work, What's Our Plan B? How the Republicans Blew the Budget Fight," *Newsweek*, February 5, 1996; and the *Washington Post*'s four-part series, "Inside the Revolution," by Michael Weisskopf and David Maraniss (January 18–21, 1996).

And for additional perspectives on some of the key issues in the economic policy debate of 1995–96, one might consider the following. On the blame game, see Keith Bradsher, "Partnership in the Deficit—Parties Share Blame over Three Decades," *New York Times*, December 3, 1995. On the political management of the process, see Elizabeth Drew, *Showdown:*

The Struggle Between the Gingrich Congress and the Clinton White House (Simon & Schuster, 1996). On centralization versus decentralization, see: John J. Dilulio, Jr., and Donald F. Kettl, "Fine Print: The Contract with America, Devolution, and the Administrative Realities of American Federalism" (Brookings, CPM 95-1, March 1, 1995); Daniel Patrick Moynihan, Introduction to "The Federal Budget and the States, Fiscal Year 1994," 19th edition (Kennedy School of Government and Office of Senator Moynihan, 1995); Sylvia Nasar, "The Bureaucracy: What's Left to Shrink?" *New York Times,* June 11, 1995; and William F. Weld, "Release Us from Federal Nonsense," *Wall Street Journal,* December 11, 1995. For arguments in support of a flat tax, see "Unleashing America's Potential," the 1996 report of the commission established by Senator Dole and Speaker Gingrich and chaired by Jack Kemp; and "The Flat Tax: 'Nutty' It's Not," *Wall Street Journal,* February 22, 1996. On the possible privatization of Social Security, see: U.S. Advisory Council on Social Security, *Final Report* (GPO, 1996); and Martin Feldstein, "Time to Privatize Social Security," *Wall Street Journal,* March 8, 1996. And for perspectives on the general problem of growing middle-class entitlements, see: Richard Darman, "The Problem of Rising Health Costs," Testimony before the Senate Finance Committee, April 16, 1991, and "Capping the Rate of Growth in Mandatory Spending" (OMB, March 1992); Matthew Miller, "Cap Gains," *The New Republic,* May 27, 1996; and Robert J. Samuelson, *The Good Life and Its Discontents: The American Dream in the Age of Entitlement, 1945–1995* (Times, 1995).

On this last issue, entitlements, I would add one further comment: It has long been clear that restraining the growth of middle-class entitlements is key to solving the federal spending problem. But little progress was made on this in the Reagan years. The first serious restraint came with the 1990 budget agreement, but was far short of what was needed. Still, if the entitlement issues had been strictly budgetary, the problem might have been addressed relatively easily. The problem was more complicated, however, than the straightforward math might have suggested. Addressing entitlements involved not only the conventional questions of the middle class's obligations to the poor. The entitlement problem also entailed very hard questions of the middle class's obligations to itself. Most of the taxes and benefits at issue were to be paid, received, or relinquished by the middle class. But the middle class was hardly uniform in age, vulnerability, or comfort with risk. The entitlement and tax issues, therefore, involved more than shuffling financial obligations from one pocket to another. They also involved such questions as these: In an economy predicated on risk taking, but with a large portion of the population feeling insecure, how should the balance of risk and safety be struck? Who, within the middle class, should be protected against exactly what risks? What are the obligations of working generations to generations too young or too old to work, and to generations yet unborn? To what degree should risk protection be assured by collective governmental action, and to what degree by private individual action?

Neither of the co-Presidents offered much to help understand these hard problems. Indeed, they did more to avoid them than to clarify or confront them. The looming retirement of the baby-boom generation— and the inadequacy of the Clinton-Gingrich policies with respect to this demographic reality—promised to make the problems even harder. The struggle over entitlements, debt, and taxes is therefore bound to remain on the agenda. And it is understandable that the middle class, hence the representative political system, has been profoundly conflicted in trying to sort this out.

For a set of concise essays on twentieth-century Presidents, focusing on the dimension that I think most important—and most conspicuously wanting in the period of the Clinton-Gingrich co-presidency—see Robert A. Wilson, ed., *Character Above All* (Simon & Schuster, 1995).

Populism and the Center

The concepts of "populism" and "the center," used frequently here and in conventional political commentary, are overly broad. I do not think that is such a bad thing; it allows more opportunity for coalition building. Neither this book nor this note seeks to clear up what confusion it may cause. I mean simply to acknowledge that I am aware of the problem.

Meg Greenfield (a slightly leftish sensible centrist) has argued that labels and placements along the American political spectrum are not only confused but misguided; see "The Tyranny of 'the Spectrum,'" *Washington Post*, September 18, 1995. For more on labels and the spectrum, see: David S. Broder, "Search for the Sensible Center," *Washington Post*, December 20, 1995; John B. Judis (TRB), "Off Center," *New Republic*, October 16, 1995; Joe Klein, "Stalking the Radical Middle," *Newsweek*, September 25, 1995, and "Character, Not Ideology," *Newsweek*, November 13, 1995; Michael Lind, "The Radical Center or the Moderate Middle," *New York Times Magazine*, December 3, 1995; William Safire, "Of Mainstreams and Movements," *New York Times Magazine*, March 16, 1996; and Robert J. Samuelson, "The New Reactionaries," *Washington Post*, May 24, 1995, and "Pseudo Conservatives," *Washington Post*, June 7, 1995. Most of these, I should note, accept the notion of a "sensible center" or a "moderate middle," while also pointing to the complications and contradictions among labels arrayed along the American political spectrum.

The label most in fashion recently has been "populist." It is not exactly on the ideological spectrum; it is better understood as on an attitudinal spectrum. I have suggested that where centrism is often sensible, populism is often (though not always) angry. To that extent, its recent strength is consistent with the increased polarization of American politics. But, of course, anger is not a characteristic that is sufficient to define populism. Populism is, to a degree, defined by its antipathy toward concentrations of power or privilege that are perceived as unfair by large numbers of ordinary people. Still, since there are populists of left, right, and center, it is a label with compound potential for confusion. It reaches from the would-be tax-increasing Ross Perot to the anti-tax class of 1994 House Republicans and from Oliver Stone to Newt Gingrich.

For a sample of thinking on the subject of late-twentieth-century American populism, see: Jeffrey Bell, *Populism and Elitism: Politics in the Age of Equality* (Regnery, 1992); Richard L. Berke, "Vox Populist: Just Regular Ruling Class Guys," *New York Times*, February 4, 1996; Max Boot, "Down with Populism," *Wall Street Journal*, December 8, 1994; Alan Brinkley, "A Swaggering Tradition," *Newsweek*, March 4, 1996; *Business Week*'s cover story, "America's New Populism," March 13, 1995; Richard Darman, "Observations on the New Populism," *New Populist Forum*, May 9, 1986; Jason DeParle, "Class Is No Longer a Four-Letter Word," *New York Times Magazine*, March 17, 1996; E.J. Dionne, Jr., "Populist Politics," *Washington Post*, February 13, 1996; Thomas B. Edsall, "Buchanan's Populist Pitch May Pose Problem for GOP," *Washington Post*, February 14, 1996; Paul Gigot, "Why 'Princeton Populist' Is No Oxymoron," *Wall Street Journal*, February 2, 1996; William Greider, *Who Will Tell the People: The Betrayal of American Democracy* (Simon & Schuster, 1992); Lloyd Grove, "The Castle Storms Back," *Washington Post*, February 23, 1996; William A. Henry III, *In Defense of Elitism* (Doubleday, 1994); Michael Kazin, *The Populist Persuasion: An American History* (Basic, 1995); Michael Kinsley, "Populist, Shmopulist," *Washington Post*, December 2, 1993; Charles Krauthammer, "Infantile Conservatism," *Washington Post*, February 23, 1996; Christopher Lasch, *The Revolt of the Elites and the Betrayal of Democracy* (Norton, 1995); Jack Newfield and Jeff Greenfield, *A Populist Manifesto: The Making of a New Majority* (Praeger, 1972); Norman Ornstein, "Elite Men of the People," *Weekly Standard*, March 18, 1996; Kevin P. Phillips, *The Emerging Republican Majority* (Arlington House, 1969), *Post-Conservative America* (Random House, 1982), and *Arrogant Capital* (Little, Brown, 1994); Gerald F. Seib and John Harwood, "With Populist Themes, Surging Buchanan Puts Squeeze on Own Party," *Wall Street Journal*, February 14, 1996; Steven Stark, "Right-Wing Populist," *Atlantic Monthly*, February 1996; *Time* magazine's cover story of January 23, 1995, featuring Robert Wright, "Hyper-democracy," and Richard Corliss, "Look Who's Talking"; *Time* magazine's cover story of February 26, 1996, *Grand Old Populists*, featuring Richard Lacayo, "The Populist Blowup," Richard Stengel, "The Making of Buchanan," and Dan Goodgame and John Dickerson, "The Search for Alexander"; Alvin and Heidi Toffler, *Creating a New Civilization: The Politics of the Third Wave* (Turner, 1995); and Richard A. Viguerie, *The Establishment vs. the People: Is a New Populist Revolt on the Way?* (Regnery, 1983).

Without having cleared up any of the confusion, I would simply note that the following might be observed of the "center" and "populism," using these terms in the way that most people would generally understand them. In America, there is a very large political center, with a profoundly stable commitment to America's Constitutional democracy, but with weak or fluid party identification. There is also a populist force, sometimes latent, but always ready to activate itself to correct narrowly based accumulations of excessive power. The dynamics of centrist inertia and populist correction shift power around among the competing parties and partisans in a process that rarely causes a fundamental change of direction, but is, rather, a continuous course correction along what is, in general, a progressive centrist path.

For a view of how Americans have recently distributed themselves along the political spectrum, and other categories of political interest, see "The People, the Press and Politics: The New Political Landscape," Times Mirror Center for the People and the Press, September 1994. And for a sample of perspectives on how the current mix might sort itself out (or might have already sorted itself out), see: Dan Balz and Ronald Brownstein, *Storming the Gates: Protest Politics and the Republican Revival* (Little, Brown, 1996); A. Lawrence Chickering, *Beyond Left and Right: Breaking the Political Stalemate* (ICS Press, 1993); E.J. Dionne, Jr., *They Only Look Dead: Why Progressives Will Dominate the Next Political Era* (Simon & Schuster, 1996); Albert R. Hunt, "GOP Ranks Swell, but Diversity Brings a Tangle of Tensions," *Wall Street Journal*, March 8, 1996, and the related *Wall Street Journal*/NBC News poll conducted under the direction of Peter Hart and Robert Teeter.

Values and De-civilization

This is an enormous subject that stretches from Aristotle to Zen. It is not the principal subject of this book. But since I state that it is a problem of greater importance than the fiscal problem, and that attention to it is essential, I offer a few references that suggest my point of view. For general perspective see Michael Barone, "High Anxiety," *American Enterprise*, July/August 1996; and for recent facts, attitudes, and politics related to values, see Ben J. Wattenberg, *Values Matter Most* (Free Press, 1995). For a selection highlighting more particular elements of the problem, see: William M. Adler, *Land of Opportunity: One Family's Quest for the American Dream in the Age of Crack* (Atlantic, 1995); Geoffrey Canada, *fist stick knife gun: a personal history of violence in america* (Beacon, 1995); Michael Medved, *Hollywood vs. America: Popular Culture and the War on Traditional Values* (HarperCollins, 1992); and Robert D. Putnam, "Bowling Alone," *Journal of Democracy*, January 1995. For a reminder that problems and solutions may be a great deal more complex than is suggested by such nostalgic nostrums as "We must restore the traditional American family," see Stephanie Coontz, *The Way We Never Were: American Families and the Nostalgia Trap* (Basic, 1992). And for responsible conservative thought on the legitimacy of a role for the state in promoting values within a free society (to be distinguished from the substantial body of irresponsible thought on the same subject), see: Margaret Thatcher, "The Moral Foundations of Society," *Imprimis*, March 1995; and George F. Will, *Statecraft as Soulcraft: What Government Does* (Simon & Schuster, 1983).

Baseball as Metaphor

Last but not least, I turn to a subject that will undoubtedly have been an annoyance for those who are not appreciative of what was once America's national pastime. For the unappreciative, I hereby make one final attempt at conversion. I recognize, of course, that baseball is slow. But that is one of its virtues. It allows time for thought. Indeed, there are many moments when it is only as interesting as the thought one brings to it. That may be why baseball is so often treated as allegory. And since it is a spectator sport that, unlike most, provides much opportunity for parents to talk with children, the use of baseball as a metaphor often runs to issues of character and values.

For those who are not yet converted to this element of baseball's virtue, I respectfully suggest a short course in the connection between baseball and values. I would begin with three movies: *The Natural* (TriStar, 1984), *A League of Their Own* (Columbia, 1992), and *Field of Dreams* (Universal, 1989). I would then move to the fundamental primer on the ethics and metaphysics of the Red Sox' struggles, Dan Shaughnessy's *The Curse of the Bambino* (Penguin, 1991). For use of a hero as an opportunity for reflection by great writers (with two contributions by John Updike), see Lawrence Baldassaro, ed., *The Ted Williams Reader* (Fireside/Simon & Schuster, 1991). See also the op-ed pieces in the *Washington Post* on the occasion of Cal Ripken's tying the Lou Gehrig record on September 5, 1995: "Baseball's Ordinary Hero" by E.J. Dionne, Jr., and "Nonstop Ripken" by George Will. Then, for a bit tougher going, one might move to the detailed defense of puritanical virtues found in George Will's *Men at Work: The Craft of Baseball* (Macmillan, 1990). And finally, for the perennial conflict between romantic and anti-romantic perspectives on baseball and life, one might consider Donald Kagan, "George Will's Baseball—A Conservative Critique," and George F. Will, "The Romantic Fallacy in Baseball—A Reply," both of which are found in *The Public Interest*, Fall 1990.

ACKNOWLEDGMENTS

I COULD NOT have had the opportunity to serve at high levels in government if it were not for formative influences that helped me at earlier stages in my life. I therefore thank especially: first, my parents, Eleanor and Morton Darman; my sister and brothers, Lynn Darman, Robert Newton Darman, and John Marshall Darman; my teachers at the Harris School, The Rivers School, and Harvard; and a few special friends from Harvard College, Ann Douglas, Charles Pierce, and my Eliot House roommates, Jeffrey Forbes, Scott Harshbarger, Richard Keyes, and Robert Lea. I am grateful, also, to Harry Palladino, who gave me my first private sector job, at fourteen, mowing lawns and doing landscape construction; and to Michael Timpane, whom I was fortunate to have met at Harvard, and who got me my first job in the federal government when he returned to the Department of Health, Education, and Welfare.

Once in government, I benefited from a succession of truly extraordinary mentors who were willing to entrust me with responsibility for which I will always be grateful: Lewis Butler, Laurence Lynn, Elliot Richardson, James Baker, and George Bush. Over the years, I was also fortunate to have had the support of a remarkably able and dedicated group of deputies and associates, especially Barry Anderson, Margaret Brackney, Robert Damus, William Diefenderfer, Sara Emery, Deborah Frankenberg, Kimberly Gibson, Robert Grady, Janet Hale, Francis Hodsoll, Robert Howard, Patricia McGinnis, Janet McMinn, John Palmer, John Rogers, Thomas Scully, Daniel Sprague, David Taylor, Suzanne Woolsey, and Robert Zoellick. These people not only contributed to successes with which I was associated. Many also suffered for my failings, and nonetheless remained supportive through thick and thin. I am grateful to colleagues in the Reagan White House, Bush White House, and Bush cabinet—many of whom remain close friends. Among friends in the press, I thank especially those who showed genuine kindness toward my family. I am appreciative, also, of those in the private sector who gave me a home when I was out of government: James Billington at the Woodrow

Wilson International Center for Scholars; James Edwards and William Stitt at ICF; Graham Allison at Harvard; James Robinson and James Johnson at American Express-Shearson Lehman Brothers; and at The Carlyle Group, former partner Steve Norris and current partners Jim Baker, Frank Carlucci, William Conway, Dan D'Aniello, Ed Mathais, and David Rubenstein.

When our son Willy was gravely ill, I had a chance to learn how caring a community could be. For me the lesson was wonderful. I offer deepest thanks to all those who were then helpful to our family. Had they not been so, I doubt this book would have been written. But that is the least of what I will always feel I owe them. What might have been a profoundly saddening experience was ultimately made rewarding thanks to the extraordinary kindness of many of the friends already noted, along with the following additional people, who were particularly helpful. Among medical professionals my family and I thank especially our pediatrician and diagnostician, Robert Tolson; the team led by Dr. Kevin McGrail at the Georgetown University Medical Center, including Drs. Val Abassi, Jorge Kattah, Robert Martusa, Marianne Schuelein, and all the committed doctors and dedicated nurses of the Georgetown pediatric intensive care unit; Drs. Raymond Adams, Gilbert Daniels, Pierson Richardson, Ann Young, and Nicholas Zervas at the Massachusetts General Hospital; and Dr. David Rosenthal at the Harvard University Health Services. Among important other helpers and supporters, we especially appreciate: William Myers, the Rector of St. John's Church in McLean; the Potomac Upper School community led by Andrew Watson and David Civali, and including thoughtful teachers and advisers like John Drew and Heydon White Rostow; along with our and Jonathan's and Willy's many school friends, whose consistent attention was genuinely inspiring; at home, the wise and helpful Rosa Perez; among our extended once-governmental family, special friends like Barbara Bush, Susan Baker, and Anne Richardson; at Harvard University, William Fitzsimmons and Neil Rudenstine; and the many more who kindly called or wrote or stopped by with expressions of concern or advice or hope—in some cases nourishing us literally, in all cases nourishing us spiritually.

In a different vein, I am grateful to several friends who were kind enough to read parts or all of this book in draft form. Among them, I thank especially: John Thomas Smith, Bill Diefenderfer, Lesley Stahl, Bob Grady, Kim Gibson, Meg Brackney, and members of my family who gave me both helpful advice and important early encouragement; Bob Zoellick, who gave me his usual tough-minded and incisive criticism; and Margaret Tutwiler, who generously took on the difficult (some might say impossible) task of trying to protect me from myself. Others helped with corrections large and small for which I am appreciative. Some of these friends disagree with my perspective, and should not be presumed to endorse it simply for having been kind enough to give me the benefit of their advice. At Simon & Schuster, I was helped enormously by the legendary editor Alice Mayhew and her very able deputy, Roger Labrie. Among many other important contributions, they led me to think that what I originally had in mind was really two different books, and that only one of them should be fit between these covers. They were right (though I may return to the other book someday). Marie Florio, Joann DiGenarro, Victoria Meyer, and Cathy Saypol took on the challenge of gaining a wider audience for this book, for which I am appreciative. And Bob Barnett served as my lawyer for this project, providing a valuable mixture of professionalism, entertainment, and wise counsel. I have never been known to be easy to work with or anxious to accept the criticism of others. So the usual disclaimers and thanks apply at least doubly to all those who have tried to help me.

Last but certainly not least, I wish to thank the members of my immediate family, to whom this book is dedicated: Kath, Will, Jonathan, and Emmet Darman. In most acknowledgments, authors seem to treat writing as a burden upon their families. In my case, every family member old enough to write views writing as a valuable calling. (Emmet, who was born as this was being written, has not yet expressed an opinion on that. But given his mother's strong, wise, and sensitive influence, I suspect he, too, will agree one day.) Kath, Will, and Jonathan are all better at writing than I am, and probably wish I would have spent more time at it rather than less. For them, my service in government was in many ways the burden. I will always be deeply grateful for their support, which has been essential, and for their inspiration, which for me has been profoundly important.

Dick Darman
June 21, 1996

INDEX

abortion, 180, 324
acid rain, 180
Adams, John, 41
advertisements, negative, 14–15, 307
Ailes, Roger, 192
Alexander, Lamar, 15, 16, 200
Allen, Dick, 49, 51, 52, 57
American Business Conference, 264
American Revolution, 18, 28
American Romance, 17, 32, 35, 168, 269, 319, 351*n*–52*n*
Anderson, Barry, 298
Anderson, Marty, 56, 75, 76–77, 84, 93
Arab oil embargo, 19, 142
Archer, Bill, 256
Armey, Dick, 311
Armstrong, Neil, 29
Atlantic Monthly, 103–10, 111, 112
Atwater, Lee, 129
automatic signature pens, 61

Baker, Howard, 66, 99, 100, 116, 182
Baker, James A., III:
  Atlantic affair and, 107, 108
  in budget negotiations, 206, 208, 209, 264–65, 275, 276
  as Bush's campaign manager, 188, 189, 190

Darman's relationship with, 37, 38, 133–35, 196, 214, 236, 258
  Economic Recovery Program and, 83, 84, 86, 91, 93, 97, 99, 100, 101, 103, 115, 116–17, 154
  as moderate, 14, 37–38, 83, 84, 86
  in presidential campaign (1984), 127, 131, 133–35
  proposed resignation of, 73
  Reagan assassination attempt and, 47–51, 56–57, 58
  Regan's job switch with, 48, 139–40, 145
  as Secretary of State, 206
  as Secretary of the Treasury, 139–40, 145, 146, 172
  tax reform and, 149, 151, 152, 153, 154, 159, 160, 161, 162
  as White House chief of staff, 37, 38, 41, 127, 139–40, 158, 288, 294, 296
Baldrige, Malcolm, 169
Ball, Bob, 116
banking industry, 149, 180
Barnett, Barney, 67
Barry, Marion, 307
baseball, 9, 157–58, 159, 164–67, 197, 218–19, 230–31, 238, 298, 346–49, 364*n*
Bay of Pigs invasion, 313
Bennett, Bill, 16, 234, 323, 337

Bentsen, Lloyd, 161, 205, 226, 227, 245, 256, 258, 270
Berlin Wall, fall of, 289
"Beyond the Deficit Problem: 'Now-Now-ism' and the New Balance" (Darman), 219–22
Birnbaum, Jeffrey, 152
"black bag," 55
Bonfire of the Vanities (Wolfe), 221
Book of Virtues, The (Bennett), 337
Boren, David, 150
"Born in the U.S.A.," 123
Boskin, Michael, 223, 228, 237, 246
Boston Red Sox, 157–58, 159, 164–67, 230, 238, 347
Bradley, Bill, 152, 153, 160, 161
Brady, Jim, 54, 58, 247
Brady, Nick, 206, 209, 215, 222, 224, 226, 228, 229, 232, 246, 247, 248, 250, 251, 256, 258, 260, 261, 262, 263, 264
Brockway, David, 152
Broder, David, 115, 306
Buchanan, Pat, 15–16, 20, 21, 22, 290, 291, 294, 296, 311, 317, 320, 327
Buckner, Billy, 166, 167, 197, 238, 298
budget, Bush administration (1990), 198–287
  Baker's role in, 206, 208, 209, 264–65, 275, 276
  balancing of, 198, 200, 203, 204, 229, 235, 277–78
  baseball analogy for, 218–19, 238
  Big Fix for, 215, 232, 233, 244, 245
  bipartisanship for, 204, 205, 208, 209, 214–15, 216, 218, 236–37, 242, 248–49, 257, 260, 272, 273
  breakfast agreement on, 262–66, 269, 275
  Budget: Big Bipartisan Agreement (BUBBA) on, 248–49, 257, 274
  Bush's support for, 215, 216, 217, 223–25, 227, 233, 243, 245, 246, 248, 250, 251,
    252–53, 254, 257, 259, 260, 262–66, 272, 273–74, 277, 278, 279–80, 348
  compromise for, 202, 265, 271, 272–73
  congressional approval of, 199–205, 214, 258, 259, 261
  conservative criticism of, 216, 227–28, 230, 249, 259, 272–87, 296
  Darman's memos on, 206–9, 210, 215–16, 217, 232–33, 243–49, 257–58
  Darman's role in, 198–287, 297–98
  Darman's speeches on, 219–22, 237–38
  Darman's testimony for, 236–237
  deficit and, 198, 202–10, 216, 217–18, 220, 221, 225–32, 236, 237, 240–45, 248, 257, 266, 273, 275, 276–77, 286
  Democratic opposition to, 199–208, 210, 214–15, 225–27, 229, 232, 233, 236–46, 248, 251–52, 254–55, 264, 265, 273
  director's introduction to, 235–36
  Dole and, 205, 248, 249, 251, 255, 259, 260, 264, 270, 272, 278
  economic growth and, 199, 202, 206–7, 222–23, 227, 229, 237, 241, 243–44, 257, 274, 275–76, 285–88
  flexible freeze in, 198–99, 200, 201, 207, 208, 225
  Gingrich's role in, 218–19, 228, 238–39, 248, 249, 254, 255, 256, 259, 260, 264, 272–87, 295
  government shutdown and, 277
  Greenspan's policies and, 201–2, 216, 222–23, 228, 229, 237, 244, 257, 275–76, 279, 285, 294
  "lame duck" session for, 258, 259, 261

budget, Bush administration, *continued*

mañana syndrome in, 222

media coverage of, 214, 218–19, 222, 225, 228, 235–36, 249–59, 262–66, 270–71, 275, 278, 280

middle-class entitlements in, 198, 199, 201, 216, 217, 225, 226, 227, 229, 232, 236, 240, 242, 244, 246, 259, 261–62, 265, 304

Mitchell's role in, 205, 225–27, 229, 248, 249, 251, 255, 256, 257, 258, 260, 261, 262–63, 264, 265, 272

negotiations on, 201, 202, 205, 208, 214–19, 226–27, 229, 237, 244, 245, 246, 247–65

Nixon's views on, 200–201, 209–10, 266

populist support for, 269–70

public reaction to, 231–32, 240, 264–66, 272, 274, 285–86

Quayle's role in, 204–5, 246, 247, 272

Reagan budgets and, 198, 205, 206, 214, 224, 272

Republican support for, 199, 200–201, 202, 203, 205, 233, 237, 239–41, 242, 247–48, 254–55, 263–64, 272–73, 285

resolution for, 208, 260, 272–287

Rostenkowski's role in, 209, 242–43, 245, 246, 247, 249–50, 255, 258, 264

sequester for, 207, 214, 215, 216, 217, 223, 229, 235, 237, 243, 250, 259, 277

spending reductions in, 198, 199, 201, 203, 216, 223–25, 232, 234, 239, 240, 241, 242, 244, 250, 255, 260, 262, 265, 271, 274, 278–79, 285, 293

stock market and, 242, 243

strategy for, 206–9, 215–16, 232–33, 265–66

summits on, 201, 247–65, 269–78, 304

Sununu's role in, 206, 215, 216, 217, 223–24, 228, 232, 243, 245–52, 255, 256, 260–65, 280

tax increases and, 199–202, 205, 209–10, 214, 216, 224–29, 231, 234, 235, 237, 239, 240–47, 251, 254–66, 272, 275, 279, 285, 286, 287, 291, 293, 294, 296

Ten Required Characteristics for, 246–47, 250

trust and, 251–52, 260, 261, 265

two–step approach to, 200–201, 210, 216, 217, 219, 220, 222, 225, 226–27, 231, 232

Ted Williams approach to, 231–32, 233, 234, 235, 247, 257, 293

Budget: Big Bipartisan Agreement (BUBBA), 248–49, 257, 274

Budget Review Board, 118

Building a Better America, 214

Burger, Warren, 41

Bush, Barbara, 194–95, 211, 212, 264, 266

Bush, George, 187–298

"balance" of, 212–13

in budget negotiations, 215, 216, 217, 223–25, 227, 233, 243, 245, 246, 248, 250, 251, 252–53, 254, 257, 259, 260, 262–66, 272, 273–74, 277, 278, 279–80, 348

budget of, *see* budget, Bush administration (1990)

cabinet of, 234

conservative opposition to, 272–87, 289, 293, 296

conservatism of, 212, 303

credibility of, 224, 227, 235, 275, 286

Darman's relationship with, 194–95, 210–13, 222, 230–31, 263, 281, 284–85, 296–97, 348

Dukakis's debates with, 194–95

economic policies of, 66, 223, 237, 257, 274, 276, 282

Economic Recovery Program and, 94, 145

foreign policy of, 246, 289–90

inaugural address of, 215

majority coalition of, 213,
288–89, 292–93, 302–3, 323
media coverage of, 192, 212,
213, 214
personality of, 187, 210–13, 289,
348
populist appeal of, 187, 188,
212–13, 290, 293
as President-elect, 194–97,
210–13
presidential campaign of
(1988), 187–95, 198–99, 205,
206, 207, 208, 216, 224–25,
251, 325
presidential campaign of
(1992), 216, 286–91, 293–94
"Read my lips" tax pledge of, 76,
191–92, 210, 213, 214, 216,
217, 224, 225, 228, 231, 232,
239, 243, 247, 251, 262–66,
275, 291, 293
Reagan assassination attempt
and, 49, 50, 54–55, 57, 59, 62
Reagan compared with, 187, 212
tax reform and, 150
"vision thing" of, 190, 287,
288–92, 318, 319
business depreciation allowances,
77
Business Roundtable, 245, 264
Byrd, Robert, 269–70

Camp David, 31, 131, 211, 233,
248–49
Cannon, Lou, 127
caps, spending, 111, 244, 265, 304,
305, 342
Carlucci, Frank, 96
Carter, Jimmy, 28, 30, 31, 33, 35,
42, 74, 81, 82, 97, 140, 142,
180, 182, 200, 283
Casey, Bill, 55
Chasen's restaurant, 175–77
Cheney, Richard, 14, 99, 102, 217,
277
Chevrolet, 123
Chicago Eight, 35
China, People's Republic of, 181,
266
Chrysler-Plymouth, 123
Clark, Lindley, 275

Cleaver, Eldridge, 35
Clemens, Roger, 165–66, 230
Clinton, Bill:
budgets of, 294, 302, 303–5,
314–15, 316, 326–27, 330–32
cabinet of, 305–6
as centrist, 10–11, 14, 16, 21–22,
299–300, 303, 306, 318–19,
335
character issue for, 293–94
"co-presidency" of, 299–320,
323, 324, 361n
credibility of, 286, 301
deficit reduction program of
(1993), 273
economic policies of, 66, 302,
303
ethics of, 305–6
health care plan of, 13, 303, 334
inauguration of, 297
Kennedy and, 13, 17, 299
leadership of, 301, 302, 306,
307–8, 319–20
liberal agenda of, 285, 293, 299,
301, 303, 308, 320
majority coalition of, 299–303,
319, 323
media coverage of, 12, 13–14,
304, 305, 306–7
as New Democrat, 11, 285, 303,
335, 337
presidential campaign of
(1992), 286–87, 290, 293–94,
302, 327
presidential campaign of
(1996), 11–14, 16, 21–22, 300,
315, 320, 330, 335
public image of, 12–13, 287,
290, 291, 347
Reagan's influence on, 13, 17,
299
State of the Union address of
(1995), 306
State of the Union address of
(1996), 12–14, 17, 18, 22
tax policy of, 73, 286–87
vision of, 13, 287, 294, 299, 302,
327
Clinton, Hillary Rodham, 299, 303
Cogan, John, 214
Cohen, Richard, 306

communism, 62, 72, 181–82, 289–90

Community Action Program, 74, 79, 341

Conable, Barber, 75, 79, 102, 116

Congressional Budget Office, 218, 273, 276, 304, 316

congressional elections (1982), 114

congressional elections (1986), 168

congressional elections (1990), 229

congressional elections (1994), 10, 13, 20, 300, 307, 325, 326

conservatives:
  in budget negotiations, 216, 227–28, 230, 249, 259, 272–87, 296
  Bush opposed by, 272–87, 289, 293, 296
  Darman opposed by, 36, 83, 91, 115, 227–28, 280–84, 285, 286, 294, 295
  Dole influenced by, 10, 11
  moderates vs., 20–22, 36, 83, 84, 323–24
  Reagan supported by, 29, 33, 36, 37, 38, 39, 179, 181–82, 283
  in Republican party, 14–17, 20, 21–22, 83, 114–15, 181, 213, 311–12

Constitution, U.S., 33, 52, 53–56, 58, 59, 149, 180, 182, 183, 262, 277–78, 309, 324

consumer price index (CPI), 275

Conte, Silvio, 253, 259, 260

Contract with America, 300–301, 307, 308, 309, 310, 317

Control car, 176–77

Coolidge, Calvin, 42

"corpocracy speech," (Darman) 168–70, 172–73, 226, 337

corporations, 113, 147–48, 168–70, 172–73, 226, 337

cost-of-living increases, 245, 260

Council of Economic Advisers, 75, 103, 118, 275

Cox, Archibald, 53

credit unions, 149

crime rate, 327, 339

"crises crisis," 31

Crisis (Jordan), 31

Crowe, Bill, 223

Cuban missile crisis, 30, 132, 142

Curse of the Bambino, The (Shaughnessy), 164–65, 364n

Dale, Ed, 106

Damus, Bob, 298

Danforth, John, 150, 160–61

Darman, Emmet, 348

Darman, Jonathan, 89, 165–67, 195, 196, 211, 212, 214, 216, 307, 348, 349

Darman, Kathleen Emmet, 36, 165, 196, 211, 212, 214, 216, 298, 307, 348

Darman, Richard:
  Atlantic affair and, 103–10, 111
  background of, 38–39, 143
  as baseball fan, 9, 157–58, 159, 164–67, 197, 218–19, 230–31, 238, 298, 346–49, 364n
  confirmation hearings of, 88–91, 211, 213–14
  conservative opposition to, 36, 83, 91, 115, 227–28, 280–84, 285, 286, 294, 295
  as Deputy Secretary of the Treasury, 140, 144, 145, 146, 172, 188
  Economic Recovery Program and, 75–76, 84, 85, 86–91, 97, 99, 100, 101, 116–17, 154
  media coverage of, 154, 156, 169–70, 172, 218–19, 222, 235–36, 280, 281, 294–95, 297
  as moderate, 21–22, 35, 36–37, 84, 120
  Nancy Reagan and, 130, 131, 133, 134, 135–39
  as OMB director, 88–91, 107, 138, 139, 195–298, 317–18
  in presidential campaign (1984), 125–42
  in presidential campaign (1988), 187–95
  proposed resignations of, 73, 91, 125–26, 130–39, 202, 280–83, 295–97
  as public servant, 36–38, 88–91

Reagan assassination attempt
  and, 47–62
speeches given by, 154–59, 164,
  167–70, 172–73, 219–22,
  237–38, 280–18
as White House aide, 35, 38–43,
  136
Darman, William, 165–67, 195–96,
  197, 211, 214, 217, 298, 348
Davis, Rennie, 35
Deaver, Mike, 48, 49, 60, 83, 107,
  108, 109, 115, 135–36, 137,
  138, 139
defense spending, 77, 88, 95–97,
  101–2, 105, 117, 124, 178–79,
  192, 199, 200, 203, 217,
  223–29, 232, 235, 241, 262,
  277, 290, 326
deficit:
  budget negotiations and, 198,
    202–10, 216, 217–18, 220,
    221, 225–32, 236, 237,
    240–45, 248, 257, 266, 273,
    275, 276–77, 286
  economic growth and, 145–46
  Economic Recovery Program
    and, 72, 73, 76–80, 83, 88–91,
    93–103, 110–13, 116, 118,
    119, 124, 145
  projections for, 179–80, 304
  reduction of, 15, 34, 45–46, 72,
    73, 111, 116, 150, 154, 273,
    305, 315, 327, 329, 330
Democratic Leadership Council,
  299
Democratic party:
  in budget negotiations,
    199–208, 210, 214–15,
    225–27, 229, 232, 233,
    236–46, 248, 251–52, 254–55,
    264, 265, 273
  congressional control by, 91,
    173, 181, 199, 200–201, 203,
    210, 233, 239, 265, 273, 286
  Economic Recovery Program
    supported by, 79, 86, 94–95,
    97, 100
  liberal wing of, 11, 17, 302
  Reagan opposed by, 65–66, 82,
    85, 119, 173
Deng Xiaoping, 181

Devroy, Ann, 251
Diefenderfer, Bill, 152, 160, 298
"Director's Introduction to the
  Budget," 235–36
District of Columbia, 309, 343
Dole, Bob:
  in budget negotiations, 205,
    248, 249, 251, 255, 259, 260,
    264, 270, 272, 278
  as centrist, 10–11, 16, 20–21
  conservative influence on, 10, 11
  deficit reduction and, 15, 116
  populist appeal of, 188, 194, 322
  presidential campaign of
    (1996), 15, 16, 20–21, 330
  tax policy of, 75, 79, 145, 160
  tax reform and, 145, 160
Domenici, Pete, 66, 101, 201, 256,
  259–60
drug abuse, 313, 314, 343
Duberstein, Ken, 84, 116–17
Dukakis, Kitty, 194
Dukakis, Michael, 187, 190–91,
  194–95, 225

Eastwood, Clint, 187, 191, 192, 193
Economic Recovery Program
  (1981–82), 66–119
  Baker's role in, 83, 84, 86, 91,
    93, 97, 99, 100, 101, 103, 115,
    116–17, 154
  bills for, 68–70
  Bush's role in, 94, 145
  "children's allowance" in, 80
  coalition for, 83, 116–17
  compromise on, 76, 78, 79, 80,
    83, 86–87, 91, 110–16, 118,
    123–24
  congressional approval of, 70,
    79, 86–91, 93–95, 112,
    116–17, 145
  corrective measures for, 87–91,
    93–103, 110–13
  Darman's role in, 75–76, 84, 85,
    86–91, 97, 99, 100, 101,
    116–17, 154
  defense spending and, 77, 88,
    95–97, 101–2, 105, 117, 124
  deficits and, 72, 73, 76–80, 83,
    88–91, 93–103, 110–13, 116,
    118, 119, 124, 145

Economic Recovery Program, *continued*
  Democratic support of, 79, 86, 94–95, 97, 100
  economic impact of, 72, 74–75, 79–80, 91, 95, 98, 101, 103–10, 111
  enactment of, 68–70, 79–86, 179
  Fall Offensive for, 90, 93–119
  federal debt and, 73, 78
  government shutdown and, 101, 102, 109, 110
  incrementalism violated by, 74–75, 111–12, 113
  leaks on, 95, 105, 114
  mañana syndrome in, 102, 112–13
  mandate for, 82
  media coverage of, 68, 69, 70, 75, 103–10, 111
  moderate support of, 83–86
  "mouse" analogy for, 103, 110, 111
  Ping-Pong game analogy for, 100, 101, 102, 110
  populist support of, 81, 82, 85, 157
  Reaganauts and, 75, 76, 86, 107
  Reagan's support of, 64–71, 80, 81, 85, 86, 87, 94–97, 99–102, 103, 110, 113, 124
  Republican support of, 79, 98–99, 100, 102, 114–15
  Rosy Scenario for, 98, 103
  signing of, 68, 69, 71, 74, 78, 92, 93, 94
  spending reductions and, 77, 78, 79, 80, 81–82, 84–85, 94–99, 102–3, 110, 112, 114, 123–24
  Stockman's role in, 64, 72, 75–77, 79, 80, 83, 84–85, 88–91, 93, 94, 95–110, 116–17, 154
  tax cuts in, 64–71, 72, 74–76, 78–79, 83, 84, 86, 88, 89, 91, 101–2, 117, 118, 146, 148
  "three-legged stool" formula for, 97, 98, 99, 100, 101, 102, 145
  voter support for, 78–79
  Weinberger's role in, 94, 95–97
education, 168, 173, 241, 270, 287, 316, 328, 334–35, 338, 343

"Education of David Stockman, The" (Greider), 103–10, 111, 112
Eisenhower, Dwight D., 27, 61, 323
employee benefits, 148–49
energy crisis, 142, 274
entertainment deductions, 147, 149
entitlements, 15, 20, 45, 58, 70, 73, 77, 78, 88, 99, 102, 111, 123–24, 192, 303, 305, 314, 329–30, 341, 360n–61n
  in budget negotiations, 198, 199, 201, 216, 217, 225, 226, 227, 229, 232, 236, 240, 242, 244, 246, 259, 261–62, 265, 304
environmental issues, 180–81, 316
Equal Rights Amendment, 182
Evans, Michael, 32
Evans, Rowland, 214

families, dysfunctional, 313–14, 338
farm price supports, 77, 180, 198, 226, 271
Federal Employee Hiring Freeze, 40–41
Federal Reserve Bank, 72, 82, 116, 201–2, 216, 222–23, 228, 229, 237, 244, 257, 275–76, 279, 285, 294, 330
Feldstein, Marty, 118
Fielding, Fred, 52–53, 56
Field of Dreams, 221, 319
Fischer, Dave, 49
Fisk, Carlton, 238
Fitzwater, Marlin, 251, 264
Foley, Tom, 215, 229, 248, 249, 251, 258, 260, 261–62, 272
Fonda, Jane, 35
Forbes, Jeff, 242
Forbes, Malcolm S. (Steve), Jr., 14–16, 20, 21, 317, 322
Ford, Gerald R., 30, 35, 38, 133, 142, 200, 202, 283
Fowler, Wyche, 255, 256, 257, 272
Freedom Brigade, 122
free lunch theory, 65
Frenzel, Bill, 245, 248, 259
Friedersdorf, Max, 84

Frum, David, 181
Fuller, Craig, 84, 93, 106, 114, 133, 196

Gang of 17, 111
Gates, Bob, 224
Gephardt, Dick, 152, 153, 250, 255, 260, 261, 262, 272
Gergen, Dave, 83, 93, 106
Germond, Jack, 136–37, 225
Gideon, Ken, 152
Gigot, Paul, 236
Gingrich, Marianne, 278, 283
Gingrich, Newt:
  ambition of, 279, 283–84, 285, 309–14
  in budget negotiations, 218–19, 228, 238–39, 248, 249, 254, 255, 256, 259, 260, 264, 272–87, 295
  as conservative, 272–87, 309, 311–12
  Contract with America and, 300–301, 307, 308, 309, 310, 317
  "co-presidency" of, 299–320, 323, 324, 361n
  Darman's relationship with, 193, 218–19, 228, 238–39, 254, 280–84, 285, 295
  Dole's relationship with, 10, 11
  extremism of, 10, 21, 22, 279, 281–82
  flat tax as viewed by, 15
  government reform and, 45
  government shutdown and, 314, 315, 316
  "laptops" proposal of, 309, 313
  leadership of, 311–14, 317, 318, 319–20, 345
  orphanages supported by, 310, 313–14
  "revolt" by, 272–87, 295
  rhetoric of, 310, 311, 313–14, 343
  tactical mistakes of, 315–17
  unpopularity of, 301, 317
Glenn, John, 88–89, 115
"God Bless the USA," 123, 141
Goldwater, Barry, 181

Gorbachev, Mikhail, 182
government, federal:
  administrative overhead of, 43, 44
  bureaucracy of, 44, 125, 152, 181, 327
  debt of, 73, 78, 180, 199, 202, 210, 220, 232, 316, 329
  deficit of, see deficit
  economic role of, 19–20, 65, 326–27
  "f.w.a." (fraud, waste, and abuse) in, 77, 81–82
  popular distrust of, 15, 18, 19, 28, 81, 169, 285, 290, 293, 311, 325–28, 332, 344
  reform of, 44–45, 308
  shutdown of, 101, 102, 109, 110, 277, 314, 315, 316
  size of, 11, 13–23, 33, 34, 43–45, 64, 65, 68–69, 114, 117–19, 174, 175, 179, 292, 320, 324, 326, 335, 337, 346
  social programs of, 19, 74, 79, 241, 327, 341
  spending reductions for (budget negotiations), 198, 199, 201, 203, 216, 223–25, 232, 234, 239, 240, 241, 242, 244, 250, 255, 260, 262, 265, 271, 274, 278–79, 285, 293
  spending reductions for (Economic Recovery Program), 77, 78, 79, 80, 81–82, 84–85, 94–99, 102–3, 110, 112, 114, 123–24
  state government vs., 44, 180, 314, 331, 342–43
Grady, Bob, 214, 298
Gramm, Phil, 15, 145, 201, 249, 255, 259, 260, 270, 272
Gramm-Rudman-Hollings law, 145–46, 192, 198, 203–7, 214–18, 223, 224, 229, 232, 235, 237, 243, 250, 259, 276, 277, 279
Great Society, 19, 74, 79, 241, 327, 341
Green, Stephen, 169–70
Greenspan, Alan, 82, 116, 201–2, 216, 222–23, 228, 229, 237,

Greenspan, Alan, *continued*
244, 257, 275–76, 279, 285, 294
Greenwood, Lee, 123, 141
Greider, Bill, 103–10, 111, 112
Gridiron Club, 249–50
gross domestic product (GDP), 14, 20, 29, 78, 98, 146, 174, 179–80, 198, 202, 240, 241, 272, 315, 326, 329
Group of Seven, 172
Gulf War, 14, 274, 277, 290, 341

Haig, Alexander, 49–56, 59, 175, 177, 310
Haldeman, Bob, 50
Hale, Janet, 298
Hamilton, Alexander, 238–39, 248
"Hard Choices Ahead" (Darman), 210
Harper, Ed, 106
Hatfield, Mark, 259
Health, Education and Welfare Department (HEW), 36, 44
health care, 13, 45, 292, 294, 300, 303, 327, 330, 333–34
Helms, Jesse, 114
Herblock, 254–55
"Heresy: The Politics of the Economic Program" (Darman), 75–76
Heseltine, Michael, 278
"Historic Tax Reform: The Populist Correction" (Darman), 154–59
Hobbs, Roy, 238
Hodsoll, Frank, 298
Hollings, Fritz, 145
House Appropriations Committee, 253
House Ways and Means Committee, 159–60
Howard, Bob, 298
Hubbell, Webb, 305
Hussein, Saddam, 276
hyperinflation, 111

immigration, 15, 17, 18
Imus in the Morning, 306
inflation, 70, 72, 81, 101, 111, 112, 199, 202, 223, 224, 226, 259, 303
insurance, 149
health, 45, 292, 294, 327, 330, 333–34
social, 20, 241
unemployment, 114
interest rates, 98, 206, 222, 257, 274, 276, 305
investment incentives, 72, 118, 226, 244–45, 247, 265, 272
Iran-contra scandal, 164, 170–72, 173, 178, 179, 182, 183
Iranian hostage crisis, 19, 32, 122, 142

Jackson, Reggie, 278
Janklow, William, 114
Jarvis, Howard, 81
job creation, 72, 287, 343
job training, 335, 343
Johnson, Lyndon B., 27, 35, 74, 142, 327
Jordan, Hamilton, 31
Joseph and the Amazing Technicolor Dreamcoat (Lloyd Webber), 332
Junior Tuesday primaries, 20
Justice Department, U.S., 55

Kassebaum, Nancy, 333
Kasten, Bob, 152, 153
Kean, Thomas, 114
Kemp, Jack, 14, 102, 152, 153, 188, 202, 221, 222, 228, 234, 296, 309, 311, 353n
Kennedy, Edward M., 31, 35
Kennedy, John F., 13, 17–18, 19, 20, 29, 30, 41, 47, 49, 55, 56, 57, 64, 122, 132, 142, 183, 196, 220, 240, 299, 307, 313, 319, 352n
Kimmitt, Bob, 189–90
King, Martin Luther, Jr., 19
Kissinger, Henry, 282–83, 285, 295
Kramer, CeCe, 158
Krauthammer, Charles, 17, 237
Kristol, Bill, 14, 222, 323
Kuwait, Iraqi invasion of, 257, 276–77

Laffer curve, 65, 80, 81
Laxalt, Paul, 99, 110, 126–27,
    130–31, 133, 136
League of Women Voters, 124, 141
Legislative Strategy Group, 39, 84,
    102
Lewis, Anthony, 306
Lewis, Drew, 209
Libyan shootdown, 177–78
Lincoln, Abraham, 63
Lloyd Webber, Andrew, 332
Lofton, John, 40
Long, Russell, 79, 150, 161–62
Lott, Trent, 99, 102
Louvre Accord, 172

McCarthy, Joseph, 16
McClendan, Sara, 259
McCullough, David, 250
McNamara, Johnny, 166
Magaziner, Ira, 13, 303, 334
Malabre, Alfred, 275
mañana syndrome, 102, 112–13,
    222
"Mapping Backward from Possible
    Sequester" (Darman), 217
market economics, 18–19, 32, 37,
    72, 167, 179, 180, 292–93,
    302, 308, 326–27, 330, 334,
    335
Matsunaga, Spark, 150–51
Maximum Feasible Misunderstanding
    (Moynihan), 74
Mayaguez crisis, 30
means testing, 232, 304
media, mass:
    budget negotiations and, 214,
        218–19, 222, 225, 228,
        235–36, 249–59, 262–66,
        270–71, 275, 278, 280
    on Bush, 192, 212, 213, 214
    on Clinton, 12, 13–14, 304, 305,
        306–7
    on Darman, 154, 156, 169–70,
        172, 218–19, 222, 235–36,
        280, 281, 294–95, 297
    on Economic Recovery Program,
        68, 69, 70, 75, 103–10, 111
    influence of, 19, 30, 31, 57, 59,
        69, 70, 100–101, 120, 121,

122, 126–28, 182, 213, 236,
    254, 270, 326, 338, 339
    on Reagan, 28–29, 32, 42,
        49–50, 51, 57, 59–60, 68, 69,
        70, 127, 128, 132–33, 141,
        176, 178
    on Reagan Revolution, 28–29
    tax reform and, 154, 156,
        162–63
Medicaid, 314, 316, 331
Medicare, 77, 180, 198, 236,
    270–71, 273, 278, 304, 314,
    316, 326, 331
Meese, Ed, 43, 75, 77, 84, 93, 95,
    96, 107, 171, 177–78
Meet the Press, 228
"Mega" proposal, 44
Mentz, Roger, 152
Merrill Lynch, 48
Michel, Bob, 100, 205, 248, 249,
    251, 256, 259, 260, 264, 272,
    273, 283
milk price support bill (S-509), 58
Miller, Jim, 145
"misery index," 81, 124
Mitchell, Andrea, 228
Mitchell, George, 205, 225–27,
    229, 248, 249, 250, 255, 256,
    257, 258, 260, 261, 262–63,
    264, 265, 272
Mondale, Walter, 115, 125–42, 182
money supply, 202, 222–23,
    275–76, 285
Moral Compass, The (Bennett), 337
Morris, Dick, 306
motor pool management, 43, 45,
    77
Moynihan, Daniel Patrick, 74,
    79–80, 85, 116, 117, 119, 150,
    161, 236–37, 249, 303, 341
Mubarak, Hosni, 230, 231
Mulroney, Brian, 180
Murphy, Dan, 53, 54
Murray, Alan, 152

National Association of Manufac-
    turers, 157, 164
National Command Authority, 52
National Economic Commission,
    209

National Governors Association, 237–38
National Security Council, 39
Nation of Immigrants, A (Kennedy), 17, 352*n*
Natural, The, 88, 238
"Neo-Media-Pop-ism," 280, 284
New Balance, 212, 222, 229
New Democrats, 11, 285, 303, 335, 337
New Populist Forum, 193
Newsweek, 133, 163, 218
New York Mets, 165–67
New York Times, 78, 169, 214, 235, 306–7
Nicklaus, Jack, 158–59
Nixon, Richard M., 27, 35, 36, 42, 53, 56, 57, 74, 116, 140, 142, 172–73, 200–201, 209–10, 266
Nofziger, Lyn, 58
Noonan, Peggy, 191–92
North, Oliver, 170–71, 178
Novak, Robert, 214, 306
"Now-Now-ism," 219–22, 226, 229, 337
nuclear arms reductions, 179, 211
Nussbaum, Bernard, 305

Office of Management and Budget (OMB), 69, 304
  Darman as director of, 88–91, 107, 138, 139, 195–298, 317–18
  Stockman as director of, 43, 44, 97, 107, 138, 139, 145, 294, 304
oil industry, 149, 274, 276
O'Leary, Dennis, 58
O'Neill, Paul, 200
O'Neill, Thomas P., Jr., 53, 94–95, 116
Operation Desert Storm, 14, 274, 277, 290, 341
Opportunity Society, 312
Orr, Robert, 114
Osgood, Charles, 305

Packwood, Bob, 149, 151, 152, 160, 161, 259

Panama Canal treaty, 182
Panetta, Leon, 205
Parker, Fess, 175–76
Parkinson, Paula, 189
Parr, Jerry, 47–48
pay–as–you–go system, 111, 271
Pearlman, Ron, 152
Penny, Tim, 245
Perot, Ross, 14, 286–87, 290, 291, 294, 296, 301, 306
Phillips, Howard, 114–15, 182
Phillips curve, 65
Plaza Agreement (1985), 172
Pledge of Allegiance, 191
Poindexter, John, 170
politics:
  change in, 9–11, 120, 183, 340–44
  coalitions in, 83, 167, 213, 288–89, 292–93, 299–303, 319, 320, 323, 324, 358*n*
  control in, 22, 23, 27–28, 34, 59, 62, 63–64, 120, 175–83, 345–46
  correction in, 23, 32, 179, 212–13, 308–9
  crises in, 29, 30–32
  iconography in, 120, 121–23
  incrementalism in, 63, 66, 74–75, 111–12, 113, 148, 150
  middle ground in, 10, 21–22, 23, 63, 80, 86–87, 153, 182, 273, 289, 293, 296, 319, 321–44, 345, 346, 349
  polarization of, 10, 21–22, 23, 86, 212–13, 215, 273, 282, 321–44, 345
  restructuring of, 340–44
  rhetoric of, 9, 10, 14, 33, 76, 120, 129–30, 168–69, 214, 310, 311, 313–14, 326, 337, 343
  status quo in, 80–81, 153–54, 156, 291, 294
  symbolism in, 41, 66–67, 69, 71, 120–44, 164, 178–79, 191
  system of, 120, 163, 182–83, 242, 275, 278, 308, 325, 340–44, 345, 349

populism:
  budget negotiations and,
    269–70
  Bush and, 187, 188, 212–13,
    290, 293
  and "centrism," 322–23, 324,
    325–26, 361n–63n
  communication and, 143–44,
    191, 292
  as corrective reaction, 308–9
  Darman's speeches on, 167–70
  Dole and, 188, 194, 322
  Economic Recovery Program
    and, 81, 82, 85, 157
  as ideology, 12, 15, 16, 32, 33,
    81, 82, 85, 167–70, 322–23
  Reagan and, 81, 82, 124, 152,
    169, 173–74, 187, 289
  tax reform and, 144, 147, 148,
    152, 153–59, 168
Porter, Roger, 214, 246
Powell, Colin, 14, 20, 21, 301, 319,
    321, 322
prayer, school, 180, 324
president, U.S.:
  as agent of change, 120, 183
  audience appeal of, 121
  capabilities of, 141–42
  as commander-in-chief, 52, 55,
    171
  leadership of, 61, 63–65, 66, 87,
    128, 152, 301, 302, 306,
    307–8, 319–20, 329, 345–49
  mandate of, 27–28
  motorcade for, 175–77
  national agenda for, 329–44
  symbolic communication by,
    120–44
  transfer of power for, 33, 49,
    52–58, 59, 62
  vision of, 13, 190, 287, 288–92,
    294, 299, 302, 318, 319, 327
presidential election (1980), 82,
    94, 325, 354n
presidential election (1984),
    114–15, 124–42, 146, 182,
    286, 290, 324, 325
presidential election (1988),
    187–95, 198–99, 205, 206,
    207, 208, 216, 224–25, 251,325

presidential election (1992), 216,
    286–91, 293–94, 302, 327
presidential election (1996), 9–23,
    300, 315, 317, 320, 325,
    328–44, 345
Presidential Lecture Series on the
    Presidency, 250
Primary Colors (Anonymous), 13
Project Apollo, 290, 313

Quayle, Dan, 188, 189–90, 192,
    204–5, 246, 247, 272
Quayle, Marilyn, 189, 258

Rancho del Cielo, 67–70
Rather, Dan, 191
Ray, Robert, 114
Reagan, Maureen, 136
Reagan, Nancy, 38, 60, 61, 67, 68,
    130, 131, 133, 134, 135–39,
    172, 176, 191
Reagan, Ronald, 27–183
  as administrator, 39–40
  age issue for, 128–29, 132, 133,
    141
  Alzheimer's disease of, 40
  assassination attempt against,
    47–62, 71, 83, 175, 177
  big government opposed by, 34,
    68–69, 114, 117–19, 174, 175,
    179, 320, 324, 326
  "brutalization" of, 126–27,
    136–37
  budgets of, 15, 19, 31, 34, 42,
    43, 73, 102, 111, 118, 119,
    139, 179, 180, 198, 205, 206,
    214, 224, 272, 303, 315
  Bush compared with, 187,
    214
  cabinet of, 41–46, 77, 139
  Clinton influenced by, 13, 17,
    299
  colon cancer of, 150–51
  as communicator, 120–44, 152,
    182, 191
  conservative support for, 29, 33,
    36, 37, 38, 39, 179, 181–82,
    283
  convention speech of (1988),
    188

Reagan, Ronald, *continued*
 as "cowboy," 28, 33, 34, 67–70,
  121
 Darman's relationship with,
  39–40, 41, 60–61, 125–42,
  263
 Democratic opposition to,
  65–66, 82, 85, 119, 173
 economic policies of, 14, 34, 42,
  43, 62, 64–71, 82, 103–10,
  111, 113, 114, 118, 119,
  179–80, 282, 303
 Economic Recovery Program
  and, 64–71, 80, 81, 85, 86, 87,
  94–97, 99–102, 103, 110, 113,
  124
 as film star, 28, 67, 121
 foreign policy of, 181–82
 as governor, 133, 142, 275
 honeymoon period for, 82–83,
  85
 hospitalization of, 48, 50, 51,
  55–56, 57, 58
 ideology of, 33–34, 39–40, 59,
  62, 71, 81, 115–16, 173–74,
  309, 323, 324
 inauguration of, 33–35, 40
 leadership of, 61, 63–65, 66, 87,
  128, 152, 320
 legacy of, 62, 64–65, 178–83
 legislation supported by, 58,
  66–71
 majority coalition of, 167, 289,
  301, 320, 324, 358n
 mandate of, 29, 82, 153
 media coverage of, 28–29, 32,
  42, 49–50, 51, 57, 59–60, 68,
  69, 70, 127, 128, 132–33, 141,
  176, 178
 Mondale's debates with, 125–42
 personality of, 10, 39–40, 95,
  109, 176
 popularity of, 115, 121, 178, 324
 populist appeal of, 81, 82, 124,
  152, 169, 173–74, 187, 289
 presidential campaign of
  (1980), 82, 94, 325, 354n
 presidential campaign of
  (1984), 114–15, 124–42, 146,
  182, 286, 290, 324, 325
 press conferences of, 128

 public image of, 28, 33, 34,
  67–70, 81, 121, 122
 ranch of, 67–70
 Republican support for, 114–15,
  119, 167
 sense of humor of, 42, 58, 113,
  114
 signature of, 58, 61, 68, 69, 71
 State of the Union address of
  (1983), 113, 115–19
 State of the Union address of
  (1984), 179
 State of the Union address of
  (1987), 173–74
 tax policy of, 29, 64–71, 111,
  113, 116, 118, 141, 150–51,
  272, 285, 286, 324
 tax reform and, 118, 140,
  146–47, 151, 152, 153, 154,
  156, 162
 TV performances of, 100–101,
  121, 122, 126–28, 182
 whistle-stop campaign of,
  129–30
 White House staff of, 37, 38, 41,
  126–27
Reaganauts, 29, 33, 36, 37, 38, 43,
  45, 58, 75, 76, 86, 107, 123
Reagan Revolution:
 big government opposed by, 23,
  33, 64, 179
 impact of, 46, 58–59, 62, 74,
  107, 115, 120, 164–74,
  178–83, 321
 media coverage of, 28–29
 reality vs. rhetoric of, 10, 33
 as revolution, 28–29, 42–43
 symbolic importance of, 121,
  123, 178–79
recessions, economic, 72, 73, 103,
  142, 182, 223, 237, 257, 274,
  276, 282
Regan, Don, 84
 Atlantic affair and, 107
 Baker's job switch with, 48,
  139–40, 145
 Reagan assassination attempt
  and, 48, 57
 tax reform and, 150, 151, 152
 as White House chief of staff,
  139–40, 145–46, 171–72

Republican party:
  in budget negotiations, 199,
    200–201, 202, 203, 205, 233,
    237, 239–41, 242, 247–48,
    254–55, 263–64, 272–73,
    285
  congressional control by,
    274–75, 300
  conservatives in, 14–17, 20,
    21–22, 83, 114–15, 181, 213,
    311–12
  Economic Recovery Program
    supported by, 79, 98–99, 100,
    102, 114–15
  moderates in, 20–22, 36, 83–84,
    213, 303, 311, 323–24
  primaries of (1996), 14–17,
    20–21
  Reagan supported by, 114–15,
    119, 167
research and development (R&D),
    169, 220, 244, 342
Richardson, Elliot, 36–37, 44, 53,
    262
Ripkin, Cal, Jr., 347–49
Rivlin, Alice, 200
Rodman, Dennis, 338
Rogers, John, 42
Roosevelt, Franklin D., 63–64, 74,
    117
Rostenkowski, Dan, 79, 86, 152,
    153, 159, 160, 161, 162, 209,
    242–43, 245, 246, 247,
    249–50, 255, 258, 264
Roth, William, 150
Rubin, Jerry, 35
Rudman, Warren, 145
Rukeyser, Louis, 16
Ruth, Babe, 164–65

Sanders, Deion, 309
Sasser, Jim, 205, 256, 257
Saturday Night Massacre, 36,
    53–54, 91, 172
savings and loan (S&L) scandal,
    207, 211
savings rate, 118, 148, 180, 244–45,
    247
Schiraldi, Calvin, 166
Scowcroft, Brent, 214, 217, 223,
    224, 297

Scully, Tom, 298
Secret Service, 47–48, 176, 291
Senate Budget Committee, 101,
    205
Senate Finance Committee,
    149–51, 156, 157, 159, 160–
    62
"sensible center," 322–24, 345
service sector, 147, 148
Seymour, Rita, 70
"Shamrock Summit," 180
Shaughnessy, Dan, 164–65, 364n
Shaw, Bernard, 194
Shearson Lehman Brothers, 188
Shiraa, Al, 170
Showdown at Gucci Gulch (Murray
    and Birnbaum), 152
Skinner, Sam, 234, 288
Smith, William French, 55
Social Security, 29, 77, 99, 100,
    111, 114, 115–16, 117, 119,
    123, 145, 180, 198, 207, 209,
    225, 229, 232, 235, 236–37,
    241, 244, 245, 260, 278–79,
    324, 326, 330, 331, 335–36
Social Security Commission, 111
Soviet Union, 62, 102, 181–82
space shuttle, 71
Speakes, Larry, 49–50, 51, 106
Spencer, Stu, 129, 133–35, 137,
    138–39, 172
Springsteen, Bruce, 123
Stahl, Lesley, 50, 103–5
Stanley, Bob, 166
Stark, Pete, 303
Stein, Herbert, 327–28
Stern, Howard, 338
Stigler, George, 113
Stockman, David:
  Atlantic Monthly story on,
    103–10, 111, 112
  Darman's relationship with,
    84–85, 88–91, 103
  deficits as concern of, 72, 76–77,
    88–91, 93, 94
  Economic Recovery Program
    and, 64, 72, 75, 76–77, 79, 80,
    83, 84–85, 88–91, 93, 94,
    95–110, 116–17, 154
  memoir of, 88, 89–91, 109–10,
    183

Stockman, David, *continued*
  as OMB director, 43, 44, 97, 107,
    138, 139, 145, 294, 304
  in presidential campaign
    (1984), 127
  proposed resignation of, 107–10
  "woodshed" luncheon of, 107–9
stock market crash (1987), 79,
    116, 173, 204, 209, 218
Strauss, Bob, 209
student loans, 77, 198, 271, 326
Sununu, John, 114, 206, 215, 216,
    217, 223–24, 228, 232, 243,
    245–52, 255, 256, 260–65,
    280, 281, 288
Superfund program, 180–81
supply-side economics, 62, 64–65,
    73, 75, 95, 98, 104–5, 113,
    118, 119, 156, 202, 228, 237,
    241, 287–88, 297, 311, 341
Sutton, Willy, 45
Symms, Steve, 150

Taft, Will, 224
taxes:
  "acceleration" of, 116, 119
  alternative minimum, 148
  brackets for, 81, 147, 153, 159,
    201, 259
  "bubble" rate for, 147, 161
  Bush's policy on, 76, 191–92,
    210, 213, 214, 216, 217, 224,
    225, 228, 231, 232, 239, 243,
    247, 251, 262–66, 275, 291,
    293
  capital gains, 147, 216, 219, 226,
    227, 228, 244, 246, 251, 292
  Clinton's policy on, 73, 286–87
  consumption, 118, 148, 244,
    247, 259, 293
  corporate, 113, 147–48
  cuts in, 29, 64–71, 72, 74–76,
    78–79, 83, 84, 86, 88, 89, 91,
    101–2, 117, 118, 142, 145,
    146, 148, 151, 294, 304, 310,
    324, 325, 331, 340, 341
  deductions in, 147, 148, 149, 155
  deficit reduction and, 15, 72, 73,
    111
  energy, 114, 232, 244, 245, 247,
    258, 260

  flat rate for, 15, 75, 118, 148,
    150, 154, 179, 304, 330
  gasoline, 114, 232, 245
  income, 70, 77, 118, 147, 148,
    226, 240, 244, 247, 260, 272,
    273, 285
  increases in, 15, 20, 72–73, 111,
    113, 116, 123, 181, 182,
    199–202, 205, 209–10, 214,
    216, 224–29, 231, 234, 235,
    237, 239, 240–47, 251,
    254–66, 272, 275, 279, 285,
    286, 287, 291, 293, 294, 296,
    334
  loopholes for, 72–73, 77, 88,
    102, 113, 147, 149, 198, 210
  progressive rate for, 118
  Reagan's policy on, 29, 64–71,
    111, 113, 116, 118, 141,
    150–51, 272, 285, 286, 324
  revenues from, 102, 112, 154
  sales, 247
  shelters for, 148, 149, 244
  "sin," 232, 260, 336
  state, 148
  user fees and, 279
  value added (VAT), 247, 288
tax reform, 145–63
  Baker's role in, 149, 151, 152,
    153, 154, 159, 160, 161, 162
  baseball analogy for, 157–58,
    167
  Bush's role in, 150
  congressional approval of,
    149–54, 156, 159–62
  Darman's role in, 149, 151,
    152–74
  Darman's speeches on, 154–59
  deficit reduction and, 150, 154
  Dole and, 145, 160
  enactment of, 144, 153, 171
  media coverage of, 154, 156,
    162–63
  opposition to, 149–51, 160–61,
    162
  populist support for, 144, 147,
    148, 152, 153–59, 168
  provisions of, 147–49, 154
  Reagan's support for, 118, 140,
    146–47, 151, 152, 153, 154,
    156, 162

Regan's role in, 150, 151, 152
revenue neutral provision for, 154
status quo vs., 153–54, 156
strategy for, 159–63
Taylor, David, 298
Teeter, Bob, 194, 196, 198, 206, 209
TEFRA, 72–73
television, 19, 57, 59, 69, 70, 100–101, 121, 122, 126–28, 182, 213, 236, 254, 270, 339
term limits, 309
"Thanksgiving turkey," 114
Thatcher, Margaret, 278
"Thinking About Budget Strategy as of Early December" (Darman), 206–9
This Week with David Brinkley, 218–19
Thurmond, Strom, 53
Time, 32, 123, 136, 162–63, 218
Toffler, Alvin, 310, 311
Tokyo Summit Communiqué (1986), 172
Tower, John, 224
Treasury, U.S.:
  Baker as Secretary of, 139–40, 145, 146, 172
  Darman as Deputy Secretary of, 140, 144, 145, 146, 172, 188
  Office of Tax policy of, 152
  supply-side economics in, 75
Trewhitt, Henry, 132
"trickle down" theory, 241
Triumph of Politics, The (Stockman), 88, 89–91, 109–10, 183
Truman, Harry S., 27, 129
Tutwiler, Margaret, 158, 189, 308
Twenty-fifth Amendment, 53–56, 58

unemployment, 81, 98, 114
United States:
  as "city upon a hill," 18, 32, 43, 67, 112, 308, 349, 352n
  competitiveness of, 168, 292
  culture of, 168, 219–21
  democratic process in, 271, 323, 346
  economy of, 14, 15, 18–20, 32, 37, 64–71, 72, 73, 98, 103, 124, 142, 145–46, 148, 173, 179, 180, 182, 199, 202, 206–7, 222–23, 227, 229, 237, 241, 243–44, 257, 274, 275–76, 282, 285–88, 302, 305, 330–31, 337–38
  exceptionalism of, 33–34, 71
  idealism in, 17–18, 30, 35, 319
  living standards in, 31–32
  pluralism of, 18, 37, 323
  pragmatism in, 37, 322–23
  self-confidence in, 31, 32, 33–34, 81, 302
  space program of, 19, 29, 64, 71, 142, 220, 290, 313, 341
  spirit of, 120–21, 22, 123, 124, 168, 178, 179, 346
  traditional values of, 13, 167, 181, 270, 302, 305, 310, 313, 324, 327, 337–40, 348–49
  as world leader, 18, 243–44
U.S. News & World Report, 173

Values Matter Most (Wattenberg), 337
veterans benefits, 77, 198, 271
Vietnam War, 19, 27, 29, 122, 142, 178, 224, 242
Vietnam War Memorial, 122
Viguerie, Richard, 114–15, 182
Volcker, Paul, 72
von Damm, Helene, 60, 107
"voodoo economics," 66, 303
voter turnout, 9

Waiting for Godot (Beckett), 237–38
Wake Me When It's Over (Germond and Witcover), 136–37
Wallace, George, 81
Wall Street Journal, 17, 89, 115, 156, 162, 178, 235–36, 275
Wall Street Week, 16
Walters, Barbara, 128
Wanniski, Jude, 79
Washington Post, 28, 104, 105, 106, 114, 251, 278, 280, 281, 288, 316
Washington Times, 162, 169
Watergate scandal, 19, 36, 53–54, 56, 142
Watkins, Jim, 234

Wattenberg, Ben, 337
Weaver, Earl, 347
Weber, Vin, 279, 281–82
Webster, Bill, 224
Weekly Standard, 13–14
Weidenbaum, Murray, 64–65, 76, 93
Weinberger, Caspar, 52, 94, 95–97
welfare reform, 173, 181, 308, 312,
    314, 330, 331, 343
White, Joseph, 83
Whitewater affair, 306
Whitten, Jamie, 253, 256, 257
Wildavsky, Aaron, 83
Will, George, 52, 182, 218
Williams, Ted, 197, 230–32, 233,
    234, 235, 247, 257, 293, 298,
    346

Wilson, Mookie, 166
Wilson, Pete, 145
Wilson, Woodrow, 61, 63–64
Winthrop, John, 32
Wirthlin, Dick, 128–29
Witcover, Jules, 136–37, 225
Wolfe, Tom, 89, 221
work ethic, 18–19
World Series (1986), 164–67
Wright, Jim, 86

Yang, John, 251

Zoellick, Bob, 288